Economics, the Social Order, and the Ron Paul Revolution

Jorge Besada

Copyright © 2008 By Jorge Besada

All rights reserved. Permission must be secured from the author to use or reproduce any part of this book, except for brief quotations in critical reviews or articles.

ISBN 978-0-9796591-4-0

Version 0.9.2

Cover pictures:

Bryan W. Diaz, courtesy of his dad William Diaz

Herbert Spencer http://commons.wikimedia.org/wiki/Image:Herbert_Spencer_2.jpg

Carl Menger http://commons.wikimedia.org/wiki/Image:Menger.jpg

Ludwig von Mises and Henry Hazlitt courtesy of the Ludwig von Mises Institute www.mises.org, via http://en.wikipedia.org/wiki/Image:Misessuit.jpg and http://en.wikipedia.org/wiki/Image:Henry_hazlitt.jpg

F.A. Hayek http://en.wikipedia.org/wiki/Image:Friedrich_Hayek.jpg

---

Visit www.capitalistworld.com for updates/errata and more resources.

Author can be reached at hayekian@gmail.com

To Henry Hazlitt
To regular folks like you and me
To present and future Ron Paul supporters everywhere

"The solution to the present problem of massive, overwhelming poverty is nothing other than the science of economics. As should be increasingly clear, economics is a science which can make possible the construction of a social and political system in which human success is a feature of normal, everyday life everywhere. It is truly the humanitarian science, and only those who have studied it well and who are prepared to implement its teachings deserve to be called friends of mankind. The most important charity which true friends of mankind can pursue is to disseminate knowledge of this vital subject as widely and as deeply as they know how."
—George Reisman

"We haven't convinced the majority. Is this because the majority just won't listen to reason? I am enough of an optimist, and I have enough faith in human nature, to believe that people will listen to reason if they are convinced that it *is* reason. Somewhere, there must be some missing argument, something that we haven't seen clearly enough, or said clearly enough, or, perhaps, just not said often enough.

A minority is in a very awkward position. The individuals in it can't afford to be just as good as the individuals in the majority. If they hope to convert the majority they have to be much better; and the smaller the minority, the better they have to be. They have to think better. They have to know more. They have to write better. They have to have better controversial manners. Above all, they have to have far more courage. And they have to be infinitely patient." — Henry Hazlitt

CONTENTS

Acknowledgments ix
Disclaimer x
Preface x

I. INTRODUCTION 13

America's dire economic path. 13
Who is Ron Paul? 14
Ron Paul is obviously an antiquated ideologue, right? 15
The human ant-farm and the market process 17
Capitalism and Communism introduced 19
A tribal brain in a modern world 22
Wealth as a transformation of matter and the main difference between the tribal and modern worlds 29
Market process vs. Government. South vs. North Korea 32

II. ECONOMICS AND THE MARKET PROCESS 35

The ongoing cycle of production and consumption 35
Self-sufficient vs. market oriented societies. The division of labor and knowledge, and their impact on the human ant-farm. 35
Market oriented societies as supercomputers 38
The growing interdependence of knowledge 39
Money 39
Prices. The quantity theory of money 43
Human action and the quest for increasingly more beneficial states of well-being. 46
The value of goods. Carl Menger's Subjective Theory of Value 47
The importance of trading 48
Value, ownership and private property 50
The creation of useful knowledge 52
Thinking about progress and its destruction. 53
Inflation 55
   The destructive rearrangement of the human ant-farm. 55
   Inflation's redistribution of wealth 58
Inflation and the natural selection of sound money 59
Hyperinflation and historical examples 60
Progressive vs. recessive rearrangements of the human ant-farm. Profitability as a signal of progress. 62
Companies and how employee wages are determined 65

Banking 69
The lending industry 70
Interest rates 72
The efficient distribution of resources 74
Economic booms and busts and the business cycle 76
Competition. The forced and beneficial spreading of knowledge and rearrangement of society. 85
How the social organism calculates what to produce. The average rate of profit 91
How living standards and real wages rise 93
Bringing the future closer: the effects of, and importance of saving .. 96

III. GOVERNMENT PLANNING VS. THE MARKET PROCESS 103

Our strong instinct to form groups. 103
The origins of governments 105
The recent evolution of law and the emergence of the modern socialist mindset 107
The birth of American Capitalism. 117
What is seen and what is not seen. The wisdom of Frederic Bastiat 121
The Public Sector vs. The Market Process. The wisdom of Herbert Spencer 126
Government regulation 133
    Food and Drug Administration(FDA) and American Medical Association(AMA) 136
More Spencer 145
Government finance basics 147
    Taxes 147
    Inflation 149
    Borrowing 150
On democracy 151
The modern political zoo and its inevitable road to serfdom 153

IV. THE ENVIRONMENT 159

Why we are not running out of natural resources 159
Dealing with pollution 161
Global warming 162
The conservation of species 165
Conclusion 167

V. CULTURAL EVOLUTION 169

Cultural evolution. Hayekian selection introduced 169
Understanding religion 180

Comments on drug prohibition, its history, and race relations 190
Ideology. Democrats, Republicans and Libertarians 196
    Libertarians and traditional conservatives 196
    Modern day Republicans 197
    Democrats / Liberals 200
Review 201

VI. THE RON PAUL REVOLUTION 204

The fallacy of needing to "protect our interests" overseas and police the world. Non-interventionism 204
The nonsense of mainstream economists 207
    Alan Greenspan tries to save face and our needed return to the gold standard 207
    Bernanke's economic nonsense and his "stimulus" package 210
    John Maynard Keynes. The grandfather of our mainstream economorons 211
    Franklin Delano Roosevelt: America's drastic turn towards Socialism 215
Governmental foreign aid does not help 216
Terrorism and national security 218
    Government monopolies cannot protect us 218
    Why do they hate us 219
    The destruction of the American social order via military spending 227
    Lockheed and Loaded: The Company that Runs the Empire. By Jeffrey St. Clair 229
    The coming mushroom cloud? 237
    Bin Laden's embarrassing victory. Brought to you by American tribalism and economic ignorance 239
    A few answers 240
The real motivation for the Ron Paul Revolution 242
Common libertarian ideological mistakes 243
    Government is not evil. Hayek's most alarming lesson of modern history 243
    Preaching freedom for freedom's sake and ignoring economics as part of the freedom message. 249
Some final thoughts 253
Henry Hazlitt's inspirational words 253

APPENDIX 263

A few speeches by Dr. Paul before congress 263
    Has Capitalism Failed? 263
    Statement on Ending US Membership in the IMF 266

Lift the United States Embargo on Cuba 268
Statement Opposing the use of Military Force against Iraq..........270
Arguments Against the Iran Sanctions Enabling Act of 2007 276
Repeal Sarbanes-Oxley!...277
Federal Reserve has Monopoly over Money and Credit in United States 278

INDEX..**294**

Acknowledgments

I would like to thank my father Jorge L. Besada and long time friend William Diaz, not only for comments on early drafts of this book, but for their help and encouragement in many ways throughout my life.

I would like to thank my friend Ted Chang, who became my sort of intellectual mentor soon after I met him, and whose many suggestions have greatly helped me reach whatever understanding of the world I might have today.

I would like to also thank the various individuals and publishers that have given me permission to quote their material and especially Dr. George Reisman, Richard J. Maybury, the Libertarian Press for Carl Menger's quotes, the Foundation for Economic Education for Henry Hazlitt's 70th birthday speech and quotes, and the Ludwig von Mises Institute for Mises' quotes.

I would like to thank my family, beginning with my grandfather Jorge Besada Ramos for having set such a great example and having rescued my immediate family and so many other family members from Cuba's Communism. My mother Sara I. Besada for her endless love and support, and Cynthia, my little sister for telling me from time to time that she misses me. Also thanks to Catherine Yohn for her encouragement, Jennifer Spencer and her family as well as the Branson family for their many wonderful meals and company in my home away from home in Omaha.

And finally a huge thanks to Dr. Paul and all of his supporters everywhere in the world and my friends from the Omaha/Council Bluffs Ron Paul Meetup group.

Disclaimer

This book is not endorsed by or associated with Ron Paul or his campaign.

Preface

The presidential campaign of ten-term congressman Dr. Ron Paul has helped spark a capitalist revolution that is sweeping across America. Regardless of Dr. Paul's presidential success, this movement is poised to continue its Internet dominance and ultimately help spread the proper understanding of free-market economics throughout the USA and the rest of the world.

The purpose of this book is to help the layman understand, not only how Capitalism is the economic system that creates the most prosperous social order, but just as importantly, why due to our tribal human nature we so easily fear and misunderstand it and blindly fall for the share-the-wealth socialist ideologies which inevitably bring socioeconomic hardship.

The book provides a concise yet in-depth introduction to what economists refer to as "the market process", which is the economic process that gives an efficient and productive order to the nearly 7 billion human beings that make up our global human ant-farm. This introduction to economics and everything else in the book begins from scratch and should be within a high school student's grasp.

An introduction to cultural evolution, based on the ideas of 1974 Nobel laureate in economics F.A. Hayek is also provided. This introduction to cultural evolution is a crucial ingredient needed to understand the important evolution and interplay between human nature, religion, morals, laws and economic forces.

This intellectual foundation is then used to examine the detrimental effects of government involvement in the economy, environmentalism, religious and political ideology, and finally the successes, failures, and future of the "Ron Paul Revolution". The ultimate purpose of this book is to spread an understanding of Capitalism and show how individual freedom and small government, instead of leading to social chaos and great injustices as most people fear, leads to the greatest social order and prosperity humanly possible.

Unlike most books, this book is a POD(Print-On-Demand) title. When a copy is ordered, the latest version of my manuscript is printed and shipped to the customer. This differs from the traditional model of publishing where a book is finished, then printed in large quantities, stored, and then shipped as orders come in. What all of this means is that the contents of this book can and will change often as I expand/refine/evolve much of the book. This is one of the first versions(0.9.2) and is in need of much editing, but nonetheless I feel like regardless of these shortcomings the book is very useful in its current state. We are so used to seeing books as having concrete beginnings and ends because we have been limited by the traditional way of publishing, which makes the publishing of frequent updates to books prohibitively expensive. But things no longer have to be this way. Why should an author have to wait months or years to "finish" a book when early drafts can already be valuable to potential readers? Society progresses not because we get things "right", but because we do them better than we used to, and the same applies to books, especially this one.

Most of the book's content is taken from drafts of a larger project that will include more in-depth coverage of the concepts discussed here, as well as other topics and a chapter on race relations, particularly the rise and dominance of Hip-Hop culture and its impact on America and the rest of the world. The close proximity of the 2008 presidential election, the never ending need to spread an understanding of economics, as well as the "Ron Paul Revolution" itself is what has prompted me to quickly put this book together. So I apologize in advance for various parts that will be somewhat lacking in flow as well as the long sentences, misplaced commas and errors that the book still contains.

I. Introduction

America's dire economic path.

In 2001 the annual percentage increase in health insurance premiums went up by 10.9%, then another 12.9% in 2002, 13.9% in 2003, and another 11.2% in 2004[1].Prices at the pump have more than doubled in last five years[2]. According to collegeboard.com, in the school year 2007-2008, the average cost of a college education at a public university has gone up 6.6%[3]. Since 1971, college has become more expensive by about 6% each year[4]. As the picture in the book's cover shows, for most of our country's history, average prices were stable with a slight downward trend, but over the last century, especially since the early 70s, prices across the entire economy have been skyrocketing.

Until about the early 70s, every new generation of Americans inherited a bigger slice of material prosperity than the previous one, and had to work less and less to be able to afford more and better products. But since then that trend has stagnated and is now clearly in decline. The idea of a middle class family having a single working parent being able to pay a mortgage on a home, have a family car, 20th century medicine, some money left over for vacation, and some reasonable savings is now a laughable joke. Sure technology has improved and we have things like computers and the Internet, but instead of all of these things being sort of added to a growing slice of prosperity, the slice's ingredients have changed to include these wonderful new things, but overall it has been getting smaller due to the increasing costs of other things like a college education, healthcare and pretty much everything else.

The U.S. Government already owes over 9.2 trillion dollars which is over 30,000 per man, woman, and child. We are not just taxed to pay for our federal bureaucracies, we are taxed over 400 billion dollars per year just to pay for the interest on this massive credit card[5]. This figure is the national debt, which represents how much the government has already borrowed, but the government has also promised to pay for about 60 trillion dollars worth of future benefits. Most of these benefits are medical care for retirees and social security payments. Our current economic troubles and deteriorating condition is a result of decades of fiscal irresponsibility by our economically ignorant elected ideologues. David Walker, comptroller general of the United States, our government's top accountant and head of the Government Accountability Office, understands the situation and has spent the last two years traveling on a

"Fiscal Wake-up Tour", trying to get the word out about our deteriorating economic condition and how it will only get much worse unless drastic action is taken. In a 60 Minutes interview, he says, "I don't know anybody, who has done their homework, has researched history, and who's good at math, who would tell you that we can grow our way out of this problem."... "We are mortgaging the future of our children and grandchildren at record rates, and that is not only an issue of fiscal irresponsibility, it's an issue of immorality"[6]. Fortunately for all of us, there is one man running for president that has a profound understanding of what Mr. Walker is referring to and his name is Dr. Ron Paul.

Who is Ron Paul?

Ron Paul is a ten-term Congressman from Texas running for president of the United States. Amongst many accolades, he is a doctor who has delivered over 4,000 babies and most importantly for our purposes, he has a profound understanding of economics.

Early in his life, Dr. Paul read "The Road to Serfdom" by F.A. Hayek who would later go on to win the Nobel Prize in economics in 1974. The important lesson that one walks away with after reading Hayek's book is that without the proper understanding of economics, governments tend to grow to the point where they destroy their economies and people essentially become serfs of a gigantic dictatorial bureaucracy, hence "The Road to Serfdom". Hayek and like-minded economists are referred to as "The Austrian School of Economics", because like Hayek himself, other early proponents of this pro-Capitalism school of thought were born in Austria. As Dr. Paul explains in his short pamphlet titled "Mises and Austrian Economics":

"My introduction to Austrian economics came when I was studying medicine at Duke University and came a cross a copy of Hayek's The Road to Serfdom. After devouring this, I was determined to read whatever I could find on what I thought was this new school of economic thought—especially the works of Mises"[7]

To Dr. Paul, the "Austrian School" could properly explain past economic downturns like the Great Depression[8] and make accurate predictions about the future effects of current policies. Dr. Paul could clearly see how our mainstream economics establishment and bureaucrats in D.C. were continually making all the wrong moves based on flawed economic principles.

Economics is at the heart of everything, not just material prosperity but the morals and attitudes of people and international conflicts. Alarmed by the path our nation was taking, those familiar with the "Austrian School" worked feverishly to educate and take action.

"I decided to run for Congress because of the disaster of wage and price controls imposed by the Nixon administration in 1971... I decided that someone in politics had to condemn the controls, and offer the alternative that could explain the past and give hope for the future: the Austrian economists' defense of the free market...Americans need a better understanding of Austrian economics"9
— Ron Paul

Ron Paul is obviously an antiquated ideologue, right?

Ron Paul refers to himself as a "strict constitutionalist", which means that he believes that the Federal Government should be limited to the few things specified in the US Constitution. This means no Food and Drug Administration that attempts to ensure the safety of our food and drugs, no American Medical Association that decides who can or cannot practice medicine and what they must learn in order to do so, no federal Department of Education, no Social Security or Medicare that attempts to take care of us in old age, no government assistance to the poor via welfare programs, no Securities and Exchange Commission which regulates our nation's financial sector, no to countless other things that the federal government tries to do, and most importantly for our purposes, **no central bank, the Federal Reserve, manipulating our nation's economy.**

To most people this seems like a recipe for chaos. For example, with respect to abolishing the Federal Reserve and going back to the gold standard, as well as their views on the U.S. Constitution, their thoughts quite logically might be as follows:

"Don't the brightest economists work for the Federal Reserve? Aren't they the graduates of our finest universities? Isn't the gold standard a thing of the past? If it were so great, why don't other countries use it? Are the countless market-watchers, experts, authors, and business magazines part of some massive conspiracy out to benefit themselves at the expense of society? Or are they all just wrong, and the right ones are Dr. Paul and his tiny group of anti-fed-obscure-PhDs? How could Ron Paul, a man who does not even have a degree in economics, think that he knows better than all these people? C'mon, I find either of these scenarios to be highly unlikely. And with respect to Dr. Paul's "strict constitutionalist" views, it should be obvious to anyone who is not blinded by ideology like Dr. Paul and his supporters that the Constitution was fine for the 1700s, but that today's world is much larger and complex, and therefore needs a larger government to manage it."

This type of reasoning makes a lot of sense, yet it is wrong. Dr. Paul is correct and our mainstream economic/financial establishment is wrong. We would all be tremendously better off if we abolished the Federal

Reserve and our money was backed by gold or silver as mandated by the Constitution and if we privatized as much as possible and got rid of the aforementioned federal bureaucracies. Now, before the reader quickly concludes that this book is written by some crazy fool, please just read the next few paragraphs.

William E. Simon, former Secretary of the Treasury for presidents Richard Nixon and Gerald Ford, fills us in on the incompetence of the nation's "most prominent economists" during the financial crisis of the 1970s:

"The Wall Street Journal interviewed several dozen of the most prominent economists in the United States on the causes of the recession and on ways to prevent a recurrence. They disagreed about virtually everything save this: that there was much economists did not yet understand. The details of the economists' ignorance are of interest, but I stress here the overriding conclusion to be drawn from their statements: **The economists who had been advising our Presidents simply had not known what they were doing**"[10]

"…Gerson Green, formerly of the Office of Economic Opportunity, summed up the attitude of many of his colleagues when he observed caustically, "The change I discern is that **none of us knows what to do**. In those days, we thought we did. The country has taught the social engineers a lesson."… So who was running the store? The answer is: nobody. **Not one human being in the whole vast realm of political control over the American economy has *ever* known what he was doing**…For forty years the American ship of state has been lunging erratically toward economic disaster, with no awareness of its direction…"[11]

Ben Bernanke, the Chairman of the Federal Reserve and our establishment's top economist, admits that the Federal Reserve itself was largely to blame for the infamous Great Depression where up to 25% of the labor force was unemployed when he said:

"Let me end my talk by abusing slightly my status as an official representative of the Federal Reserve. I would like to say to Milton and Anna: Regarding the Great Depression. You're right, we did it. We're very sorry. But thanks to you, we won't do it again."[12]

The history of mankind is full of episodes where the commonly accepted knowledge was wrong compared to what most of us know or accept as right or just today. Thousands of years ago the idea that a woman had the same rights as a man was unheard of, and the same applies to mistreating or enslaving someone from another group, race, or tribe. When it comes to economics, during the 20th century millions were lured by communist ideology and inadvertently brought misery upon themselves. Many of these communist economists where white men with blue eyes, and not only that, they even had impressive sounding Russian last names. How could they have possibly failed?! Yet they did so miserably. Socialism/Communism did not spread and destroy much of the 20th century because of a few bad apples or tyrants; it first spread through the minds of the intellectuals that then gave the future tyrants the moral and intellectual justification for their actions. As 1974 Nobel laureate in economics F.A. Hayek tells us:

> "It is necessary to realize that the sources of many of the most harmful agents in this world are often not evil men but high-minded idealists, and that in particular the foundations of totalitarian barbarism have been laid by honourable and well-meaning scholars who never recognized the offspring they produced." [13]

The point of these last few paragraphs is to open up the reader's mind to the possibility that mankind is in the middle of a monumental ideological shift, and that our entire mainstream economics establishment is wrong. We must not make the mistake of believing that pompous looking white men[14] who are good in math and have degrees from prestigious universities necessarily know what is best for society. Mainstream economists are as wrong about economics and as likely victims to following popular fads in their field as psychologists were when they said that homosexuality was a mental disorder, that masturbation would lead to insanity, and that black slaves wanting to flee captivity "suffered" from a mental disorder called Drapetomia.[15]

The human ant-farm and the market process

Imagine you are looking at the earth from a spaceship. From high above humanity looks like a human ant-farm. Billions of people moving here and there, cars and planes going in and out of cities. Did anyone plan the human ant-farm? No. Even though the human ant-farm is the result of human action it is not the result of conscious human design. The human ant-farm and its amazing complexity shares this trait with language. Language too is the result of human action yet it was not consciously invented. No human being ever thought, "Hum... I think developing language would really help us communicate" and neither did a single person or group of people design and plan the amazing complexity of the human ant-farm. The human ant-farm and its amazing complexity is the result of a process, a process which is known to economists as **the market process**. The market process is what creates efficient, complex, and seemingly purposeful arrangements of human beings. It is what gives the human ant-farm, especially the human ant-farms of modern economies like the American and Japanese ones, their incredibly complex yet wonderfully ordered productive structures. Just like human beings were inadvertently developing language and at the same time language became an indispensable tool for their continued survival and evolutionary success, we are inadvertently creating the market process and it too is an indispensable tool for our continued survival and evolution.

If we could go back in time 1,000 years and look at the human ant-farm from high above, what would it look like? Today's social order is vastly more complex and productive compared to the one of 1,000 years ago. Today's human ant-farm is ordered in such a way that it can feed almost 7 billion people and have many live twice as long and in more material comfort than they did one thousand years ago. It also contains a vastly superior amount of knowledge spread throughout its billions of human brains, the knowledge required to transform matter in the ground into things like planes, cars, skyscrapers, computers, medical equipment, medicines, etc. If we compare today's American human ant-farm to that of Africa one we find that the American one produces about 13 trillion dollars worth of goods and services, while the African one produces only half a trillion even though the African human ant-farm has over twice as many people. What does this tell us? It tells us that the American human ant-farm has a more efficient and productive order.

Why is it that the American human ant-farm is ordered much more efficiently than the African one? 1000 years ago both human ant-farms were more or less the same in terms of material prosperity compared to what we have today, but why is it that over the last 1000 years the American human ant-farm managed to grow to the complex network that produces so much while the African one didn't? Because the market process has been working in America and therefore the people living and moving to America have been integrated into an ever more productive and technologically advanced social order. The market process has been more or less constantly rearranging the American human ant-farm, and slowly over time it became the most productive one in the world, and one vastly more productive than the African one. Unfortunately, Americans, and even more so Africans, have no understanding of what the market process is or how it works and we instinctively act in ways that slow it down and cripple it, and therefore slowing down and crippling the very progress of mankind.

Imagine it is the year 2050 and the whole world is doing great, there is no poverty and everyone can afford great products and health care and even the environment will be perfectly taken care of, but not just our environment over here, even the moon is being transformed via a rapidly growing space tourism industry. The human ant-farm of the year 2050 will obviously have to look different than today's. There will be new cities, new buildings, new knowledge that guides the actions of people in ways that will lead to this more efficient arrangement of society. If this prosperous future is in the cards, there is a sequence of steps that must be taken by every single human being in order to transform today's human ant-farm into this awesome one of the year 2050. How will we know which steps to take? Is it something we can plan? If 50 years ago the government hired the brightest minds and tried to plan for the year 2008, their plan would have been based on the ideas and technology that existed in the 1950s. There would have been no cell phones, no personal computers, no Internet and the tremendous advances that flow from these technologies. The smartest minds would have failed miserably in coming even close to designing a human ant-farm like the one we have today. The progress of mankind cannot be planned, but fortunately, the market process, if properly understood by all human beings, can be allowed to ensure that the steps we take are as efficient as humanly possible or pretty close to it. Just like following a few simple traffic rules, like go on green light and stop on red light, help coordinate the driving of millions of cars and in a more indirect manner have been crucial rules for the entire functioning of modern society where automotive transportation plays such a vital role, the market process also grows out of the adherence to a few simple rules. The rules basically come down to these two laws:

1. Do all you have agreed to do[16]
2. Do not encroach on other persons or their property

How adherence to these two rules/laws is what 'turns on' the market process and how it in turn creates our social order is one of this book's most important purposes.

Capitalism and Communism introduced

Capitalism in its purest form is an economic system where the government essentially enforces two simple laws, they are:

1. Do all you have agreed to do
2. Do not encroach on other persons or their property

The first law is the basis for what we call contract law, and it ensures that people keep their word and do not defraud each other. The second one makes all acts of theft and violence illegal which forces all human beings into peaceful interaction. In a purely capitalist society no one can be forced to do anything that they don't want to do. The only amount of money or resources that the individual would have to give the government would be those needed for the government to enforce the two laws, which for our purposes we'll limit to national defense, courts, law enforcement and that's about it. No public education, social security, welfare, funding of the arts or sciences, regulation of businesses or health care practices, etc., because in order to pay for these things the government would have to violate law #2 and forcibly take money from people who might not want to fund these government programs/functions as well. This is the essence of government in a 100% capitalist society; it protects the freedom of the individual to do with his money/property as he wishes, period. It is important to note that Capitalism is synonymous with individual freedom, and that there is no visible entity managing or controlling the economy or whatever social order emerges out of the interactions of these free individuals. It almost seems like a recipe for social chaos.

The opposite of Capitalism/'100% individual freedom', is Communism or 100% government control. In a pure communist society there is no private property, everything is owned and controlled by the government including the people. A communist society can be seen as a society where the individual is taxed at a rate of 100%. If you are taxed at a rate of 100% then you do not have the means with which to buy or own anything, and everything that you need like education, health care, housing, food, etc., must be provided by the government at no cost. In a communist society, since the government provides everything for its citizens, it has no choice but to take away their freedom in order provide these services. It should be obvious that for the government to provide services to society all people cannot be free to do whatever they want, people have to work for the government in order for it to function and the more services the government provides for people the more people have to work for the government.

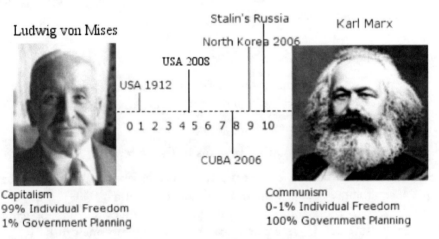

Above we have a figure showing pure Capitalism on one side represented by Ludwig von Mises and pure Communism on the other, represented by its most famous proponent, Karl Marx. All governments fall somewhere in between, for example, today's North Korea might have the most government controlled and therefore communist economy in the world, so it would land near the 9. Stalin's Russia during the 1930-40's might be considered to be even more government controlled/communist so it is closer to 10. The United States near 1912 was at around 1, people were relatively free, there wasn't even an income tax, the government provided very little in terms of services and social planning. Americans and the companies they created provided for all goods and services. Americans had a lot of freedom and control over the fruits of their labor. We can see that by 2008 the United States has moved towards Communism quite a bit. Today's USA has a much bigger government which does much more social planning. It provides many services like public education well into adulthood, welfare for the have-less, medical care/retirement for the elderly via social security, regulates and orchestrates how to practice medicine, who can or cannot be a doctor and what they must do in order to be one, what can or cannot be a medicine, how much money someone can legally work for, how to build homes/cars/planes/ladders/toys to make them safe etc. Pretty much everything these days has to meet some government issued requirement. All of these things are obviously done in good faith, most of us believe that this makes the world a better place and we often gladly vote for higher taxes in order to give the government even more things to do. Today's US government does these and countless other things which it did not do in 1912 because at the time it did not have the legal power or ability to take the needed resources from the private sector to pay for the administration and oversight of all of these things. In order for it to do so much in 2008 it has to tax and take from Americans a much larger amount of money and resources than it did in 1912. For our current purposes it does not matter whether a capitalist or communist government is democratically elected, a monarchy, military dictatorship, theocracy, run by "good" or "evil" people, or which one might be better or preferred by members of society. All we want to accomplish is to define them and understand their main difference which is the amount of economic freedom enjoyed by individuals, or in other words, the proportion of resources and decision-making power controlled by either free individuals or combinations of them(companies), i.e. the private sector, or the government/public sector. The more the government does/oversees/regulates, the more communist a society is, the less the government does/oversees/regulates and therefore the more the private sector/'free individuals' do/oversee, the more capitalist/free is a society.

  Finally, we need to briefly discuss Socialism. Anything that is 'socialized' means that it is run by the government. For example, in the United States, a single 30 year old male has to pay for health care directly by purchasing health insurance from a company in the private sector or paying his own medical bills. If the people via their politicians decide that the

United States government should offer everyone health care regardless of his/her ability to pay, then we say that health care/medicine has been socialized, it has gone from being provided by the private sector to the government/public sector. The more sectors of the economy are socialized the closer to Communism the economy becomes. When all sectors of an economy are socialized and therefore managed by government, we have 100% Socialism or Communism. So once everything is socialized we say we have Communism, until then, we have various levels of Socialism, with 100% Socialism being Communism. Throughout the book I will often times refer to Socialism and Communism as if they were equal because in essence they are the same, they are about government control as opposed to individual control/'private sector'.

A tribal brain in a modern world

In order to understand the world's socioeconomic troubles and get humanity on the path to peace and prosperity we have to focus on a drastic change in the recent social evolution of man, the transition from simple self-sufficient tribal societies to our modern complex economies.

The environment where we evolved, in other words, the environment where our genes, instincts, and "tribal morals" have been shaped by evolution was a world very different from the one we currently live in. It was a world more like that of our close cousins the chimpanzees and bonobos which slowly changed into that of the stereotypical caveman and tribal existence. In the simple tribal societies everyone was of the same race, even the neighboring tribes. This was the case because people had not developed ways of traveling distances that were long enough to run into people that were significantly different from each other. And if we go even farther back in time, biological differences would have been too small to even classify different groups of people as belonging to different races like we might do today. There was little division of labor which was mostly based on sex and age, women might have gathered fruits and vegetables and men took care of the hunt and fighting with the neighbors. There was a fixed amount of resources in the environment where people lived. We were not smart enough to learn to adapt to new environments so we were limited to a regular living area, which could only support a limited amount of people. For example, there would only be so much food that could be gathered from the land without waiting for it to re-grow naturally, if some people had lots of food others would have less. An environment where there is a fixed amount of resources and some have plenty at the expense of those that have little, or also where for every winner there is a loser like in a tennis match or a fight to the death, this type of environment economists and evolutionary psychologists refer to as a zero-sum environment. A zero-sum environment is like a 10 inch pizza, the more pizza one person gets, the less there has to be for the rest.

Tribes were small(25-150 people) and most people knew each other personally. There was little technological progress and it was too slow to be noticed, for example, for the last 2.5 million years until maybe the last 20,000 years our most useful tools were mostly stone axes and knifes, clubs to bash people's heads with and fire. We were self-sufficient and consumed or "used up" most of the things we created ourselves. Life was simple and easily understood. An adult more or less had a good idea of what everyone else did and how the community worked. All tasks were relatively simple and involved at most the interactions of few easily identifiable people. Our minds and instincts have been shaped to live in this kind of world but the world has changed drastically over the last 20,000 years, and especially so during the last 200.

Today's advanced societies are very different, it is normal to see people of different races and even if a single race is the majority in a particular city it is very common to travel and interact with people of other races. There is lots of division of labor, members of a modern society are highly specialized compared to the members of tribal societies, some are mechanics of different kinds, doctors of different specialties, computer programmers and so on. Most professions take years to master unlike the simple tasks carried out by members of tribal societies. And by far the most important difference is that our modern world is not a zero-sum environment because rapid technological progress and the ability to produce more and better things increases the amount of goods available so that even though some might have much more than others, everyone can have more and will be better off compared to his previous state. In other words, the pizza or global economic pie constantly gets bigger and bigger, very, very fast and without limit. We are not self-sufficient. Instead of consuming the things we create ourselves, we trade the goods we make or the labor we sell for money, and then use this money to buy the things we need. Money plays a crucial role in our modern world and how it works and helps coordinate our modern human ant-farms is something we do not intuitively or even consciously really understand. We live in cities of millions of people most of whom we will never personally deal with. The world is very complex and it is impossible for a single person to fully understand how everyone else does his job or how a single thing is created.

Even what seems like a simple task in today's modern economies is incredibly complex, and is the result of the interactions of millions of people going back in time for generations. Just think about buying a computer. Unlike a task in the tribal world which was carried out by easily identifiable people and at most required the knowledge and skills of those few human beings, your computer was put together and came to your store due to the interactions and knowledge of millions. Many companies and groups of human beings worked and in some way or another your computer made it to your nearby store thanks to the interactions of these individuals. Not a single one of them knows who you are and not a single one of them woke up that morning thinking about your need for the computer you are going to buy. Some computer parts were made in Taiwan, others in Japan, some assembly might have taken place in Singapore, the transportation of parts took place on large ships built in England built years or decades ago, ships composed of thousands of different components, many of which were imported from many different countries, built by a multitude of people, and you get the point; all of these interactions are impossible to trace and go far back in time, yet it was this network of interactions that mattered.

In the tribal world everything involved the interactions of a few people with their natural environment, and there was no complicated web of production like we just described. In today's modern economies it is not the abilities and character of a few people that matter when it comes to getting things done, it is the arrangement and coordinated actions of millions of people. This is something that we do not intuitively understand because we evolved in a much simpler world. We care about the smiles and trustworthiness of our elected leaders just like we would have cared about the trustworthiness of fellow tribe members in the past. But in today's world, it is the structure and well coordinated actions of millions of people over generations that get things done, and more importantly, it is the market process that shapes all of these things and not particular individuals.

Another one of the most important differences between our tribal world and today's is that in the tribal world, everything that was created by man was designed or planned with a specific purpose in mind while in today's modern world, although most things are still designed or planned with a specific purpose in mind, the human ant-farm/'social organism' and its mind-boggling complexity is not the result of conscious human planning or design, it is the result of the market process, something that didn't exist in our tribal/ape-like past. Things like the Internet depend on computers, which in turn depend on microprocessors which in turn depend on transistors and on and on, yet none of the things in the lower levels were designed with the purpose of someday contributing to the Internet and all that in turn depends on it. Since everything in our tribal past that was made by human beings was also designed by human beings and everything was relatively simple, in today's modern world we have a propensity to think that human beings can design/plan/regulate the economy/'human ant-farm' and this is one of the reasons we feel like we need a huge government apparatus to help give the human ant-farm order. But this is a mistake, which is rooted in our tribal propensity to plan and easily understand the much simpler tribal social order, and lack of an understanding of what the market process is and how it works.

Whenever one of the many tasks the government tries to do is screwed up enough to get the necessary public attention, like the recent handling of hurricane Katrina[17], we always look for people to blame because it comes naturally to us to think that the only way to create purposeful and coordinated arrangements of people is through top-down delegation where some people plan what needs to be done and they delegate all the way down the man-made hierarchy. We have this type of mentality because in our tribal world it worked. Even the most complicated of tasks in our tribal past could not employ more than the entire population of the tribe, say at most 150 people. You just delegated parts of the tasks to a relatively small number of personally known, and therefore easily identifiable people, whose skills and abilities were more or less the same and whose trustworthiness was probably the most important asset. Tasks were relatively simple and could be designed by few human brains and carried out without much change in order to accomplish the original goal. But today's world is much more complex and tasks are carried out in a different manner. We still use delegation, which we are very familiar with, but unknowingly we also use something new, something we do not instinctively truly understand because it is a new invention in the world that our tribal brains have not evolved to understand. We use *the market process* and its many components like, money, prices, the banking and lending industry, stock markets, interest rates, and other institutions that play a crucial role in developing our modern human ant-farms. All of these things are new to us, like language they too exist thanks to the actions of human beings but they provide a function that is independent of our conscious design. It is the market process which ultimately allows us to create the kinds of complex arrangements of human beings that give the modern world its amazingly complex and productive order, not the top-down delegation which we instinctively associate with such arrangements. We do not realize that no matter who is in charge of large groups of people and resources, it is the way these thousands or millions of resources interact and not the trustworthiness, or good intentions, or our personal relationship with the people at the top that matter. We do not know what the market process is or how it works and therefore we don't realize that only the market process can arrange these resources in a productive and orderly fashion. Unfortunately the market process does not have a face, it does not smile, and it can't hold babies and take pictures and talk to us and tell us how it will "plan" the efficient structuring of society.

It makes sense for most of us to look at the vast complexity of the world and think that someone or some entity must help guide or keep it orderly and "fair", and we think that it is government that greatly helps us achieve this. This is why we constantly vote for and pay taxes to fund things like government run welfare system for the poor, government run education, government oversight of health care, government sponsored unemployment benefits, anti big business laws, and also fear a world where everything is privatized and people have to pay for everything and if they don't have the money and there isn't enough private charity tough luck. A world where the government does not take care of the poor or elderly, does not educate people, does not interfere with businesses regardless of how big and rich or successful they become, and lets employers hire and fire people for whatever reason or lack thereof, might be a scary thought for most of us, and for most of my life I too would have been scared at such an idea. Most of us feel like without much government management there would be social and economic chaos. It seems obvious to some that without government intervention the "white man" will oppress the minorities, that health care costs would soar because the greedy companies can charge lots of money for vital health care services, that businesses will pay employees less than a "living wage" because of our inherent greed and exploit them, that all of our jobs will be shipped overseas and we will be poorer because of it, that any idiot can pose as a doctor and harm people and so on. We also know that we are not 'perfect' and that it is in our nature to do bad things and we believe that by using the government we can help ourselves be better than we would otherwise be, but all of this is wrong. It is an almost inevitable mistake given our lack of an understanding of how the market process works and how it creates the modern world.

Most people would acknowledge the fact that the government/'public sector' is not perfect, that yes, it can be bureaucratic at times and that sometimes there are corrupt politicians etc. So we constantly look for ways to improve it, to 'cut the waste', or 'make it more accountable', to 'run it in a business-like fashion' and all kinds of other well meaning ideas. But what very few people understand and will seem shocking to most is that **even if everyone who works for the government were completely unselfish, with a heart as pure as that of a Mother Teresa or the Pope or an angel from heaven, and if on top of that they were also as smart as your favorite historical genius like Einstein perhaps, this government created arrangement of people, with its lack of corruption and overabundance of good intentions and intellect, would still destroy more social order and prosperity than it would create.** Most people think that the problem with government is related to corruption or the people who are in charge of it and so on, but that is not the case. Let's state it again, even if all the wonderful things governments try to provide for society were to be carried out by incorruptible geniuses, it would still provide a worse result for everyone, rich or poor, than the private sector with its average human beings and all of their so called faults and vices. The reason for this, as will be explained in the coming chapters, is because the market process, which creates the productive order of human beings and technology we associate with progress and civilization, only works in the private sector, and that whenever the government interferes with the privates sector, no matter how great the final outcome might seem to us, the vast majority of times it creates far more problems than it solves. Hopefully this will all make better sense soon.

The fall of communist Russia should have taught us that having government try to provide solutions to the needs of mankind was an utter failure, but that is not what we learned. We learned that if we could just have "good" people running the government then everything would be ok, and it is for that reason that we feel like spreading democracy is what will fix the world. We feel like with a democracy, should "bad" people control the government then we just suffer a little, but then we can vote them out and replace them with "good" people and everything will be great. No matter how hard Russian communist revolutionary Vladimir Lenin tried to have government plan and provide for his people, the inevitable growing inefficiency of his government apparatus kept leading to an unproductive chaos. Lenin, as well as most of us, believed that "the key feature is people, the proper choice of people", and if we could just have the right people with the right values government management would work. But Lenin was wrong. In today's modern world, the personal abilities of individual human beings are not as important as they were in our simpler tribal past, and nowhere near in comparison to the importance of the workings of the market process. What the fall of communist Russia should have taught us is that government management does not work period, regardless of whether the government is created via democracy, theocracy, military dictatorship or how nice, caring, or smart its members might be.

Unfortunately we have not evolved to instinctively understand economics, what the market process is, why government programs inevitably cause way more problems than they solve, and much less learn anything from the history of economic policy. I can talk to a monkey and tell him how to properly use the bathroom, how to do various jobs and live like a human being, but no matter how correct I might be in my instructions, it is not in the monkey's nature to understand and process our powerful languages and be able to do things as well as we can. Something similar applies to human beings and our ability to understand how the market process shapes an increasingly productive social order and everything we associate with civilization above the tribal level. The failure of government planning compared to individual economic freedom constantly stares us right in the face, yet we have not evolved to see their difference, just like a monkey has not evolved to understand my clear instructions on how to live like a human. We think government planning/regulation leads to order, social justice, a clean environment, and equality, while individual economic freedom leads to chaos, social injustice, irresponsible pollution, and inequality via haves and have-nots. But the truth is that we actually have it backwards, government planning/regulation leads to economic chaos, social injustice, pollution, and inequality, while individual economic freedom leads to the most productive and efficient social order, justice, a clean environment, and material equality. The only way we can really see this, is by training our minds to properly understand the new world in which we live, and we do this by learning about economics and how the market process works.

Society and civilization are the products of an evolutionary process just like our bodies are. The ability of this evolutionary process to create order, whether it is biological order or socioeconomic order, is far beyond what we could possibly consciously achieve. To think that electing people to a government whose task it will be to organize, plan, or manage the functioning of society is as big a mistake as is asking a doctor to create 50 trillion cells and piece them together to make a human being. Right now, most Americans and the same applies to pretty much everyone in the modern industrialized countries, believe in the ideology of a democratically elected government that more or less takes 50% of the wealth generated by the private sector via taxes and so on, and uses it to provide so called essential services and regulate the functioning of the economy. This big government, democratic-high-tax-spend-regulate ideology is a mistaken one that is slowing down the very progress of mankind and destroying the lives of many.

Our tribal nature is maladapted to the modern world but fortunately we have reached a point where we can understand this and overcome the problem. Our strong desire for "equality", our jealousy or contempt for the rich, or those that "have too much" and do not "share" their wealth, in other words, the anti-capitalist-eat-the-rich-take-from-the-haves-to-give-to-the-have-less mentality that seems to spread so easily amongst most of us, is a result of our inherited instincts from our tribal past and we are doomed unless we can see this fact and transform our cultural values to be in synch with the rules and laws, that although they might scare us instinctively, we can rationalize and understand how they are truly in our best interest. The next step in the evolution of man has nothing to do with our genes or personal abilities, it will be the wide spread understanding of how the market process works, in other words, an understanding of Capitalism. To do this we need to understand why our brains are highly susceptible to the idea of having government plan and regulate society.

Wealth as a transformation of matter and the main difference between the tribal and modern worlds

The fundamental difference between our tribal world and our modern market-process-coordinated world is that our tribal world was a zero-sum environment where the nature-provided, and therefore limited amount of resources, created conditions where in order to have resources for your survival you had no choice but to be very "evil" and have an us vs. them mentality. When a lion takes over a pride and kills the existing cubs in order for the females to be available for mating with him and to devote resources to his future progeny/genes, most of us accept this as part of nature, we don't say the lion is "evil", yet the lion as well as ourselves owe our existence to such "evil" acts and brutality committed by our ancestors. The world was a pizza of a given size and the more others had the less there would be for you. There was no political correctness or much in the way of morals to a tribal brain. All that mattered and existed were strategies that led to success. This "zero-sumness" of the world we evolved in is at the heart of explaining why we can be so selfish and even enjoy the misfortunes of others. If the world had an infinite supply of everything you could possible want, would there have been any need for anger, or jealousy, or selfishness? Not really. But in the real world, especially in our tribal world, there was always a limited supply of resources, and anger, jealousy, selfishness was needed to ensure we got enough to survive.

In the modern market-process-coordinated world our fates are determined by the workings of our human ant-farms much more so than our personal abilities. It is not the doctor that cures us, it is the tremendous amount of easily affordable technology/medicines/training which allows an average human being to help us cure our diseases. But we cannot possibly care about or protect a system whose very existence we are not even aware of as is the case with the market process. In today's world, our global human ant-farm can be seen as, and in fact *is*, like a new living thing, one that survives by transforming the world around it in a way that feeds and meets the needs of its individual human ants/parts/cells. A process fundamentally no different than the way our body interacts and transforms the external world for the benefit of the cells that make it up and therefore keep us alive and in order.

In the modern world we are not limited by what nature naturally replenishes, we create new wealth by transforming matter. Physics teaches us that matter cannot be created or destroyed, all wealth is really just a transformation of matter from a state that is useless to people to one that is useful to us. We evolved in a world where we had no ability to transform nature, so whatever nature provided was truly finite as far as we were concerned and that is how we more or less see the world today. The fact that when we integrate ourselves with the social organism via the market process, we become a sort of super-robot that works at transforming the thousands of cubic miles of matter that the entire planet is made of into new wealth, constantly increasing the economic pie for everyone, is completely foreign to us. As economist George Reisman tells us:

"...from the perspective of physics and chemistry, all of production and economic activity consists merely of changing the combinations and locations of the chemical elements. The production of automobiles or refrigerators for example, entails the movement of some part of the world's supply of the element iron from locations such as the Mesabi range in Minnesota to places all across the country and the world. In the process the iron is broken out of combination with certain other chemical elements such as oxygen or sulfur and put into combination with different chemical elements such as chrome or nickel. The overall quantity of each of the elements in the world remains exactly the same as before. The only difference is in the relationship of the chemical elements to human life and well-being, which is obviously vastly improved by man's productive activity. Iron buried in the hillsides of Minnesota is useless, but changed by human productive activity to take the form of automobiles, refrigerators, bridges and skyscrapers and countless other products it is of immense utility."[18]

What really is a refrigerator? It is an arrangement of elements/chemicals/natural resources found in the planet that have been relocated from one set of coordinates to a different one. The refrigerator was once broken up into millions of pieces of matter deposited in mountains or beneath the earth, and it was the workings of the human ant-farm that relocated and transformed those elements/matter into a refrigerator that is useful to us. So once again we can see that wealth is about transforming matter and reorganizing it in a way that helps us in our continuous quest for superior states of well-being. Wealth is a transformation of things from states where they have little to no use from our human perspective to states where they are more valuable to us. Let's quote another great economist just because it's cool and he has an impressive sounding name, this time Eugen von Böhm-Bawerk:

"To "produce": what does this mean? It has been so often said by economists that the creation of goods is not the bringing into existence of materials that hitherto have not existed—is not "creation" in the true sense of the word, but only a fashioning of imperishable matter into more advantageous shapes..."[19]

Let's think about food, which has been the most important source of wealth for most of our evolution. Food is a package of chemicals that we can consume in order to maintain our orderly structure. The chemicals that make up our food are found on the earth and by nature's workings they are gathered by plants and therefore transformed from various coordinates in the earth to new sets of coordinates where they happen to be of use to us in the way of edible plants, and also through further transformations into the animals that feed on these plants. Before plants transformed these chemicals, they were useless to our continued orderly existence, the chemicals were not organized into human usable wealth, but after their transformation by nature they became wealth, the food we ate. Before humanity stumbled upon the market process and it transformed us into being members of the 'social organism'/'market-process-coordinated human ant-farm' like we are now, nature, and nature alone transformed the chemical elements into wealth and this is what limited our ability to grow and prosper beyond our inevitably brutal zero-sum existence. As members of the global market-process-coordinated human ant-farm we now transform matter for our benefit in ways that we have not evolved to intuitively understand. A few miners today, using building-sized trucks and other machinery, can mine and begin the transformation of matter to wealth in ways that are thousands of times more productive than they were just a couple of hundred years ago, and our ability to transform the various elements we need to nourish our bodies has also increased tremendously compared with the rate at which nature performed this transformation before we stumbled upon agriculture and the many other improvements generated by the social organism. The fact that the computational ability of the human ant-farm, in other words, its ability to unconsciously calculate the paths that matter must take as it is transformed into human usable wealth, continuously increases as more human brains are added to it, is something we have not evolved to understand and we find counterintuitive.

Contrary to what most of us believe, so called "overpopulation" is not a problem, it is a blessing. This happens because the rate at which the human ant-farm transforms matter into wealth increases much faster than the rate at which our increasing population can consume such wealth. The human ant-farm is in fact aided by a large population which simply helps make it a more efficient matter-to-wealth machine. But more on this later. For most of us, without an understanding of the market-process there are only so many bananas in the trees, and the more people the less bananas, which happens to be the opposite of the truth in our new world, where the more people the more bananas appear, but fortunately understanding this radical change, from depending on nature to transform matter into wealth to allowing the 'social organism'/'human ant-farm' to perform this transformation, is something that can be easily understood by learning how the market-process/economics works.

Market process vs. Government. South vs. North Korea

Just a few pages ago, I compared the American human ant-farm to the African one, let's have another comparison along the same lines. This time North Korea, a communist country where government is what manages the actions of the human ants it controls and therefore plans the social order, and South Korea, a much more capitalist country where it is the market process which coordinates and gives order to its human ant-farm.

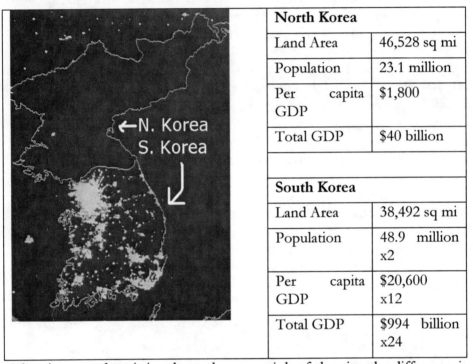

North Korea	
Land Area	46,528 sq mi
Population	23.1 million
Per capita GDP	$1,800
Total GDP	$40 billion

South Korea	
Land Area	38,492 sq mi
Population	48.9 million x2
Per capita GDP	$20,600 x12
Total GDP	$994 billion x24

The picture and statistics above do a great job of showing the difference in the types of productive social orders that are created by both systems. The picture was taken at night by the US department of Defense and shows how the South Korean human ant-farm is brimming with cities which can power themselves at night, while the North Korean human ant-farm barely has a little spec in its capital city. South Korea is a smaller country in terms of land area yet it houses a population that is over twice as large as that of North Korea. Each South Korean on average can produce about $20,600 worth of wealth, which is about twelve times more than the $1,800 that his northern brother can. Since South Korea has over twice as many people who are each about twelve times more productive, the total domestic production is about twenty four times greater for South Korea than it is for North Korea. Forty billion dollars worth of goods and services for the North Korean human ant-farm vs. 994 billion for the South Korean human ant-farm. Once again try to picture the two human ant-farms from high above. The South Korean human ant-farm is a very efficient matter-to-wealth transformation organism. Thousands of tons of raw materials come in, or are dug up, and are transformed into human usable wealth(cars, tools, computers, gadgets, medicines, etc.), some of which is then traded with other human ant-farms like the USA/Japan/China/'rest of world' for other types of wealth. The North Korean human ant-farm has a less efficient and less orderly structured human ant-farm, it is an inefficient and inferior matter-to-wealth transformation organism compared to the South Korean one. The North Korean human ant-farm has a visible entity trying to achieve an efficient productive order, the government with its many bureaucracies and regulations acting like tentacles moving the human ants around, yet the productive social order cannot keep its people alive, much less in any sort of material well-being. The South Korean human ant-farm does not have a visible entity telling the millions of human ants that make it up what to do and how to do it, its productive order is created by the market process, by the emergent behavior of human beings going about improving their condition, by people coming together via companies here and breaking up there, always more or less following our two fundamental laws.

One of the most important lessons that can be learned from this short comparison is that race, or genetics, has nothing to do with socioeconomic prosperity and advancement since both Koreas were a single nation with a common people until the end of World War II. From 1910 to 1945 the Korean peninsula was occupied by the Japanese. When the Japanese lost WWII, communist Russia and semi-capitalist USA did not come to an agreement as to how to "liberate" the Koreans, so it was split into the Russian influenced and therefore communist North, and the American influenced and therefore more pro-capitalist South.

---

[1] Kaiser/HRET:1999-2004

[2] http://www.gasbuddy.com/gb_retail_price_chart.aspx

[3] http://www.collegeboard.com/student/pay/add-it-up/4494.html

[4] http://www.fool.com/college/college01.htm

[5] http://www.federalbudget.com/

[6] http://youtube.com/watch?v=OS2fI2p9iVs A "60 Minutes" interview given by Steve Kroft

Also visit this link http://www.gao.gov/newcomers.vid.html in the GAO's website for more educational videos put out by Mr. Walker.

[7] Paul, Ron. "Mises and Austrian Economics", page 4.

[8] See Murray N. Rothbard's "America's Great Depression" in Amazon.com and compare its glowing reviews to top mainstream economist, Federal Reserve Chairman Ben Bernanke's "Essays on the Great Depression"

[9] Paul, Ron. "Mises and Austrian Economics", Page 3

[10] Simon, William E. "A Time For Truth". McGraw-Hill Book Company. 1978, page 121-122 ISBN 0-07-057378-6 . Originally references The Wall Street Journal, August 18, 1976. I have added emphasis on a few words by printing them in bold.

[11] Ibid. 122-123. Here too I have used bold font to emphasize a few words and the word "ever" shows up in italics in original publication.

The statement made by Garson Green is referenced to "The New York Times. November 27, 1976"

[12] Ben Bernanke, "At the Conference to Honor Milton Friedman, University of Chicago, Chicago, Illinois November 8, 2002"

http://www.federalreserve.gov/BOARDDOCS/SPEECHES/2002/20021108/default.htm

[13] F.A. Hayek, Law Legislation and Liberty, Volume I Rules and Order. The University of Chicago Press, published 1983, page 70

[14] no pun intended. If it weren't for my accent, I could pass for a white guy. I'm guy in blue on back cover.

[15] http://en.wikipedia.org/wiki/Drapetomania

[16] These laws I like to refer to as Maybury's laws, named after Richard J. Maybury. Author of the wonderful Uncle Eric series of books.

[17] Lew Rockwell's speech on the inevitable government mishandling of hurricane Katrina's New Orleans devastation is a gem. Read the transcript here : http://www.mises.org/story/1934 or better yet, listen to Lew's speech here : http://www.mises.org/multimedia/mp3/ss05/ss05-Rockwell.mp3

[18] Reisman, George. Lecture given at the Ludwig von Mises Institute(www.mises.org) on 2/29/2004 , entitled "Resource Economics and Environmentalism". Audio file http://www.mises.org/mp3/MU2001/MU20.mp3 , minute 16:07

[19] Eugen von Böhm-Bawerk, The Positive Theory of Capital. London: Macmillan and Co.. 1891, trans. William A. Smart, 1891. Section I.I.13 . http://www.econlib.org/library/BohmBawerk/bbPTC1.html

II. Economics and the Market Process

The ongoing cycle of production and consumption

A human ant-farm, whether it be a single person one, or the entire global one, is in a constant cycle of production and consumption. Using our modern world as example, we can envision matter being dug up from mines, or at times recycled, and through incalculable steps it is transformed into the wealth we consume like energy, cars, planes, food, buildings, etc. This process of taking matter that is in a state that is not useful to us and reordering it into human usable wealth is called production. The process of using up such wealth for our continued existence and growth is called consumption. As we consume most wealth it eventually either ceases to exist as wealth, like food that is eaten, or wears out like cars and so on. So production increases the economic pie while consumption reduces it.

Self-sufficient vs. market oriented societies. The division of labor and knowledge, and their impact on the human ant-farm.

A long time ago people were more or less self-sufficient. Life was very simple, we were nomads just living off of whatever nature provided and naturally replenished. At some point, regardless of how we got to it, most societies centered their daily activities based on trade. Assuming people were not using money yet, they had to barter, which means that they would have to trade their goods directly for the things that they wanted. I would go to the market and trade my coconut pastries for other things like blankets, spears, knifes, baskets, milk, fish, bows, arrows, or any of the many other things people in the market produced. Why did most societies eventually go from self-sufficient to market oriented societies? Because market oriented societies were more productive and this led to more growth and eventually the overtaking either by conquest or migration of those other societies that were not market oriented. Let's take a look at why it is that market oriented societies built around trade are more productive than non-market oriented self-sufficient societies.

There is one main benefit that a society gains from trade and that is the division of labor and knowledge. Each member of a market-oriented society specializes in learning how to produce and going about producing just one or a few goods, which he later uses to trade for all the other types of goods available in the market. The division of labor and knowledge has three main advantages over self-sufficiency.

1.   You do not have to waste time switching tasks like you would if you tried to produce every good for yourself. Instead of wasting time switching, you spend that time in the continued production of the one thing you make and therefore this leads to more productivity than would have otherwise existed.

2.   By specializing in producing just one thing, you get better, faster, and more efficient at producing this one item and therefore this leads to more productivity than would have otherwise existed.

3.   You do not have to waste time learning how to make the various other things that can be produced. You only learn how to make the one or few things you specialize in. Instead of wasting time learning how to make other things, you spend that time in the continued production and betterment of the thing you specialize in and therefore this leads to more productivity than would have otherwise existed.

Point number three is of special importance for the way in which we will continue to learn about economics. There comes a point where a single human brain cannot possibly learn how to make an increasing number of things. A brain can only hold so much information and a human being can only spend so much time learning as opposed to producing the things it needs in order to survive. Imagine a society of 1,000 people where each person specialized in producing one item which he trades for other things in the market, a 1,000 member market oriented society or human ant-farm. When I go to the market I can trade my coconut pastries for any one of the other 999 goods produced. By being able to trade my pastries for them, I can make use of 1,000 different goods and only know how to produce one of them. I do not have to learn anything about basket weaving like where to find the best materials and how to weave them to make a good basket. I do not have to learn how to milk or take care of cows, or how to hunt and skin animals to make blankets. I also save everyone in society from having to learn how to safely and effectively gather coconuts, where to find them, and how to make my tasty coconut pastries. If we compare the 1000 member market-oriented society to the 1000 member self-sufficient tribal society and picture them as human ant-farms being seen from above we see that the self-sufficient society as a whole has very simple knowledge repeated through its 1,000 brains and guided by this simple knowledge people more or less just wake up, gather food, sleep, and repeat. But the market-oriented society has a much more complicated and productive human ant-farm. It contains much more knowledge, the knowledge required to build 1,000 different items, and this knowledge is not repeated in every one of its 1,000 brains, it is efficiently stored in each brain just once, leaving lots of brain power in each person left over to think about other things, like how to improve or create new products.

It is important to realize that technological improvements are mostly just a recombination of previous knowledge. There are only so many ways in which you can combine 5 products or pieces of knowledge to come up with new ones. But 1,000 products provides for many possibilities to combine them to make new products or improve the production of existing ones, in other words, to create new knowledge. For example, I used to get my coconuts by climbing a tree, using a sharp rock to cut them loose from the tree, and then I would make several trips to my house carrying as many coconuts as I could with my hands, about 5. Based on the knowledge that existed in my brain, this was the best way I knew how to go about getting coconuts. Human brains are always thinking of ways of being more productive. We are always trying to make our lives easier and this means finding new ways to do our tasks in ways that save us time and effort. One day while walking by the market I saw a guy selling baskets, he was showing off how strong they were by filling them up with rocks and lifting them. I immediately realized that I could increase my productivity by using the baskets to carry more coconuts per trip to my house. I also saw another vendor selling very sharp stone knifes, he was demonstrating their sharpness by showing how easily his knifes could cut through small thin branches. I also realized how much faster I would be able to cut the coconuts lose from the trees and process them afterwards by using the better knifes. Luckily both vendors were interested in my coconut pastries, we came to a mutually beneficial arrangement and made our trade. Thanks to my new knife and basket I went from producing 6 of my coconut pastries per day to 8. Since I produced more, now I had more to offer others in the market in exchange for their goods, I was able to afford more stuff and happier because of it.

Now let's examine what has happened in terms of the human ant-farm, its arrangement and the distribution of knowledge. Thanks to the already existing division of labor and knowledge that allowed our society to have 1,000 people each specializing and knowing how to produce one type of good, I was able to find a new way of combining goods based on existing knowledge(knife and basket) to come up with new knowledge. The new knowledge is not a new product in this example, it is a new and better way of going about producing an existing one, my coconut pastries. This new knowledge leads to a different arrangement of the human ant-farm. If we zoom into my section of the human ant-farm, I move differently, use my hands differently by using the new knife, I make less trips carrying coconuts back to my house by using my new basket. My old knowledge, which led to a certain sequence of actions on my part, has been replaced by new knowledge which now leads to a more productive sequence of actions.

The human ant-farm has transformed itself from a less productive state to a more productive one. The order in which the ants moved has been altered to be a more efficient one. The pattern of knowledge that existed in its brains has been altered for the better. Knowledge of basket and knife use was now incorporated into my brain.

Market oriented societies as supercomputers

In a market oriented society the entire human ant-farm becomes a supercomputer, constantly discovering new knowledge and restructuring itself in increasingly more productive ways. This happens because every brain constantly looks for new knowledge which can guide its actions in more productive ways. The individual brain looks in the market place for products or things or ideas that it can use to come up with more productive ways of producing its product/enhancement or new product, in other words, discovering new, more efficient knowledge to replace less efficient one like I did when I realized I could use a knife and basket to increase my productivity and therefore my own little ant-like behavior. When a human brain discovers new knowledge it can have two effects on the larger social organism, it can introduce a completely new product, which all the other brains in society can now use in their own calculations of how to go about improving their productive processes, or it can simply find a way of increasing the production of its current product, which simply increases its supply, making it more affordable, which can once again lead to new knowledge. For example, laptop computers now cost about $400, if new knowledge leads to a more efficient way of producing them so that they cost $10, this fact enters the brains of millions of people who can use $10 laptops to greatly increase their own productivity and therefore the further rearrangement of the human ant-farm in ever more efficient and productive ways.

The material progress of mankind is the result of the continued increase in productivity of the human ant-farm. This means that the human ant-farm goes from one state where its ants are ordered doing things one way to another more productive state where the ants act in a more productive way. And if the human ants are moving in a more productive way it is because they have discovered new and more productive knowledge. There are two main factors that lead to the discovery of new productive knowledge, one is the discovery of new products or services by human brains, like the knife and basket which helped me come up with a superior way of going about my production of coconut pastries. And the second is the continued reduction in price of these products or services, like how the reduction of cost of computers helped give rise to the Internet. These two factors are what constantly allow brains to recombine existing goods and services into more productive ways of acting, and therefore giving the human ant-farm its increasingly more prosperous and efficient structure.

The growing interdependence of knowledge

As the process described above continues, a complex web of interdependence of knowledge emerges. For example, the knowledge I used to gather my coconuts was very simple, find a sharp rock to cut coconuts lose from the tree, learn how to climb trees, learn how to carry as many coconuts as possible with my arms back to my house, my coconut pastries recipe. Since my new production process involves using the new stone knife and basket, it now makes use of the knowledge that went into the production of such goods, like where to find the best materials to build the basket, how to weave it, what kinds of rocks make the best knifes, where to find them, and so on. When I use the knife or basket I am a benefactor of the knowledge that went into creating them yet I do not have to know anything about this, I only have to know how to use these products to my advantage. A one hundred person market oriented society might be simple enough so that one brain can trace all the knowledge that goes into the production of the average item produced. But in a modern society like today's USA it is nearly impossible to trace and understand all the knowledge that goes into the making of your average item. A bag of chips is made up of a plastic bag which came into existence thanks to who knows how many chemical processes and is made of raw materials that had to be mined somewhere and transported using trucks with engines that where made who knows where or how, and that is just the plastic bag.[1]

Money

We have discussed the advantages of a market-oriented society over a self-sufficient one. We have seen how the division of labor and knowledge allows for the continuous restructuring of the human ant-farm into increasingly more productive and technologically advanced states. These advantages allow market-oriented societies to grow more, support bigger and more technologically advanced populations and sooner or later they spread by either conquest of other societies or by having others migrate or imitate their market-oriented ways.

There is one problem I overlooked with our current market-oriented society. What would I have done if neither the knife maker or basket maker were interested in my coconut pastries? There would have been no trade. The new knowledge I came up with would not have been able to be applied to alter my pastry making productive process, the human ant-farm would not have been improved. I would have had to ask these vendors what products they would be interested in and then try to exchange my pastries for those instead, and then get back to them to make the trade. Let's say the basket maker was looking for a blanket, I would have had to go find the blanket vendor and hope that he would be interested in my pastries so that I could trade them for a blanket and then trade the blanket for the basket. This problem is commonly referred to as "The Double Coincidence of Wants" because for a trade to happen you need the coincidence that both parties are interested in the goods they have available for trade. In a very small market-oriented society where few goods are produced this might be workable but as the market grows and more products are produced and offered for exchange, the time spent looking for trading opportunities trying to setup the trade you really want would become a limiting factor to the continued growth of society. This is where the evolution of money comes into existence. As people traded, they realized that there were some goods that most people were willing to trade for, not necessarily because they wanted to consume them, but because they knew they could be used to trade for other things they really wanted. These goods became know as money. For example, in my fictional 1,000 member market-oriented society most people liked to smoke tobacco, even if you didn't smoke tobacco, you would be willing to trade your goods for it because you knew that you could later trade the tobacco for the goods you really needed. Once people started using a common medium of exchange(money) to trade, the double coincidence of wants problem went away. Instead of spending so much time making intermediate trades to setup the trade you really wanted, that time would be spent increasing production and therefore societies that used money were able to grow bigger and more technologically advanced and overtake other societies that did not use money. Different societies in history have used a wide array of goods for money, for example pre-Revolutionary America used things like maize, iron nails, beaver pelts, and tobacco.

So the emergence of money serves to facilitate trading which is what drives the actions of the human ant-farm. The easier it is to trade, the more fluid, and faster the previously mentioned benefits of trade occur and the faster the society that benefits from them will be able to constantly rearrange its human ant-farm into increasingly more productive and technologically advanced states. Given that money greatly facilitates trade and therefore greatly increases the rate at which a society progresses we have to now consider what qualities lead to the best money. For example, let's say a society uses elephants for money, elephants are big and indivisible. You might be interested in trading some of your elephants for blankets but you feel like one elephant for one blanket is way too much, unfortunately you can't offer a quarter of an elephant. Elephants can also run away, get sick and die, and get very angry and destroy property. So a society that used elephants for trading might miss out on many trading opportunities. So what are some of the qualities that make good money?

1. Wide acceptance as a medium of exchange. You want the money to be accepted by as many people as possible, this allows you to trade for the most amount of goods and services. Goods and services that now become available to your calculating brain.

2. Should have intrinsic value. It should be seen as valuable by itself, like gold for example, it can be used as money yet it is valuable for ornaments and so on. This greatly helps meet quality #1.

3. You want money to be durable. You don't want your money to be burnt away, or die or run away from you like an elephant can. You want it to be a durable store of value.

4. Divisible and easily aggregated. You want to be able to divide the money into smaller units to enable trades for items of low value and you also want to be able to combine your money into large quantities to facilitate expensive trades.

5. Convenience. Money should be convenient to carry and transfer.

6. Money should be relatively scarce or hard to manufacture. This is an INCREDIBLY important quality, the future and very progress of mankind depends on it and we will discuss why later.

Cattle was the most commonly used form of money in early civilizations, as great economist and modern founder of the Austrian School of Economics Carl Menger tells us:

"In the earliest periods of economic development, cattle seem to have been the most saleable commodity amongst most peoples of the ancient world. Domestic animals constituted the chief item of the wealth of every individual among nomads and peoples passing from a nomadic economy to agriculture. Their marketability extended literally to all economizing individuals, and the lack of artificial roads combined with the fact that the cattle transported themselves(almost without cost in the primitive stages of civilization!) to make them saleable over a wider geographical area than most other commodities…The trade and commerce of the most cultured people of the ancient world, the Greeks … showed no trace of coined money even as late as the time of Homer. Barter still prevailed, and wealth consisted in herds of cattle. Payments were made in cattle. Prices were reckoned in cattle. And cattle were used for the payment of fines... Among the Arabs, the cattle standard existed as late as the time of Mohammed."[2]

As societies progressed and became more centered around life in cities, the daily activities of the average person dealt less and less with animals, and the "animal standard" of money was slowly replaced by the "metallic" standard which used coins made out of metals like copper, silver, and gold. Menger continues:

> "Copper was the earliest metal from which the farmer's plough, the warrior's weapons, and the artisan's tools were fashioned. Copper, gold, and silver were the earliest materials used for vessels and ornaments of all kinds. At the cultural stage at which peoples passed from cattle-money to an exclusively metallic currency, therefore, copper and perhaps some of its alloys were goods of very general use, and gold and silver, as the most important means òf satisfying that most universal passion of primitive men, the desire to stand out in appearance before the other members of the tribe, had become goods of most general desire."[3]

The change from animal standard to metallic coins did not happen overnight or in all cultures, it was a gradual change, most cultures went through periods were both standards were used at the same time.

By the 1800's as far as we are concerned the modern Western world was using gold and silver. As the human ant-farm progressed these two metals, especially gold, emerged as the best money around. Both do a great job of meeting the 6 criteria for good money. Let's just focus on gold from now on and see why.

It is widely accepted as money, everyone knows gold is valuable and willing to accept it as a form of payment. Gold does not rust or burn away, it can be stored and not decay for an eternity as far as people are concerned, it is durable. It can easily be melted and divided into smaller pieces of any size and also combined to make large purchases. It is easy to carry around, it is very heavy but by the time it gets too heavy to carry you are making very large and infrequent purchases.

So let's recap. To understand mankind, his past, and his future, is to understand the growth and characteristics which enable, motivate, facilitate, or impede the growth of the human ant-farm. Human ant-farms that don't grow are overtaken by those that do, and since we are alive right now, we happen to be part of a human ant-farm that so far has managed to grow or at least maintain and defend its social order. We always have to keep in mind that societies succeed or fail based on their growth and technology and more often than not how the previous two lead to the ability to kick butt. More productive human ant-farms can afford to feed and clothe bigger and better equipped armies. I am not saying that we are alive today because we are descendents of a single human ant-farm that stumbled upon the right economic institutions like the use of money and others we still have to discuss, this is obviously not the case. What happens is that as human ant-farms grow, conquer, are conquered, assimilate values, spread values, and so on, the technologies and good ideas and customs are more or less retained.

We saw how the self-sufficient society gave way to the market-oriented one and how the market oriented one used money to be even more productive and we discussed how better money leads to an even better and more efficient working of the human ant-farm. And finally we analyzed how gold naturally emerged as the best money for the various human ant-farms that when added together make up the whole human ant-farm, or at least the Western one which is the most important in terms of the last 200 years.

Prices. The quantity theory of money

Imagine a small island human ant-farm where there is a total of $1000 dollars held by its 100 inhabitants(each has $10). Each person produces 10 goods so that this human ant-farm produces 1000 goods(100 people x 10 goods = 1000goods) that the inhabitants consider useful and are willing to pay for and exchange amongst each other in a market. Can anything in this island sell for $1200? No, even if all the inhabitants put their money together they cannot buy a product that is being sold for that price because there are only $1000 total dollars in circulation. The $1000 have to be spread amongst the 1000 products. The average price of each good would approximately be the total amount of money in the economy divided by the total amount of goods. In this case $1000/1000(goods) = $1 per good. What if our island economy had $2000 total dollars as opposed to $1000? There would now be $2000 dollars that can be used to purchase 1000 goods. The average price of a good would be approximately $2000/1000 = $2, there are still the same 1000 goods being traded amongst 100 people. People would have twice as much money to buy goods that sold for twice as much so they would be no better or worse off. What if there was a total of $100 dollars in the economy? In this case the average price of a good would be $100/1000 = .10 or 10 cents. People would have 10 times less money but each good would cost 10 times less so once again it would make no difference, there are still the same 1000 goods being traded amongst 100 people.

Next let's imagine a couple of years go by and everyone in the island has become so good at what they do that each person has doubled his productivity by producing 20 goods instead of 10. Our economy now looks like this, $1000 dollars in circulation and 2000 goods. The $1000 will eventually be divided amongst 2000 items creating an average price of 50 cents per item. The people are better off because they each have the same $10 dollars but instead of each dollar buying them more or less one item at a price of $1 per item now each dollar buys them 2 items because the average price has been cut in half to 50 cents. Each person is better off because each person managed to produce twice as much as before and this doubling of productivity is reflected in the 50% drop in prices. Before, each good had to sort of compete against 999 other goods for dollars to buy it, and it could get about $1 spent on it, but now each good has to compete for the same $1000 dollars but there are an additional 1000 goods also competing for the same $1000 dollars. Why has the price of each good been cut in half? Because there are twice as many goods being "chased" by the same amount of dollars. Why are there twice as many goods? Because new knowledge, thanks to experience and the constant search for more efficient ways of doing things, has replaced less productive knowledge and people led by this new knowledge have acted in ways that doubled their productivity.

There are three important things to learn from the previous examples. One is that any amount of money is sufficient to help coordinate the actions of a human ant-farm, whether 100, 1000, or 2000 or a trillion dollars, the amount of money in an economy has no impact on the workings of the economy. Two, is that the increased prosperity of a human ant-farm has nothing to do with the amount of money or average price of goods and everything to do with the amount and quality of goods being produced. The island economy went from producing 1000 items per 100 people to 2000 items per 100 people. Thanks to the increase in productivity there are now more goods per person and that is a good thing. What really matters is not the specific prices of goods but the relationship of values between goods. For example, if the value of one orange is that of two apples it does not matter whether the orange is $100 and the apples are $50 or whether the orange is $10 and the apples are $5, all we care about is the relationship between the values of goods and any level of prices as long as it correctly shows this relationship is fine. And third is that as people increase their productivity prices should go down if the amount of money is not increased, as people doubled their productivity we saw how prices were cut in half, this is a good thing, it is what we should expect to happen in general in a healthy and prosperous society.

It is very important to always keep in mind this relationship of how the money supply and productivity affect prices. Let's go over a few scenarios just to practice and gain a few insights. Let's once again assume the 100 person scenario where everyone has about $10 so there are a total of 1,000 dollars in circulation and that each person produces 10 items for a total of 1,000 items in the island economy and every item more or less has an average price of one dollar. What would happen to the average price of goods if Johnny woke up one day thinking he was a prophet from God and convinced everyone to work 12 hours per day instead of their usual 6 because that was God's will? Since they worked twice as long we would expect them to produce twice as much so the average price would be $1,000/2,000\text{goods} = .50$ dollars or 50 cents. Johnny had another revelation, God was pleased and wanted everyone to go back to their usual 6 hours per day. Productivity went back down to old levels and the average price of goods went back up to $1 per good.

One day Oscar needs to buy five items and he needs a loan so he asks Mark for a $5 loan which he will pay back in a month, Mark agrees to lend him the $5, and Oscar uses it to buy his 5 items. The following night while everyone is sleeping, Ben, the money gremlin, goes to everyone's house and gives everyone $40. After a week of buying and selling the average price now settles at $5 per item because thanks to Ben there are now a total of $5,000 in circulation but still just 1,000 products being produced on average so their price is $5,000/1,000 = $5 per item. When it comes time for Oscar to pay back his $5 loan to Mark, he finds it very easy to do so given the extra money he now has thanks to Ben. Mark feels a little weird though, he had to forgo the purchase and enjoyment of 5 items in order to save the $5 he lent to Oscar last month but now the $5 he got back can only buy him a single item. Thanks to Ben, Mark got cheated to Oscars advantage, Mark lent out money that had the purchasing power of 5 items and he got back the same amount of money but this time it only had the purchasing power of a single item.

Keeping in mind that there are now still $5,000 total dollars in the economy, a few months go by and Oscar asks Jose for a loan to buy 5 items so he now needs $25, Jose agrees to lend him the $25. The next day Ben the money gremlin sneaks up again but this time he takes back the $40 he gave to everyone so that everyone goes back to having about $10 each and the economy goes back to $1,000 total and after a week of trading the average price settles at the expected $1 per item. Oscar is now in trouble, he can't sell his goods for the $5 per item that they used to sell for. At the previous price of $5 per good he could raise the 25 needed to pay back the loan by selling 5 goods, but now he needs to sell 25 of them at $1 per good and is obviously finding it a lot harder to save the $25 he owes. He borrowed money that had the purchasing power of 5 items and now he finds himself having to return the same monetary amount but it is an amount that represents 25 actual goods. He starved himself trying to save the $25 and still came up 5 short and was hanged for his crime of not paying back the full $25. This time thanks to Ben, Jose got a great deal at

Oscar's expense. Jose lent money with the purchasing power of 5 items and he got back money with the purchasing power of 20 items and poor Oscar was seen as an evil person who did not want to pay back his loan and lost his life.

The last two scenarios provided further examples of how the money supply affects prices and it also showed us how changes in the money supply affect borrowers and lenders. In the first example we saw how Ben's increase in the money supply not only increased prices 5 fold but it also made it easier for borrowers to pay back their loans at the expense of the people doing the lending. The last example showed how a decrease in the money supply made it harder and harmed borrowers for the benefit of lenders.

Our simple formula for average prices of dividing the total amount of money by the total amount of goods is referred to as the "Quantity Theory of Money". It is a slightly crude way of looking at prices and far from being their exact determinant but captures the essence of their relationship and is perfectly suited for our purposes.

Human action and the quest for increasingly more beneficial states of well-being.

People are always up to something, we are always acting in ways that we consider to be in our best interest. We act this way because we have brains. Our brains are constantly learning, calculating, ranking the many possible actions which we can take, and then acting on what it considers to be its best option. Every time we act, we do so to go from a certain state to one that our brains consider to be a more beneficial one. For example, you might be reading a book and then you feel hungry. Your brain was doing something that it considered to be in your best interest, reading the book. There are many other things that you could have been doing instead of reading the book, but your brain has something like an Action Rank System that constantly ranks all the possible courses of action that you could take, ranks them in an order that reflects how beneficial they are to you and then causes you to act out the course of action it calculated was the best one. So for a while you read, but now the state of the world has changed, the brain is receiving a signal which tells it you are low on energy, it takes this signal into consideration and calculates that you would be in a better state if you were fed so it guides your actions as you prepare yourself a meal. You acted to go from one state, the hungry state, to a more beneficial state, the full-and-no-longer-hungry state. The same thing happens when you change the channel on your TV. Whatever is being shown on the current channel is not as interesting or desirable as what you think might be on some other channel. You want the world to be in a different state, one which you feel will be more favorable to your needs or desires so you act to get to this state and press the button in the remote control to get you there. The instant you press the button and the TV changes you have reached the state you desired, a state your brain felt was a better one than the one you were in just a second ago. Once you get to the new channel, the state of the world has changed and your brain reexamines it. It turns out that the new channel you entered is not as entertaining as the one you were watching before. Once again you find yourself wanting to go from one state to a more favorable one so you act, you change the channel back to the one you were watching originally and once again your brain will examine your current state and act based on its perceived well-being and possible courses of action to increase it. So every action takes us from a less favorable to a more favorable state. Life is very much about acting, constantly using our knowledge of the world to help us act in ways that will take us from less favorable to more favorable states.

The value of goods. Carl Menger's Subjective Theory of Value

Where do goods get their value from? Value is a concept that only exists in human brains. If everyone died all of a sudden things would have no value. How valuable things are to a human brain depends on each individual brain and how useful a role the item being 'valued' plays in the brain's plans of action. The value of something can be determined by what a brain is willing to do in order to obtain it. In an advanced market-oriented society like ours the value of things is best determined by how much money we are willing to trade for it, and how much money we are willing to trade for something depends on how useful the trade will be to the person making it. If I am dying of thirst in a desert and a cup of water can keep me alive for the next mile I need to travel to reach a safe place with water, I would be willing to trade a lot for this water, I would value it more than some precious diamonds I might be carrying in my pocket. If I am safe in a major city where there is plenty of water I would value the diamonds much more than the water, not because I have any use for them personally, but because I know I can trade them for other things that I really want, like money which I can then use to act in ways that will greatly increase my state of well-being. The two situations were different and I valued the water and diamonds according to how much each would increase my well-being, the value of the water and the diamonds was reflected in my ultimate use for them as means to achieve my ends in the respective situations. People who grow up in modern market oriented societies have a concept of a "market value", which is more or less what you can expect an item to sell for.

What we have just discussed with respect to the value of goods is commonly referred to as the "Subjective Theory of Value" often credited to Austrian economist Carl Menger[4]. Subjective because it depends on the unique viewpoint of individual human beings, as opposed to something that is objective where the value, or whatever is being evaluated/measured, is fixed regardless of the people doing the evaluation or measuring. For example, a pound of butter weighs a pound regardless of who is doing the measuring or how they feel about it, but the value of a pound of butter is up to each individual and how much he is willing to trade for it.

The importance of trading

Trading is an action just like any other and given that human beings only act to go from a less favorable state to a more favorable one trading is something that benefits both parties involved in the trade. If both parties didn't benefit they would not have traded. Trades only occur when both parties go from a less favorable to a more favorable state according to their respective brains. When I buy a hamburger from a fast food restaurant for two dollars I value the hamburger more than the two dollars I give up and the restaurant values my two dollars more than the hamburger it sells me. Both of us have gone from a less favorable state to a more favorable one from our own viewpoints. After I eat the hamburger I could spend another two dollars for another hamburger but my brain no longer values the hamburger more than my two dollars, probably because I am no longer hungry and my brain calculates that the two dollars could be used at a later time to act in a more favorable way.

Let's go over a cute example. Imagine a very small human ant-farm, a 5th grade classroom where I give each student a toy at random[5]. Some of the girls get miniature soldiers and tanks while some of the boys end up with dolls and hair adornments. First I allow them to trade their toys with those who are sitting immediately next to them, we'll call this restricted trade. Some trade. When I first gave them their toys, all of them were at a certain level of well-being, those who traded did so because they valued the toys they were giving up less than the ones they were getting in exchange. After the trading, the small 5th grade human ant-farm's structure was changed and went from a less beneficial to a more beneficial state. More kids were happier, toys moved around. Next I allow them all to trade freely with anyone in the whole classroom, we'll call this free trade. Previously they could only trade with their immediate neighbor, there were only so many opportunities for trade and therefore only so many paths to increased well-being. Allowing anyone to trade with anyone else in the whole classroom greatly increased the opportunities for trade and therefore the opportunities to go from a less to a more beneficial state. Lots of trading happened. The mini human ant-farm restructured itself into an even more beneficial state where even more people were better off than when they started. Are there some kids who did not like the toys they initially got and no one wanted to trade with? Probably, those kids simply remained in their current state of well-being, but at least their state of well-being did not go down(increased jealousy and envy due to the increased happiness of others should not take away from the important point being made in this example). The trading allowed the human ant-farm to go from a certain state to a more beneficial one and never to a worse state. Free trade leads to progress. Anything that increases or speeds up our ability to trade increases the rate at which humanity progresses. Anything that slows down or prevents free trade slows down or reverses human progress.

It is important and somewhat startling to realize that the entire human ant-farm is coordinated by the billions of trades that the human ants are constantly making. Stop right now and fully realize this. As people act and trade with each other, every trade in society increases the well-being of those involved in the trading. And since all human beings are trading all the time, we are constantly going from less to more beneficial states, this is the essence of mankind's progress.

For most of us, the most important thing we trade is ourselves, our time and labor. People who don't understand how free-trade works can easily have thoughts along the lines of "I don't make anything, I've got nothing to trade, how can we call this a free-trade based economy when lots of people don't make anything to trade with?" , well fortunately our hours of labor are just as important as physical things when it comes to trading and this is one of the first and most important things one needs to realize. In a tribal, simpler, more self-sufficient world it was easy to see simple trading and production of specific goods by one or a few individuals, but in the modern world most of us combine our labor with tens, thousands, or millions of people via companies to create products/services. Whether making a pie, or a car, or anything else, labor is an ingredient as important and no different than the physical stuff that goes into making tangible products. All human usable wealth that is not directly plucked from the earth involves a combination of two key ingredients, 'natural resources'/matter and labor which helps transform this matter into human usable wealth. Next, a few examples…

Daniel is getting up in the morning to go to work, his calculating brain constantly ranks all the possible things he could do with his time, and given all the options available to him he decides that the best thing to do is to trade his time and labor with his employer in order to get the money he needs to trade for other things like food and so on. Daniel could decide not to work and live off of his savings or starve but he does not want to starve and he wants his savings for a down payment on a home which is an important step towards the achievement of other future goals/plans. When

Daniel trades his time and labor for money he is trading something which according to his brain is of smaller value for something of higher value. Daniel values his time and labor and all the other things he could be doing if he weren't working less than the money he get gets from his employer. If this were not the case, Daniel would not work. From Daniel's perspective the trade has taken him from a less favorable state to a more favorable one, a state one step closer to achieving his goals of feeding himself and buying a home. To Daniel's employer, Daniel's labor is more valuable than the money they exchange for it. Daniel's employer also goes from a less favorable to a more favorable state. By trading with Daniel, his employer will be one step closer to the successful execution of its plans whatever they might be. The Daniel human ant and his employer mini-human-ant-farm are busily trading and humming along.

Are all trades really in the best interest of both parties? Not necessarily, we often times make mistakes and buy the wrong product or service. Trading is something we do all the time, it is an action like any other and our brains are constantly making mistakes and learning from them. If there was a supreme being looking down from the heavens and knew the best course of action to take for every single human being in the human ant-farm and could constantly tell us how to act in the most efficient way given our desires, then the human ant-farm would continuously restructure itself as perfectly as possible. But we don't have a direct line to this supreme being regardless of whether one believes it exists or not. We restructure our actions constantly going from less favorable states to more favorable ones by interacting with the world via trading. This is how market oriented human ant-farms work. If other human ant-farms which did not work based on the principle of free-trade amongst individuals were a better system, they would have grown and prospered, people would have wanted to move to them and join those human ant-farms, but this has not happened. In reality, people all over the world go through great lengths to move to capitalist societies where free-trade has created the most productive human ant-farms ever. More on this later when we discuss Socialism and government.

Value, ownership and private property

Another factor that is of crucial importance in the calculations that a brain makes when assessing the value of something is whether the thing being evaluated can be safely used as part of future plans of action. What does it really mean to own an object? It means that a brain can use it as an ingredient in its plans of action. If you do not own things you cannot make plans that make use of them, or the plans that you do make have to be considerably shorter than they would otherwise be. Imagine trying to build a house if you do not own the materials and half way through its 6 month construction the materials leave your control and are employed elsewhere, or even worse, you finish the house and after living in it for 2 weeks you are driven out by invaders. If you know that there is a very high chance that this sort of thing could happen in the society you live in, instead of building a nice strong house that would take you 6 months to build you would be better off just building a small shack which did not involve too much effort, perhaps a couple of days, since eventually you would lose it. In this society people would have little incentive to produce anything because there is a high chance that it could be taken from them and at the same time you have more incentive to try to obtain things by taking them from others. People would carry and guard their possessions close to them and their plans would be limited to very short-term projects that could be closely monitored, defended against theft, and would be no major loss when taken away or destroyed in conflict. There would be little incentive to produce beyond what is necessary for subsistence, it would actually be foolish and detrimental to produce more than what could be defended against invaders.

Why do we buy houses and value them highly? Our homes are an integral part of our lives and our brains value them highly because they are an important part of many of our future plans of action like sleeping, raising offspring, protection from the weather and so on; plans of action, which like all other plans of action, are conceived by our brains to take us from a less favorable to a more favorable state. Now imagine that because of political turmoil a well intentioned dictator rises to power and next week your house will be taken away from you and you will be homeless. Your house will no longer be a part of your future plans. However important an ingredient to your future plans your house might have been, it is now close to worthless, and the day you can no longer use it at all, it will be worthless as far as your future plans are concerned. During your last week of home ownership your brain will not find it to be in its best interest to clean or take care of the house. If the house were made out of wood, it would make more sense to start tearing it apart and using the wood to build a fire to keep you warm. If someone would be willing to trade you a car which you could keep and make use of for future plans in exchange for your house, you would probably do it depending on whether your felt like a car you can use for a long time was more valuable than using your home for a single week. An hour before the dictator's men come to throw you out of your house you might easily prefer to trade the house for a meal if you could.

If the ownership of property is not secure, property loses its value for longer term plans and it creates incentives to consume resources which would be better used as building blocks for the future as our house example shows. The house lost value because it could not be incorporated into future plans and it made more sense to consume it for immediate needs, like tearing apart the wood for fuel, than as a home for many future tasks like protection from weather, privacy, and childrearing. A society that did not have laws or customs that protected private property or the right to own things would have its brains limited to short term actions and there would be a reduced incentive to produce in excess of mere subsistence. Compared to other societies that did have laws and customs that protected private property and the right to ownership, it would produce less and have little, if any, technological advancement. This would lead to a smaller, less technologically advanced human ant-farm, and eventually cultural extinction either by conquest or migration of its members to other societies which were more prosperous due to their respect for private property. This has been the history of the 20th century's exodus from communist/socialist countries to free-market/private property/capitalist societies, but more on this later.

Human ant-farms grow or perish depending on how their human ants act. We have already briefly discussed how a human ant-farm is like a supercomputer which constantly discovers new and superior knowledge that guides its human ants in ever more productive ways. All the resources available to a human ant-farm enter this social supercomputer when a brain takes ownership of a given resource and begins calculating how to best use it for its own plans of action. Since we live in a market oriented society where in order to obtain the goods and services that we want we first have to offer something to the social organism in exchange, it is in the best interest of all brains to look for the best way of combining and incorporating into productive plans all of the things they own and are under their control. If something is not owned or is owned by many brains, whatever the item might be, it cannot be incorporated into future long term plans because you never know who might control or use up the resource. In communal ownership the best strategy is to just use up as quickly as possible whatever the item being shared might be and to exclude it from long term plans. This severely limits the possible beneficial uses of resources and eventually leads to less productivity than would otherwise have existed if the items in question were privately owned and controlled by a single entity.

The creation of useful knowledge

Let us step back for a second and once again think about some fundamental characteristics of the human ant-farm. The human ant-farm constantly creates and selects useful knowledge for survival and eliminates less useful knowledge. As previously mentioned, the human ant-farm is a supercomputer which lives and grows thanks to the useful knowledge that leads its ants into ever more productive courses of action. Given that the history of mankind can be seen as a competition between human ant-farms, human ant-farms that allow for the emergence and spread of inefficient knowledge, and let this inefficient knowledge be the basis for the arrangement of their human ants, will be somehow overtaken by other human ant-farms which found a better way of discovering and acting on better knowledge.

In a market-oriented society every human being is in the business of serving the larger social organism, i.e. the market. We have to create things that are ultimately desired by society. Somehow we have to produce something that people are willing to trade their money for and helps them move from an inferior to a superior state of well-being. Whatever it is that we produce is based on some knowledge, if the outcome of this knowledge is a product or service that no one is willing to trade their money for, I have to discover some other knowledge that leads to me acting in a different way so that I produce something that the rest of society wants. Let's say Bob has an idea for a hole-making business which works as follows, people bring Bob things and he uses his drill and gun to make holes in them. Bob has certain knowledge, the knowledge required to create and operate his hole making business and offer his hole making service to society. Bob opens his business, gets the word out via some advertising but unfortunately for Bob his hole-making service seems to be of no use to the human ant-farm. Bob is not producing anything of value, since he is not producing anything of value Bob has nothing to trade for the money he needs to later trade for all the other things he wants like food and shelter. So Bob's savings get alarmingly low, he abandons his hole-making business and trades his ability to learn and show up on time with a fast food restaurant. In a few weeks Bob's useless hole-making ideas have been replaced by burger and fry making knowledge which are of use to the human ant-farm. Bob's brain has been altered by the natural workings of the market-oriented human ant-farm. Bad knowledge has been forcibly replaced by more useful knowledge. The market process naturally fills brains with productive knowledge which guides them into being the best little ants they can be for the larger human ant-farm.

Thinking about progress and its destruction.

Let's brainstorm about what progress really means. When most of us think about progress we think about better technology, better medicines, the ability to live longer and disease free, not having to work as hard. There has obviously been great progress during the last few thousand years. Sure there have been lots of bad things along the way, but overall most of us owe our lives to the highly efficient and productive arrangement of human beings that has occurred in the last few thousand years, especially since the industrial revolution. Many of us don't work a day in our lives until we are well into our 20s, an option which would only have been available to royalty or the relatively very rich in the past.

Let's imagine we are looking down from above at three societies governed by their respective kings that are at the same stage of social and technological development. Since people are always thinking and discovering new and superior knowledge and improving their methods of production we can expect these three societies to progress into more advanced states as time goes by. Let's assume that every week society B's king takes away 25% of everything that his subjects produced, the king of society C takes 50% of what his subjects produced, and the king of society A leaves his subjects alone. Unlike modern governments who take wealth from society and then redistribute it to build roads, provide government schools, national defense, courts, police, resources for the poor and other things which supposedly help society, the kings just build themselves fancy castles and don't give anything back that is useful to their societies. After a hundred years, which society would we expect to have progressed further? We should expect society A to be the most advanced, followed by society B and then C. Building a home in society A would take about 6 weeks of work gathering materials. In society B it would take about 8 weeks because every week one fourth(25%) of the materials would go to the king so more work and time would have to be spent to make up for the lost wealth taken by the evil king. In society C it would take 12 weeks because half the wealth was taken and therefore twice as much time had to be spent producing the same amount of wealth. This sort of delay would happen not just in building a home but in other productive processes and therefore lead to an overall slowing of the rate at which human ant-farms B and C would progress compared to A.

The general slowdown in the progress of human ant-farms B and C would be no different if instead of evil kings removing their productivity, it were due to large waves of criminals stealing and consuming the same amount of resources. In the example, the kings took away 25 and 50 percent of all new things produced to use as they pleased, but a more realistic example is if they taxed everyone's money and then used the money to buy resources and bring them under their control that way. In one way, the king's henchmen periodically show up at everyone's doorstep with a wagon and say "give me 25/50 percent of all the new things you have produced" and take the goods that way. And in another way the henchmen show up at everyone's door and simply ask for 25/50 percent of people's money, which they later use to buy products to fill their wagons and take them to the kings. So whether the kings have 25 and 50 percent of new production going to their plans directly by confiscation of the real physical wealth or whether they take people's money and then use the money to buy resources which are then employed for the kings' plans it makes little difference. The moral of this story is that when wealth is destroyed or wasted the progress of mankind is slowed down.

A final but very important thing about progress is that for most of our evolution there was none of it and therefore it is not something we have evolved to understand. When we think of lost wealth, or the type of oppression the kings imposed on their subjects in our last example, it is easy for us to understand the hardship and injustice of having what you've worked for taken away from you, but the important fact that the very technological progress of mankind is stopped or slowed down is something we don't instinctively take into account and should constantly keep I mind.

Inflation

The destructive rearrangement of the human ant-farm.

Inflation is the increase in the price of goods brought about by an increase in the supply of money. In the previous section entitled "Prices. The Quantity Theory of Money", we learned how what determines the price of goods is the amount of money in circulation. We saw how doubling the amount of money would more or less lead to a doubling of the prices and so on. In this section we are going to learn a few key things about how and what can happen when the money supply is increased. In order to better prepare our minds for a good understanding of inflation let's try to envision a 1,000 person market-oriented society where most of the people produce a single type of good which they use to trade amongst themselves and that they also use paper dollars just like we do, and that there are a total of $10,000 in circulation. Once again try to picture it from high above, with ant-like human beings going about their daily tasks of producing goods/services, trading their goods for money and using this money to buy other goods. In each of their brains there are pages of information specific to the knowledge related to the products/services they offer to the market. Every member of the society does the best he can to enjoy his life. Most people realize that the best way to enjoy the most material comfort is to focus on producing the products they specialize in, they all more or less do this because based on their knowledge this is the best they can do. No one directs the human ant-farm, the human ant-farm is the emergent behavior that arises out of the selfish interest of the individual human brains. The human ant-farm is currently structured as best as it could possibly be given the knowledge that it contains dispersed throughout its many minds.

When a person realizes that something is valuable he or she is willing to take steps to its acquisition. When we grow up in a market-oriented society we are taught that money is a very valuable thing and we structure a large part of our actions in a way that maximizes our ability to get money. Money is like cheese for a mouse in a cartoon, you can use it to lure people to do stuff, it is the primary means by which one can rearrange the human ant-farm. One day Alan the schoolteacher invents a printing press, prints himself $10,000 and starts offering people a lot of money to build himself a castle. Alan offers enough money to lure 500 of the 1000 members of the human ant-farm to work on building his castle. These 500 people realized that they could make more money by working for Alan than by continuing to produce whatever it was they made before. The human ant-farm's productive structure, in other words, the sequence of actions taken by its 1,000 members, has been drastically altered. Assuming it takes 6 months to build Alan his castle, let's see some of the changes that are happening to the human ant-farm.

As the 500 people start working on Alan's castle, given that these 500 people were half the population of the whole town and they are no longer producing whatever it was they used to produce, the total amount of goods and services in this town has been cut in half. The $10,000 in circulation now will be spent in half as many goods so there will be a tendency for prices to rise until they eventually double. But now we also take into consideration the extra $10,000 that Alan is adding to the economy as he pays the 500 people who work on building his castle. This slow doubling of the money supply further doubles the prices again. Let's assume that before Alan used his new money to restructure the human ant-farm there were about 10,000 goods produced and the average price was $10,000/10,000goods = $1 per item. When half the people went to work on Alan's castle this changed to $10,000/5,000goods = $2 per item. Towards the last days of building Alan's castle when he had already added most of his new $10,000 to the economy in the way of wages for his employees and before they went back to producing the things they used to produce, things would look like this: $20,000(money in economy)/5,000(goods produced) = $4 per good. For 6 months even though people were getting more money they were actually poorer because ultimately there were half as many goods being produced that were available for them to buy regardless of how much money they were earning. For half the population, the knowledge in their brains was increased by castle-making related knowledge. After spending 6 months building a castle some of their proficiency at producing what they used to produce must have been lost, and all the knowledge and new ideas which could have increased their productivity at producing their old products, and the possible improvements that they might have discovered during the six months of additional experience failed to come into existence because their minds were preoccupied with an entirely different subject. With the exception of Alan who thanks to his printing press can afford to buy anything no matter how high prices get, and who has a new impressive castle, the average member of society is worse off. Six months of his life have passed by and his material well-being was actually reduced during this time.

If Scott had $100 in savings before Alan's inflationary spending, Scott's $100 could have bought him 100 items at the old price of $1, the purchasing power of each dollar was one item, but after Alan's gimmicks his $100 could only buy him 25 items. Alan's inflationary spending robbed Scott of his money's purchasing power and therefore his savings. At some point in the past, Scott had worked and increased the economic pie by adding wealth(haircuts, bananas, berries, whatever Scott did), and it is thanks to these products/services which he added to the economic pie, things which people felt they could incorporate into their plans to improve their lives, that they gave him the $100 which he managed to save. The $100 Scott saved, were a sort of claim on 100 goods, but Alan's inflation ultimately robbed him of 75 of those goods. So we see how the wealth stolen via inflation reflects itself in the lower purchasing power of the monetary unit.

With the exception of Alan, the human ant-farm is in a worse state after the six months than before. The knowledge in the 1,000 brains is less useful than it would have otherwise been, and there is less production. After a few weeks the human ant-farm will rearrange itself into a productive structure similar to what it was like before Alan used his printing press to distort the ant-farms structure of production solely for his benefit.

The 500 people that were employed in the building Alan's castle were producing things, some mined rocks, others created ladders and other tools needed for the building of the castle, but this new production does not increase the well-being of the 1,000 human beings that make up the human ant-farm. They are not products that the 1,000 people that make up the human ant-farm can incorporate into their plans to improve their lives.

By controlling the money supply the entire productive structure of the human ant-farm can be altered to work and produce for the benefit of those who control the money as opposed to for the human ant-farm or social organism at large. Before Alan altered the structure of the human ant-farm for his benefit people worked for the benefit of everyone else through the complicated network of mutually beneficial trades of daily life. As soon as he started increasing the money supply we saw how people were duped into altering their productive activities which were truly in their best interest for working on the desires of those who controlled the money supply.

It is important to realize that as far as the well-being of society's members is concerned, it would not have made a difference if Alan was an evil king who instead of using inflation to restructure the human ant-farm to his benefit, taxed and took away half of everyone's money by force in order to raise the money needed to hire people to build his castle. The fundamental difference here is that nothing is seemingly taken away from the members of society when inflation is used. We have evolved to easily understand that when something is taken away from us we are worse off. One is just as worse off if prices double and your money can buy you half as much, as if a thief steals half of your money while prices remain unchanged. When a thief steals your money you know who is doing the redistribution of wealth and this is something that even monkeys and less intelligent animals can figure out, but when it comes to inflation we are clueless. We have not evolved to deal with and understand money and therefore we do not understand inflation.

Inflation's redistribution of wealth

Inflation does not just restructure the human ant-farm to the benefit of the ones increasing the money supply like it did for Alan, it has another bad and more subtle effect. Let's name the medieval town, where Alan has distorted the human ant-farm to work to his benefit, town A. Let's imagine that there are two other towns nearby. Town B is located 5 miles east of town A, and town C is located another 5 miles east of town B. So on a map they look something like this.

Town A-------------Town B------------Town C

As the prices rose in town A because of Alan's increasing of the money supply and the fact that there are less goods being produced, people started going to town B to buy stuff where prices were now relatively cheaper than in town A. As people from town A started buying goods from town B, town B got a large increase in money and saw its goods being shipped to town A, so town B saw an increase in the money supply and a reduction in the amount of goods, so in town B there would now be more dollars chasing a smaller amount of goods so prices eventually rose there as well. People in town B saw that prices in town A were already very high so they took their new money to town C to take advantage of the lower prices. New money came to town C and goods in town C were shipped to towns A and B and prices rose again in town C. Unfortunately for the people in town C their new money could not get them much from towns A and B where prices were already high. Town C was the biggest loser, they saw their real wealth, the real goods they produced leave their town and all they got was paper which could not buy them as much from towns A and B as what they gave up in exchange for the paper. All thanks to Alan manipulating the money supply to his advantage.

In the previous example we can see that as the new money spreads through the economy, those who are closest to where the new money entered the economy get a benefit and those that are furthest away are harmed the most, there has been a redistribution of wealth as the gradual increase in prices worked its way through the entire economy. Alan was the biggest winner. Instead of first producing economic-pie-increasing wealth and then trading it for money and using the money to reduce the economic pie via his consumption, he simply created the money without previous pie-increasing-production, leading to pure consumption of the economic pie, or pure theft from society. The next benefactors were his employees, then his town as a whole as they bought things from town B. Many in town B suffered higher prices and not being able to buy from the already-expensive town A but at least they got to use some of the additional money to buy from town C whose members really got cheated.

Inflation and the natural selection of sound money

In the previous section entitled "Money" we discussed some of the important characteristics that make good money but we did not go into detail for the 6th quality which read "Money should be relatively scarce or hard to manufacture." After having discussed inflation and its evils it is easy to understand why this quality is of vital importance. This is why we don't use sea-water, or grass, or dirt for money. If the money is easy to manufacture, then people have more incentive to create knowledge that leads to finding more money, and they act in ways that create money as opposed to acting based on knowledge that adds useful products and services to society. A society that uses an abundant thing like dirt for money would have the products it produces brought into the possession of people that came up with the best way of creating money/dirt as opposed to the people that added useful products or services to the human ant-farm/'economic pie'. Once again try to picture it from high above. When Alan started using money to build his castle, the most important things in society, the people and their brains were drawn and directed away from productive activities that were good for the whole human ant-farm, activities which increased the economic pie of useful goods. The useless and damaging knowledge of counterfeiting was rewarded. Given that money can be used to restructure the actions of the human ant-farm it is of vital importance to societies that those who obtain money do so by producing things of value to society, in other words, by increasing the economic pie of socially desirable goods, goods that people are willing to trade their money/wealth for. If Alan would have produced many great things of value to society in exchange for money and then used his large savings, which came from previous socially beneficial production to build his castle, although the effects would have been similar(prices would have first declined as Alan removed money from economy as he saved it, and later increased as Alan injected his savings back into the economy), society would have benefited in the past from all the great things Alan produced which would have strengthened it or improved it in some way.

The destructive effects of inflation will plague societies that make the mistake of using money that can be easily manufactured. Their productive structures will be distorted leading to a weaker and less productive human ant-farm. Good money forces every brain to think of a way to add something to the economic pie that society values and is willing to trade for(for most of us we add our labor). It forces everyone to be a good little ant, always taking part in the endless pie-increasing-cycle of production-trade-consumption. Good money can be trusted to show the optimal relationships between the values of goods in society and make efficient social calculation possible. Bad money will cause a society to have its structure distorted for the benefit of the people controlling the money supply like Alan did in our simple example, or as is the case in real life, governments and their well-intended-yet-economically-ignorant politicians. Later we will discuss in more depth why gold has emerged to be the best money and why we should strive to abolish our central bank, the Federal Reserve, and go back to the gold standard.

Hyperinflation and historical examples

When inflation increases very fast because the increase in the money supply is much greater than the increase in the production of real goods and services, we have what economists call hyperinflation. Modern governments have often times destroyed the productive structures of their human ant-farms by essentially acting like Alan. Instead of printing money to restructure the human ant-farms to create castles, they use the money to restructure the human ant-farms to carry out wars, to "try" to provide government services like education, medicine, elderly care, to strive for "equality" and "social justice" and just about everything the unfortunately economically ignorant citizens expect their politicians to do. When governments tax their citizens directly to pay for the real costs of having the government manage all of these services, the true costs of maintaining a hugely bureaucratic, inherently corrupt and inefficient structure like the government provide for such services becomes known, and the citizens would be unwilling to pay such high taxes, but with the printing press, the governments can still rearrange the human ant-farm to try to provide such services but the real cost is not paid by taxes but by higher prices which the population blames on greedy businessmen and everything else imaginable except for the real cause of the problem, government econumorons creating money and using it to rearrange the human ant-farm to their liking, but more on how government really works later.

Here are just a few of the many lessons history teaches us about hyperinflation. Politician's knowledge of economics is limited to the following "I need to solve my country's problems. Resources cost money. I get the banks to give me the needed money. I buy resources and bring prosperity to my people and history will remember me as the greatest president of all time". The fact that what they need is increased production so that there is more real wealth to go around, and all that printing money to buy stuff is going to do is to distribute wealth, damage society's productive structure and increases prices does not enter their minds, and even if it does, they need to do something to justify their existence and appeal to the unfortunately ignorant masses. So here is just a sample of the results that are so common in Latin America and keep the people there stuck in the third world[6].

1. In 1985 the Bolivian government tax revenues covered only 15% of their spending. If the government spends the same amount of money that it takes from its citizens via taxes there is no new money created and therefore no inflation, but since it only collected 15% via taxes it essentially printed new money to pay for the remaining 85%, every year. In 1980 it took 24 Bolivian pesos to trade for a US dollar, by 1988 it took about 2 million pesos to buy a US dollar. A hard working Bolivian who in 1980 might have saved 120,000 Bolivian pesos to retire on, which would have bought him wealth equivalent to what $5,000 USD could have bought, would only be able to trade his 120,000 for wealth equivalent to about six US cents by the year 1988. His savings were stolen via inflation.

2. In 1980 it took 2,000 Argentinean pesos to trade for a US dollar, by 1988 it took 60 million.

3. In 1980 it took 70 Brazilian Cruzeros to trade for a US dollar, by 1988 it took 140,000.

4. Perhaps the most famous of all is the German hyperinflation following WWI where an item that might have cost you one German mark in July 1914 would cost you 726,000,000,000 marks in Nov 1923. At times prices doubled every 49 hours.

Once again it is important to keep in mind that we have not evolved to understand money and how it works. Most politicians responsible for the inflationary collapses of their countries have little understanding of what it is they are doing, and the masses that vote for them are equally clueless. Most people think inflation is some kind of natural phenomenon that needs prestigious looking white men armed with complicated mathematical equations to understand and control or manage. But this is not true and based on the few simple concepts that we have already discussed it should be obvious to see that inflation is caused by those who control the money supply and all that is needed to stop it is to simply put an end to the creation of additional money.[7]

Progressive vs. recessive rearrangements of the human ant-farm. Profitability as a signal of progress.

How do we know whether the planned actions of human beings lead to a progressive or a recessive rearrangement of the human ant-farm. In other words, how can we ensure that society progresses, that our actions lead to pie-increasing wealth as opposed to more pie-decreasing consumption. At the beginning of the book we envisioned a more utopian year 2050 and we know that to reach such a level of prosperity the human ant-farm will be ordered differently, how do we calculate our actions so that we know that they are steps in the right direction? We do this by ensuring that all our actions lead to profitability.

Every company or mini social order is involved in a constant cycle of production, exchange and consumption. For example, thousands of Microsoft employees coordinate their efforts to offer Microsoft's products and services to the world which increases the world's economic pie of wealth, these goods and services are then traded for money as they are sold to the public and the money is then traded for wealth via the food, homes, cars, fuel, etc. that Microsoft employees consume and remove from the economic pie. So on the one hand, the economic pie is increased due to a company's production of wealth and on the other it is decreased due to the wealth a company must consume in order to maintain its productive social order. The sales revenue of a company is a measure of how much wealth it has added to the world's economic pie. For example, if Microsoft sells 40 Billion dollars worth of goods and services in a year it has added about 40 billion dollars worth of wealth to the economic pie. The costs of maintaining a company or social order is reflective of how much wealth is consumed from the economic pie, for example if 20 of the 40 billion dollars in revenue are used to pay for employee's wages, rent/etc., those 20 billion will lead to the consumption of homes, cars, energy, doctor's visits, and so on, which reduces the world's economic pie by 20 billion dollars worth of wealth. The difference between how much wealth a company has added to the economic pie, in other words its revenue, and how much wealth the company needed to consume in order to maintain its social order(its costs) is the profit, which is a measure of by how much wealth the entire economic pie has been increased. So profitability is what allows us to know whether our actions add more wealth to the economic pie than what they consume, profitability is the signal of progress.

Entrepreneurs are always using monetary calculation looking for a profit, which at a more fundamental level is just another way of saying that they are trying to transform matter from states where it is less useful to states where it is more useful therefore increasing the amount of useful wealth in the economic pie. Guided by profitability one knows that one is consuming less than what one adds. Let's go over another example.

Joe has an idea for a medical screening device that can be used to screen for 90% of all diseases known to man in about 5 minutes and describe a cure. All the patient has to do is stand inside a large refrigerator-like enclosure, and breathe into a small tube for 5 minutes. If Joe felt like manufacturing one of his machines would cost 5 trillion dollars it means that every American would have to trade about half of everything they produced in a year in order to bring one of Joe's machines to existence, a machine which most people would not even be able to use. 5 trillion dollars worth of wealth would be consumed by the thousands or millions of people employed in the process of creating this one machine. Would Americans or the American ant-farm calculate that this was in its best interest? Would the production of all the other things that would have to be given up in order to produce this one machine be worth postponing? Would the restructuring of society needed to create such a device be a step in the right direction as calculated by the millions of Americans? Obviously not.

Just like the Bob's hole-making business idea discussed in the section entitled "The Natural Selection of Useful Knowledge", the market process would quickly put an end to Joe's idea or at least his attempt to create such a device. Joe's brain grew up and was molded in a market-oriented society and it would be smart enough to know that if the costs associated with producing item A were greater than what would be offered in exchange for it, then it is a bad idea to produce item A. If Joe attempted to create the device he would not have the money to bring it to creation, he would have wasted time pursuing something that could not be done as opposed to continue working in his regular job adding useful hours of engineering time. The modern world is a descendent of market-oriented societies, societies that survived because they created the right incentives for the brains that made them up to act based on useful knowledge. A human ant-farm that allows its resources to be squandered in projects that are not beneficial to growth and continued progress are overtaken by those societies that do a better job of discovering useful knowledge and letting it reshape society's structure.

Now let's assume that Joe's device can be manufactured for a cost of one million dollars per unit as opposed to 5 trillion. Lest assume that it currently costs $50,000 and a wait of 3 weeks to conduct all the tests that Joe's new device can perform in 5 minutes. Assuming Joe charged the $50,000 that it currently costs to get tested, people would still prefer it because they would only have to wait 5 minutes and it saves them a ton of time. Instead of wasting time driving and taking time off from work people could remain working and increasing the productivity and progress of the human ant-farm. Joe's machine would pay for itself with just 20 customers. So at $50,000 per set of tests Joe's machine would be a great benefit and improvement to society. In order for Joe to produce his screening device for a cost of one million per unit he needs to build a large manufacturing plant with an efficient assembly line making use of expensive and highly sensitive machinery and a highly trained staff of scientists and other staff. The costs of the manufacturing plant would be about 5 billion dollars.

Joe's brain needs to calculate whether his attempted restructuring of the human ant-farm will be a beneficial one to society. His 5 billion dollars will lure employees, raw materials and other goods from other possible lines of production towards the building of his manufacturing plant. How do we know that Joe's restructuring of the human ant-farm takes society from a less developed to a more developed or beneficial state? Prior to Joe's restructuring of the human ant-farm we could say that all of the resources that he will rearrange in the human ant-farm are worth 5 billion dollars to the human ant-farm. The employees, trucks, buildings, land, machinery, raw materials and so on, they are more or less worth 5 billion dollars because that is what he needs to offer in exchange for them. Joe calculates as follows, 5 billion for manufacturing plant and everything needed to manufacture and operate 1,000 machines all across the country. He is convinced that at least 10 million of the 300 million Americans and countless of foreign visitors from other countries will be willing to trade their $1,000 in order to gain the benefits of using his machine. In order to serve the 10 million people, each of his machines would have to diagnose about 30 people per day which could easily be done since each use of the machine takes just 5 minutes. By diagnosing 10 million people at $1,000 per customer Joe figures he will make 10 billion dollars in just the first year. So Joe will have taken about 5 billion dollars worth of resources from the human ant-farm and transformed them into something that the human ant-farm is willing to trade twice as much for, 10 billion dollars. His company would have consumed 5 billions dollars in terms of food, homes, energy, etc, as it engaged in the production of 10 billion dollars worth of wealth in terms of medical services, leaving the economic pie of wealth bigger by 5 billion dollars worth of wealth. And again, Joe uses monetary calculation at every step of the way.

The same applies to individuals. As we work we increase the economic pie of wealth by whatever it is we help produce with our labor. Our wages are reflective of how much society values the wealth we have helped produce. Then with our wages we consume food, cars, homes from the economic pie. If you have savings left over, you are profitable. You have helped add more wealth than that which is being consumed. But more along these lines shortly.

Joe does not have to be concerned about whether his rearrangement of the human ant-farm is a better one for society, he could be an "evil capitalist" concerned only with making a profit. But it just happens to be the case that in a market-oriented society, the only way to make a profit is by transforming existing resources from a less valuable state, as seen through the eyes of society, to a more valuable state regardless of the "niceness" or "evilness" of those making the profitable transformation. Market-oriented societies turn man's innate greed and competitive instincts into motivation for production which benefits all members of society.

Companies and how employee wages are determined

As briefly mentioned in the introductory chapter, the entire human ant-farm is one gigantic matter-to-human-usable-wealth transformation entity. For the most part, matter is first dug up in some mine somewhere and through countless transformations it becomes the physical wealth that we associate with the tangible products we use. When it comes to food it is no different, the various chemicals which we need to survive exist in the world and are transformed and packaged in a way we can absorb via the work of plants and the animals we eat. Let's imagine a simple economy where a man(Marc) is by himself in an island and he requires a fish per day to maintain his life/'orderly structure'. Every day Marc interacts with the world and transforms it in a way that produces enough wealth for him to live, his transformation involves throwing a spear several times in the water until eventually he catches a fish. When he catches the fish he has increased the world's economic pie of human usable wealth by one fish. He needs to consume the fish in order to maintain the ongoing consumption of nutrients that keep his body functioning. If Marc can continue to produce the one fish per day he will be able maintain his internal order, if he goes hungry for too long, his internal order will not have the necessary nutrients and energy needed to keep the whole thing in order and it will break down. Whether it is the heart, liver, kidneys, or something else, eventually something will not function good enough to provide whatever service it provides for all the other parts that depend on it and this part's failure will trigger many other failures until eventually the entire orderly structure(Marc) will break down in a way that even if one were to sort of jump-start his heart it would be too late to get all the other organs/'orderly structures' to restart appropriately. But Marc is crafty, he gets better at fishing and now he catches five fish per day. Now he has an amount of wealth greater than that which is needed for his mere subsistence, he has a profit, a profit of four fish.

The same concepts just described for a living biological thing like a human being extends to companies. Similar to how cells are the orderly structures that combine to make a larger human enterprise, human beings are like the cells that interact/trade to make up companies. And just how humans, like Mark, need to act in ways that create the necessary wealth to maintain the parts they are made of, so do companies have to act in ways which produce enough wealth to feed/maintain their internal structures like employees, machinery, etc.. Let's look at an example.

A farm that sells ready to cook chickens coordinates the production of food in a way that yields more wealth than would have otherwise naturally existed. The company transforms stuff/parts(employees, chickens, electricity, machinery) into a product that can be exchanged for more wealth than the total sum of each individual part. Every month the farm manages to sell $30,000 worth of chickens from which $20,000 will go to maintain the farm's productive structure, in other words, to maintain its overall orderly structure by paying employee wages, chicken feed, power, maintain equipment, etc., and $10,000 will be its profit, which once again, is the amount of wealth created above that needed to maintain the entity/farm's orderly structure. If we assume that the farm sold each chicken for 2 dollars, it sells about 15,000 chickens per month. These 15,000 chickens per month is the amount of wealth that it adds to the world's economic pie which it then trades for the $30,000 it gets in revenue. Again, with the $30,000 it got in revenue, now the farm has to consume/use some of it to maintain its orderly structure. This is just like our fisherman Marc having to consume one of his fish in order to maintain his internal order. When the farm pays 3,000 per month on an employee's wage and the employee trades some of his money in a supermarket for milk, in a way, thanks to the wonders of money and the market process, it is as if he traded some of the chickens he helped grow for the milk. If the farm does not produce enough wealth to maintain its internal order, the entire chicken farm enterprise breaks down. It might not make enough money to pay for the electricity which powers some of its equipment so that part fails, causing a failure to the whole orderly structure, if it does not pay enough in wages the employees leave, if it doesn't buy enough chicken feed the chickens will not grow and so on. Each of these sub-parts must maintain their orderly structure and continue to interact with each other in a way that leads to the production which will eventually help maintain them, just like Marc's heart/lungs/organs do for his orderly structure.

A company is like a small or mini human ant-farm where people coordinate their actions to produce goods or services which it then trades for money with the market/public/'social organism'/human ant-farm. A company or mini human ant-farm has a dynamic and fluid structure. People don't just drive to work to move around in a chaotic way, there is a productive order. People move and act based on knowledge that will guide their actions in a way that will ultimately produce whatever product or service the company offers to the public for the money it needs to maintain its 'productive structure'/'orderly structure', like the wages of employees, land rent and so on. When we think of companies we think of brand names like Microsoft or Wal-Mart, we associate them with the news we hear about them or the products or services that they offer but if we use the term productive structure or mini human ant-farm it will help us visualize them more as what they really are, coordinated arrangements of human beings.

Companies only exist if they are profitable, in other words, if they add more wealth to society than the amount of wealth they consume. Companies and the actions of their members are really a complicated network of trades. We don't realize this instinctively but when we are working we are trading. In a small restaurant servers might trade their table-waiting and customer service skills for $3 per hour plus tips, the restaurant manager trades his managerial abilities for maybe $12 per hour, the cook his cooking services for $10 per hour and so on. Perhaps it would help to picture the employees as having small displays on their backs, showing the total amount of money the company trades for their services every second. Let's call it a wage-o-meter, the higher your wage rate the faster the amount displayed in the wage-o-meter goes up per hour. The wages of employees are more or less dependent on how their contribution to the overall productivity of the productive structure affects the willingness of the human ant-farm to trade its money for the company's product. For example, if a waitress leaves the restaurant, the restaurant's service will be slower, it might be too busy now and the wait time for customers increases and some customers will take their money elsewhere, the total revenue of the restaurant will be affected by a "certain amount". Assuming that the waitress did not leave, by hiring an additional waitress the service would improve, wait times would be smaller and probably revenue goes up by a "certain amount". The wage rate of a waitress will be more or less related to this "certain amount". The loss or acquisition of an additional manager or cook might have a bigger impact on the revenue of the restaurant and therefore their wage rates tend to be higher. A productive structure will only trade money for labor if the additional revenue is at least enough to pay for the new employee's wage. If it hires an employee for $2,000 per month but the revenue only goes up by $1500 per month the company suffers a loss and eventually has to dissolve itself into the human ant-farm. The employees will get other jobs by trading their labor with other productive structures, the restaurant's building will be rented or sold to someone else and so on.

The knowledge and actions of the employees, mixed with the ovens and tables and building, coordinate to create meals which the restaurant trades with the social organism for money which it will use to maintain its productive structure by paying its employees, land rent, equipment and so on. If the meals and service are not calculated by the larger social organism to be in its best interest, in other words, if not enough customers want to trade their money for the restaurant's food and service, the restaurant will lose money, it will have to offer less in exchange for the services of its employees in the form of lower wages. At some point the employees will realize that they can trade their services with a more productive and socially desirable company which does offer a product or service that the social organism is willing to exchange more money for. Employees leave the less productive structure and join other productive structures which are ordered in a way that does allow them to be self sustaining or "alive" or profitable. They join other companies that are structured in a way that brings in more money than what the costs needed to maintain their internal structures are. This is just one example of how people, the employees, by just paying attention and guiding their actions based on how much money they can get in exchange for their services find their way into productive and socially desirable arrangements of people, guided by useful knowledge.

The restaurant could have been losing money because it was paying too much for employees. If when losing money it cut their pay and they didn't leave because no other companies would make the mistake of paying them too much, then the restaurant owner has simply found new knowledge. The employees were overpaid, and now that they are paid less the restaurant is profitable and self-sustaining.

Companies also contain knowledge in their productive structures. Knowledge that is in a way greater than the sum of its parts. All of the restaurant's employees more or less had experience at doing each of the tasks they now perform in the restaurant, the cook already knew how to cook, the waitresses already knew how to wait on tables and so on. But as they work together in this particular restaurant, although they each have knowledge specific to their respective tasks, the entire restaurant as a whole contains the knowledge that makes this restaurant work in the way that it does. We all know that you don't just hire an employee and they immediately blend with your company. Even if the new employee is very knowledgeable about his duties it still takes a little while to learn how your particular company is structured. There is also the knowledge that went into picking the location of the restaurant and more. It is this knowledge that I am referring to. And also unlike human beings which die, companies retain their productive structure indefinitely as long as they provide a socially desirable product or service and can therefore trade their product or service for enough money to maintain their internal structures 'alive'.

Banking

The emergence of the institution of banking was another great improvement in the way a human ant-farm works, and those societies that stumbled upon banking and used it effectively, further increased the rate at which the many brains in society created new knowledge and restructured their actions accordingly, leading to superior growth compared to other societies where banking did not evolve or failed to assimilate it. Banking is an institution that exists in every modern country which is further evidence of the fact that it had to provide an evolutionary advantage to the societies that used it over those that didn't. Ok, I should not say that just because every country does something a certain way means that it has to be good for their societies. As we will discuss later, all countries use a fraudulent, criminal and destructive banking system which leads to theft and distortions of the productive structure of the human ant farm like Alan did, but more on this important topic later.

Banking started out as a way of storing money in a safe place. Today if someone breaks into your house they might take the TV and computer but your retirement funds and family inheritance are safe in a bank and the same benefits applied in the past. So one of the main benefits was a decrease in the incentives for theft and the previously discussed benefits that emerge from this. When we think of The Wild West and Western movies, the robbing of a bank and getting to the safe is a common theme. It would be very costly for every person to buy a safe and it was cheaper and better to make use of a very good one that the banker would employ. A single good safe could house the deposits of many people instead of having everyone have their own expensive safe. This is just one of the many reasons why banks were useful for safety.

A bank that had branches in different towns also made it possible for someone traveling to take a deposit slip, issued by the bank where you deposited your money(gold or silver) showing how much money you had in the bank, to another branch location in another town where you could get your money. This way you could also travel without carrying around lots of money once again reducing the incentives and socially damaging effects of crime. This is how paper money first got popular. People would trade the bank notes they had instead of the real gold or silver that the bank notes represented.

The lending industry

The emergence of the lending industry provided another great boost to the human ant-farms where it arose. A human ant-farm has many brains, most of them constantly thinking of ways of being more productive, looking for more efficient ways of performing their current tasks or producing new products which they feel others will want to trade their money for. In other words all the human brains are constantly looking for new useful knowledge and based on this knowledge rearranging their actions to be more productive. More often than not new ideas, and especially those that are very beneficial to society, involve making large rearrangements of resources in the human ant-farm. For example, a lemonade stand business requires a small rearrangement of the human ant-farm. It is something that small children can coordinate and involves few resources(lemons, water, ice, table…) which can be obtained using the savings of a single human being. A modern and competitive car-manufacturing business requires a more substantial rearrangement of resources from the human ant-farm. Lots of people will have to be hired for a long period of time, buildings and complex machinery will have to be built and so on.

When discussing inflation we briefly mentioned how money is what is used to rearrange resources in the human ant-farm. Alan caused a large rearrangement, a rearrangement of the human ant-farm which was detrimental to its members, they worked hard to create him a castle and all they got in exchange was higher prices and less goods for it.

If there was no lending industry Joe would never be able to save the 5 billion on his own. Without a lending industry, newly found useful knowledge like Joe's invention, and the better restructuring of the human ant-farm that would flow from it would be limited by the relatively few resources that can be obtained by the savings of a small number of people, and valuable time and resources would also be wasted in matching those needing the resources with those willing to do the lending. The knowledge that resides in Joe's brain, which would lead to a better restructuring of the human ant-farm would be unable to do so. Joe would have to find someone who already had 5 billion to lend. Once again let's picture the human ant-farm from above, there is a brain that needs 5 billion dollars to carry out an improvement of the human ant-farm, there is another brain somewhere else that has the 5 billion, how do they find each other efficiently? What if there isn't a single person that has the 5 billion, or the ones that have that kind of money have already lent it to other people?

There are many people in the world whose savings in total could be more than 5 billion but they are held in small individual accounts. Joe could place an ad in the newspaper looking for people to lend him the money and spend the rest of his life trying to raise the 5 billion.

Lending allows many more useful ideas to restructure the human ant-farm which would otherwise not have been able to do so. When a new idea comes into existence it is not limited by the relatively few savings controlled by the brains closest to the brain discovering the new knowledge, it is now limited by the total amount of savings the human ant-farm is willing to lend it via the institution of lending. With lending, as soon as a new idea comes into existence it can use the savings of others and quickly apply this new knowledge to transform the human ant-farm into a better one. This provides a great advantage compared to societies that don't have a lending industry and therefore those that do have lending out compete and overtake those that don't.

Given that banks are a place where people stored their money, it came naturally for the institution of lending to be closely tied to that of banking and most of us see banking as performing both functions, keeping our money safe, lending us money, and giving us incentives to lend our money via CDs, investment funds, free checking, online account management services, debit cards and so on.

So lending is great and we can see how it further enhances the progress of the human ant-farm, but how do we decide who gets to use the money that is saved? It should be obvious to realize that it is in society's best interest that superior ideas and productive plans be paired with the resources needed to implement them. Societies that lend their saved resources to good ideas like Joe's will grow more prosperous and powerful compared to societies that squander their resources by making them available to someone like Bob so they can implement their silly and less beneficial or destructive ideas. The efficient pairing of savings and socially beneficial ideas is where interest rates play a key role and will be discussed next.

Prior to discussing interest rates let's observe a few things that happen when you save and invest by lending your savings. First is that when you save and then lend your money you are giving up your ability to alter the structure of the human ant-farm and giving that ability to whoever borrows your money. Instead of you buying a car or hiring people to build yourself a home, by saving your money you are refraining from doing so and therefore reducing your consumption of the resources that you would be bringing into your control. And by lending your money to someone else you are giving this other person the means with which to rearrange the human ant-farm, like buying stuff or hiring people. Second is that sometimes when you spend your money you spend it in ways that lead to pure consumption, like buying food, clothes, TVs, movie rentals, flights, these are things that are used up and cease to exist or are transformed in a way that causes them to lose their value, they are consumed and therefore the world's economic pie is reduced. And third is that when you lend your money whoever borrows it and has to pay it back, has to use your money in production as opposed to consumption. Whoever borrows your money can't use it for travel and leisure because he has to pay you back, therefore this person has to use it for productive purposes so that he can exchange whatever he produces for the money he will use to pay you back. Actually, they can use it to go on vacation and so on, but the bottom line is that in order to pay you back they need money, and that money comes into their control the only way it can in a free-market economy, by producing something and increasing the world's economic pie, and then trading that produced good or service for money which they can then use to pay you back. So when you lend money the borrower is forced to increase the economic pie by an amount at least equal to the size of the loan plus the interest agreed upon as opposed to decreasing it by consumption.

Interest rates

An interest rate is the price a borrower pays for the use of wealth he does not own and is usually expressed as a percentage of the amount loaned. For example, if I borrow $1,000 for a year at an interest rate of 10%, at the end of the year I would have to pay back the original amount of the loan($1000) plus 10% of the original amount loaned (1,000 x 0.10 = 100) for a total of $1,100. The higher the interest rate someone is willing to pay on a loan, the more incentive people have to lend this person money. Let's say I have $10,000 saved and Mike and Gina would like to borrow the money, Mike is willing to pay me 20% interest and Gina 10%. It is in my best interest to lend the money to Mike. Both Mike and Gina have knowledge in their minds as to how they are going to employ the money I lend them, both need to put the money to productive use, something that will enable them to offer a good or service of enough value to the human ant-farm to earn enough money to pay me back with the added interest agreed upon. Their ability to offer me a high interest rate is representative of how beneficial to the human ant-farm is the knowledge in their brains. Mike wants to use the money to setup a tree and branch removal business, we just had a hurricane pass by and the human ant-farm is showing its desire to have trees removed from inappropriate places by offering lots of money in exchange for tree-removal services. Mike is confident in his observations of the human ant-farm's needs and feels like he can use the $10,000 to buy the necessary equipment and get him started in what he feels like will be a very profitable plan of action. Profitable enough to pay me back on time with the 20% interest, a total of $12,000 after one year. Gina wants the money to open up a coffee shop, she feels like her coffee shop will be a successful rearrangement of the human ant-farm, in other words, she will be profitable, but not enough to pay back the loan with anything more than 10% interest. Mike's knowledge will lead to more profitability because society will value his contribution more than Gina's. And how do we know that society will value Mike's knowledge and contribution more than Gina's? Because society will trade more of its money for his services and that is what leads to more profitability for Mike as opposed to Gina and thanks to his higher profitability he can offer a higher interest rate for my loan. By me lending the money to the person offering the highest interest rate, not only am I benefiting myself, but I am allowing the plan that is of most use for society to be carried out, Mike's plan as opposed to Gina's. Without having to know anything about either Mike's or Gina's plans by offering my money to the one willing to pay me the highest interest rate I have contributed to the efficient calculation and distribution of resources in society.

Let's go over a more realistic example that also shows how lenders make their money. Let's say Tim has one million dollars saved and an idea for a business, an auto repair shop. Tim calculates that his business will yield 6% every year, this means that the business might cost Tim $1,000,000 a year to run and it brings in 1,060,000 in revenue so 1,060,000 − 1,000,000 leaves Tim with a profit of 60,000 which is 6% of 1,000,000. Banks and other lending institutions are willing to give Tim a 6.5% return if he lends them his $1,000,000. So one year invested in his auto repair shop yields $60,000 and lending his money to the banks yields $65,000. Tim is better off lending his money to the bank instead of going ahead with his plan for an auto repair shop. The bank either has borrowers willing to offer it an interest rate higher than 6.5% or the bank feels like it can invest the money itself in ways that will also yield more than 6.5% and keep the difference as its profit. For example, the bank could lend the 1,000,000 it gets from Tim to EasyPhone Inc. at 7% for a year and at the end of the year it would get back 1,070,000 back from EasyPhone Inc and then pay Tim his 1,065,000 and keep the difference between the two amounts as a profit 1,070,000 − 1,065,000 = 5,000 which happens to be the amount corresponding to the difference in interest rates 7% - 6.5% = 0.5% , 0.5% of 1,000,000 is 5,000. So this is how lenders make money, they lend money at a higher interest rate than the interest rate they pay to people who lend them money and they keep the difference.

So Tim's money will be put in the control of brains that have more socially useful and desirable knowledge. How do we know that this is the case? Because the borrowers have a more profitable idea, an idea that will produce goods and services that when offered to the human ant-farm in exchange for money will yield enough profitability to pay back those loans made in higher than 6.5% interest rates. Maybe Joe went to the bank looking for his 5 billion for which he will gladly offer 10% in interest. In this case the bank would pocket the difference between the 1,100,000 it would get back by lending Joe Tim's 1,000,000 and the 1,065,000 it has to pay back to Tim for a profit of 35,000 which is the difference in the interest rate 10% - 6.5% = 3.5%.

At any given moment there are many entrepreneurs with good ideas in need of more resources than those currently under their control, the perceived usefulness of such knowledge held in the minds of people wanting to borrow money will be reflected in how high an interest rate they are willing to pay for in the loans they take. Society is better served if those brains with the most productive ideas who are willing to pay the highest interest rates get the money and resources they need. The institution of lending and the special role the interest rate plays are what calculate who gets to put society's savings to use. But it gets much better, not only does it channel savings to those who hold the most productive knowledge, it gives incentives to those whose knowledge is less productive to lend their savings to those with more productive knowledge. This is what happened when Tim decided not to open his auto repair shop and lend his saved money to the bank which would find a more productive use for it like perhaps lending it to Joe.

The interest rate is also a number that embodies people's preference for consumption over saving, for example, if we are getting closer to Christmas we would expect savings to be lower since people are buying Christmas presents and therefore since there would be fewer savings those savings would be "auctioned" off at a higher interest rate. The less savings there are the more borrowers will have to offer in terms of a higher interest rate. Since the interest rate can be seen as the "cost" of borrowing, it makes sense that the less money there is to be loaned out the higher its price and therefore the higher the interest rate will be. When there is a lot of saved money and few borrowers we can expect the interest rate to be low, when there is less money saved or more people looking to borrow we expect the interest rate to rise.

The efficient distribution of resources

Prior to Joe's great idea for his new medical device the human ant-farm had a certain structure. Billions of people were moving around doing things, in the process of other restructurings and so on. When Joe first thought of his invention it was too costly to make. The necessary restructuring of society needed to bring his invention into existence would not have been a good one for society at the time. Let's remember that when Joe first thought of creating his machine it would have cost 5 trillion dollars, which meant that about half the income of everyone in the USA would have to go towards his project. The millions of Americans would not have made this trade, giving half of their money to create Joe's machine at the time would not have taken them from a less beneficial to a more beneficial state so they would not have gone for it. As Joe's brain learned more and perhaps the technology or means that existed in society changed, Joe's brain came up with new knowledge, a different and cheaper way of creating his invention. Joe went to a bank/lending institution to get the money. The lenders would have to employ some of their brains to check whether Joe's knowledge is really useful or not, it could have been Bob asking for 5 billion in order to create a huge hole-making machine with fancy diamond tipped drills that could drill holes on just about anything, oh yeah. The lenders and their brains serve as a check on the usefulness of the knowledge that is going to be put in control of so much money and resources. It is in the best interest of the lenders to ensure that Joe's knowledge will lead to a successful and therefore profitable rearrangement of the human ant-farm. Joe and the lenders reach an agreement, the lenders tell Joe that they will have the money for him in 3 months and Joe agrees to pay 10% interest on the loan. The lenders contact other lenders/financiers/banks and borrows money from them say at 7%, it offers its customers a higher interest rate say from 5% to 7% for them to lend them money. Most other banks and lenders are currently offering the general public 5% interest rate on money loaned to them so at 7% people flock to Joe's lender to lend them their money. There are people like Tim who instead of using his money to restructure a small part of the human ant-farm to create his auto repair shop in a way that would yield 6% now lend their ability to transform the human ant-farm to Joe's project which will be much more socially desirable. There is also a wealthy investor, Carl, who instead of lending money to John, who wanted to build a new small plane manufacturing plant which would have yielded 6%, now lends his money to Joe's lender because he can get a higher return on his investment by doing so as opposed to investing on John's knowledge and plans. Had John acquired the necessary financing from Carl, he would have hired builders, and engineers, bought raw materials, and have restructured the human ant-farm in a certain way but he did not get the financing, the money was placed under the control of Joe's brain, to implement his more socially beneficial plan. It is important and amazing to realize that neither Tim nor Carl, nor the countless of other people who would now find it in their best interest to lend their money to Joe's lender, have the slightest clue as to how all of them are performing the human ant-farm's resource-allocation calculations and are cooperating in the carrying out of Joe's plans. The superior and more beneficial knowledge to the human ant-farm was matched with the money it needed to restructure the human ant-farm.

The market process works in a way that puts resources under the control of the brains whose knowledge and plans are the most beneficial to society. This involved calculation. Thousands of people altered their plans in a way that enabled Joe's plan to go ahead. This calculation was not done and could not be done by a single brain, it was done by all the individual brains each calculating the return on their productive plans compared to simply lending their money. Unknowingly they were deciding whether their plans or Joe's were better for society. Joe hired people, bought raw materials, perhaps some of the very same engineers and builders that would have worked in John's plane manufacturing plant ended up working for Joe. Actually let's imagine that through an unlikely twist of fate even John now ended up working for Joe. Joe was able to do this because the money, and therefore real goods and services that can be exchanged for it and which would have been employed in some other way, was now placed under his control. The resources, which Joe now can control, were going to be used as part of other plans, but less profitable and therefore less socially useful ones. The human ant-farm has been restructured in as good a way as humanly possible.

Economic booms and busts and the business cycle

Economic booms, busts, depressions, recessions and any other bad things that happen to an economy are not products of the market process, they are the products of government interference with the market process. Just like in the section entitled "Hyperinflation and Historical Examples" we briefly discussed how governments inadvertently create economic chaos in their human ant-farms, the same applies here. Understanding how government economorons create economic problems is cool, let's see how they screw things up by creating the booms and busts that are so common in our modern economies.

Before getting to the heart of this section let's prepare our minds by going over the following scenario. Let's imagine that there are two couples each with a toddler who want to go out with their friends but there is only one babysitter available. Regardless of how much money either couple has and is willing to offer the babysitter, since there is only one babysitter, only one of them will be able to successfully execute their plans. All the money in the world can't change this, right? This should be obvious. In order for both couples to be able to accomplish their plans we need more wealth(another babysitter), not to make billionaires of the two couples, because offering higher and higher amounts of money to the one babysitter, is still not going to help both couples accomplish their goals. Ok, with that in the back of our minds we continue.

Let's assume that the average interest-rate across the human ant-farm is around 5%. If your knowledge and productive plans would yield more than 5%, say 30%, then you borrow money at 5%, use that money to bring under your control resources from the human ant-farm to implement your plan in a way that produces goods or services that yield 30% and you profit the difference. For example, you borrow $1,000,000 at 5% to implement your business ideas, the business' revenues are $1,300,000 of which $1,050,000 are paid back(the original $1,000,000 + $50,000 for the interest) so you are left with a $1,300,000 − $1,050,000 = $250,000 profit. Prior to your borrowing, the human ant-farm had a certain structure, millions of human beings doing the best they can given their knowledge about their skills and abilities and the piece of the human ant-farm they interact with. Many of these people did not have productive plans which could restructure a piece of the human ant-farm in a way that yielded more than 5% so they lent their money to banks/lenders and by doing this they left those resources that they could have brought under their control to be brought into the control of other brains. As money goes from saver to bank/lender to borrower so does the ability to control real resources from the human ant-farm. It should be obvious that one cannot save and lend a million to some people and at the same time use the million. By saving and lending, some people are giving up their ability to restructure the human ant-farm and transferring that ability to others(the borrowers) who have better ideas and this is what makes the lending industry such an advantage to human ant-farms advanced enough to have them.

At a 5% interest rate there are borrowers with ideas and productive plans that lead to a return higher than 5%, and there are savers whose ideas would lead to a return lower than 5% who instead prefer to lend their money and ability to restructure the human ant-farm. As the people with ideas that are more profitable than 5% borrow money, they reduce the supply of loanable funds which will increase the interest rate. For example, when Joe went to the lenders asking for his large sum of 5 billion we saw how the bank increased the interest rate it offered people in order to entice them into lending them money so that they could in turn lend it to Joe. We saw how during those 3 months where Joe's lender was increasing the interest rate it offered as an incentive for savers to lend them their money the interest rate went up from 5% to 7%. As the interest rate rose from 5% to 7% all of the plans which would have been worth implementing which would have yielded between 5-7% return have been abandoned in order to provide the necessary means/savings to rearrange the human ant-farm so that Joe's project can be implemented.

So interest rates are now at 7%, Joe as well as other borrowers with better than 7% return ideas have been bidding up the interest rate bringing money into their control, and other people, the lenders, have been giving them their money and therefore refraining from bringing into their control resources from the human ant-farm. Someday in the future, as Joe and those others who borrowed and pushed the interest rate higher bring their products and services to the market, we will have all this great new stuff and the world will be that much better. We know that this will be the case because the very reason why Joe and other borrowers borrowed so much money, which ended up increasing the interest rate, was because they knew that the product or service they were creating, would eventually be profitable enough to pay back the loans and make some additional money to increase their personal well-being and take them from a less to a more beneficial state.

Let's briefly jump to a separate example for just one paragraph that that shows us how important interest rates are for businessmen/entrepreneurs and social calculation in general. Let's say you have a business idea which needs an initial investment of $1,000,000 and you think will yield 10% per year. If interest rates are low at say 2%, you borrow the million, implement the business which brings in $1,100,000, pay back the loan plus 2% interest($1,020,000) and pocket the $1,100,000 – $1,020,000 = $80,000 difference. But what if interest rates are at around 8% instead of 2%? In that case you would have to pay back 1,080,000 which would leave you with a smaller profit of 20,000 instead of 80,000, a profit perhaps too small to entice you to risk a possible business failure so you abandon the idea. If the interest rate was at 10% then you wouldn't make any money at all once you paid back the loan. So as the example shows, low interest rates encourage people to attempt business ideas which otherwise would not have been worth the trouble, and they are a crucial component of a business's profitability, and thanks to this it is easy to see why businesses are always asking government/'The Fed' for low interest rates. Politicians love low interest rates because they help "stimulate" the economy by allowing all of these businessmen to get the money they need to put people to work implementing their business plans. As consumers we also loves low interest rates so we can make smaller payments on our home mortgages and car loans. Bottom line, given our economic ignorance and its ultimate reflection in our elected leaders, lower interest rates, regardless of any long term consequences is what we want, and that is what our elected economorons give us because it seems obvious to all economorons involved in politics that it is the right thing for America.

In order to bring the interest rate down from 7% to say 2% the government economorons via the FED have to increase the amount of loanable funds, so through a somewhat complicated process which we won't go into, they essentially allow the banks to create as much money as needed to bring the interest rate down to 2%. This process of increasing the amount of loanable funds, or credit, is also referred to as the process of credit expansion. Before the government did this, the interest rate was the *natural interest rate*, it was the number that arose naturally and was calculated by the human ant-farm supercomputer, it measured/evaluated/ranked and properly allocated savings to the productive plans of every brain in the economic system as good as humanly possible.

The new much lower interest rate is the *artificial interest rate*, one calculated and determined by a few economorons who instead of spending their youths trying to have sex and working productively they spent that time learning mathematics believing that they were somehow better than other people and that someday they could be the geniuses that give the world order. Ok, I'm just kidding obviously, let me stop fantasizing about young rappers making fun of those pompous economorons and get back to the economics.

So the interest rate is now at an artificially low 2% due to a large injection of money/credit into the banking system. The first thing we need to keep in mind is that new money will be entering the economic system without any previous increase in production. Having already discussed the relationship between prices and goods and inflation, one should understand that this increase in the money supply will eventually increase prices and bring about inflation just like Alan did.

Prior to the artificial lowering of the interest rate, when the interest rate was at around 5-7%, many ideas that yielded for example 4% or all the way up to about 7% were abandoned and the money and therefore ability to restructure the human ant-farm was given up by those who saved, and given to those who borrowed at the higher interest rates(the Joes and other business men with superior knowledge) so that they could implement their superior plans. At the new 2% artificial interest rate, suddenly many of those previously socially inferior plans, whose restructuring of the human ant-farm were abandoned to make way for the more socially beneficial plans, seem beneficial/profitable once again. This is where the boom begins, as previously unprofitable projects will be able to get the financing they need and begin to break ground and we seem to be headed for an unexpected or higher than normal amount of prosperity. Another side effect of this artificial lowering of the interest rate that should be brought to mind is that potential savers now have less incentive to save because their returns will be lower and therefore are more likely to consume even more and make less wealth available for the subsistence of new projects.

Remember John? The guy who could not get financing to start his small plane manufacturing business, because the investors decided to lend their money at a higher interest rate to Joe's lender/bank, and eventually ended up working for Joe? In a world free from government economorons meddling with the interest rate he would have remained working for Joe and Joe's machine would be completed more or less on time and the world of medicine would have been revolutionized, but now John's 6% return on investment with his plane manufacturing idea seems like a great one, borrow at 2% and earn revenue of 6% means a 4% profit. So he quits working for Joe and easily gets the 500 million dollar loan that he needs thanks to the newly available money added to the banking system by the economorons. With this new money John starts bringing into his control resources from the human ant-farm that previously would have been employed by other people, like Joe and others like him. Not only does Joe have to replace John since he is short one employee, but since John has this new money which he is using to buy and bring into his possession a limited, or slow growing amount of labor, machines, computers and buildings: their prices go up. Instead of having a certain amount of money(the amount that had been saved) competing for factors of production(labor/machines/computers…), we now have the additional economoron created money competing for those very same resources so their prices go up. Joe finds that his original calculations were off, he sees that some of his employees are going off to work elsewhere, equipments costs a little more than expected and so on because suddenly there are all of this new businesses popping up like John's and others using new economoron created money to attract resources to be used for their respective plans.

When businessmen like Joe and John embark on a business venture they can be seen as builders whose objective is to build a brick house[8]. Successfully building a brick house is like successfully implementing their business plans in a way that brings in the expected rate of return in profits and successfully rearranges the human ant-farm. Prior to the artificial lowering of the interest rate, most businessmen or builders were attempting to build their houses and there were more or less enough bricks "saved" or unused for most of them to successfully build their brick houses. And it is the natural interest rate that they use to make the calculation as to whether they can build a house or not. When the economorons artificially lowered the interest rate, they made it seem like there are a lot more bricks than there really are, so many new homes/'business ventures' will break ground. As Mises states, "A lowering of the gross market rate of interest as brought about by credit expansion always has the effect of making some projects appear profitable which did not appear before."[9] But there is one problem, there are not enough bricks to finish them all, in other words, there are not enough resources at the right prices to implement all of their business plans in a profitable manner, and all the money in the world cannot change that. Let us remember the two couples needing the babysitter, all the money in the world could not help them both complete their plans, and something similar applies to businesses attempting to complete their plans in a profitable manner. Mises continues, "However conditions may be, it is certain that no manipulations of the banks can provide the economic system with capital goods[bricks]. What is needed for a sound expansion of production[more houses] is additional capital goods[bricks], not money or fiduciary media. The boom is built on the sands of banknotes and deposits. It must collapse." [10](words between [brackets] added by me)

There are several important things we want to understand as we follow what happens next and I have numbered them individually to make them easier to identify.

1.   Joe and other businessmen realize that they now need to borrow more money to complete their projects so they too borrow and further contribute to the continued increase of prices of their factors of production like raw materials, labor, machinery, computers and so on.

2.   The additional borrowing not only contributes to the increase in the prices of factors of production as just mentioned but it also reduces the amount of loanable funds which increases the interest rates once again.

3.   As the additional money from all the borrowing goes to employees(who increase consumption due to the fact that they now have higher salaries than they otherwise would have) and then to the economy, inflation starts to occur not just in the factors of production needed by the businessmen but across all goods and services in the entire economy.

4.   This inflation is also taken into account by people who lend money and further contributes to an increase in the interest rate, for the following reasons. If there is say 4% inflation per year and you lend $100 at 4% for a year, at the end of the year you get back $104 but these $104 will buy you the same amount of goods as your original $100 a year ago because prices have gone up due to inflation. Because of this when you lend your money you ask for a higher interest rate, one that takes into account the fact that the money you receive will buy you less real goods, so you might ask for 6% in order to make a real 2% gain from your loan. This asking of a higher interest rate of return on a loan to compensate for inflation will contribute to a further increase in the interest rate which is already occurring due to the increased borrowing by businessmen as they essentially use this new borrowed money to compete with each other for the needed "bricks" to finish their homes/projects.

5.   As the interest rate rises many of the plans of action which seemed profitable in the past at the 2% interest rate will now start to look like loses

and have to be abandoned. For example, imagine Andrew was one of the people who borrowed at 2% hoping to complete a project that he expected would yield 5%, but because of the continued increase in the prices of the needed factors of production(the "bricks"), just like Joe and John, Andrew needs to borrow more money at an interest that now might be at 6%, so Andrew finds himself borrowing at a higher interest rate than what his business revenues will repay profitably and therefore he will be losing money and have to abandon his project and what seemed like a profitable idea in the past turned out to be a bad one.

6. If the government economorons compensate for the additional borrowing and inflation related increase in the interest rate by once again injecting more money into the banks/loan market in order to increase the amount of loanable funds and therefore once again lower the interest rate, those businessmen like Andrew can continue to borrow at a low interest rate and try to compete for the needed bricks. But this just continues to increase the prices of the needed factors of production(bricks), and once again leads to more inflation and more borrowing by businessmen as they need more money to complete their projects. Again, there is only one babysitter, only a limited amount of bricks at right prices to complete some, but not all of the projects in a profitable manner. Some businesses will inevitably fail.

7. Two things can happen next that will bring an inevitable end to the boom:

A. The government economorons continue to inject greater and greater quantities of money into the loanable funds market to keep the interest rate low even though inflation will keep on increasing which will eventually lead to runaway inflation. With prices rising very rapidly, people's savings become worthless and there is no incentive to save, people want to spend the money to buy real things before the money buys even less, they will try to exchange it for another country's money, gold, real estate, the money will become worthless, there will be economic chaos and social upheaval until nobody accepts the government's money at all and something else takes its place.

B. Stop adding new money to the loanable funds market and allow the interest rates to increase. Once the economorons stop adding money to keep interest rates low, interest rates will increase, some businesses, like Andrew's, will not be able to borrow and complete their projects in a profitable manner and will finally go bankrupt. Their employees will be laid off and unemployment will rise. It is as if their houses remained unfinished. As some of these businesses go bankrupt and sort of break up and release their resources into the market place, some of these resources, like some of the labor, will be able to incorporate themselves and contribute to the completion of other projects, but there will be many resources that are too specific to a particular business plan and will be very substantial losses. For example, let's say John goes bankrupt, some of his ex-employees might be able to get jobs working for Joe, but highly complex and specialized airplane manufacturing assembly plant robotics will have a much harder time incorporating itself with other plans. It is as if the bricks of some of the houses that will not be able to be finished will be able to be moved and used towards the completion of other houses but other bricks are stuck being parts of incomplete homes. Other businesses like perhaps Joe's will complete their projects in a profitable manner. Even though Joe's project might have cost him more money to implement due to the additional competition for the needed factors of production as he was trying to build his business, he might be able to charge a higher price for his services later due to the monetary inflation. At this stage we are in the bust phase and soon a new restructuring of the human ant-farm based on the natural interest rate as opposed to the artificial and fictitious one will take place.

When this whole fiasco got started, one could say that there were going to be 100 brick houses built(100 profitable ideas/'rearrangements of the human ant-farm') and there were more or less enough bricks for all of them. The artificial lowering of the interest rate made it seem like 120 houses could be built with the same amount of bricks. When everyone started building houses it looked like instead of having a future with 100 nice houses we were going to have a future with 120 houses, we had a nicer than expected economic boom. Politicians and economorons take pictures and congratulate each other, many young students aspire to be wise economorons and pay a high price to attend prestigious universities and learn useless mathematics. As the houses are being built and there are less bricks to complete all the houses, the additional borrowing is used to compete with other homebuilders/entrepreneurs to attract the bricks to their respective houses. In the end some cannot continue to borrow and compete for bricks so their houses remain unfinished and others are able to finish theirs, but ultimately instead of having 100 houses society has 60 completed houses and 60 incomplete ones. Although society is better off than it was at the moment the government economorons artificially lowered the interest rate, it is far worse off than it would have been should the economorons not have messed with the interest rate. Our modern world would have progressed much faster into a more prosperous future if governments would not have interfered with the interest rates creating these booms and busts which ultimately leave us worse off than we would have otherwise been. As Mises tells us :

"The characteristic mark of economic history under capitalism is unceasing economic progress, a steady increase in the quantity of capital goods available, and a continuous trend toward an improvement in the general standard of living. The pace of this progress is so rapid that, in the course of a boom period, it may well outstrip the synchronous losses caused by malinvestment and overconsumption. Then the economic system as a whole is more prosperous at the end of the boom than it was at its very beginning; it appears impoverished only when compared with the potentialities which existed for a still better state of satisfaction."[11]

Every business venture is an attempt at morphing the social order in a way that it produces more than it consumes, i.e. is profitable. Under the free circumstances, business ventures are spawned, they munch on real savings, and increase the economic pie by more than that which they have consumed. With the artificial lowering of the interest rate, many more different social restructurings begin to take place, consuming just as much wealth as they would have should interest rates not have been artificially lowered, but this time many will not be able to complete their projects, therefore ending up having consumed more than what they added, leaving society worse off.

It is important to stress the fact that once a boom has been created it is inevitable that there will be a bust which is needed in order for the human ant-farm to properly realign its productive structure. The bigger the boom and therefore the bigger the deviation from what is truly possible, the harder the bust and realignment phase will be. As the human ants go from being parts of unprofitable, unrealizable plans, to feasible ones, there will be some unemployment. If government economorons decide to once again artificially 'stimulate' the economy in order to put these men to work doing who knows what, it will only slow down or further aggravate the bust/realignment phase. In Hayek's words:

"And, if we pass from the moment of actual crisis to the situation in the following depression, it is still more difficult to see what lasting good effects can come from credit-expansion. The thing which is needed to secure healthy conditions is the most speedy and complete adaptation possible of the structure of production … determined by voluntary saving and spending. If the proportion as determined by the voluntary decisions of individuals is distorted by the creation of artificial demand, it must mean that part of the available resources is again led into a wrong direction and a definite and lasting adjustment is again postponed. And, even if the absorption of the unemployed resources were to be quickened this way, it would only mean that the seed would already be sown for new disturbances and new crises. The only way permanently to "mobilize" all available resources is, therefore, not to use artificial stimulants—whether during a crisis or thereafter—but to leave it to time to affect a permanent cure by the slow process of adapting the structure of production to the means available for capital purposes."[12]

We just look at the world and think that money is all we need. We are so used to using money and having money really be what brings us wealth, that we completely overlook the fact that it is not really money that we need, it is increased production, we need more bricks. But again, such a simple and obvious fact, is completely foreign to our nature.

A perfect example of an economoron at his best when it comes to messing around with interest rates was president Lyndon B. Johnson who in his State of the Union message in January 1967 put it bluntly :

> "Given the cooperation of the Federal Reserve System, which I so earnestly seek, ... I pledge the American people that I will do everything in a President's power to lower interest rates and to ease money in this country. The Federal Home Loan Bank Board tomorrow morning will announce that it will make immediately available to savings and loan associations an additional $1 billion, and will lower from 6 percent to 5 3/4 percent the interest rate charged on those loans."

This concludes our discussion on how the lending/finance industry and the interest rate are a crucial part of what turns the human ant-farm into the world's most powerful supercomputer. Next we move on to another crucial mechanism employed by the market process, competition.

Competition. The forced and beneficial spreading of knowledge and rearrangement of society.

Market oriented societies force their members to cooperate in ways that are beneficial to society. Let's think about how a modern productive structure like an auto manufacturing company comes into existence. First of all, the automaker idea comes into existence in a brain or a group of them. As highly evolved creatures, we are always thinking of ways of increasing our production, we grow up and our minds are trained to want to make money and to do this we have to be productive. We could have grown up in another society where instead of putting values in a brain that encouraged working and enjoying large homes and comfortable cars and leisure, the cultural symbolism could have molded our brains to enjoy meditation in search for the inner self all day. But we are the cultural descendents of societies whose cultural symbolism encouraged reproduction, growing families, and these things required a culture of hard work and a desire to make money and this is something that is very much in the minds of most of us. Making money is all about rearranging resources to make them more valuable. The more valuable in the eyes of other brains I make things, the more I can get in exchange for them. Let's assume I am young and unemployed and watch TV all day. I would gladly exchange my hours of comfy TV watching time for money but no brain is willing to make this trade with me, I cannot steal the things I want because I live in a society that does not permit this, a society that has reached the level of prosperity it has because it has prevented theft and actions by its members that are detrimental to the social order. I need to find something else to offer for exchange or I will starve. So I transform myself from a couch potato to a human being that can show up to work on time, learn to do simple tasks, and do as I am told by a manager. I have transformed resources, myself, from something that had zero exchange value to something with some exchange value, this is usually good enough for an entry-level job at a fast food restaurant. The market-oriented society has forced me into contributing to society.

After years of managing a SuperAuto car manufacturing plant Tom feels like he can create a car company that can sell better cars for ½ the cost. This means that the productive structure Tom would create, based on his newly found superior knowledge, embodies a better arrangement of people and resources than the SuperAuto one he works for. Tom feels like his car manufacturing company could make a great $4000 car, while he sees that the current SuperAuto productive structure averages about $8000 per car. Assuming Tom was successful in building his company and manufacturing the cars at that price, Tom would have made the world a better place. He discovered a way of arranging people and resources in a better way. He would have improved the structure of the human ant-farm compared to how it used to be and we would be one step closer to the more utopian year 2050 briefly mentioned at the beginning of the book.

The entire progress of mankind is based on producing more and better products at a smaller price and with less effort. We again want to remind ourselves that society is always in a constant cycle of production and consumption. Producing something at a smaller price simply means that we have to consume less as we are producing. The more expensive to produce something is, the more wealth has to be consumed as wealth is produced. Building a car manufacturing plant is more expensive than a lemonade stand because thousands of employees will be consuming cars, energy, food, etc., as they produce the plant, compared to the couple of sandwiches and water consumed by a kid while he produces the lemonade stand.

When Tom starts selling cars for half as much as every other company that maintains its structure by trading cars for money, they start to lose money. This loss of money is a signal to the people that own the other car-making companies which let's them know that the resources that make up their company are no longer being used as best as possible. It let's them know that its arrangement of resources would be better used if those resources were placed in the hands of different companies. The reason why the resources they employ can be used better elsewhere is because Tom's company has found a better way of satisfying the needs of the human ant-farm. The social organism has found new knowledge, and as customers trade their money for Tom's cars as opposed to cars from other manufacturers, the social organism is placing money, and therefore the ability to maintain and further expand this newly found and useful productive structure, in the hands of the brains that are responsible for the better knowledge, Tom's and his team. Money and therefore the ability to restructure the human ant-farm in the future, are being pushed closer and in control of a more productive structure and are being withdrawn from the less productive ones(other car makers). The owners of other car companies would be smart enough to realize that the reason why they are losing money is because new and superior car-making knowledge has come into existence. The owners can do several things, one of them is to learn how Tom's company is structured and replicate this structuring in their own companies. If SuperAuto can restructure itself to do things like Tom's company then it would produce cars as cheaply as Tom. SuperAuto is in a position where it is forced to replicate the efficient structure of Tom's company. If SuperAuto did not do this they would have continued to lose money and at some point the owners of the SuperAuto productive structure would have found it in their best interest to sell their company to Tom and then Tom would reorder its structure to be more efficient or perhaps there is some other brain out there, who knows, perhaps one of Tom's current plant managers, who feels like he can rearrange the SuperAuto productive structure to be even more productive than Tom's. As you can see by now, this process, is a natural process that will occur in the free-market based on the selfish interests that every human being has. This process replicates the best knowledge across society. If Tom's engineers had superior knowledge and that was part of what allowed Tom to make better and cheaper cars, eventually this knowledge would also spread and replace inferior knowledge either because SuperAuto was able to see how Tom built his cars and copy the superior knowledge found in his productive structure or because SuperAuto owners found it to be better to just sell their productive structure to someone who felt like he had the necessary knowledge to turn it into a profitable and therefore socially useful one. Either way, the human ant-farm reorganizes itself from a less productive state to a more productive one. The superior knowledge that was embodied in Tom's company was replicated across the human ant-farm.

    This last example shows what most of us would refer to as competition. Unfortunately, the word competition carries with it a very primal "I win, you lose" mentality that is largely responsible for the fear that drives so many to instinctively attack the free-market and Capitalism.

Competition is more like the forced and beneficial spreading of superior knowledge and the rearrangement of the human ant-farm that this new knowledge entails. As previously mentioned, a human ant-farm powered by the market process is like an efficient supercomputer, constantly discovering new, more productive knowledge and restructuring itself accordingly, growing more powerful and technologically advanced. When new knowledge pops up into one of it's many brains, the knowledge improves the structure of a company or leads to a new company as in Tom's case. In Tom's case the new superior knowledge was expressed in the lower price of Tom's cars. The human ant-farm starts to restructure itself accordingly, millions of brains who are constantly calculating how to improve their actions now update their calculations and improve them, instead of buying an $8,000 car they buy one for $4,000. This also triggers in their brains new ideas, which would not have been profitable at the higher car prices, causing further beneficial restructurings of the human ant-farm. Since the human ant-farm is now trading with Tom's productive structure as opposed to the other car making productive structures, these other structures have less money to maintain themselves. The loss of revenue by other productive structures causes them to either replicate the new superior knowledge or to simply break up and dissolve the structure into the social organism by selling off the various assets that make up their productive structures like buildings, factories and so on. Even though the millions of brains in the human ant-farm are only concerned and excited about the new cheaper cars they can afford they are actually performing the social organism's calculations. By giving their money to Tom's company they are selecting his superior knowledge and placing in his hands the money and therefore resources needed to further expand his superior productive structure and at the same time they are communicating to Tom's competitors, via a lack of revenue on their part, that they need to restructure themselves or sell off their assets to those that can best use them.

Some productive structures will be successful at replicating the superior knowledge that led to Tom's success. They hired some of Tom's employees, reverse engineered some of his cars, visited Tom's plants and were able to copy and replicate Tom's superior ways. Some other companies were too slow to do this or attempted different restructurings that ultimately led to inferior products, products that the millions of brains in the human ant-farm did not feel were as good as the alternatives for their productive plans. The owners of these productive structures decided to cut their losses and sell their assets, they did not feel like they had knowledge that if implemented would lead to continued profitability and therefore useful employment of their productive structures. Since they did not posses this knowledge they decided to sell their buildings, and factories, and other assets to the human ant-farm, to the thousands of brains who would incorporate these assets into their productive, profitable, and therefore socially beneficial plans. Let's say that Magic Autos was one of the companies whose owners decided to sell their assets. Another thing that could have happened is that Magic Autos simply went bankrupt because it could not pay for the loans it took to pay for the various assets it used, like a mortgage or rent on a factory building. In this case Magic Autos' assets would now belong to its creditors and it would be the creditors selling off the buildings and equipment that belonged to Magic Auto. From now on I'll just assume in our example that Magic Auto went bankrupt and that its former assets are now controlled by its creditors like the banks and lenders that loaned Magic Autos money. If Magic Autos' managers and employees had a hard time making a profitable use of all of their combined resources, their creditors will have less of a clue since they are not in the car making business and therefore they will most likely try to sell them off to the highest bidders. During the sell off, or liquidation phase, what happens is that resources which were part of a plan which was no longer calculated by the millions of brains in the human ant-farm to be in their best interest(expensive cars compared to Tom's), will be placed in the control of brains who will incorporate these assets into their useful and profitable plans. Magic Auto's assets will be sold to the highest bidders, selling the assets to the highest bidders ensures that the assets will be in the hands of those whose plans are the most profitable and therefore the most useful for the human ant-farm. We would not want a building previously in the control of Magic Auto to be sold for 10 million dollars to a large furniture store which the human ant-farm would trade 5 million dollars for the products it would ultimately offer, when the building could be sold to Joe for 20 million and he could use it to create his wonderful medical device which society would value more, which would be reflected in society's willingness to trade 10 billion dollars for the services offered by Joe's productive structure. By selling the assets to the highest bidder not only do the creditors rightfully get as much money as possible but also the real assets are placed in the control of the brains that have the best knowledge and plans for their use.

    We have just seen how new knowledge inevitably spreads and restructures the human ant-farm to the benefit of its members. At any point in time, the human ant-farm is structured to produce things a certain way, given that people are always looking for cheaper and better ways of producing whatever products or services they offer to the human ant-farm for exchange in order to increase their profits, we should expect prices to continuously fall and quality to rise. Tom's example showed how this happened in the auto industry, the same thing can be said about today's computer industry where the prices of computers and laptops always go down and the quality improves. Competitors are always learning from each other and therefore restructuring their respective mini human ant-farms to act based on the best knowledge that has arisen in society. This process of human brains thinking of new ways to improve and restructure the mini human ant-farms(companies) that they can control, and the spreading of this more productive ways throughout the other productive structures that are in the same industry, occurs in all industries. A car mechanic benefits from the continuous drop in prices and increase in quality of products and services offered by the auto industry in the way of cheaper and better cars; the consumer electronics industry in way of cheaper and better TVs, stereos, MP3 players; the travel industry in way of cheaper and fancier airplanes which lead to cheaper flights; and on and on throughout every industry. This is what people who understand the market process should expect. We should expect things to get cheaper and better all the time across all industries.

Having reached a point where we have discussed the workings of interest rates and competition we need to briefly reflect on their importance. These two concepts are what really help turn individual brains into the social supercomputer, which is what the human ant-farm/'social organism' really is. At the very core, humanity is a supercomputer that is discovering knowledge which ultimately guides the actions of its billions of human ants as they go about transforming matter into human usable wealth and growing its orderly structure.

The market process goes about discovering knowledge in a simple way. If there is an existing need for anything, whether it'd be improved safety, a faster car or whatever, this need is reflected in an amount of money/wealth that is being offered for it and reflects the relative importance or urgency of this need/desire. This is what economists refer to as consumer demand for something. This amount of wealth lures brains in the social organism/supercomputer into figuring out the best way of meeting this need. And the process of competition ensures that the best ideas are naturally selected. This process, the market process, is universal. Whether you want to figure out the best way to educate a child or the best way to increase the safety of a car, if what you are looking for is a way, in other words, knowledge, the market process is as good as human beings can possibly do. It is very important to realize that competition is competition between ideas and knowledge of how to go about doing things, and not some struggle for survival. The things that are being naturally selected for survival are knowledge and ways of doing things as opposed to our lives and well being. Competition just forces everyone into updating their knowledge to reflect the latest technologies and ways of doing things.

With respect to the market process, no one in the world has yet to come up with a more efficient way to discover knowledge that ultimately guides our actions. No one even invented this fabulous mechanism. It was one of the many unplanned/inadvertent innovations which allowed the pro-Capitalism human ant-farms to flourish and expand their ways all over the world. No smart philosopher ever designed this system. As people inadvertently tried to make the most of their savings by lending them, and out of their own selfishness tried to get the best rate of return, they were inadvertently creating the world's most efficient mechanism of pairing the best plans/knowledge with the necessary savings/money/means to carry them out. And with respect to competition, people never realized that by freely spending their money on the things that were best for them, they were performing a crucial selective role that allowed for the best knowledge to flourish and spread throughout society. These market process mechanisms were not consciously invented by anyone, they inadvertently arose and invented us! At times the Christian/Western world prohibited lending at interest but they got around it, unfortunately lending at interest is still strongly prohibited in the Islamic world and this is obviously one of many things that keeps their human ant-farms materially/technologically backwards compared to the Christian world.

How the social organism calculates what to produce. The average rate of profit

The prosperity of a society depends on the productive actions of its members. We have already discussed many of the features in a market oriented society that keep the human ant-farm constantly discovering new knowledge and restructuring the actions of its members in increasingly productive ways. Seeing society as one large super-computer, how does this super-computer decide what to produce? We have already seen how the lending industry and the interest rate answer this question, but let's look at it again from a different perspective.

Let's assume that the auto industry is in its infancy, people have started making cars and since they are such wonderful inventions which brains realize can greatly help them increase their production and well being they offer lots of money for these automobiles. This means that the automobile industry is very profitable. Let's assume that a company is put together with an investment of $1,000,000 per year and it sells $2,000,000 worth of automobiles. It has received a 100% return on investment. In the human ant-farm there are many other brains like bankers, lenders, investors with access to people's savings looking for the best places to invest this money, places with the highest return on investment, and high profits in any industry are a signal to such investors that that is where they should invest. High profits are a signal to the social organism that whatever sector or product is generating such high profits is very useful and desirable to the social organism. It is very useful to society because the millions of brains that make it up are willing to trade more of their money and resources for this new product or service than for other things and it is this strong desire which leads to the high prices that people are willing to pay and to the large profits. So just like the bankers loaned Joe money based on the higher profits he would earn which allowed him to offer a higher interest on loans, the bankers and lenders invest their money in the new and highly socially desirable car industry.

As more automakers enter the car manufacturing industry the profits will be reduced. Let's assume that our first automaker, Cool Autos, sold cars for twice their cost and made a 100% return on his investment, let's assume they cost $500 to make and were sold for $1,000. The second car manufacturer, Luxor Autos, also has about the same costs of $500 per car and sells them for $900 in order to lure Cool Auto's potential buyers. Selling cars for $900 when they cost $500 to build is still a large profit margin of 80%. Let's assume that Cool Autos lowers its price to about the same $900 dollars so that both companies each more or less has about 50% of the auto manufacturing market, this is still a very profitable sector compared to the many other industries where bankers, lenders, investors and so on could be investing their money. So investors and people with savings help finance more car manufacturing companies so that even if Cool Auto and Luxor had some kind of evil price fixing agreement the high profits that they make thanks to such an agreement would only serve to signal further competitors into entering the auto industry. Tanaka Autos enters the car manufacturing business and let's assume that it still costs them $500 to make cars and they sell them for $650. This is still a 30% return on investment, if we assume that the average return on investment across all industries in the whole society is about 8% there is still a lot of incentive for saved money and resources to be invested in the auto industry. So what will happen is that eventually the auto making company's profits will be comparable to those of any other industry and due to the competition and continuous lowering of prices instead of huge profits for auto makers you have average profits for auto makers and huge savings for consumers.

We have just seen how high profits are a signal to the many brains in the social organism that transfers knowledge indicating that there is a highly desirable and useful product or service to be made, in this case it was autos. And we saw how the market process channeled resources into that sector and how competition eventually brought profits down to the average level, which exists across all branches of production in a society. The high profits made by companies will never last long due to the increase in competition that this signal will bring from other sectors of the market. The high profits are usually reinvested into making the product better in order to keep up with competitors. Eventually the high profits disappear and they become savings for consumers due to the lower prices that the competitive restructuring process brings about. Although this example showed how this process works in the auto industry, it is a process that is constantly occurring in all sectors of the economy.

Another important thing to take away from this section is to realize that it is impossible for companies to "exploit" workers by paying them too little and making huge profits because of it. If a company is making huge profits because it is paying its employees very little, this is just a signal to the many brains/entrepreneurs in society that they can start a competing company, pay the "exploited" employees a higher wage to lure them to work for them and now the new competitor is making a large profit, although not as big as the original "exploiter" because it is having to offer higher wages. What was once a single "exploiter" now has to compete with the new "exploiter" to the great benefit of the employees. If the two companies are still making profits substantially above the average rate of profit, this is once again a signal to more brains/entrepreneurs out there and more competition comes to offer hire wages to employees, until eventually the opportunity for so called "exploitation" dries up, all companies are making close to the average rate of profit, and the employees' wages are truly reflective of their productivity. Falling for the "exploiter/exploited" mentality is an error rooted in our tribal/brutal mentality where we might have been used to really exploit and take advantage of people by force in a more tribal past, but even if we still quite naturally have tendencies to see things this way and even consciously believe that we are exploiting people, as long as there is economic freedom and the market process is allowed to operate, a human being's contribution to the world will always tend to earn him an amount that is truly reflective of his contribution.

How living standards and real wages rise

Imagine you are a new immigrant in a large island populated by 1,000 people and each inhabitant has a machine that can transform sand and seawater into a variety of nutritious and tasty meals like chocolate cakes, pizza, lasagna, and many others. Since people's nutritional needs are so easily taken care of, their needs and desires are channeled to other things. One person wants to build a large house, another one wants to build a boat and there is always the desire to keep up with the neighbors. When you go look for work, given that everyone has an endless supply of food thanks to their special machines, many will end up offering you at least more food than you could have gotten on your own by fishing or finding coconuts or killing birds and so on. In the eyes of the islands' inhabitants they trade food that they have in abundance and is of little value to them because they can create it so easily for something that is scarce and they value more, your labor. Since everyone can easily offer you all the food you need they probably offer you at least that plus something else in order to compete for your labor. Mike might offer to help you build a small shack to live after you help him build his big house. Bob might offer to let you use his boat when he does not need it.

In the modern world instead of having 1,000 people we have thousands of groups of people producing, we call these groups of people companies, and thanks to the continued and ever more efficient restructuring of the human ant-farm, technology, machines, and so on, those companies and people are so productive that they have no choice but to offer more and more for laborers as they compete with other companies similar to how the island's inhabitants were forced to offer ample food as they competed for your labor. Since human beings, thanks to technology and interactions with increasingly more efficient productive structures, are always more productive, we have no choice but to offer more to lure labor to join us in our productive endeavors. This is the essence of why the living standards of every human being must inevitably increase, because producers inevitably find it easier and easier to produce more and more, and in order for them to remain in business they have no choice but to offer more wealth in exchange for the labor they need, just like the people in the island had to at least offer ample food and more as they competed with each other for your labor.

Cheaper and better ways of producing stuff forces everyone to produce as cheaply and as best as possible. For example, why do the prices of computers always go down? Because the knowledge and means to create them for a lower price eventually come into existence in a human brain and those who do not take advantage of using this knowledge by selling expensive and lower quality computers will see the money go towards their competitors who produce computers based on the better knowledge. If there are currently no competitors the new knowledge must have come into existence in the brain of someone and that person will have the incentive to go into the computer business therefore bringing a competitor into existence and eventually forcing this superior knowledge to spread to others. The incentives that exist in a market-oriented society are such that new knowledge inevitably alters the human ant-farm in ways that lead to increased production and progress. And the more wealth is produced, the more wealth has to be offered in exchange for people's labor.

It should be clear by now how the human ant-farm is a vast and complicated network of trades by human beings. The human ant-farm can be seen as a tool, kind of like a robot that works to create wealth for human beings. When a person integrates into the economy or human ant-farm by producing something in exchange for money and then using the money for his own purposes, the person is using the robot to achieve infinitely more than the he could without the robot. For example, I can flip burgers for a month and use the money I earn to buy a computer that would have been impossible for me to build on my own. So the robot(the entire human ant-farm) is an incredibly useful tool. My right or ability to use the robot is the money I have earned by previously working and contributing to the robot's functioning. When I spend my money I am interacting with the robot to get what I want from it and at the same time I am helping fine-tune the inner workings of the robot by giving my money to some parts of it and not to others.

The robot has a certain efficiency, or ability to produce wealth for people. Let's assume the average human being living somewhere in medieval Europe in the year 1,000, spent 70 hours on a given week working the land and was able to exchange his labor for enough money to buy 20 meals. A "poor" person working for minimum wage at the present time in the US makes $5.15 per hour and if this person works 70 hours he will have $360.50(we'll forget about taxes for now). With the popular "dollar" menus at most fast food restaurants our American worker can get a burger, fries and a drink(with free refills☺) for about $3.20 which means he can buy about 111 meals compared to 20 in the year 1,000. And let's also keep in mind that the 21st century fast food meal will be a better tasting and more sanitary one, served in a nice air conditioned building with no need to cook it or clean up afterwards. But let's forget about all that and just stick to the number of meals, 111 compared to 20. This is 5.5 times more food in the present compared to the year 1,000. This is because the human being in the year 1,000 was using a less advanced tool, a less productive and technologically advanced human ant-farm. It is like a farmer who farms by hand and one that uses a modern tractor. We tend to refer to technology as gadgets and machines and physical tools but this is a mistake or perhaps a current limitation or deficiency in our vocabulary, technology is the continuous concentration of productive knowledge and social order. When one uses a supermarket as opposed to growing your own food you are using a productive structure, a tool, the supermarket, no differently than using a hammer to hammer a nail compared to pounding it with a rock. Productive structures and companies can be seen as tools, they are technology, just not concentrated into a lifeless physical object.

There is one vitally important difference that must be pointed out between the human ant-farm/tool/supercomputer of the year 1,000 versus today's. Today's human ant-farm has almost 7,000,000,000 (7 billion) brains compared to the 300,000,000 (300 million) brains of the year 1,000. That is 22 times more brains in the present compared to the year 1,000. The more brains the human ant-farm has the more powerful and productive it becomes. Every time a human being incorporates himself with the human ant-farm by trading with it, not only does he gain the benefits that it brings but he also makes it a little smarter and more powerful so that the next person who joins and trades with the human ant-farm gets even more productivity from it and further increases the functionality of the human ant-farm for the next person to use and on and on and on. This is something that reality easily verifies. We have a vastly larger amount of people in the world and at the same time every human being is more productive and can enjoy a bigger and better slice from a constantly increasing economic pie. This continuous smartening and increase in productive capacity of society is something completely foreign to our instincts, and as will be discussed later, is the key to overcoming our fear of running out of natural resources as well as environmental concerns. During our millions of years of evolution our minds have been shaped to deal with a zero-sum world where other people's loses were our gains and we were limited by the few resources replenished by our natural environment. Our productive plans were limited by the intelligence of a few minds making use of the simplest of tools if any tools were used at all.

What we have just discussed should once again help us realize that there can be no "exploitation" of labor. Even if given our human nature, a manager or business owner might enjoy or derive pleasure from paying someone less so that he can enjoy more, such "greedy" or "evil" mentality cannot be maintained because the increasing amount of wealth that other employers around him are generating and inevitably offering in exchange for labor, will lure away his "exploited" employees. So the key to higher wages and material prosperity for employees, is the increased productivity that inevitable comes as the market process rearranges humanity into increasingly productive states, and not asking the government to simply take from the haves to give to the have-less, but more on that later.

Bringing the future closer: the effects of, and importance of saving

We have already discussed some of the role that savings plays while discussing interest rates, banking and lending and the business cycle. The money saved and invested by those who lack ideas whose rate of return is greater than the current interest rate, becomes the money borrowed and spent by others that do have ideas that are more profitable than the current interest rate. This way, money is always paired with and enabling the carrying out of the most productive ideas/plans/'rearrangements of the human ant-farm'. As this happens the human ant-farm constantly morphs itself into increasingly more productive and technologically advanced states, increasing the rate at which it transforms matter into wealth, increasing the economic pie, which eventually has to be offered in greater quantities to labor as productive structures/businesses/companies compete for such labor in order to continue their productive activities. This is the essence of the progress of mankind, it is wonderful and it gets much better when we understand the effects of saving.

Imagine a man stranded in a deserted island who needs to catch a fish per day on average in order to survive. If he spends 3 days gathering the necessary materials and building himself a net he will be able to catch 3 fish per day instead of one. If we compare the two states of this simple single-ant human ant-farm, the state after the man has built himself a net is more technologically advanced and productive, it would be a world with a more efficient matter-into-human-usable-wealth-transformation structure thanks to the net. A world where it takes less human effort to achieve the same level of production than it used to. In order to get from his original state to this more productive state he will need to save 3 fish in order to stay alive/'maintain his orderly structure' during the three days it will take him to build his net. So for several days he either works harder and saves the additional amount of fish he might catch during the day, or he reduces his consumption and goes a little hungry in order to save. After he has saved 3 days worth of fish, he can then embark on the morphing/rearrangement of his productive structure by gathering materials and building his net as he consumes the 3 fish he had saved. By saving and then investing he has transformed his state from a less productive/'technologically advanced' state to one that is more so. The man could have chosen to save at various rates, if he saved one tenth of his single fish daily catch, it would have taken him ten days to save one fish worth of food and 30 days to save the total needed to fund his transformation. If he increased his rate of saving to 1/4th of his daily catch, it would have taken him 4 days to save enough for one fish, and 12 days as opposed to 30 in order to save for all three fish. By saving more he would have brought the more technologically advanced future closer to his present, in a way accelerating the rate at which he progresses. Whatever other ideas for the improvement of his condition he might have in the future, he will be able to save the necessary amount of food and carry out such improvements much sooner thanks to the fact that after he has his net it will take him less time to save for further investments/transformations than if he had not saved and built his net. In other words, he would be moving into a more technologically advanced future faster. The more productive the man is, the faster he can build up and save the necessary wealth which he will need in order to make further investments. Having discussed how savings and investment work at a single man solitary economy let's see how it affects the modern human ant-farm.

If there is little savings there is little money/wealth available for lending. If people did not save money, there might not have been enough savings to fund the necessary restructuring of the human ant-farm needed to bring Joe's wonderful medical device to life. Every new company/'productive structure' needs to live off of savings while it creates itself and begins to produce a good/service which it can later trade for the necessary money to maintain/expand its productive order. Joe needed 5 billion in order to pay his employees and building costs as he restructured the human ant-farm, and it wasn't after many months when he was able to start selling his medical diagnosing services and make some money. No one would have worked for Joe or loaned him the necessary materials for however long it took him to bring his product to market and then get paid. If there is little savings in the economy, Joe's would-be employees would not even have had the savings necessary to live off of while they worked on Joe's enterprise until it was complete and able to finally pay them. So in order to start any new business/'rearrangement of the human ant-farm' you need savings.

If a human ant-farm has little savings, if pictured from above, it will have a very sort of repetitive or slow-changing rate of transformation into increasingly productive states. As was the case with our new discussion about Joe's project, if there is little savings, there is little money to fund and maintain alive new restructurings of the human ant-farm, in other words, you need savings to start companies, companies need to live off of savings while they bring a product/service to market. So if there is little savings, the rate at which new companies/businesses/'restructurings of the human ant-farm' come to life is slowed down. The human ant-farm simply continues in its old productive patterns and consumes most of its wealth as opposed to saving some, which is what would be needed for providing a subsistence fund for the new companies to live off of while they bring their new products/services to market. People are more or less doing the same old thing in their jobs, producing the same amount of stuff, and consuming most of it, and repeating.

If there is little savings and many people have profitable ideas which would restructure the human ant-farm into more productive/profitable/advanced states, then the competition for the few available savings by the businessmen who want to borrow in order to execute their plans would raise interest rates quickly and make a lot of these ideas no longer profitable. For example, if interest rates are at 20%, only ideas which can yield higher than 20% will be able to borrow at such high interest rates and carry out their restructurings of the human ant-farm. So we can picture the human ant-farm sort of stuck in a rigid pattern of production and consumption with little savings, and a new restructuring here and there when a really great idea which will surely yield a higher than 20% return comes along. This is bad for society because there will be many more people whose ideas could transform resources to yield 3,5,6,10,15…20% increases in production, but because interest rates are above 20% these ideas will not be profitable and therefore unable to morph the human ant-farm into more productive and prosperous states. The lack of savings, which reflects itself in the high interest rate, prevents these possible beneficial restructurings of the human ant-farm from having enough money/resources/bricks to be carried out.

Now let's assume that people do save a lot which will increase the amount of loanable funds and bring down the interest rate to say 2%. Now, instead of being limited to carrying out only the most beneficial/profitable of ideas/transformations, those whose profitability was greater than 20%, we can still carry out the very profitable ideas that yield 20%+, but now we also have enough savings to 'give life to'/fund many more ideas/transformations, those that yield a 2 to 20 percent return on investment. If we picture the human ant-farm from above in our new scenario where people save more, we see a human ant-farm that is constantly morphing into increasingly more productive/technologically advanced states. As soon as new ideas come there are savings/'bricks' saved up which they can borrow/use to implement their plans/restructurings/'brick houses'. Speaking of bricks. We already discussed the futility of artificially lowering the interest rate to make it seem like many more restructurings of the human ant-farm are sustainable when they are not. As already discussed in our previous section about the business cycle, when interest rates are artificially lowered, by simply adding money into the banking system, and are not truly reflective of the amount of wealth that is saved, the human ant-farm will begin to morph itself and seem very dynamic for a while during the early stages of the boom, but as we know, many of these restructurings will eventually fail, and there will be less production and increased unemployment during the bust as the human ants align themselves with truly productive and self sustaining enterprises.

So we have just discussed a topic that is of monumental importance for the prosperity of mankind. Saving and investing is the way in which we bring the future closer to us. What is the difference between the hypothetical more utopian year 2050 I introduced earlier in the book and our current state? The productive alignment of the human ant-farm. And we get there from here by morphing/restructuring our actions via profitable realignments/investments. The more we save now, the easier we make it to fund increasingly productive restructurings of the human ant-farm, which will bring us an increasingly larger amount of wealth/technology in the future. The less we save, the longer it takes to build up the necessary savings that can give life to such restructurings and therefore the longer it takes to bring their productive/technological benefits to us, slowing down the rate at which we could possibly advance into the future.

The more we save by giving up our current consumption the more 'fish' we make available for those who need to live off of them while restructuring/morphing the human ant-farm into more productive/technologically advanced states. As people who understand the market process, we have a say in how fast we move into a more prosperous future, we can either consume and enjoy our current level of prosperity more, or we can give up on this consumption to save and enable the future to come to us faster, and by future I mean things like better medicines/cures, cheaper and more powerful computers, gadgets, technologies that will make cleaning and taking care of the environment much easier and cheaper, and the one I really believe can come during my lifetime, immortality.

It is important to realize that money/wealth that is saved does not just sit idle. To save money is to spend money, but as opposed to spending money in a manner that leads to pure consumption, the money is spent in a way that has to be paid back, which involves pie-increasing wealth production. If I take $50,000 and consume them via a car, travel, energy, etc. the economic pie has been decreased by such amount of wealth, but if I save/lend/invest the $50,000, whatever entity borrows the money, has to pay it back plus interest, and this can only be done by first increasing the economic pie with wealth and then trading such wealth for the needed money to pay me back. Again, it is the difference between giving a man 5 dollars which he uses to buy a sandwich and trading the 5 dollars for an hour of his labor. In the first case the economic pie has been reduced by a sandwich. In the second case it has also been reduced by a sandwich which the man consumed, but it has been increased by an hour of human labor and whatever product/service such hour helped create.

When businesses/individuals save money by choosing the cheaper alternatives offered by competitors, they are not only helping select superior social order and knowledge, that of successful competitors, they are increasing the amount of saved wealth that inevitably competes for labor and therefore increases the wages and overall economic pie available to the masses. So again, one of the most important points to iterate is that saving is just another way of spending. Again, for the third time, if we just assume the simple case that savings are made available via lending, then the money is spent by borrowers as they go about producing wealth, enough wealth to later trade for enough money to pay back the loan, plus interest, which is reflective of the growth in the economic pie that is taking place, and then there is additional wealth, the profit that the borrowers get to keep, plus all the benefits that occur as savings lower the interest rate and soon.

And lastly I would like to stress the importance of realizing that things like money and banking and the workings of the market process itself were not the result of conscious human design, that just like life itself has been created by an evolutionary process, so have these and other socioeconomic institutions. Men simply acted based on their immediate self interest when they stumbled upon things like money without having the slightest clue that money was going to become to the social organism what something like nerves that carry information might be for a living animal. Today we look at a living organism in wonder of how all the parts work together in unison and think that a designer had to design them all together at the same time given their interdependence, yet there was no need for a designer, and in the social organism we have further proof. When we look at a modern economy we see complex institutions like money, banking, the interest rate, and the necessary legal framework to support such institutions which are integral parts of the social organism yet the crucial role they play was not consciously intended by men. In the words of Carl Menger :

"Natural organisms almost without exception exhibit, when closely observed, a really admirable functionality of all parts with respect to the whole, a functionality which is not, however, the result of human calculation, but of natural process. Similarly we can observe in numerous social institutions a strikingly apparent functionality with respect to the whole. But with closer consideration they still do not prove to be the result of an intention aimed at this purpose, i.e., the result of an agreement of members of society or of positive legislation. They, too, present themselves to us rather as "natural" products(in a certain sense), as unintended results of historical development. One needs, e.g., only to think of the phenomenon of money, an institution which to so a great measure serves the welfare of society, and yet in most nations, by far, is by no means the result of an agreement directed at its establishment as a social institution, or of positive legislation, but is the unintended product of historical development. One needs only to think of law, language, of the origin of markets, the origin of commodities and of states, etc."[13]

Hayek:

"We have never designed our economic system. We were not intelligent enough for that. We have stumbled into it and it has carried us to unforeseen heights and given rise to ambitions which may yet lead us to destroy it."[14]

[1] Search for "I, pencil" . A classic short essay by Leonard E. Read where a pencil describes the complexity involved in bringing him to creation. At the time of this writing it can be found here: http://econlib.org/library/Essays/rdPncl1.html

[2] Carl Menger, *Principles of Economics,* (Libertarian Press, Inc.: Grove City, PA, 1994), page 263-264. www.libertarianpress.com

[3] Ibid. 266

[4] There were others who also stumbled upon such views. See "15 Great Austrian Economists" published by the Ludwig von Mises Institute, 1999. ISBN 0-945466-04-8

[5] This example came from a great mises.org article by Arthur E. Foulkes which can be found here http://www.mises.org/story/2207

[6] The first three examples came from Gerald Swanson's "The Hyperinflation Survival Guide: Strategies for American Businesses" sponsored by Figgie International, Inc. ISBN 0-9741180-0-1 Page 5

The last example and many other great historical examples of hyperinflation can be found at http://en.wikipedia.org/wiki/Hyperinflation

[7] This short 60 second video shows how the US creates worldwide inflation and why the US dollar is quickly losing value and the potential for much higher inflation

http://www.youtube.com/watch?v=9fv1DqIen28

[8] This 'brick house" analogy comes from Roger Garrison's lectures on the business cycle available at http://mises.org/media

[9] Ludwig von Mises' Human Action . Published by the Ludwig von Mises Institute ISBN 0-945466-24-2 Page 558

[10] Ibid, page 559

[11] Ibid, page 562

[12] F.A. Hayek, Prices and Production, Published by George Routledge & Sons, LTD. Second Impression, January 1932, Page 86-87

[13] Carl Menger, *Investigations Into the Method of the Social Sciences*, (Libertarian Press, Inc.: Grove City, PA, 1996), 106. www.libertarianpress.com. The underlining of various words in quote represent emphasis placed on those words by Menger himself

[14] F.A. Hayek, Law Legislation and Liberty. Volume 3. Published by the University of Chicago Press. ISBN 0-226-32090-1, page 164. In the original text Hayek used italics on the words I have underlined

III. Government Planning vs. The Market Process

In this chapter we are going to see how government intervention in the private sector, or in other words, government interference with the market process, via its confiscation/redistribution of wealth and regulation of the economy leads to most of our problems, and discuss how much better off we would all be if the government just stuck to enforcing our two fundamental laws as opposed to trying to fix the world by catering to our fears. But before getting into the purely economic aspects of this, let us first discuss a few things about human nature as well as the evolution of government itself and a little history.

Our strong instinct to form groups.

Amongst the many social characteristics of humans, our instinct to belong to and make alliances with groups is key to understanding our current troubles. Once animals can cooperate, the genes of these animals that enable cooperation can become more important than genes that help the animal be better at individual things. Once an animal can cooperate, he now has two ways of being more successful than others, he can out-compete others at an individual level, he might be stronger in a fight etc, or he might out-cooperate him in some other way. If you can form an alliance with another guy, then even if you are weaker than your opponent you can gang up on him with your friend and have a much higher chance of being victorious. When we think of gangsters the leaders are not necessarily the biggest and strongest, they are the best cooperators, the ones that have little by little built alliances based on favors and loyalties earned at the right times. Social status takes on a new importance that does not exist in non-social animals. A high social status means that you have power that lies outside of your physical means. If you are of high social status you have more people that will come to your aid in a fight and you can also count on their help in your aggressive adventures. If you are a person of low rank, few will come to your aid and few might want to join in an alliance with you. It takes powerful brains to calculate which group to join, who to help, for how long, should I desert and so on. An important part of our intelligence has been shaped by these kinds of decisions. In a world where groups and alliances are competing against each other, as has been the case for most of our evolution, you better make sure you are part of the successful group which in our tribal past usually meant the larger one, and being alone is always a losing option.

For millions of years, from our tribal existence and going farther back to times where we shared common ancestors with current day chimps and bonobos, natural selection has been selecting mutations/traits that have made us better at forming alliances. If we do not have friends or feel like we do not belong to a larger group we get depressed and the feeling of loneliness motivates us to belong to a larger group.

Group formation is a dynamic process that is constantly happening. Our instinct to join groups evolved because of the advantages it gave us over being loners and because of the necessity to compete against other groups/alliances. If we are all part of the same group and I get no benefit over you because you too are a member of this all encompassing group then there is little benefit to being a member of the group at all. In a group this large the formation of a small group within the larger group would now be advantageous to the members of this small subgroup. Local kids from the neighborhood form neighborhood gangs that compete with other neighborhoods, but within this neighborhood gang there can be smaller groups, perhaps a group of 4 or 5 friends from the same building. And even between this smaller group there might be a stronger bond between two best friends. If we live in the same territory as others we have a strong incentive to make an alliance and see each other as cooperators against outsiders because we need to protect the environment that provides for our livelihood. You might dislike your neighbor but you will fight amongst him the invading enemy.

Another important aspect of belonging to a group is how it alters our incentives and behaviors. When a brain finds itself as part of a crowd it gains lots of power and it changes the risks associated with certain actions. As members of a crowd we can be much more brutal and ignore the moral brainwashing that makes us behave in a more civilized manner. Men who would make nice guys in civilian life often go on to take part in rape, murder, and all kinds of atrocities common in war. This is due to the power found in numbers and to the gain of anonymity that makes the individual have little chance of ever having to face retaliation from his actions in the future. Crowds cannot reason like individual people can, the bigger the crowd the simpler the concepts that can be successfully absorbed by all the brains that can lead to the kind of collective action that gives a crowd an advantage. Just knowing that the local sports team is from our town, from our territory, is enough to awake that 'groupish' instinct that motivates us to belong to the fan base as if we were getting ready to protect our turf or expand it. Common riots in soccer games have their roots in our small tribe groupish instincts. Being part of a large group feels good. If there is a problem that concerns you as well as everyone else you know that you will not be alone in having to deal with it. The school-of-fish mentality where we just follow along with what the crowd or masses are doing comes naturally to us.

Patriotism is an extension of our groupish instincts. We are suckers for it, and in our zero-sum world of inevitable conflict it paid off to be patriotic but in a world were human beings can understand human nature and how the market process works to build the greatest possible world for all, patriotism becomes one of the greatest detriments to mankind. In reality there are only human beings at different coordinates moving around doing our ant-like thing, this is something that can be easily observed when we look at the human ant-farm from above and not a silly map with political boundaries. But our groupish instincts are very strong and we see each other as belonging to different countries and so on.

The origins of governments

In our tribal world, just like in the lives of our closest relatives bonobos and chimpanzees, we(especially men) were always seeking power and were members of a pecking order. More power eventually translates itself into more food, more backup, more females and therefore more copies of power-seeking genes spreading through the population. If you are not looking for more power and ways to exert power over others to your advantage, others will be trying to exert power over you and you will be at a disadvantage and therefore there will be less food, backup, and females for you and your "peaceful" genes will not make it on to future generations. We are all descendents of the power hungry types. If it is somewhat in our nature to seek power over others, it is also in our nature to resist such power.

The very root of government can be found in this desire to exert power over others, especially men for the benefit of increased access to females. But we know that modern governments are not the result of men trying to increase their access to females, although there can be no doubt, that being a powerful politician with thousands of people treating you as their leader often times translates to lots of confidence, prestige, power and ultimately success with women. But this is obviously not the real characteristic from which our modern governments descended. Our simple tribal dominance hierarchies have another important trait that is not based on the strong/powerful wanting to subdue the weak/powerless. Dominance hierarchies were crucial for collective and coordinated actions of the group, actions where the entire group had to act towards a common purpose. A group of human beings finds itself in many situations where most members of the group need to act as one towards a common goal, we need to coordinate things like migrations and hunting, but most importantly we need to act as one for war/conquest/defense.

For most of our evolutionary history war/defense was the most important activity that needed collective action. War can be painful and cost us our lives yet men have been naturally selected to love it, it is exciting to be out there taking out the enemy, it gives us a great sense of purpose. Young men full of testosterone are suckers for it, whether wars are just or not, who cares, we have not evolved to reason what is just or not when it comes to war, all that matters to our instincts is us vs. them, we are the good guys, they are the bad guys. By killing others we are making the world safer and more plentiful for ourselves. In every country being against or not supportive of its troops is a major sin. Every country also has its own unique uniform to solidify group identity and cohesion which is so important for successful unified action. Since unity has usually been the most important factor in war, it should be no surprise that desertion has traditionally been punishable by death. Societies that did not enforce such unity would not have been as successful in war and have been naturally selected against, therefore we are all cultural descendents of societies/groups that took a strong stance against desertion, and for unity.

In our market process coordinated modern world, unity is no longer the most important factor in war, the market process and its ability to easily/cheaply transform matter into powerful weapons is what gets the job done. Unity, courage, fearlessness, valor were the most important traits in a tribal world where there was no market process and all human beings were more or less equal in their physical and technological abilities. The most united, bravest, fearless, and patriotic American Indians were no match for the "white man"'s technology and neither were the Japanese when fighting an American army powered by the most efficient market process coordinated human ant-farm the world had ever seen.

Another important function of government is to enforce the rules which society follows and help give it a more stable and productive order. Let's imagine a 100 person government-less tribe, if there is no fear of a government-like power hierarchy of people enforcing rules of conduct then the incentives for extreme selfishness and things like theft become much greater. A strong-man might take advantage of surprise/circumstance to subdue/steal from others and since there is no alliance that enforces rules against theft, in other words, since there is no concept leading to what would be considered a primitive government, this strong-man would be able to get a way with it. But this would only mean that two or three men could form an alliance, a group, to use their combined strength to subdue others. This government-less tribe would be plagued by internal strife and be easily overtaken by an external tribe who avoided such internal violence, and even if this government-less tribe did not face extinction due to external competition, a natural government hierarchy would still form because in order to exploit the solitary members of society effectively, other members would have to form alliances which were mutually beneficial where their members followed certain rules of reciprocity essentially leading to a government structure. Rules like "I help you and you help me", then "we agree to not attack each other", or to "defend each other when attacked by others". Following these rules would allow those who follow them to increase their dominance over others and eventually rise to the top and in doing so bring a primitive government and more stable social order where there was none before. We have been under the influence of some kind of government or dominance hierarchy for during our recent evolution. Chimpanzees and other primates have political structures, with powerful males and their network of alliances liked together by a history of favors. This naturally evolved into our stereotypical tribal world with its elder leaders or similar types of power hierarchies.

The recent evolution of law and the emergence of the modern socialist mindset[1]

If we compare the values and ideologies of the past to those of the modern world, it is easy to see that there have been some major changes, like a more equal treatment of women, and a more equal treatment and tolerance of people of different races. These changes have been good for mankind and they have been possible thanks to the fundamental change from an inevitably brutal zero-sum world to our highly productive non-zero-sum market-process-coordinated world. Unfortunately our ideas of what law is and how it should work have changed in a bad way.

In today's modern societies most of us are familiar with the concept of 'separation of church and state'. This is a rather new concept for mankind, if we go back in time just 500 years or so we see that most of the world was ruled by religion, the church/mosque/temple served both moral and political functions. In Europe, where our modern Western civilization grew out of, some form of Christianity was more or less both church and state. Law was not created via what we call legislation, where politicians decide what is right/wrong/lawful/unlawful, and anything can be voted into law and be considered just or unjust like it is today. For a considerable part of our history, law was whatever people thought God's laws and justice were, not what we decided it ought to be. As Hayek mentions:

"This medieval view, which is profoundly important as background for modern developments, though completely accepted perhaps only during the early Middle Ages, was that "the state cannot itself create or make law, and of course as little abolish or violate law, because this would mean to abolish justice itself, it would be absurd, a sin, a rebellion against God who alone creates law." For centuries it was recognized doctrine that kings or any other human authority could only declare or find the existing law, or modify abuses that had crept in, and not create law. Only gradually, during the later Middle Ages, did the conception of deliberate creation of new law –legislation as we know it– come to be accepted." [2]

Today's newer way of looking at law, the law that is deliberately manmade via politicians and whatever the masses want, what we also refer to as legislation, is called Positive Law or Political Law. The older law, the one that human beings felt they were discovering, as if they were universal laws of nature, created by he who creates nature, God, is called Natural Law. Let's look at one of the most important Natural law based documents in the history of mankind, The United States Declaration of Independence, which begins as follows:

> "When in the Course of human events it becomes necessary for one people to dissolve the political bands which have connected them with another and to assume among the powers of the earth, the separate and equal station to which the <u>Laws of Nature and of Nature's God entitle them</u>, a decent respect to the opinions of mankind requires that they should declare the causes which impel them to the separation.
> We hold these truths to be self-evident, that all men are created equal, that they are endowed by their Creator with certain unalienable Rights, that among these are Life, Liberty and the pursuit of Happiness."

The underlined words clearly show a Natural Law mindset on the part of their author, Thomas Jefferson, and that of the intended audience, the American 'insurgents' who refused to put up with a British government they felt was unjust. So why is natural law better than positive/political law? Am I suggesting we go back to some sort of theocracy? No... Before we really answer this question let us think about what law really means to the human ant-farm/society.

The laws of physics tell us how billiard balls work and thanks to this knowledge we can plan our shots, derive and predict the behavior of the balls, and go about accomplishing our goal of getting the balls in the pockets. Imagine if the laws of physics were different on each half of the pool table. Let's say that on one half the laws are how we expect them to be as usual, and on the other half the balls don't roll on the table, they slide, and therefore slow down much faster than if they rolled. Your original goal of getting the balls in the pockets just got a little more complicated because you have to take into account two sets of laws as opposed to one. But that is not that big a deal because at least these new laws of physics are still predictable. Now imagine if the laws of physics change in an unpredictable manner depending on where the balls are on the table. Let's say every time a ball crosses the middle of the pool table it changes direction in an unpredictable manner. Now the easiest of shots becomes unpredictable even for the greatest of pool players. The laws of physics are to playing billiards what the laws of society are to the workings of the human ant-farm. The same sort of chaos and increased difficulty to plan ahead, which having many or unpredictable laws caused in our billiards example, applies to the actions of human beings. It is thanks to laws that human beings can predict how other people will act, and based on these predictions we can successfully plan our interactions with others in ways that are harmonious with everyone's interests. No matter how many balls there are in a pool table, a single understanding of the laws of physics is all that is needed to predict how all the balls will behave, and it is this ability to predict the behavior of the balls that allows the player to plan ahead. When it comes to the actions of human beings, the same predictability and therefore stability of law is crucial to make the most of our brains' ability to plan our actions.

Imagine the social chaos that would occur if people did not act according to what they had previously agreed upon. Our entire modern world is based on people/companies/'productive structures' acting in accordance to what they have previously agreed upon. Contracts are the glue that holds the human ant-farm together, they are what ensure that the 'human ants'/'billiard balls' act in a predictable and dependable manner and that is what the first law("do all you have agreed to do") refers to. The second law, "do not encroach on other persons or their property" is what forces everyone to achieve his/her goals by first producing something of use to the human ant-farm and then peacefully exchanging it for whatever he/she desires. It ensures peace and forces every brain that makes up the social supercomputer to think about the needs of everyone else and inevitably and inadvertently leads to the emergence of the market process and therefore the very progress of mankind. Human ant-farms have been more or less naturally selected for due to their ability to follow these two laws because they are what 'turn on' the market process and the growth of a complex, highly stable and powerful social order. Again, we have not evolved to understand this obviously. Since these two laws provide the 'physics' for the most powerful human ant-farms, we can expect to see them as being integral parts of those societies that prosper and we can see that the world's major religions are very good at enforcing these two laws. Major religions expect their members not to lie and keep their word(law 1), and also not to steal or kill and mess with other people's property(law 2). If these two laws are laws of God and are protected by Him, or if they cannot be tampered with somehow, then the human ant-farms that adhere to them will not have their prosperity jeopardized.

The reason why Natural Law, which forms the basis for what is better known as Common Law, is better, is because Natural Law is not up to politicians and the unfortunate ignorance of the masses to play around with and constantly alter. Natural Law is stable, it is predictable and one can easily and safely derive conclusions from it. Positive or political law is impossible to predict or to make assumptions about what is right or wrong because it does not follow any general principles. It is completely up to the discretion of the political machine with its likely corruption and well-meaning yet disastrous policies. Instead of right and wrong being defined by some general and lasting principles, principles that prove their effectiveness by creating the very social order of the society that contains them, right and wrong becomes whatever the current ideology of the times call for. When human beings think that they can just re-engineer society by changing the laws, they are changing the 'physics' of society which can lead to unexpected and unforeseen detrimental effects. Human beings are sort of instinctively egalitarian, if some have more than others, the obvious solution will seem to take from the haves to give to the have-less via a big powerful ape(government). And given a chance they will usually vote for 'equality', in other words, they instinctively ask for Socialism/Communism.

Some people make fun of the very religious nature of Americans, especially many Europeans who can boast the fact that they are seemingly more scientific minded, and how a much higher percentage of people in European countries believe in evolution while so many Americans stick to their 'irrational' religious values. In a recent survey[3] of 34 developed nations, which measured how many people believe in evolution, the U.S. was second to last. Although I disagree with Americans on their religious beliefs and believe natural selection to be the "creator" of life, there can be no doubt that it is in some part thanks to religion, to America's inherited Christian traditions and its respect for private property(Exodus 20:15 Thou shalt not steal) and to the belief that there is a higher authority dictating the just relationships between men(their laws), that Americans did not fall prey, as hard, to the "geniuses" and "social scientists" in Europe that helped spread Socialism/Communism. Unknowingly, American's faith and religious traditions saved them from an 'abuse of reason' by human beings. Many Americans despised Communism, not necessarily because of its economic policies, because as we have already hinted at, we are sort of instinctively egalitarian and therefore highly susceptible to Communism and Americans are unknowingly voting themselves closer to Socialism/Communism with every trip to the voting booth they take today, but because they saw how Communism was essentially atheist and violated their Christian morals and its strong family centered, as opposed to government centered, way of life. As Hayek mentions, "even an agnostic aught to concede that we owe our morals, and the tradition that has provided not only our civilization but our very lives, to the acceptance of such scientifically unacceptable factual claims."[4]

In 1933 US President FDR decided to officially recognize the brutal Russian/Stalinist regime and told Russian representative Maxim Litvinov, "That's all I ask, Max — to have Russia recognize freedom of religion."[5] But the Soviets felt too smart to put up with religious nonsense and let the inherent individual freedom in religion get in the way of their attempt at having government bring a superior order to society. They trounced individual freedom, not only with faulty economic insights(with their lack of sufficient reason), but with their destruction of tradition(religion) which held far more intelligence than their human "reason".

It was the stability and immutability of Natural Law and its respect for private property in the societies where there was this 'Higher Law' that helped prevent human beings from inadvertently bringing Communism upon themselves, or at least slowing it down. These people were more likely to believe that God and 'thou shalt not steal' came before their egalitarian instincts and the wishes of politicians to take from some to give to others to reach an 'equality' that appealed to the masses' egalitarian instincts. An equality that would inevitably destroy their social order like it has and will continue to do to all countries that either consciously attempt(Cuba, former Soviet Union...) or inadvertently slide towards(every other country USA included) Socialism/Communism.

Why the change from Natural law to positive manmade law? Another important addition to our modern mindsets, which was virtually inexistent 500 years ago, was the concept of science and its ability to explain how the world works. For most of mankind's history we did not understand the forces of nature that shape our world and that is one of the main reasons why everyone believed in an all-powerful God that gave the world order. Many of the first famous scientists were priests who were trying to make sense of Gods laws, and the first universities in Europe grew out of churches and monasteries. Famous astronomer Johannes Kepler whose laws of planetary motion gave order to the heavens gives us a perfect example of what people's mindset with respect to science was at the time, "I was merely thinking God's thoughts after him. Since we astronomers are priests of the highest God in regard to the book of nature, it benefits us to be thoughtful, not of the glory of our minds, but rather, above all else, of the glory of God." And the great Isaac Newton tells us, "Gravity explains the motions of the planets, but it cannot explain who set the planets in motion. God governs all things and knows all that is or can be done." and "I have a fundamental belief in the Bible as the Word of God, written by those who were inspired. I study the Bible daily."

Newton's invention of calculus and his ability to use mathematics to discover his laws of motion and gravitation and more, gave humanity a consistent understanding of the mechanical workings of the world. The idea that the world could be explained with mathematics also began to tighten its grip on the minds of future scientists and social philosophers. To Newton and many others this might have seemed like further proof of the genius of God and that just like there are God's laws of nature there were also God's laws of justice, but at the same time it became easier to understand the laws of physics, and discard God and his ultimate sense of justice as well. God was still above everything and we tried to discover his physical laws as well as his moral laws and therefore justice, but the idea of giving society a human 'rational' order, which would have to violate or replace God's laws, would spread through our minds with every scientific discovery, especially those that clearly refuted scripture. Science was doing away with God and his laws and morals as a by product, and man began to create his own laws via legislation.

If one had to pick a single point in recent history to pinpoint this changing of the guard from a society built around God's laws to a society planned by human reason, a good candidate or example would be the French Revolution(1789–1799). The French Revolution was partly inspired by The American Revolution, and it too had a strong sense of Natural Law as can be seen in Article 2 of their "The Declaration of the Rights of Man and of the Citizen" which states: "The aim of all political association is the preservation of the natural and imprescriptible rights of man. These rights are liberty, property, security, and resistance to oppression." And article 17 "Property being an inviolable and sacred right, no one can be deprived of private usage, if it is not when the public necessity, legally noted, evidently requires it, and under the condition of a just and prior indemnity". It is important to see how the respect and protection of private property, which is the most important ingredient of a market oriented society, and the very progress of mankind, was "an inviolable and sacred right".

I mentioned how Natural/Common Law was superior to Political/Positive Law but Natural Law was not perfect either. If kings had 'The Devine Right of Kings' on their side they can obviously, and quite frequently, turn into despots and bring great hardship on their subjects. France at the time was structured into three classes, the king and Catholic Church(First Estate), the Nobles(Second Estate), and the peasants/workers/merchants/traders who were lumped into the 'Third Estate' and paid all the taxes to support the first two. Inspired by their natural rights and other circumstances, the Third Estate rebelled, chopped the king's head off, confiscated the Church's property and made the Church subordinate to the State . All of this was great in a way, supposedly we were bringing equality under the law to all men and curbing the power of oppressive governments/kings/religious entities, but at the same time something else was beginning to happen, something that would enslave men for a new purpose in a new way. Socialism, the idea that government could be used to plan and better orchestrate society. Now government and man-made laws were above the Church, above Natural Law.

As the French Revolution was getting rid of an "evil" ruling class, science was accelerating its breakthroughs and inspiring influential thinkers like Saint-Simon, the founder of French Socialism. Saint-Simon wanted to organize a great "Council of Newton" made up of "three mathematicians, three physicists, three chemists, three physiologists, three authors, three painters and three musicians" who would then use their superior genius to tell everyone else what to do. This is obviously a recipe for complete government control, for Communism, for the inadvertent destruction of the market process and the entire social order, but with good intentions of course. Just a couple of generations later, Charles Darwin's discovery of biological evolution would make it even easier for man to discard God and His Natural Law as an unfortunate byproduct. It was this overall increase in man's ability to understand the world, the believe that science and technology would usher in a new way to socially engineer mankind for the better and man's subsequent departure from God's justice, that were amongst the key factors in transforming natural law and its strong respect for private property into positive law/legislation with its anything goes attitude towards private property and human life itself. The nature of government would slowly begin to change from an entity that was supposed to protect the individual rights of its citizens to an entity that could be used to engineer society for the better. But to engineer society one inevitably has to curb the freedom of the individual in order to implement the social engineer/government's plans. As Adam Smith said with respect to the social engineer/leader/politician/"the man of system":

"The man of system, on the contrary, is apt to be very wise in his own conceit; and is often so enamoured with the supposed beauty of his own ideal plan of government, that he cannot suffer the smallest deviation from any part of it. He goes on to establish it completely and in all its parts, without any regard either to the great interests, or to the strong prejudices which may oppose it. He seems to imagine that he can arrange the different members of a great society with as much ease as the hand arranges the different pieces upon a chess-board. He does not consider that the pieces upon the chess-board have no other principle of motion besides that which the hand impresses upon them; but that, in the great chess-board of human society, every single piece has a principle of motion of its own, altogether different from that which the legislature might chuse to impress upon it. If those two principles coincide and act in the same direction, the game of human society will go on easily and harmoniously, and is very likely to be happy and successful. If they are opposite or different, the game will go on miserably, and the society must be at all times in the highest degree of disorder."[6]

Communist Russia's revolutionary founder Vladimir Lenin was "the man of system". As he tried hard to give a more "just" and "equal" order to the

Russian human ant-farm via government planning as opposed to letting the market process and individual economic freedom do so, he acknowledged and said the following, which seems like the perfect and unfortunate compliment to Adam Smith's recent quote/wisdom:

> "The machine refused to obey the hand that guided it. It was like a car that was going not in the direction the driver desired, but in the direction someone else desired; as if it were being driven by some mysterious, lawless hand, God knows whose, perhaps of a profiteer, or of a private capitalist, or of both. Be that as it may, the car is not going quite in the direction that the man at the wheel imagines, and often goes in an altogether different direction."[7]

It is important to realize that if man is free to trade and keep the fruits of his labor and do business with anyone he believes is in his best interest there can be no tyranny and oppression. It is that simple.

In Richard J. Maybury's fantastic "Whatever Happened to Justice" with respect to today's deterioration of law he says:

> "Courts today do not seek justice, they enforce law. The courts have no concept of justice–no notion of right and wrong–except whatever the law says.
>
> There was a day when two people who had a disagreement would say, 'We'll let a court decide.' Today the suggestion of a lawsuit is a threat, an act of aggression. Everyone knows that the expense of a lawsuit will be outrageous and the outcome based not on known principles but on the whims of an arbitrary legal system.
>
> The notion that an innocent person has nothing to worry about is laughable. We all know people who have been dragged into court and seriously mistreated, perhaps even bankrupted by the cost, even though they had done nothing to harm anyone.
>
> In short, to threaten a lawsuit is, itself, an assault.
>
> Today's legal system is not a way to prevent harm, it is a way to cause it. It's a weapon."[8]

This change in law and mindset has been affected, or sort of co-evolved with other things like the large differences in wealth that our increasingly productive human ant-farms have created, the increased complexity of our human ant-farms, and the perceived shrinking and zero-sumness of the world due to our increased ability to travel and begin to think that the world seems finite.

During the last 200 years the rapid increases in technology and productivity have led to large perceived differences in wealth which have aggravated our instinctive egalitarianism. Instead of the Church, which was supposed to be a sort of representative from God who always had the best interest of everyone and the poor in mind, we began to see large concentrations of wealth in capitalists/investors/businessmen who were out to seemingly "hoard" as much wealth as possible to themselves and "obviously" leave less for the rest. The idea that all this wealth was created by mankind's increased ability to transform that which was previously useless, was, and still is, not understood by people, which further aggravated our egalitarianism and anti-capitalist mentality setting the stage for egalitarian/socialist/communist/distributive policies. With the rise of mechanical power like steam engines and trains, our jobs have become less physically demanding. This too is something new. We saw a raise in new industries like finance, investing, banking, insurance and a change in the proportion of people employed in manual labor compared to non-manual labor. For most of our evolution, wealth was directly related to our ability to physically transform nature, this involved hard physical labor and sweat. Many of us sort of instinctively consider jobs where we sweat and really have to physically exert ourselves to somehow be more 'real' than jobs where you are not necessarily involved in the production of a tangible physical good with manual labor. In our tribal past anyone who had wealth and did not sweat for it, there was a good chance he stole it, tricked someone to get it, or hoarded it when he should have shared it.

As the world was advancing technologically so did the complexity associated with the production of most items. Until recently, the steps taken for the production of most items could be traced by a single mind. For example your potatoes were grown by a farmer who used a plow made out of copper dug up by some miners from a nearby mine. The potatoes were brought to the market in a carriage made of wood chopped from a nearby forest. Things were complex but still possible to trace. As societies grew in complexity thanks to the market process, the complexity of the interactions grew to an incomprehensible network of trades, which made it seem chaotic to most of us given our lack of an understanding of the market process. It became "obvious" that things like competition were wasteful, "why have different producers each doing things differently, wouldn't it be better if they all shared their knowledge and gained the benefits of standardization?" As we should know by now competition is needed to discover the best ways of doing things, but unfortunately this is not the idea which seemed obvious to most. Our instinct to give order to, and plan our actions, naturally translated itself into believing that we could give society a better order than the seemingly 'chaotic' and 'unfair' mess that capitalism was creating. And quite naturally we felt like it was the task of government planners to achieve this more perfect and "just" order, similarly to how in our tribal past an elder leader might orchestrate a large hunt or migration.

The idea of natural selection via evolution creating the biological order is beginning to be adopted or accepted by the majority of the modern world, because here it is obvious that we did not design the complex processes that create/maintain the biological order. We also almost see the process via our advanced knowledge of DNA/genetics. But the social order fools us into believing that we are responsible for it because it is our actions that are responsible for it. Yet we are not, it is the market process, which requires individual freedom and is destroyed by government's confiscation/redistribution of wealth.

The world's major powers like France and England and just about anyone who had the means were trying to colonize a world which seemed smaller and smaller all the time. Thanks to the telegraph and then the phone, trains, and faster and cheaper ways to reach as well as know about all corners of the world, the world was shrinking, which made it seem more zero-sum and also seemingly easier for a central planning body to attempt to orchestrate it.

Our misunderstanding of the modern world due to reasons already discussed has also brought new monsters that didn't exist before like the "evil corporations", "the white man", "the rich", "the minorities", "cheap foreign labor", "the drug companies", "unemployment" etc. which are seemingly too large and powerful for individuals to tackle on their own so we feel like we need to pool our resources together via government to help fight such monsters which would inevitably bring great inequalities, injustice, and economic hardship.

Before finishing this section I need to mention something that in a way contradicts much of what this section has implied. Natural law, which I seem to have been touting as being superior to deliberately man-made law/legislation does not have to be better. The laws which human ant-farms follow are what give rise to their social order and stability. Whether the laws are derived from man's theology or some higher power or deliberately man-made via legislation, natural selection does not care, it just selects the more stable and powerful social order; laws, customs, luck, and everything else that led to this social order included. If I became the world's dictator one of the things I might do is to force everyone in the industrialized world to read Henry Hazlitt's Economics In One Lesson 3 times. Instead of, or in addition to people reading and memorizing their religious scriptures moving their heads back and forth deep in concentration, I'd have everyone memorizing Hazlitt's great book and it's fundamental lesson. Actually, let's move our heads back and forth and memorize Hazlitt's heavenly sent wisdom right now:

"The art of economics consists in looking not merely at the immediate but at the longer effects of any act or policy; it consists in tracing the consequences of that policy not merely for one group but for all groups."

This would be an example where positive/man-made legislation is probably superior to natural law principles. From the author's perspective there is no natural law with some higher principle from which human beings derive their inalienable rights, there is only natural selection selecting human ant-farms and their respective laws. It is a great thing, a real miracle of sorts, that the laws that yield the most powerful and prosperous human ant-farms happen to be those that give man the greatest amount of freedom. I touted natural law as being superior because that is what seems to have been the case in the last few centuries and this is a very simplified book. Again, whether laws have a basis on some higher power which in a way shields them from man's meddling in ways that lead to bad results as in the 20th century's emergence of Socialism/Communism, or whether they are deliberately made by men via legislation, ultimately what matters is the social order that emerges from the laws/customs themselves.

The birth of American Capitalism.

In the birth of the United States we find a government which grew out of a desire to end or contain the oppression of governments over people. The United States was a country made of people who were running away from government oppression whether it be religious or economic. One of the most important things to realize about early America was the simplicity of its productive structure compared to the modern world's. In early America people were used to families and human beings being the ones that were responsible for the social order, in other words, in their minds, the private sector accomplished almost everything. Prior to the Industrial Revolution, and subsequent growth in the complexity of the American human ant-farm, life was considerably simpler. Most people were farmers and there was more self-sufficiency compared to today. The world wasn't so complex and therefore the need to give 50+% of their wealth to some gigantic bureaucracy that controlled various sectors of the economy would have seemed ridiculous at the time. Unlike England, France, and Spain, the American colonies did not have to fund large militaries for constant war/defense. For centuries having to be taxed to fund the official government sanctioned church/aristocracy and military adventures was part of the European mindset, which was not to be the case in America because both of these great historical functions/excuses for government were missing. People came from a world where government related taxes/'confiscation of wealth' was one of the main sources for their lack of material prosperity and they could see this clearly. A world of little to no taxes, where many people could actually keep everything they earned was just an unbelievable dream come true at the time, and of course, America had a lot of land available for farming. No wonder the word spread so quickly and so many wanted to come over here. In such a world everyone knew that if you didn't make it, you were most likely of bad character and your lack of material prosperity was justified. There was also still too much racial and religious squabbling amongst most people for anyone to be ok with having his money go to help someone from a different religion or ethnic background. And either way, if people feel like the only way you fail in America is if you are lazy or of bad character, what possible justification could there be for taking from some to give to others, or creating some bureaucracy to administer such equality? The equality Americans wanted was equality for everyone to keep the fruits of their labor. This does not mean that there was no charity of course. People lived in communities where everyone knew each other, it was possible to truly monitor the character of people, for people to build reputations.

If the social order is still relatively simple, one can easily calculate whether what you get from the government is more or less equal to what you give it in terms of taxes, and for colonial America this was a calculation which led to revolt and our independence from the British government. America was a nation founded by tax rebels, by insurgents! It is estimated that about one fifth of the adult white male population had either read, or had been read aloud to them, Thomas Paine's Common Sense whose very second paragraph contained the words "…government even in its best is but a necessary evil; in its worst state an intolerable one…" Paine's writings were so important and reflective of colonial America's ideology that fellow influential American founder and third US president John Adams said "Without the pen of Paine, the sword of Washington would have been wielded in vain". George Washington would distribute Paine's writings to his troops[9]. Paine's Common Sense and the ideology of Americans at the time was at the forefront of everything we have discussed about Natural Law, its evolution, and its ability to protect economic freedom.

Americans were a deeply religious people at the time. Paine's Common Sense used biblical arguments to show the illegitimacy of monarchs to rule and expropriate wealth from people. To him, and the deeply pious Americans of the day, government was needed because human beings were not 100% virtuous. In Common Sense Paine writes:

> "Here then is the origin and rise of government; namely, a mode rendered necessary by the inability of moral virtue to govern the world; here too is the design and end of government, viz. freedom and security."

In the next sentence he warns us not to let our senses and prejudices deceive us into wanting government to provide anything but the aforementioned freedom and security:

"And however our eyes may be dazzled with show, or our ears deceived by sound; however prejudice may warp our wills, or interest darken our understanding, the simple voice of nature and of reason will say, it is right"

And immediately after the above statement we stumble upon one of those many gems of wisdom and foresight that clearly show us how history repeats itself and what a genius Paine was. With respect to government in general he says:

"I draw my idea of the form of government from a principle in nature ... that the more simple a thing is the less liable it is to be disordered, and the easier repaired when disordered; and with this maxim in view, I offer a few remarks on the so much boasted constitution of England... Absolute governments(tho' the disgrace of human nature) have this advantage with them, that they are simple; if the people suffer, they know the head from which suffering springs, know likewise the remedy, and are not bewildered by a variety of causes and cures. But the constitution of England is so exceedingly complex, that the nation may suffer for years together without being able to discover in which part the fault lies, some will say in one and some in another, and every political physician will advise a different medicine."

Wow! If every American had a complete understanding of the previous quote, all of our problems would be solved. "they know the head from which suffering springs, know likewise the remedy", they sure knew how to deal with government created evils back in the day, these white men obviously had plenty of mojo. By 1776, England and its government had been in existence for many centuries, growing more bureaucratic and cancerous on its population like all governments inevitably do. Obviously the same applies to our current American government and its millions of laws and government employees, but more on this shortly.

For Thomas Jefferson "a little rebellion, now and then, is a good thing" as "a medicine for the sound health of government." Needless to say, the American founders and their morals and ideology would have them incarcerated in today's America.

The piety and religious nature of Americans cannot be stressed enough. As Alexis De Tocqueville mentions in his 1835 classic "Democracy in America":

"There is no country in the world where the Christian religion retains a greater influence over the souls of men than in America; and there can be no greater proof of its utility; and of its conformity to human nature, than that its influence is most powerfully felt over the most enlightened and free nation on the earth."

Our founders and Americans at the time were doing more than just fighting for what they considered to be just and in their material best interest. They were inadvertently fighting to protect the laws which 'turned on' the market process and would continue to reorder the American human ant-farm into the most advanced and productive one the world had ever seen. Our founders were not economists trained in an understanding of how the market process works, for the most part they just got lucky. It just happened to be the case that the more one protects individual freedom the better the market process works to bring about material prosperity for everyone, but unfortunately our socialist/communist human nature would slowly catch up with us and undue the American miracle. Even the great Thomas Jefferson believed that the preservation of a simple agricultural society was needed for liberty, in other words, he too would probably have felt the need to abandon individual economic freedom and turn towards government planning/Socialism as the world became more complex☹.

Before continuing with this chapter we should also stress that just like the social order is not the result of conscious human design neither is government. The US 'public sector'/government is a gigantic social entity with more employees than many countries and it does not answer to a single human being or group of them. It is not controlled by a few masterminds like so many people tend to think. Government is neither "good" nor "evil", such concepts do not really exist, they have been inherited from our more religious/spiritual past, but have little to do with how the real world works. And the same applies to the people who run the public sector and whose livelihoods depend on it. Although I am sure there are many people who work for the government who blatantly use it to steal money from the taxpayers or maneuver it for ideological pursuits which cause a lot of harm, most politicians and public sector employees have good intentions and they believe wholeheartedly that their actions make the world a better place, and that should they really come to understand the truth, that their actions are the single most destructive force in the history of mankind, they would immediately work with much of their might to change the system and greatly reduce the size and impact of government on society, even if it meant that they had to quit their government jobs and find private sector ones. This is something that government employees, politicians, and all of us will only understand once we understand economics and clearly see how much better the world will be once we get as many people as possible employed in the private sector as opposed to the public one.

It is a central theme of this book to clearly state that no one is to blame for the world's problems, not even the economically ignorant politicians, nor the masses that elect them, or "the big corporations", "the rich", our inherent greed, "evil" people, etc.. In many ways government in general is a reflection of our best intentions and qualities. The vast majority of us don't rebel by not paying our taxes, and as burdened as we already are, most of us are always willing to pay that extra tax if it will really solve problems and we feel like the politicians in charge can be trusted. Most of us see government as the entity which enforces the egalitarianism which we have evolved to feel comfortable with. We don't have a problem being taxed to raise other people's kids or take care of their parents or the less fortunate. Many rich people are big fans of high taxes that take from the rich to give to the "less fortunate". So again, government is a complex entity, it is part of our modern worlds because natural selection has selected it and therefore it has played a crucial part in the evolution and survival of our modern social orders. Hopefully as an understanding of economics/'the market process' spreads, the institution of government as we know it today will cease to exist or play a much smaller role, sort of like a vestigial organ like our appendices, a structure which served a purpose in a long forgotten evolutionary past, but is useless, or close to useless in the present.

What is seen and what is not seen. The wisdom of Frederic Bastiat

The great 19th century French economist Frederic Bastiat wrote a classic economics essay titled "What Is Seen and What Is Not Seen" which begins as follows:

"In the economic sphere an act, a habit, an institution, a law produces not only one effect, but a series of effects. Of these effects, the first alone is immediate; it appears simultaneously with its cause; it is seen. The other effects emerge only subsequently; they are not seen; we are fortunate if we foresee them.

There is only one difference between a bad economist and a good one: the bad economist confines himself to the visible effect; the good economist takes into account both the effect that can be seen and those effects that must be foreseen.

Yet this difference is tremendous; for it almost always happens that when the immediate consequence is favorable, the later consequences are disastrous, and vice versa. Whence it follows that the bad economist pursues a small present good that will be followed by a great evil to come, while the good economist pursues a great good to come, at the risk of a small present evil."

If something about Bastiat's introduction to his essay seems familiar, it is because it was the inspiration for Henry Hazlitt's fundamental lesson.

At the core of everything we will be discussing in this chapter lies our inability to realize that most visible goals that the government attempts to accomplish, will destroy a great quantity of unseen goals, and that the 'social value' of the destroyed unseen goals is far greater than the gained value of the government achieved goals. As the human ant-farm morphs itself to attain one goal, it inevitably has to give up working on other goals. For example, as the government provides free education, health care for the elderly, welfare for those that have less than others etc., it has to tax and take away wealth from the private sector. Should this wealth have been left in the private sector, it would have been traded for the production of other things, unseen things that were never able to come into existence because such wealth was taken by the government in order to provide the aforementioned services.

The main task of this chapter is to help the reader see how no matter how wonderful/tempting/beneficial the government mandated and visible goal/project/'restructuring of the human ant-farm' might be, the alternative path of just leaving the human ant-farm alone is a much better one, and that the reason why we have a hard time understanding this is because, once again, we have not evolved to instinctively understand how the modern market-process-coordinated world works to shape our social order.

Bastiat's essay contains a very simple example showing how easy it is for us to ignore all that is lost as we only focus on that which is immediately visible. His example goes something like this: A kid throws a brick and breaks a shopkeeper's window. At the sight of such calamity, bystanders feel a need for philosophic reflection and some see good in what has just happened, they figure that now $200 will go to provide employment for the glazier that will replace the window and then the glazier's newly acquired $200 will be spent to provide employment for a barber, and on and on the money will seemingly provide employment for many things as it ripples through the human ant-farm. People figure that if the window never broke, this visible chain of employment and productive activity would disappear making the world poorer. How is the glazier to make a living if windows never break? So far from being a menace, thanks to seemingly ingenious economic insights, the kid helped improve society. What we don't see and is unseen is that the original $200 still would have been spent on something, like a suit perhaps. In this case a tailor would have received the $200 in exchange for the suit as opposed to the window maker, and then the tailor would have bought a bicycle providing employment for the bicycle-maker who would then provide employment for someone else and on and on the money would seemingly provide employment just like it did before, but the important thing to see here is that either way the $200 would still have been employed helping to stimulate productive activity.

We have traced through both scenarios, the one where the window is broken and the one where it was not and have seen how the $200 still rippled through the economy stimulating an equal amount of production and wealth. So what is the difference between the two scenarios? The difference becomes easy to see if we once again look at things from high above. After the sequence of events in the first scenario we have a new window, an angry shopkeeper who had to spend his $200 to replace the window, and a happy bunch of people(glazier, barber…) who got additional business due to the shopkeeper's $200 expenditure that originally went to replace the broken window. In the second scenario, we have a working window that was never broken, plus a new suit, the shopkeeper is happy because he traded his $200 for a new suit as opposed to replacing a broken window, and we also still have a bunch of happy people(tailor, bicycle-maker…). The second scenario depicts a better human ant-farm because it has a working window and a new suit instead of just a new window, and let's not forget, a happier human being as well. As opposed to producing wealth to replace lost wealth, leaving the human ant-farm more or less in the same state as it used to be, wealth was added to the existing stock of wealth leading to a wealthier and more materially prosperous human ant-farm.

Having gone over this simple example our minds should be better trained to understand one of the most popular and gigantic economic fallacies, that the economic destruction caused by things like hurricanes and other natural disasters and wars are actually good for the economy. People immediately realize that many people will have to be employed to rebuild houses or entire cities and how this will provide employment and create wealth as people work on resurrecting homes/buildings. This is what is visible, but what they don't see is that the same amount of money which would have gone to provide jobs rebuilding the human ant-farm, just getting it to where it used to be, would have been spent in countless unseen ways which would have led to the production of new wealth, wealth which would have been added to the total wealth in the city/town as opposed to have gone towards replacing lost wealth. Instead of employing builders, people's money would go to who-knows-what unseen things like perhaps new cars, new medical services, new homes and buildings in addition to the existing ones, leaving the human ant-farm considerably better off and more advanced than if it had to spend its energies rebuilding just to get to a past state as opposed to moving into the future. This economic fallacy shows up every year during hurricane season where I live in Miami. Iraqis must be so happy as they look forward to rebuilding their entire country. Wars/'undesired destruction of private property' are NEVER good for an economy.

The two examples we have discussed, the broken window, and the rebuilding due to natural disasters/wars give us a taste for how easily we can fall victims to believing that the visible scenario is better than the unseen one. The root of this mistake is once again our usual culprit, our inability to instinctively understand the workings of the modern world. If we just envision the same scenarios in a more tribal, more self sufficient setting, where there is no money being traded for services/employment we would never fall victims to seeing any kind of destruction as being good. If instead of a window, say your son broke your bow, now you have to visibly spend days crafting a new one, this is an obvious loss. If a fire burns your hut, now you have to visibly sweat it and build one yourself.

In a simple tribal world, it is easy to notice all the things that are foregone as the small human ant-farm restructures itself for the attainment of a specific goal, and to go about correcting any needed problems or to simply accept the fact that the tribe is better off giving up on other things in order to achieve this important goal. Again, this is the case in small human ant-farms of 20-150 people, the kind we have spent millions of years in, and we have been naturally selected to more or less instinctively understand. In this type of environment most people can clearly measure what is gained and what is lost at the human ant-farm level as projects that involve many people are carried out. In the tribal world, as well as today, we have no problems understanding how choices and decisions affect a single individual. If you go on a vacation to Atlanta, you cannot work in Miami, so being able to think ahead and calculate what outcomes are best for the actions of a single individual are easy now, and were just as easy in our tribal days. The problem comes when we try to calculate what is gained or lost when we deal with actions that involve the interactions of many people. Our brains are powerful enough to deal with society when it is small and simple, with few billiard balls(people), adhering to our egalitarian/communist ethics/laws, but when we try to understand what is gained or lost as many(thousands/millions) people do one thing over the other in today's society, we inevitably make mistakes and greatly overestimate our ability to predict whether our envisioned rearrangements of the human ant-farm will leave us better off or not. Today's social order is vastly more complex and it exists due to the workings of the market process which is something we have not evolved to understand because it did not exist in our tribal/ape-like evolutionary past.

Every time the government tries to provide something, whether it be free education, health care, assistance to the poor, etc., it inevitably has to take wealth via taxes from the private sector to provide for these things. The things that the government tries to accomplish are highly desirable and visible social goals. Goals that inevitably come at the expense of countless other goals which would have been pursued by people should they have been free to keep the money that the government took via taxes to fund all of these wonderful social programs.

Whenever the government interferes with the market process, by for example taxing the haves to provide free "education" for the have-less, the government will rearrange/morph the human ant-farm in a way that will lead to a different social order than would have otherwise existed should it have left it alone under the ordering forces of the market process. The government managed education would be a visible goal to the concerned citizens and their elected representatives. As the government removes funds from the private sector to pay for this education it is altering the structure of the human ant-farm in order to attain the visible goal of having free education for everyone. The human ant-farm will develop two different social orders with its human ants going about doing things differently. In one social order it is left free of government intervention and there will be no free education paid for by the haves under the threat of incarceration/death, and in the other social order the government removes wealth from the haves against their will and uses it to morph the human ant-farm in a way that provides free education for everyone. If the government interferes we will see the many freshly painted new school buildings coming into existence, jobs provided for the builders who work on them and how these builders will be able to provide for their families, children sitting in classrooms learning how to read and write. We know something has to be given up in order to do this, but that is something that we will never be able to envision because the billions of tax dollars/wealth needed to fund the free education will be spread in smaller chunks across the entire human ant-farm, small chunks that on their own can't seemingly create something as big and wonderful as the previously mentioned benefits.

In our tribal past it would be easy to see what the human ant-farm would be gaining and giving up as it restructured to attain this free education goal, but in our modern world, it is impossible for a single mind to foresee all the things that are given up as the billions of dollars go towards our free education goal, much less know whether we will be better off or not. Imagine being in a simpler tribal world and a small group of 5 men propose that if everyone in the tribe feeds them for 3 months they will build a fire pit where everyone could sit around and stay warm. We'll assume that this fire pit was something very important for survival, but you, as well as every other adult in the tribe, can envision the same task being carried out by just a couple of people in two days instead of three months, so everyone refuses to go along with the men's plans. In our modern world the group of five men could be seen as government and the building of the fire could be seen as any of the important visible goals/services which government tries to provide like education, health care, ensuring safety, etc.. Amongst the problems we are faced with is that in the modern market process coordinated world we live in, all of the visible goals we want accomplished are not solved by the easily coordinated actions of an identifiable small group of people, they are solved by impersonal complex social structures/'mini human ant-farms' that can only be efficiently ordered by the market process, and that since only the market process can create this social order, no human being can know what the real costs in nourishing/funding this social order is.

Want we want to overcome is our seemingly instinctive desire to have a visible entity(government) force the human ant-farm to pursue a visible goal. And as an inevitable consequence of this, allow for an invisible entity(the market-process/freedom), made up of selfish individuals, to freely accomplish invisible goals, and to fully appreciate how much better off we all are when we let this happen. In much simpler terms, the goal is to help us see how much better off we are when people get to keep their money and go about solving their problems by themselves as opposed to having the government solve them.

The Public Sector vs. The Market Process. The wisdom of Herbert Spencer

Everything we have discussed about the market process and its various mechanisms and institutions like banking and lending, profitability, and the interest rate and competition, all serve to create a private sector that is as lean and mean a matter-to-wealth transformation machine as humanly possible. Thanks to these things the market-process-ordered private sector is always in a cycle of production and consumption that leaves the economic pie with a continuously increasing amount of wealth, as well as technology, which makes it even easier to continue to increase the economic pie in the future. This is what progress is all about. Compared to 100 years ago, we have more and better quality wealth and have to work less for it.

The main problem with the public sector/government is that only the market process can give an efficient order to millions of people. Since the public sector is a monopoly, immune to the market process' social-order-shaping-knowledge-sharing mechanisms like competition and interest rate coordination, all government created social orders or bureaucracies are misaligned and produce little wealth compared to how much they drain from the economic pie. The public sector takes over a third of all newly created wealth every year and simply consumes most of it giving back very little in terms of useful services. Most people only wake up to the inefficiencies of the federal government when all eyes are on it like FEMA's handling of Katrina, but FEMA is no different than every other government bureaucracy. They are all given shape by the same purely bureaucratic mechanism.

Some readers might have heard of the famous "Bridge to Nowhere"[10], a government funded project that would build a bridge in Alaska between the town of Ketchickan, with a population of 8,000 residents, and Ketchickan Airport located on Gravina Island(pop. 50), a bridge nearly as long as the Golden Gate Bridge and taller than the Brooklyn Bridge which would cost 315 million dollars. The bridge would be replacing a 7 minute ferry ride which currently gets the job done. This project, the brainchild of Senator Ted Stevens, is a perfect example of the kinds of destructive realignments of the human ant-farm that the Washington D.C. brain is constantly doing. 315 million dollars worth of food, homes, cars, energy were consumed from the economic pie by everyone involved in its construction, and such wealth was in a way traded for a bridge that helped a few thousand people make it to the airport with a little more convenience than they did before. This was a bad decision, the American tax payer suffered at the hands of the politically connected like the companies that build the bridge, etc. Another obvious example of government waste is the thousands of people who 'fight terrorism' in our airports by asking old ladies to empty their liquids. Wealth which should it have been left in the private sector would have been traded for more useful wealth is simply traded for longer lines in airports. Time after time, studies show that explosives and weapons can easily make it by our airport's 'terrorism experts'.

In the private sector there is something I'll refer to as the average moral values, which ensures a certain level of cooperation and effort by most of its participants. We know that in the private sector employees cannot be too lazy, because if they are, their lack of productivity will ultimately affect the company's revenues, and should there be too many lazy employees then the company's revenues will eventually not be enough to cover the costs needed to maintain the company's internal structure(wages, rents…) and it will go bankrupt due to competition from other companies whose employees did not give sub-par performances. The same reasoning applies to countless other things. Employees who are a part of a productive structure cannot be too rude, have too bad of a personal hygiene, cannot make fun of or be disrespectful to their coworkers, they have to have a certain level of tolerance of others, they have to be punctual, reliable, trustworthy, work with a certain amount of focus and hustle, be willing to learn to do things differently as new and better ways of doing things are discovered, and many more. The bottom line is that competition not only spreads productive knowledge across society, it also helps shape the behavior/morals/values of people to be more in synch with that which leads to the most productivity, which inevitably forces people to treat and welcome each other as equals.

For the reminder of this section we will briefly discuss various quotes from Herbert Spencer's essay entitled "Over-legislation" where he compares the differences between the public and private sectors in England during the mid 1850's. Spencer's essay not only shows off this man's intellect, but the fact that it was written over 150 years ago gives us a perfect example of how history repeats itself and how little we learn from it, as well as how maladapted to the world's increasing complexity we are.

"Officialism is habitually slow. When non-governmental agencies are dilatory, the public has its remedy: it ceases to employ them, and soon finds quicker ones. Under this discipline all private bodies are taught promptness. But for delays in State-departments there is no such easy cure."

"How invariably officialism becomes corrupt every one knows. Exposed to no such antiseptic as free competition—not dependent for existence, as private unendowed organizations are, upon the maintenance of a vigorous vitality; all law-made agencies fall into an inert, over-fed state, from which to disease is a short step. Salaries flow in irrespective of the activity with which duty is performed; continue after duty wholly ceases; becomes rich prizes for the idle well born; and prompt to perjury, to bribery, to simony."

Given our somewhat inevitably selfish nature, it is easy for us to take actions which benefit us at the expense of others in various unfair ways. This is true whether a person works in the private sector or in the government sector, but in the private sector, as already discussed, these bad morals/vices lead to their own downfall, they are naturally selected against due to competition. Corruption, bribery, being overpaid due to good connections as opposed to true productivity, these are all ways of acting, they are ingredients that reflect the knowledge of how to get things done that is embodied in companies, and since these ways of acting are simply inferior knowledge, they get naturally selected against as if they were bad designs for a product. Spencer again:

"Consider first how immediately every private enterprise is dependent upon the need for it; and how impossible it is for it to continue if there be no need. Daily are new trades and new companies established. If they subserve some existing public want, they take root and grow. If they do not, they die of inanition. It needs no act of Parliament, to put them down. As with all natural organizations, if there is no function to them, no nutrient comes to them, and they dwindle away. Moreover, not only do the new agencies disappear if they are superfluous, but the old ones cease to be when they have done their work. Unlike law-made instrumentalities…these private instrumentalities dissolve when they become needless."

One of the great things about human beings, is that we are all alike. What is good for me, is probably good for you as well. This means that as the billions of brains that make up humanity are thinking of ways to improve their lives, the ideas/improvements they come up with are often times likely to improve the lives of the rest of us. Thanks to the banking/lending/finance industry such ideas can quickly gather the necessary funds to create companies and morph the human ant-farm into ever more productive and advanced states. These companies can only come to existence if they are of use to society, in other words, if other human beings find it in their best interest to trade their money for this new product/service. The new company has to "subserve some existing public want", and not necessarily an existing public want, new inventions which did not exist before are not existing public wants, but become so once they come into existence and people realize that their lives can be improved by them. These new companies "take root and grow" in a way that is more or less proportional to how useful they are to the social organism/public. Microsoft, Wal-Mart, Toyota, these and every other company exists and grows thanks to the wealth it offers mankind in return. As the productive knowledge of the human ant-farm changes some companies inevitably cease to provide a useful product/service because something better comes along. As this happens the companies whose products are becoming less useful receive less revenue with which to maintain their orderly structure and eventually "dissolve when they become needless" and their parts(employees, buildings…) merge with other productive structures which are of use to society because they have the necessary knowledge needed to incorporate such parts into economic-pie-increasing transformations, or in other words, profitable plans. It is important to realize that this reordering of the human ant-farm happens without a single visible entity telling people what to do, "It needs no act of Parliament". It happens automatically as knowledge spreads throughout society's brains and they update their actions/plans and what companies/'social orders' get the needed life sustaining money/wealth. As this is happening and we think about the person who might lose his/her job in the process, we should always keep in mind that as a whole, the entire human ant-farm is becoming a more efficient matter-to-human-useable wealth machine, and that the more wealth is created the more of it has to be offered in exchange for labor which is why even if people lose a job from time to time, overall, their living standards, or size and quality of their economic pie, constantly increases. To prevent or slowdown this mechanism/'the market process' is to prevent or slow down the very progress of mankind. Spencer:

"Again, officialism is stupid. Under the natural course of things each citizen tends towards his fittest function. Those who are competent to the kind of work they undertake, succeed, and, in the average of cases, are advanced in proportion to their efficiency; while the incompetent, society soon finds out, ceases to employ, forces to try something easier, and eventually turns to use. But it is quite otherwise in State-organizations. Here, as everyone knows, birth, age, back-stairs intrigue, and sycophancy, determine the selections, rather than merit. The "fool of the family" readily finds a place in the Church, if "the family" have good connections. A youth, too ill-educated for any active profession, does very well for an officer in the Army. Gray hair or a title, is a far better guarantee of naval promotion than genius is. Nay, indeed, the man of capacity often finds that, in government offices, superiority is a hindrance—that his chiefs hate to be pestered with his proposed improvements, and are offended by his implied criticism. Not only, therefore, is legislative machinery complex, but it is made of inferior materials."

In the private sector people earn money in proportion to how much wealth they help produce. Hard-working, and experienced people tend to be more productive so their labor tends to create more wealth and therefore it can trade for more money. If one is not as smart because perhaps one's brain just doesn't work as well as someone else's then it is still in that persons and society's best interest that the free-market/'market process' finds whatever place people can productively fit themselves in.

"If two people both want to be an automotive engineer, and the better qualified succeeds, while the less qualified ends up as an auto mechanic, the better qualified one can raise the productivity of the poorer-qualified one by designing a better car for him to work on. If their positions were reversed, this would not be possible."[11](George Reisman)

Once again, when human beings integrate themselves into the social organism via the market process, we become part of a matter-to-wealth transformation machine and it is in the best interest of everyone, especially for the less able, for the most able to be placed higher up telling the less able how to do things. Thanks to the tremendously productive order the market process has given our American human ant-farm over the centuries, even the laziest and dumbest of Americans can enjoy a material comfort which would have been impossible to achieve even for the wealthiest of kings just a few centuries ago, not to mention the smarter and harder working people in third world countries.

In the private sector every market participant is involved in an ongoing process of trading. A person's ability to consume wealth from society depends on how much this person adds to society via his labor. This labor has to somehow increase the economic pie of wealth. You cannot just work and sweat all day at digging holes in your backyard and expect a high wage, or any wage at all. The labor a person adds to the world is then freely traded for money and it is not until this point that we know how valuable that labor was in monetary terms. If a man digs a hole in his backyard his labor might be useless because no one values it, no one is willing to trade anything for it because the labor did not help anyone increase their state of well-being. If the same man digs a similar hole in someone else's backyard who values the hole because she will plant a tree in it, then the value of this mans labor can be measured by the amount of money the woman gave him. The more valuable the labor that a person performs is, the more money will be traded for it by those who can judge such value and the more wealth this person will be able to later consume. This is the way things work in the private sector, but when it comes to government work, a person's ability to produce has little to do with how much wealth this person adds to the economic pie, or earns in wages. Most government jobs have pay-scales which are based on how long you have been on the job, so you basically sit on your butt and your salary goes up every year. Public sector employees get the best pensions, insurance coverage, national holydays off, the peace of mind that comes from knowing that you will never lose your job.

I remember one time I was at some court building trying to get some problem with my license taken care off. As usual there was a long line with countless of irritated people. Someone had made some remark to the county employee and the county employee proudly replied with something along the lines of "Buddy, I work for the county, I'd have to kill someone to lose this job". With respect to government jobs, the US Bureau of Labor Statistics website says "Competition is expected for some Federal positions, especially during times of economic uncertainty, when workers seek the stability of Federal employment."[12] So not only does government itself create "economic uncertainty" as we will discuss in more detail shortly, but you can always count on government coercion to inadvertently pillage the private sector for that comfy yearly raise in pay and benefits, even at times when the private sector is licking its government made economic wounds. All this is partly reflected in the bottom line, federal employees get substantially higher wages and benefits than private sector ones.

According to the US Bureau of Labor Statistics[13], a government source, as of Sep. 2006 private sector employees get an average of $25.52 dollars spent on them per hour while government employees get $37.91. That is a difference of $12.39 per hour for an almost $500($495) per week(40 hours), $1982 per month, or a whopping $25,771 per year, $78,852.80 for government vs. $53,081.60 for private sector employee.

According to another report issued by the Cato Institute[14] the figures are even more in the federal government employee's favor.

According to this report based on government provided statistics issued by the US Bureau of Economic Analysis, in 2004, the average federal government employee received $100,178 in wages and benefits compared to $51,876 for private sector employees. Looking just at wages, federal workers earned an average $66,558, 56% more than the $42,635 earned by the average private sector worker. The report also mentions how the advantage in federal pay over private sector pay has increased from 19% to 51% from years 1950 to 1980 and a whopping 93% from 1990 to 2004 or almost double as the initial figures show. Two indicators of the cushiness of federal government jobs are the following : fed workers are likely to be fired or laid off at one-quarter the rate of private sector employees, and they also quit their jobs at one-quarter the rate of private sector employees.

Once a government employee has been sitting on his job for 20 years and is now getting great pay, benefits, and a growing pension, he knows that if he leaves his job chances are that he might have to start at the bottom of the pay scale in some other government job, or with considerably less pay in the private sector. Pay which would be truly reflective of this person's contribution to society and not how long he has been doing something.

In the public sector there is little incentive to actually save money. In the public sector your department gets a certain budget, if you come up with money-saving ways to perform your duty you do not get to keep the money, the money will probably just go to another department that was as inefficient and chaotic as usual, so managers have no incentive to come up with more efficient ways of doing things. It is actually the opposite, you want to make sure you spend it all to keep as many employees happy and dependent on your benevolence and if you go over budget a little, great, that just means that you have an excuse to ask for more money for next year's budget because it obviously wasn't enough to properly serve the public for which you so tirelessly work for. How often do you hear of a government bureaucracy actually finding a way to do things cheaper and giving the saved money back to taxpayers? But this sort of thing is constantly happening all the time in the private sector. Companies are forced via competition to adopt cheaper and better ways of doing things as they arise, which inevitably translates into savings for the consumer and increased profits for the companies/investors. Profits which for the most part are saved and go to provide the necessary funds to make further profitable and pie-increasing rearrangements of the human ant-farm.

When you can profit from a superior rearrangement of the human ant-farm, you are motivated to take action and make the world a better and more efficient place. Making money motivates us to overcome what Spencer refers to as "organic conservatism" below:

"That organic conservatism which is visible in the daily conduct of all men, is an obstacle which in private life self-interest slowly overcomes. The prospect of profit does, in the end, teach farmers that deep draining is good; though it takes long to do this. Manufacturers do, ultimately, learn the most economical speed at which to work their steam-engines; though precedent has long misled them. But in public service, where there is no self-interest to overcome it, this conservatism exerts its full force; and produces results alike disastrous and absurd. For generations after book-keeping had become universal, the Exchequer accounts were kept by notches cut on sticks." Exchequer = sort of tax collector in England.

"A further characteristic of officialism is its extravagance. In its chief departments, Army, Navy, and Church, it employs far more officers than are needful, and pays some of the useless ones exorbitantly…These public agencies are subject to no such influence as that which obliges private enterprise to be economical. Traders and mercantile bodies succeed by serving society cheaply. Such of them as cannot do this are continuously supplanted by those who can. They cannot saddle the nation with the results of their extravagance, and so are prevented from being extravagant."

Government regulation

Besides government inefficiency and waste, another major source of unintended government mischief comes via government regulation of the economy.

As already discussed, the market process essentially turns every human brain into a large social supercomputer that at a fundamental level transforms matter into the human usable wealth that sustains and grows the social order. This supercomputer is vastly more intelligent than individual brains or large groups of them when it comes to figuring out in what is the best way of doing things. A government regulation is essentially a "way" of doing things, it is knowledge. But unlike knowledge that arises from the social supercomputer, it arises out of a few brains in Washington D.C.

The governmental brain, good intentions and all, believes that it can better figure out the way to orchestrate the actions of millions of people as it tells the private sector how to care for the elderly, produce energy, cure disease, ensure safety, and so much more. All of these things, anything that we want and care about, require figuring out what is the best way to go about doing them, and that is precisely what the market process does best, discovering productive knowledge. What really matters is where does the knowledge that guides human action come from. The more such knowledge arises from the private sector, the better it will be, the more it arises from a central planning authority, the worse it will be. When the government completely socializes an industry, say health care, it will inevitably grow more bureaucratic and cancerous. As the government regulates, it begins imposing its bad ideas from the top down at the point of a gun. As it begins and expands its regulation, the knowledge that guides human action comes less and less from the social supercomputer and more and more from the central planning body, a planning body, that regardless of the good intentions and genius of its members will inevitably lead to inferior decisions compared to those of the market process coordinated private sector. And I am not even taking into account special interests like corporate salesmen influencing the bureaucrats to help them get that juicy government contract at the expense of the public. That we'll touch upon in a second. Bottom line, as the Ludwig von Mises said : "Progress is precisely that which rules and regulations did not foresee."

So why do we feel like government regulations are good things? Again, in our tribal past, there was no need to have a way of discovering the knowledge required to give complicated human ant-farms order like we need today. The knowledge was simple, rarely ever changed and was easily understood by everyone. The main factor was honesty and fear of punishment for not doing things right, and this is basically what government is all about. It is about using its power of coercion to make sure everyone does things the way they are supposed to and to help enforce our sort of instinctive desire for equality. Government is the big ape that enforces our egalitarian tendencies. Figuring out what this "way they are supposed to" is, in our complex world is something that can only be done by the market process.

In today's world, we still want to make sure that if things don't get done right, that there is a penalty to pay(backed by force if necessary) but we depend on the market process and its competitive knowledge discovery mechanisms to be the one that finds out what that right is and that is what contracts and law #1("Do all you have agreed to do") are for. The government does not need to dictate how things get done, it only needs to ensure that what has been agreed to is met, and not how the market process goes about discovering the best way of meeting such contractual obligations. A contract specifies the terms of a trade, if the terms have been met, the trade has occurred as desired by both parties and both parties move from inferior to superior states of well-being. There is no need to consume resources trying please a third party.

If I want a home that is strong and can withstand a category 5 hurricane and other criteria, all I need is for the home builder to agree in contract to build me a home that satisfies my conditions. If the builder agrees to do this for a certain price and then fails to do so there has been a violation of law #1("Do all you have agreed to do"), and the government needs to step in. That's all, not regulate how my house should be built. Spencer continues…

> "In the case of bad house-building, also, it is obvious that a cheap, rigorous, and certain administration of justice, would make Building Acts needless. For is not the man who erects a house of bad materials ill put together, and, concealing these with papering and plaster, sells it as a substantial dwelling, guilty of fraud? And should not the law recognize this fraud as it does in the analogous case of an unsound horse? And if the legal remedy were easy, prompt, and sure, would not builders cease transgressing?"

Again, we do not need to be concerned with how things get done, competition figures that out, we just need to ensure that the expectations are met and that therefore there is no fraud, and that should there be fraud that the government acts swiftly. Unfortunately, we call on government 'superintendence' to create all kinds of codes and building/safety/etc. regulations, which we need an army of government inspectors to sign off on increasing the costs of our homes and countless other things.

> "So is it in other cases; the evils which men perpetually call on the State to cure by superintendence, themselves arise from non-performance of its original duty."

The 'original duty' being that of properly enforcing our two fundamental laws.

A popular type of government regulation is when it sets a price control to be lower than what the free-market price is. Again, all done with good intentions. This depresses the profits or turns them into losses for the manufacturers involved in the production of whatever item is being considered, removing the incentive to produce the product/service. Spencer gives us an example where by not allowing cabs to raise their prices to properly reflect the costs and incentives of doing business during a snow-storm, cab services were not supplied when they were needed most. Spencer:

> "The late snow-storm, indeed, supplied a neat antithesis between the two orders of agencies in the effects it respectively produced on omnibuses and cabs. Not being under a law-fixed tariff, the omnibuses put on extra horses and raised their fares. The cabs, on the contrary, being limited in their charges by an Act of Parliament which, with the usual shortsightedness, never contemplated such a contingency as this, declined to ply, deserted the stands and the stations, left luckless travelers to stumble home with their luggage as best they might, and so became useless at the very time of all others when they were most wanted!"

A couple of sentences further down Spencer mentions how government regulation causes many unforeseen evils, and how only the private sector can efficiently serve society and its ever changing needs.

> "Again, the recently-passed Smoke-Bill for London, which applies only within certain prescribed limits, has the effect of taxing one manufacturer while leaving untaxed his competitor working within a quarter of a mile; and so, as we are credibly informed, gives one an advantage of £1,500 a year over another. These typify the infinity of wrongs, varying in degrees of hardship, which legal regulations necessarily involve. Society, a living, growing organism, placed within apparatuses of dead, rigid, mechanical formulas, cannot fail to be hampered and pinched. The only agencies which can efficiently serve it are those through which its pulsations hourly flow, and which change as it changes."

The perfect contrast between government regulation and the lack thereof can be seen in the differences between the health care and technology sectors of the economy.

The technology sector is one of the freest sectors in the economy. You do not need a government issued license to create a website or to work as a computer programmer. Yet these "unlicensed" computer programmers write the software that runs critical medical equipment that maintains lives, the software that keeps planes in the sky, and all the other software that has become an indispensable tool for the maintenance and growth of our modern world. Computers get cheaper and better all the time. The Internet gets more amazing by the day and gives away more and more stuff for free, yet everyone who works in the IT/technology field is making a great living.

Food and Drug Administration(FDA) and American Medical Association(AMA)

When it comes to health care, instead of getting better quality for lower prices like in the technology sector, we get higher and higher prices, and a very slow increase in technology that just barely crawls through the regulatory apparatus. The cost and time involved with getting a new drug through the disastrous FDA's regulatory apparatus is astronomical, **nearly 800 million dollars**[15]. The FDA itself recently authored a report[16] on just how incompetent it is, and by its own admission it is in a state that can only be described as incompetent chaos. Here are some of its findings:

3.1.1 Finding: FDA does not have the capacity to ensure the safety of food for the nation

3.1.4 Finding: The FDA science agenda lacks a coherent structure and vision, as well as effective coordination and prioritization

3.3.4 Finding: The FDA IT infrastructure is obsolete, unstable, and lacks sufficient controls to ensure continuity of operations or to provide effective disaster recovery services

These are just 3 of 11 "findings" that make it clear that the FDA is a complete failure. In a video about the report[17], Bill Hubbard, a former FDA associate commissioner, said, "Imagine having an e-mail system so old, they have to bring technicians out of retirement because current technicians have never seen equipment that old". The computer systems are down frequently, paralyzing all progress. Stuff is done in paper and gets lost, etc. So this is where the 800 million go, to feed and clothe thousands of people who are disordered, and produce little wealth in terms of verifying/testing drugs, while inadvertently slowing down such an important function for the progress and well-being of humanity.

The FDA, as well as ALL other government created regulatory agencies/bureaucracies are well intentioned MONOPOLIES. They are created purely via delegation, which won't cut it for the types of complex arrangements that are needed to properly coordinate, and prioritize the actions of thousands of people interacting with thousands of other persons and companies. The competitive-knowledge-discovery-sharing mechanism that occurs in the private sector is lacking, therefore the FDA inevitably grows more redundant, inefficient, and chaotic as time goes by. In a government bureaucracy, which is a monopoly, knowledge can only be discovered within that monopoly/firm/'social body'. In the private sector, knowledge is discovered in the companies, *as well as in competitors*, and the superior knowledge and ways of doing things inevitably force their way throughout the social order, which cannot happen in a government monopoly. And I'm not even bringing up the wholly different sets of incentives which we already briefly discussed. Bottom line, it is IMPOSSIBLE for the FDA to do its job efficiently. Rep. Rosa DeLauro(D-Connecticut) , a critic of the FDA, said "I for one am not going to provide funds for an agency that has no management structure in place, doesn't have any idea of how to utilize the funds that the congress is providing to them" . Little does Rep. DeLauro know, that the "management structure" that has the right "idea" of how to give an efficient order to resources will never come via a government monopoly. Eventually Rep. DeLauro will blame the people in the FDA, and maybe change the leadership with more seemingly competent individuals. But the result will inevitably be the same.

The same can be said about the American Medical Association and its decisions as to what is a safe or unsafe medical procedure, and what is the best way of filling a brain with the necessary knowledge to provide medical services. An eye doctor(optometrist) once told me that she could train a motivated apprentice to do her job, of checking people's eyes for the right lens to use as well as vision related illnesses, in about a year. But, although I don't remember her exact words, she felt like her long, arduous, and expensive journey through medical school, so she could get the *legal right* to do her simple job, was still a good thing because it ensured a certain professional demeanor to the profession. So thanks to our AMA bureaucracy, society trades countless hours of a person's youth, plus a couple hundred thousand dollars worth of wealth that is consumed by an overpriced education for a "professional demeanor to the profession". The costs of maintaining this often times unneeded educational bureaucracy(repaying her student loans), are then passed on to the consumer in terms of the higher prices she has to charge to pay this back. She, as well as every other optometrist, can safely pass this cost on to the consumer because the government grants them a legal monopoly over providing their services. Her apprentice cannot just open up shop and charge people less because she does not have to pay back a huge loan. If she does this, she is a criminal for practicing without a license. The AMA's regulation of the medical profession essentially says: "There is only one way to practice optometry and you have to do it via this type of training." It is a mandated piece of knowledge, which can only be changed by a slow bureaucratic AMA process. This also makes going into the medical field a much more unnecessarily grueling task than it would otherwise have to be, greatly diminishing the supply of people who enter the field, leading to shortages of doctors and disproportional higher salaries for those who jump through the hurtles. And then there are the costs involved in opening up a practice and learning how to stay legit and work within the heavily regulated insurance world, causing more money and wealth to be consumed by a misaligned bureaucracy, ultimately rising prices for the consumer, and eating away at their diminishing pie of prosperity.

Perhaps the biggest of all flaws in how the AMA goes about regulating the world of medical practice is in the assumption that doctors have to be some of the brightest and most dedicated people around, which it achieves by making entry into medical school and early training such an arduous process. But this is not true, what cures people is not hard working bright individuals, it is the tremendous amount of knowledge and cheap technology that the market-process-coordinated world puts at their finger tips. The brightest, most experienced and motivated doctor from the year 1900 would be at a huge disadvantage compared to a motivate biology student with access to google and modern technology.

This flaw is not specific to the AMA, it applies to our entire educational establishments and much of how we look at the world. We force future computer programmers and engineers to learn useless mathematics, making such degrees to be much more challenging in ways that have little to do with being productive. I'm not saying that placing a challenging barrier in someone's path in order to test their ability is not a good thing, it can be, but who is to decide which roadblock to use, if a road block at all? Why should the best way of training an engineer or computer programmer involve learning how to prove some mathematical theorem? Here we can once again look to the Information Technology sector for a great example of how the free-market naturally evolves the best way of filling brains with productive knowledge. IT companies who reach a large enough size ultimately due to the great services they provide, and therefore *useful/profitable* knowledge they contain, like Microsoft, IBM, and countless others, go about creating their own educational institutions which train and test people using their products and technologies. Products and technologies which are solving real problems and have been shaped by years of fluid competition. At every bookstore you will find a huge section of IT related books helping the members of this most thriving industry keep up with the latest and most productive ways of doing things. There are over 2.1 million[18] individuals worldwide who have become Microsoft Certified Professionals(MCPs) by studying for and passing exams created by Microsoft. These exams change frequently to reflect the never-ending cycle of knowledge generation that exists in the free and unregulated world. It is beautiful I tell ya. Did the government plan the emergence of this beautiful industry and its highly evolved educational system? Of course not. It is thanks to the fact that it did not force its regulatory tentacles into the sector, that the market process was able to discover and propagate the needed knowledge with which to guide the human ants in such a wonderfully productive way.

Some people immediately say, "Oh but medicine is different, you can't experiment on people like you can with computers. You have to be a lot more careful". True, you do have to be a lot more careful but at a fundamental level this does not change things one bit. You are still looking for knowledge of how to do something. It doesn't matter whether you have to be very careful or not, the process is the same, and is best achieved by competition in the free-market.

If the AMA-imposed and well intentioned regulatory hurdles were suddenly removed, doctor's paychecks will come, not from the fact that they have a government granted monopoly on the right to provide this vital service to society, but on their effort and ability to learn and properly apply the latest knowledge discovered by the market process. Doctors today help us cure our diseases and most care greatly about their patients(I like to believe), but by inadvertently being part of our medical bureaucracy and preventing the market process from shaping their field via their well intentioned regulations, they are actually the biggest detriment to our health, because they inadvertently stand in the way of what would otherwise be a much better solution. As long as doctors do not understand this, they have their innocence, and like a 9 month old baby that throws a temper tantrum and hits a loving bystander, they can be forgiven, but once they understand this, and fight to keep the system the way it is, they sort of become accomplices to murder, not because they kill you directly, but because the stand in the way of better treatments which would keep you alive.

This helps explain how regulation affects the incentives of both individuals and investors. There are millions of people whose current jobs depend on government regulation, some of these people make a lot of money like medical professionals. If regulations are removed and the market process quickly reduces to costs of great medical care by say 90% in a couple of years, which I think is a good estimate, one type of doctor that makes say $300,000 per year might suddenly find himself out-competed by superior ideas and now find a job that only pays say $50,000. He wouldn't be able to afford the prestigious doctor life anymore. Some types of jobs might completely disappear. Some doctors might make even more, the cost of some of the medical technology they need might drastically go down, who knows. But ultimately everyone will be much better off. Ah I can just envision it, within 5 years there would be a device like Joe's in every Wal-Mart/Target/Mall in the country easily affordable to everyone.

I remember needing to get a root canal redone and doing research about it. In a root canal the nerve/insides of your tooth are taken out and the empty space is filled with some chemical(who some believe could be very dangerous) that helps prevent bacteria from growing in the empty space and causing problems. I don't remember all the details of my research at the time, but it seemed like the better choice would be to just get a fake tooth or a bridge and this way I would not have to worry about some bacterial infection growing inside to old tooth and surrounding tissue(again). I could not find any convincing evidence that keeping the old tooth was a better choice, even the American Association of Endodontists(our government monopoly on how to deal with root canals and related troubles) website[19] just said that it is always better to keep your natural tooth but no mention of statistics to back this up, and none of the endodontists I visited could make a strong case over removing the tooth. So what if it is simply better to get a new tooth when an old one needs a root canal? What if this new knowledge suddenly arises? What happens to people who have spent years and thousands of dollars learning everything about root canals when suddenly getting fake teeth becomes an overwhelmingly better option? These people would no longer be able to make a living doing root canals, and thanks to our regulation, if they wanted to do some other specialty, they would have to shell out another 50,000 and years in medical school to practice some new specialty and not go to jail for it. So assuming that I might be right here, I could be wrong, but this does not change the validity of this example. What are the incentives of endodontists in this case? What are the personal incentives of the millions of people whose futures high wages, or wages at all, would be uncertain if regulations were dropped? I do not want to say that all of these people would selfishly fight this to the detriment of mankind but human beings are human beings and incentives matter, especially in cases like this. And doctors have HUGE egos. Only if they understood economics really well and could clearly see just how quickly the world would progress, and more than make up for whatever losses people might suffer in the short run, would people be much more willing to more openly cheer for the dismantling of such regulations. That, coupled with people who work in the non-regulated sectors also putting legislative and social pressure to remove the regulations.

Do IT professionals fear the removal of any regulation that forces people to do things a certain way to become an IT pro? These thoughts never even enter their minds because there are none. But it is a whole different matter with doctors and other medical related professionals. Thanks to technology your average neighborhood pharmacist is an overpriced, overeducated pill counter, whose high salary and self esteem would fear the removal of the regulatory framework. Countless of expensive doctor visits are made just so that we get the legal right(doctor's prescription) to use medications. Sure we want to prevent people from misusing drugs, but people lie anyways to get the drugs they want, and in the end all of this just ends up increasing the costs of health care and getting in the way of superior results. It prevents good outcomes because of the fear of a few bad ones, which are needed anyways to help society discover the true consequences of actions and to learn from them.

So back to the FDA and drugs. Yes, we want these things to be safe, but how do we discover the best way of doing so? How do we find the ideal balance between preventing deaths due to early adoption of bad drugs, and saving the lives of those who would otherwise die as they waited for drugs to be approved? How do we discover the optimal way of keeping costs and time down while taking into account the countless other factors involved? I know nothing about the world of drug testing, but my basic understanding of economics and how the market process works, clearly let's me know that the solutions that would arise from the market process coordinated interactions of the millions of patients, doctors, entrepreneurs, etc., would be far superior to what any centrally planned bureaucracy could ever come up with. Does France have a software quality control agency? No, they buy the best software they can find which happens to be made in the USA. The same reasoning applies to figuring out what medical procedures are best, and how to go about filling a brain with health care related knowledge. This discovery can best be done by freedom and competition, by the market process.

When someone in the technology sector has an idea, he is free to go after it so long as he does not violate our two laws. The entrepreneur can devote almost 100% of his mental capacity to looking for better ways of serving society. It is easy to figure out when you might be violating our two laws and steer yourself in the right direction. Unlike the IT entrepreneur, the health care entrepreneur is clueless as to what he can legally do and what will have him incarcerated. The only way to figure this out is to spend thousands of dollars on medical legal experts learning to stay legit, and as you do so you are forced down a path "of dead, rigid, mechanical formulas", which can only be changed slowly and expensively by a bureaucratic process. This bureaucratic hurdle is a cost everyone has to overcome and is passed on to the consumer increasing our premiums by about 10 percent per year. Filling us with fear, launching us straight to Socialism as we ask the big ape to solve the problems.

Why is health care so heavily regulated compared to other industries? Our instincts for equality and our fears and concerns are obviously very strong when it comes to something as vital as health care and therefore we are even more demanding of some visible entity to ensure that things get done as well and as equitably as possible. Few things can spark our envy and inherent desire for equality more than knowing that some richer fellow can easily afford better medical care while we have to fear for the lives of our children. Since medicine is so important to us, courageous and well meaning revolutionaries have strived to make it available for free or as a 'right' for everyone. Russian communist leader Vladimir Lenin said that "medicine is the keystone in the arch of socialism", and quite naturally, as was the case in the early 1900s when the egalitarian moral impulses of the Russian masses rose Lenin to the top, equality in health care is increasingly becoming the major issue which we use to put our charismatic leaders in power. This strong concern translates itself into more government regulation, which serves to burden and force down a certain rigid path of knowledge the countless of brains that are trying to discover the best ways to organize the sequence of steps needed to best take care of our health. As economoron Sen. Edward M. Kennedy(D-Mass) said "We have it in our power to make the fundamental human right to health care a reality to all Americans."[20] And also buddy economoron Sen. John V. Kerry(D-Mass) "I'm committed to universal health care coverage because, in America, health care is not a privilege, it's a right."[21] And last but not least, new popular economoron Sen. Barack Obama(D-Ill) "believes firmly that health care should be a right for everyone, not a privilege for the few."[22] Whether such government run health care, with what will surely be millions of employees, is organized in a way that consumes 100 times more wealth from the economic pie than it would ideally need and eventually bankrupt the country, or whether it is a way that is conducive to the technological improvements that are so key to finding better medicines and cures, these factors, which can only be solved by the market process, are not part of our thinking.

Our FDA, AMA, and medical industrial complex bureaucracies will inevitably collapse. This can happen in one of two ways. One, they continue to aid the growth of inefficiency to the point where the entire economy collapses, or two, because there is still too much freedom for the market process to work, and they themselves are out-competed by people getting care *overseas*. Government regulation eventually turns the entire medical sector of the economy into one gigantic company which is shaped by the inefficient bureaucratic process and therefore becomes increasingly consumptive and expensive, while the countless medical cities *outside* of the US are free from such regulation and are shaped by real global competition and therefore continue to lower costs and improve care compared to the US medical sector until it is finally forced to change. This gives us an opportunity to understand why it is so important for the march towards global government to be stopped. The trend towards global government via international organizations will begin to regulate and prevent competition on a global level, ensuring that market process paralyzing regulation stamps out even the last resort of global competition.

Further proof of our maladapted thinking is how politicians are always "fighting for health care", "fighting for better education", "fighting for the elderly", everything is a fight against an implied enemy, that enemy being the haves and inherent selfishness and greed of human beings, because that is all that mattered in our tribal world. If there wasn't a guy with resources in the tribal world, then it would be obvious that there was no need to fight over anything, but as long as we have inequality in our modern human ant-farms, the 'fight' will be against the haves and inadvertently, against the workings of the market process and against the productive order of civilization.

As a final example of government regulation at least one paragraph has to be devoted to our public school bureaucracies. The average yearly per pupil costs are now over $9,000 and in some state like New York they are over $14,000[23]. That is from $180,000 to $280,000 to "educate" 20 students for one year. There are 12 states that for every classroom teacher there are two additional employees doing who knows what[24]. Regardless of how good a teacher is, or how useful the information she teaches might be, teachers get paid based on how long they have been sitting on the job and how many useless degrees they add to their resume. Yes, I said "useless degrees" because that is exactly what they are. While in college and later as teacher, I asked many who were teachers or taking the necessary coursework to become one, about the usefulness of the content of such classes. All of them agreed with me that the classes were useless. They were mostly what I like to call psychobabble. Oh, wait, there was one benefit to the classes. A classmate once told me, "George, why are you whining so much? Look at it this way, those classes are very easy and they help your GPA."

So government regulation has two main drawbacks, number one is that the regulations themselves force the social order to morph itself down a less than ideal path to begin with. Second, is that a tremendous amount of wealth and mental capacity has to be diverted in order to comply with such regulations. The millions of lawyers, compliance experts, government employees, their secretaries, plus the smaller industries that grow from the need to support such regulatory social orders, all consume wealth from the economic pie. Yet their services are not really of value to society, they are only valuable in the sense that they prevent companies and entrepreneurs from being locked up by not being legit. But compared to the more prosperous social order that would emerge should the government not regulate, a social order where these same individuals would still consume but now add truly economic-pie-increasing wealth, their jobs are a detriment to mankind.

The key to understanding government evils lies in understanding the simple fact that social order depends on knowledge needed to coordinate the continuous cycle of production and consumption in a way that it produces more wealth than it consumes. When an industry is socialized, all knowledge of how it should order the human ants that work in it comes from government, and is therefore bound to be a social cancer which consumes more and more wealth while adding less and less in return. When the government regulates the private sector, the private sector begins to lose its "privateness" in terms of where and how it discovers the best way to do things. As opposed to the competitive market process spreading knowledge through society, it begins to do things via inferior knowledge generated via the bureaucratic process. So its human ants begin to consume more and more compared to how much wealth they add to the social order. So whether it'd be figuring out how to test drugs, educate people in the health care field, or educational field, it doesn't matter. If it is productive social order we want, freedom and the market process is the *only* way to go about it. Temporarily one can believe that government solutions will work, but this is what has governments borrowing more and more, putting off the problems into the future, which is what the US is currently doing, until major economic collapses put an end to such impossibilities. Our over-regulated health care sector has grown from consuming just 1.6% of the gross domestic product(GDP) in 1960 to 4.2% in 1980[25] to a whopping 16% that was consumed in 2006[26].

To our maladapted tribal mindset, once an idea seems good to us that's all there is too it, but in our modern world, ideas are good if they ultimately out-compete other ideas in the free and unregulated private sector. It is only once they have proven their superiority in the free market that we can tell that the ideas are truly superior, and even then, that will only be from our individual and subjective standpoints, there could always be another idea, in another brain, in another part of the world that is better and spreading its superior order and we just don't know it yet.

A recent Business Week article titled "Do Cholesterol Drugs Do Any Good?"[27] once again brought to the forefront the fact that cholesterol lowering drugs barely do any good at all. The difference between 100 people taking the leading drug Lipitor and a sugar pill was that 3 people with sugar pill got a heart attack while only 2 taking Lipitor did. Yet an amount of wealth equivalent to that produced by a small country like Nicaragua, about 28 billion dollars is forked over by over 12 million people to pay for these "statin" drugs. Dr. John Abramson, clinical instructor at Harvard Medical School and author of the highly recommended "Overdosed America" says : "We should tell patients that the reduced cardiovascular risk will be replaced by other serious illnesses"[28]

Anyways, this is not a book about giving statistics about how disastrous our bureaucracies inevitably become. We are mostly focused on the fundamental economic principles here. Once those are properly understood, there should be little need to look for such damaging statistics.

More *Spencer*

In another great essay by Spencer titled "The Coming Slavery" Spencer clearly sees an ideological shift taking place in people's thinking. A shift going from individual economic freedom to the belief that it is the government that can best manage everything and the expectation that it does so. It is important to realize that Herbert Spencer was living in 19th century England in the middle of the industrial revolution, which was transforming the world, taking its complexity to a new level unfamiliar to mankind. A complexity, which most people felt needed the government to manage and exploit to appease our egalitarian tendencies.

"They listen with eager faith to all builders of political air-castles...and every additional tax-supported appliance for their welfare raises hopes of further ones. Indeed the more numerous public instrumentalities become, the more is there generated in citizens the notion that everything is to be done for them, and nothing by them. **Each generation is made less familiar with the attainment of desired ends by individual actions or private combinations, and more familiar with the attainment of them by governmental agencies; until, eventually, governmental agencies come to be thought of as the only available agencies."**

Towards the end of his "Over-legislation" essay, Spencer talks about the key to England's emergence as a world power. That key being the self-reliance of people as opposed to reliance on government.

"Let any one, after duly watching the rapid evolution going on in England, where men have been comparatively little helped by governments—or better still, after contemplating the unparalleled progress of the United States, which is peopled by self-made men, and the recent descendants of self-made men—let such an one, we say, go on to the Continent[rest of Europe], and consider the relatively slow advance which things are there making; and the still slower advance they would make but for English enterprise. Let him go to Holland and see that though the Dutch early showed themselves good mechanics, and have had abundant practice in hydraulics, Amsterdam has been without any due supply of water until now that works are being established by an English company."

He continues describing how it is Englishmen and Americans who are remaking the world, and the main difference between them and the rest of the world, is their self-reliance, in other words, their cultural values which stress individual economic freedom as opposed to government management. Spencer knew it was this economic freedom/'relative self-dependence' and not something like race that set the Americans and the British apart from the rest of the world. Referring to England's rise and the rest of Europe's stagnation Spencer continues:

"Were not the inhabitants of the two, some centuries ago, much upon a par in point of enterprise? Were not the English even behind in their manufactures, in their colonization, in their commerce? Has not the immense relative change the English have undergone in this respect, been coincident with the great relative self-dependence they have been since habituated to?"

I love this next quote, where he gets to the heart of mankind's troubles, our countless laws and blind faith in government.

"The essential truth of the matter—that law had been doing immense harm, and that this prosperity resulted not from law but from the absence of law—is missed; and his faith in legislation in general, which should, by this experience, have been greatly shaken, seemingly remains as strong as ever."

We are suckers for having government pass laws and force us to do things. In our ape-like tribal past perhaps we were just used to doing what the big bad ape wanted us to do for fear of retaliation but that is not what creates our modern social order. Finally Spencer ends his "Over-legislation" essay by mentioning how our faith in government is in our human nature.

"Indeed this faith in governments is in a certain sense organic; and can diminish only by being outgrown…All superstitions die hard; and we fear that this belief in government-omnipotence will form no exception."

Damn!!! Herbert Spencer was a badass!

Government finance basics

Let's briefly go over how the government finances itself.

Taxes

Easy right? We pay taxes. When we do so, money goes from the private sector to the government, then the money is traded back to the private sector for the wealth needed to feed, clothe, house our army of public sector employees and the companies that do business with it. Very little is given back to society, or worse, we get regulation. It is much better to simply lose your wealth than to lose your wealth and also be told how to go about producing less than you would otherwise do. Wealth is not just mostly consumed, we always want to keep in mind the alternative and free social order, that which is not visible. The social order where instead of having government employees consume the wealth which has been taxed away, they actually remain integrated into profitable business plans which increase the size and quality of the economic pie.

Some readers might be familiar with "Tax Freedom Day" which happened to be April 30th for 2007. "Tax Freedom Day" is the day in which the private sector starts working to produce wealth for its own consumption as opposed to the government. The private sector works from January 1st to April 30th just to create enough wealth so that the public sector can munch on. After that day till the rest of the year the private sector gets to consume what it produces for its own well being.

Taxes also discourage the creation or expansion of businesses. Imagine a business that operates for four years whose yearly bottom lines are as follows, first year 100 million in profit, second year 50 million loss, third year another 100 million profit, and fourth year a 45 million loss. Over the four years this business made a total profit of 200 million dollars and lost 95 million for a final balance sheet of a profit of $105 million. Overall this is a good business right? Some years it has done well, others not. Perhaps on the bad years a new competitor came, but the business adapted, learned from the competition, and managed to update the productive order of its mini human ant-farm in a way that once again maintained an efficient and productive order, an order that when we take into account the four years, has managed to increase the economic pie by $105 million in value. So all this is great, the business/'social order' is increasing the economic pie and helping humanity move into a more prosperous future. Now let's assume that we have a tax rate of 55% and see what effect this has on our business. The two years with 100 million profits are now turned into two years with 45 million dollar profits because the 55% tax rate confiscated 55 million dollars each year that the company made 100, for a total of 90 million in profits instead of the 200 million. The two years of losses still bring the 50 + 45 million dollar losses for a total of 95 million in losses. Now we have a total profit of 90 million and a total loss of 95 million leaving the balance sheet with a total loss of 5 million. Taxes have turned what is truly a productive enterprise, one that maintains and gives an efficient order to a section of the human ant-farm, one that embodies good knowledge, into a bad idea, into an unprofitable idea that will have to be abandoned. What makes us think that the world revolves around our manmade concept of years? Sometimes people make good decisions which lead to useful products and services and therefore pie-increasing profits, sometimes they fail to do so, resulting in losses. It is simply too risky to run a business when the government taxes much of your gains, yet you fully suffer the losses. Given these incentives, businesses are much more cautious than they would otherwise have been, only embarking on "safe" ideas as opposed to all profitable ideas. Ultimately this is just another way in which the morphing into more productive and advanced states is greatly hampered and slowed down by government, once again slowing down the entire progress of mankind.

When we fall for taxation we often times think that we are better off when we take a little from people and then combine this amount to do something visible and great for society as we combine the money. We might think "1 dollar in each American's hand can't build anything really great, but taxing that 1 dollar can lead to 300 million dollars which can be employed on a single great thing for society". We do not see that that one dollar is savings which usually enters our investment/finance/lending industry where it can be combined with other people's single dollars to also create large amounts. The difference here is that these large amounts of money will lead to profitable investments that increase the economic pie as they produce enough wealth to cover their costs and return a profit to investors and savers.

Taxing the rich is one of the worst things we can do. The wealth of the rich is the very wealth that enters our financial sector and will sustain pie-increasing/profitable business plans. If the rich are not taxed, the working masses still get the wealth that the rich have via their wages, but they will be working in a way that increases the economic pie as efficiently as humanly possible. When the government taxes such wealth it will either give it away in some welfare scheme leading to pure consumption of the economic pie, or employ people in the public sector which still leads to mostly pure consumption by the government employees since what they give back is mostly useless and just gets in the way of real progress, especially when such government employees are regulators/etc.

The fact that the savings of the rich is the money that is loaned to brains with superior ideas that end up employing the have-less in an efficient and prosperity building manner is just something that we have not evolved to instinctively understand. To the untrained mind such additional wealth is like bananas that will rot or be used to show off, while in reality they are bananas that will feed others while even more bananas are produced. And the more bananas the rich have and inevitably save, the more bananas will have to be offered(higher wage) to the workers in order to compete for their labor.

Inflation

The government, via the Federal Reserve and our banking system essentially creates more money and then trades this money for real wealth which helps feed its bureaucracies or the politically connected companies/banks that get this money. This trade leaves the private sector with more money and less wealth, altering the ratio of money to wealth, therefore raising prices.

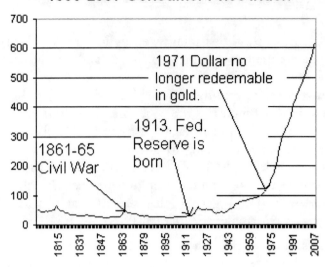

The figure above shows a historical trend of slightly declining prices under the gold standard. The amount of gold entering the economy grew slower than the amount of wealth being produced so prices went down. The quick jump in the early 1860's was due to the devastation caused by the Civil War, which naturally destroyed a lot of wealth, therefore altering the ratio of money to wealth(more money/less wealth = higher price) raising prices. In 1933 Franklin D. Roosevelt's administration confiscated the people's gold and put the American public on a purely government created paper money standard, but still redeemed dollars in gold to foreign governments. This allowed the government to spend more and pay for such spending via the printing press and we begin to see inflation pickup substantially after 1933. But eventually the dollars would go overseas, as the American public traded them for imported goods, and then come back looking to be traded for gold causing problems for our benevolent ideologues. In 1971 the Nixon administration stopped all payment in gold severing the link between gold and the dollar once and for all, allowing for more rapid inflation as the graph shows. At present time, just in the week of Aug. 20 – 27 2007 the M2 money supply grew by 65 billion dollars[29].

Borrowing

The government sells IOUs(I owe you(s)), whether they are referred to as Treasury bills, government bonds or whatever, for our purposes they are fundamentally the same thing. For example, you buy a government issued IOU, in this case a $1,000 Treasury bill, or T-Bill for short, for $970 and in a year you can redeem your $1,000 T-Bill for $1,000.

So you lent the government $970 for a year and at the end of the year it gave you back $1,000. You made $30, which happens to be the 3% interest earned by your T-Bill. In this short example you lent the government money for 1 year but money can be loaned to government for longer periods during which the government periodically pays you interest on your loan. Since the United States and its dollar has been the most stable currency in recent history, many people in the world feel like lending it money is a good and safe investment. The United States government owes what will soon be 9.2 trillion dollars of this kind of debt. This is the national debt that one often hears about, which is over $30,000 per man, woman, and child in the US, or $60,000 per working adult. In 2006 the US government had to pay about 406 billion dollars just on the interest of the debt[30], sort of like making the minimum payment on your credit card.

When government borrows, instead of savings being used to fund private sector transformations which increase the economic pie and efficiency of our social order, the money and subsequent wealth that it can buy is given to the government where it is mostly consumed for a net loss and reduction of the economic pie. Since savings are being lent to the government instead of the private sector, there is less savings available for the private sector and this reflects itself in higher interest rates, which crowds out many profitable business ideas.

Since the government does not create wealth it will have to pay it back by either increasing taxes, via inflation, or just borrow more to pay current bills while going further in debt, and creating more inflation as it pays the debt. And again, not only hurting us, but slowing down the very progress of mankind.

On democracy

The United States these days is pretty much a full-blown democracy, which means that politicians are elected by the public and their decisions reflect the average ignorance/wisdom of the very masses that elect them. Politicians cannot pass or repeal laws that the masses do not like, even if such laws or their repeal might be the best thing for them. If they do, they are voted out of office and replaced by a true representative of the people who will do as people want, regardless of what is really in their best interest. Since it is in our nature to have a certain longing for Communism/Socialism for reasons already discussed, given a chance, as a democracy provides, we ask for it with every trip to the voting booth, so as Karl Marx said "Democracy is the road to socialism." This is why what might start as a relatively free and limited democracy, as in the case of the United States, inevitably moves towards a sort of communist democracy due to our innate desire to have some alpha-male-like visible entity dictate the workings of society as opposed to the seemingly chaotic individual freedom/'market process'. A few quotes on democracy are called for:

"A democracy is nothing more than mob rule, where fifty-one percent of the people may take away the rights of the other forty-nine." – Thomas Jefferson.

"…a state which recognizes the subordination of the minority to the majority, i.e., an organization for the systematic use of force by one class against another, by one section of the population against another." – Lenin

"The best argument against democracy is a five minute conversation with the average voter." – Winston Churchill

"Sooner will a camel pass through a needle's eye than a great man be "discovered" by an election" – Adolf Hitler

"The higher the wisdom the more incomprehensible does it become by ignorance. It is a manifest fact that the popular man or writer, is always one who is but little in advance of the mass, and consequently understandable by them: never the man who is far in advance of them and out of their sight… So that, even were electors content to choose the man proved by general evidence to be the most far-seeing…there would be small chance of their hitting on the best… Their deputy will be truly representative;—representative, that is, of the average stupidity." – Herbert Spencer

In Richard J. Maybury's already mentioned awesome "Whatever Happened to Justice?" he tells us:

[31]"In fact, as far as I know, no one in the American Revolution was interested in democracy. Read the literature of 1776, try to find any mention of it. Everywhere you will find demands for liberty, but little or nothing about democracy. The Constitution says nothing about democracy.

The Founders did not like democracy and they did not trust it. They wanted liberty.

Indeed, as citizens of Britain, the early Americans probably already had more democracy than any other nation. To a large extent, this is what the war was about. The American colonists were a minority of the British population, which was governed by parliament's majority rule. Even if every one of the colonists could have voted, they probably could not have stopped parliament from voting against them….

…The Founders studied the democracies of ancient Greece and other nations before they created the Constitution. In Federalist #10, James Madison (4th US pres) wrote:

'Such democracies have ever been spectacles of turbulence and contention; have ever been found incompatible with personal security or the rights of property; and have in general been as short in their lives as they have been violent in their deaths.'

In Federalist #50 he worried that,

'The passions, therefore, and not the reason, of the public would sit in judgment.' " — Richard J. Maybury

Thomas Jefferson said, "Whenever the people are well-informed, they can be trusted with their own government", so as long as the overwhelming majority of people understand the market process, I think we will be alright.

The modern political zoo and its inevitable road to serfdom

As should be increasingly apparent by now, the talents, honesty, charisma, good intentions, loyalty, patriotism, and countless other traits which were crucial for the successful maintenance of the social order in our simpler tribal past, are insignificant in comparison to the workings of the market process in our modern world. They are insignificant to what free individuals can accomplish. However, we don't realize this, especially when it comes to politics. Millions of us spend our Saturday/Sunday afternoons watching the various political shows where they debate the sorts of things that were of importance to our tribal world. Let's go over our usual political concerns and discuss just how out of place we really are.

"Is so and so of good character and can he be trusted?" Trust was a big deal in our tribal past and you really needed the leaders not to redistribute wealth in an unfair manner, or mediate conflicts to their advantage as opposed to the equality we all want and would keep things stable. In today's world, we have contracts, how trustworthy people are is less important. As long as they adhere to the contract which describes a transaction that benefits both parties, then everything is great, if not, then this new concept of "the law" steps in to correct the fraud. But whether the people we are doing business with are 'nice' or not, it matters less. The 'niceness' of the thousands of people involved in building my car is irrelevant to the bottom line that says that should anything break down within the car's first 3 years it must be fixed at no cost to me and that I must be provided with a decent rental car in the meantime. This does not mean that we do not care about the morals and values of those we do business with, we still do, and this is still very important in our dealings, but again, in our market process coordinated world it is not as important as it once was, it is not the main factor. As already discussed, all the traits we associate with niceness are naturally selected for anyways, because niceness is one of the many ingredients that go into making a company work well and compete for the life sustaining money we feed them. In order to afford a better standard of

living it helps to be nice and have a good reputation, these traits lead to more connections/'business partners' and so on. We just naturally rather be nice. Monkeys love to have fun and get along when there is plenty to share and so do we.

"Senator X has an extensive history of military service, he has proven himself to be someone who can make a great sacrifice for our country." Obviously being a courageous fighter was a great show of altruism. You can definitely trust someone who is willing to risk his life for you, this was great back in the day, but it has little to do with the ability to give an efficient order to the millions of public servants that presidents/congressmen believe they oversee. Even if a moral and incorruptible leader is chosen and he immediately weeds out corruption and ill intent in a few layers below him, this is still nothing compared to the layers upon layers of delegation which are parts of our modern government bureaucracies. And this still misses the main point, it comes naturally for us to think that things don't get done well due to corruption, and the unproductive and selfish vices inherent in man, but this is not the main reason why government does not work. It is the lack of the competitive knowledge discovery mechanism that the market process provides in the private sector that inevitably leads to tremendous inefficiencies in the public sector, not to mention opportunities for out right corruption.

"Senator X has led many 'bipartisan' efforts before, therefore he has earned the respect of other men and will succeed in the collective action and unity needed to get things done." In our tribal days, elders and people who have lived long lives and created a rich network of friendships intertwined by favors, and felt sort of connected to the many families and nearby tribes were important in securing the necessary cooperation of many people to carry out the many tasks that required a significant proportion of the population(war/migrations/dispute resolutions). But when it comes to the tasks our modern governments embark upon, no matter how much respect and friends, or 'bipartisan' support this person might have, it will not make the slightest difference when it comes to giving a productive order to the millions of employees that the government manages, or improve the workings of the private sector via regulations.

Again, in our simpler tribal past, even the most complicated and daunting of tasks involved at most the organization of the entire clan which was a relatively small number, say 25-150 people. In this type of scenario, the unity and common purpose of everyone involved must have been a crucial factor in the completion of such large-scale projects. But in the complex economies we now live in, it is impossible for a single mind or many minds to determine whether the gigantic forced restructuring that the government forces the private sector to undertake leave society better off than before. Actually, given everything we have discussed so far, we can be certain that the result will be an inferior one. But it doesn't matter, year after year, we keep falling for the same ideas, "if we could only focus our energies and pay that extra tax that will ensure that our schools are properly funded" we think. "If we could all just get together and pool our resources we could make it happen". Over and over and over, being suckers for unity/'bipartisanship' we pool our resources to create gigantic government bureaucracies that just end up trading our tax dollars for cars, homes, and food for the millions of public sector employees and the private sector gets back little to nothing in return, or worse, paralyzing regulation.

In the tribal world, individual and easily identifiable human beings were responsible for getting things done. In our modern world, the demand for something, in other words, the amount of money people are willing to trade for something, which reflects their need/desire for it, provides the necessary incentives/signals for many brains to 'look for'/discover profitable knowledge that will provide the needed product/service. Another example of our mal-adapted nature to the modern world is how most Americans will probably know the names of at least 5-10 political figures yet they cannot name 5-10 CEOs, who are the leaders of the companies that truly add wealth and help spread well-being and a productive order to the world.

Our reliance on human beings to organize our actions as opposed to the market process also clearly manifests itself in the hero-worship of politicians. This is especially visible in more full blown communist countries like Cuba(Castro), Venezuela(Chavez), North Korea(Kim Jong-il), and the former USSR(Lenin,Stalin) and China(Mao) where large banners and parades idolize their respective leaders. Since we are all equally human and susceptible to such hero-worship, many of us do the same here in the US. There can be no doubt that our supreme leader George W. Bush has plenty of die-hard followers who idolize him. All we care about are good intentions, trustworthiness and someone who is part of and loyal to our tribe. George W. Bush prays to God often for guidance, he talks to religious leaders, he feels like he is a good person and that he is doing good for mankind by waging the battle of 'good' vs. 'evil', and that to his brain, and that of many Americans, there is 'evil' in the middle east. That it is concentrated in places like Iran, Iraq, Syria and so on. And that if we kill the 'evil' people, then we will have 'good' "freedom loving" people left over and all of our problems will be solved. Oh boy, we are in trouble, more on ideology and the middle east later.

So every four years in the US millions get excited about choosing their leader, we become volunteers in political campaigns, willing to make great sacrifices to make sure that honest and great men who will not be "swayed by power" are put in power so that they can properly enforce equality, and honestly lead the nation towards a visible and much sought after common purpose, whatever it might be. It is as if all of our problems could be solved via unity and hard work, and one obviously needs a leader that everyone will get behind with, and this is why inevitably we are fall pray to charismatic leaders and the inevitable dictatorships that follow. All of this happens not out of "evil", it is our human nature imposing itself on the modern human ant-farm.

The politician has two choices, either force everyone via taxes or regulation to go along with the master plan, or do nothing, which according to his thinking, and that of the masses that put their faith in him, will lead to things getting worse and social collapse. "Obviously" "something needs to be done". He has to act and chooses the lesser of the two evils which is to force the human ants into acting towards "the plan" that will make things better. The people who do not want to go along have to be forced or else the master plan dissolves into chaos, and cannot meet its goal and society collapses in the eyes of the fearful public. These are the "tough choices" that our great leaders make that require "exceptional men" with great "political willpower".

The moral justification for forcing the dissenters to go along can come from many sources. He has the backing of those who voted for him and also believe that it is necessary that the dissenters contribute to the master plan. Again, governments are neither good nor evil, whatever good or bad they do, for the most part is a reflection of the ideologies of the masses.

Every decision simply expands the size of government leading to a bigger need to take even more resources from the private sector which makes things worse, until things are so bad and our egalitarianism so strong that we put our power in the charismatic leader that can finally take all the wealth from the halves to give it to the have-nots or finally get everyone working together to implement the "master plan" that will fix all the problems. Our democracies begin to seem to slow. If we feel like we need our leaders to act quickly to prevent further calamities, all of this voting and bureaucracy just gets in the way, our leaders are good people, with good intentions, the hell with democracy, we just want to give them the power to do what seems like the obvious solution(take or regulate). It seems fitting to quote Hayek's Road to Serfdom which so much inspired Dr. Paul. In one of its most celebrated chapters entitled "Why the Worst Get on Top" Hayek mentions:

"We must here return for a moment to the position which precedes the suppression of democratic institutions and the creation of a totalitarian regime. In this stage it is the general demand for quick and determined government action that is the dominating element of the situation, dissatisfaction with the slow and cumbersome course of democratic procedure which makes action for action's sake the goal. It is then the man or the party who seems strong and resolute enough "to get things done" who exercises the greatest appeal. "Strong" in this sense means not merely a numerical majority –it is the ineffectiveness of parliamentary majorities with which people are dissatisfied. What they will seek is somebody with such solid support as to inspire confidence that he can carry out whatever he wants. It is here that the new type of party, organized on military lines, comes in."[32]

The public not only believes that we need a benevolent dictator; the system naturally selects him for us. A confident fool will sway more minds than a doubtful and considerate genius. It is the man who thoroughly believes that he has the right "master plan", that carries himself with the needed confidence to sway the public.

So our democracies eventually become dictatorships, then we blame the dictators, lick our wounds, and go back to democracy, which leads to new dictators and on and on. As Maybury tells us: "The latin nations still ride a pendulum that swings every few years from dictatorship to democracy and chaos, then back to dictatorship, and so on."[33]

---

[1] The reader might be better served by first reading chapter V "Cultural Evolution and Hayekian Selection" and then coming back here.

[2] F.A. Hayek, The Constitution of Liberty. The University of Chicago Press, published 1978, page 163

[3] Ker Than, "U.S. Lags World in Grasp of Genetics and Acceptance of Evolution" http://www.livescience.com/health/060810_evo_rank.html

[4] F.A. Hayek, The Fatal Conceit. The University of Chicago Press, published 1989, page 137

[5] http://www.fff.org/freedom/0401f.asp . This is a link to Dr. Ralph Raico's great series of essays titled "FDR – The Man, the Leader, the Legacy" where the quote can be found. I have yet to research the original location of the quote

[6] Adam Smith's The Theory of Moral Sentiments par. VI.II.42

[7] Lenin, speech given to Party Congress on March 1922.

8 Copyright 2004 by Richard J. Maybury. Reprinted with permission of Richard J. Maybury and Bluestocking Press (www.BluestockingPress.com) from Whatever happened to Justice, revised edition, copyright 2004, (pages 115-116).

[9] Adams, Charles. "Those Dirty Rotten Taxes", The Free Press, 1998 page 24

[10] http://www.youtube.com/watch?v=f6q__0-krUo

[11] Reisman, George. Capitalism: A Treatise on Economics. Published by Jameson Books. ISBN 0-915463-73-3, page 357

[12] http://www.bls.gov/oco/cg/cgs041.htm

[13] http://www.bls.gov/news.release/ecec.nr0.htm

[14] Edwards, Chris. "Federal Pay Outpaces Private-Sector Pay" http://www.cato.org/pubs/tbb/tbb-0605-35.pdf

[15] http://www.independent.org/newsroom/article.asp?id=1176

[16] http://tinyurl.com/2zgmjx

[17] http://tinyurl.com/29bmhg

[18] http://www.microsoft.com/learning/mcp/certified.mspx

[19] http://tinyurl.com/2arqku

[20] Alice Dembner, "Kennedy to Propose Universal Health Care," Boston Globe, January 22, 2004.

[21] Alan J. Borsuk, "Kerry Vows to Fight for Health Care," Milwaukee Journal-Sentinel, September 14, 2004.

[22] from his senate website at http://obama.senate.gov/issues/health_care/index.html

[23] http://tinyurl.com/39qfqj

[24] Michael Antonucci, Tribute for a Light: Public Education Finances and Staffing(Washington ,DS: Education Intelligence Agency, May 2001)

[25] Ronald Bailey's article from Reason Magazine titled "2005 Medical Care forever" http://www.reason.com/news/show/34979.html

[26] Marc Kaufman and Rob Stein's Washington Post article "Record Share of Economy Spent on Health Care" http://tinyurl.com/d79tp

[27] John Carey "Do Cholesterol Drugs Do Any Good?" Business Week Jan 17, 2008 http://www.businessweek.com/magazine/content/08_04/b4068052092994.htm

[28] Ibid.

[29] http://research.stlouisfed.org/fred2/data/M2.txt

[30] http://www.federalbudget.com/

[31] Copyright 2004 by Richard J. Maybury. Reprinted with permission of Richard J. Maybury and Bluestocking Press (www.BluestockingPress.com) from Whatever happened to Justice, revised edition, copyright 2004, (pages 126-127).

[32] F.A. Hayek , "The Road to Serfdom" The University of Chicago Press ISBN 0-226-32061-8 Page 150

[33] Copyright 2004 by Richard J. Maybury. Reprinted with permission of Richard J. Maybury and Bluestocking Press (www.BluestockingPress.com) from Whatever happened to Justice, revised edition, copyright 2004, (page 93).

IV. The Environment

Why we are not running out of natural resources

Another side effect of our fundamental change from self-sufficient tribal world to market process coordinated world is the importance associated with land and natural resources. We are instinctively territorial because land and the food and animals that it contained was of vital importance in our tribal past, but this is not the case today. Wealth and material prosperity needs two things, one is matter/natural resources, and the second is a process that transforms this matter into human usable wealth. In our tribal past nature provided both the matter and the transformation, today nature provides the matter and we, the market-process-coordinated social organism, provide the transformation. With respect to matter/natural resources, they are abundant, we have an entire planet filled with them. Most people are worried that we are running out of natural resources but this is not true. As the complexity and embodied knowledge of our productive structures increases, our ability and ease with which we can transform matter into wealth increases faster and faster. As George Reisman explains:

"There is no limit to the further advances that are possible. Hydrogen, the most abundant element in the universe, may turn out to be an economical source of fuel in the future. Atomic and hydrogen explosives, lasers, satellite detection systems, and, indeed, even space travel itself, open up limitless new possibilities for increasing the supply of economically useable mineral supplies. Advances in mining technology that would make it possible to mine economically at a depth of, say, ten thousand feet, instead of the present much more limited depths, or to mine beneath the oceans, would so increase the portion of the earth's mass accessible to man that all previous supplies of accessible minerals would appear insignificant by comparison. And even at ten thousand feet, man would still, quite literally, just be scratching the surface, because the radius of the earth extends to a depth of four thousand miles."[1]

Our ability to find new sources of energy seems to be increasing faster than the rate at which we consume them. For example, by the end of 1944, crude oil known reserves were 51 billion barrels worldwide. After 58 years, by 2002 we produced 917 billion barrels yet the known reserves had increased over twenty times to 1,266 billion barrels. From 1967 to 2003 2,563 trillion cubic feet of natural gas were produced yet during this time the known reserves increased six-fold from 1,041 in 1967 to 6,076 trillion cubic feet in 2003. In 1950 the world's known coal reserves were 256 billion short tons, from 1950 to 2002, 188 were consumed and at the same time the known reserves increased more than fourfold from 256 to 1,089 billion short tons[2]. It is true of course that at some point in the future if the social organism does not find better ways of producing energy these resources will eventually run out. But why make dire predictions about a future that is at least hundreds of years away based on today's inferior technology and knowledge? What are the chances that our ability to produce usable energy will not be greatly increased in the near future? Reality and history clearly show that our ability to produce energy is increasing faster than the rate at which we use it. One hundred years ago drilling miles deep into the earth and doing the transformations we are profitably capable of doing today were impossible, much less economically viable and profitable, and yet here we are, consuming more energy than ever and with more reserves as well. Today, many people who have no understanding whatsoever of how the market process works, dismiss countless sources of energy simply because they are currently too expensive or not economically viable without realizing that just about every one of today's energy sources was too expensive in the near past.

Our natural resource problems are the result of our basic problem, our inability to recognize the fundamental change from tribal world to market process coordinated social organism. Our unfortunate ignorance of economics. We have evolved with little to no changes in technology. As previously mentioned, for the last 2 million years our technology was limited to a few simple stone tools. We have not evolved to instinctively understand how technology evolves and increases the social organism's ability to transform the world for our benefit. When we think of technology, we think of individual gadgets or tools, but the word technology should have another meaning or perhaps we need a new word to embody the concentration of productive ability that is embodied in entire productive structures/companies made up of many human minds and their tools/computers and so on, each constantly improving their efficiency and therefore improving the efficiency of the whole productive structure. Again, these productive structures and how the market process shapes them via competition, prices, investing, interest rates and all the things we discussed in the economics chapter are new to us and unless we include their proper understanding as part of our weaning process we will continue to destroy the very mechanisms that have led to our own existence.

A perfect example of the social organism's ability to transform matter into wealth is the Japanese human ant-farm. Japan has a total area a little smaller than the state of Montana and it is spread over 4 large islands and many smaller ones totaling over 3000 islands. The terrain is mountainous and volcanic, with relatively few and hard to get natural resources, yet the 130 million Japanese who live there make up the most complex productive order mankind has ever seen. Thousands of tons of matter are shipped to it daily and are transformed into wealth. The Japanese aren't running out of space either, they simply transform matter from some mine somewhere to flooring that they stack on layers as they build up! Africa is full of natural resources and matter yet it lacks the most important ingredient for wealth, a complex human ant-farm capable of transforming that matter into wealth. Or better said at a more fundamental level. The African human ant-farm does not have the laws, the human physics, which allows for a productive human ant-farm to emerge, they do not have Capitalism. They do have Bono though.

Matter and natural resources are abundant, what really makes a difference in our modern world is the human ant-farm's ability to transform this matter into human usable wealth as opposed to nature. What good does it do one to be standing on large deposits of crude oil or any other natural resource if you do not have a productive structure that can transform it into wealth? The planet has had petroleum and other natural resources long before we came to exist, it is thanks to the social organisms combined intelligence and not to their mere existence that natural resources become of any use. "Because the supply of resources provided by nature is one and the same with the supply of matter and energy, the supply of economically useable natural resources is capable of is virtually limitless. It increases as man expands his knowledge of and physical power over the world and universe" [3]

Once one understands economics and the workings of the market process, such zero-sum based fears should begin to go away.

Dealing with pollution

Taking care of the environment is the easiest of all problems to solve yet the toughest to get people to understand. The key to protecting the environment is to privatize as much as possible. All of it, including rivers and oceans. If someone dumps garbage in your house they are violating law #2 (Do not encroach on other persons or their property). If all land is privatized all garbage and pollutants would have to be properly disposed of or stored or transformed into something people don't mind having around. It is that simple. There is no such thing as pollution or environmental problems in privately owned land. If rivers and streams were privately owned the dumping of toxic chemicals in rivers and streams would be a violation of the river owner's property rights and bring about a justified lawsuit. Garbage disposal and storage companies would buy large tracts of cheap and undesirable land and use it to properly store and dispose of our garbage and pollutants and they would always take the necessary precautions so that such garbage and pollutants cannot make it to other people's property. If the pollutants happen to be dangerous chemicals that can get in water supplies and pollute surrounding private property then they would have to be stored in containers raising the cost associated with disposing of such pollutants. This increase in the price associated with disposing of certain pollutants is a signal that carries with it information, the fact that properly disposing of this chemical is hard to do and requires a lot of care and resources. The companies/'productive structures' which use these chemicals will then base their calculations as to whether to use the chemical or not based on this price which embodies all the details relevant to its proper disposal and this would discourage the very use of such pollutants. If the use of such pollutants was a crucial part of some process then it would be included in the final price of whatever process the pollutant is used in and be able to pay for its proper disposal, if not, then the pollutant would not be used. For example, Larry owns a plastic making company and as a byproduct of his plastic making process a very toxic pollutant is created which requires an expensive chemical process that breaks it down into things that aren't harmful. If Larry's plastic is great stuff that people are willing to pay a lot of money for, enough money to also cover the cost of the process of transforming the pollutant byproduct into a non-pollutant, then great, Larry is in business, his productive structure is self sustaining and socially desirable, if not, then Larry needs to find something else to do or wait until a better way of dealing with his pollutant comes along.

An important thing to realize about the proper disposal of pollutants is that their disposal is nothing but a transportation and/or transformation of matter, and that this is something that market-process coordinated human ant-farms are getting better at faster and faster and faster. Every increase in the efficiency of transportation or automation improves our ability to move/store/dispose of garbage/pollutants. And as our ability to transform matter improves, sometimes we can learn to use our old garbage for new things like in the cases of profitable recycling. This is why the cleanest and most environmentally sound places in the world also happen to be the most economically advanced. Increasingly productive human ant-farms find it easier and easier to clean up after themselves. All garbage is just matter that has been transformed from a state that is useful to us to one that is less useful or uneconomically usable at a certain time. But as time passes by and our ability to transform matter to our benefit increases garbage will eventually become a usable natural resource.

Global warming

Global warming is over-hyped. I am not going to discuss or give my own scientific counterarguments against pro-doomsday global warming studies. I know very little about climatology and there are countless of books that already do a great job of using solid science to counter the global warming hysteria . What I do feel confident in discussing is the social organism's ability to adapt its productive order to a changing environment. Let's assume the very worst possible case. Let's assume that it is true that human beings are a new factor that increases the earth's temperature in ways that have never happened before and that this increase in temperature is something that will have substantial detrimental effects in the future. The first thing we need to ask is, how fast is this happening? If we are doing it, it is obviously not happening fast enough to bring about a quick extinction to mankind. To my limited knowledge, even scientists who feel like we are bringing about detrimental climate changes, the drastic changes would be at least a couple of centuries away. According to the Intergovernmental Panel on Climate Change(IPCC), surface temperature readings have increased about 1.1° F over the last 100 years. Let's assume that this rate even increases threefold to 3 degrees every 100 years. That gives us 300 years to learn how to shape the world around us to our advantage given an average temperature that is 9 degrees higher than what it currently is. Even if we increase the temperature that much, it just means that the colder places like Greenland, northern Canada, and gigantic parts of northern Asia which were part of the former soviet union now become more fertile and better suited for human life.

A hotter planet does not necessarily mean a less hospitable one. Sure some habitats might get too hot and the life that currently exists there might diminish but new life will spring up in the new more hospitable areas. Life on this planet has endured countless of drastic environmental changes, as recently as our last ice age from 70,000 to 11,500 years ago Greenland's surface temperature changed 15° F in just 10 years. Things like higher carbon dioxide levels which many feel are causing the global warming also help plants grow better.

As I write this book I am living in Miami, a place that would have been inhospitable to the millions who live here before the human ant-farm was able to easily transform the environment in a way that was hospitable to human life, by easily creating structures like buildings where there was only swamps before. And by far the most important of these transformations is air conditioning! Thanks to heating and air conditioning we can transform the environment so that many previously inhospitable places are now comfortable locations for us and I am sure that by the time the earth becomes an inferno we will have found it so easy to transform our environment to our liking that it wouldn't be a problem at all, and that is assuming that it will become an inferno. It all comes down to this, based on my understanding of the market process and its ability to give an efficient and highly adaptable order to society, a fundamental piece of knowledge which is missing from virtually ALL so called experts in predicting the future conditions of mankind, I believe that our ability to transform the earth's environment to our liking will easily outpace whatever truly negative impact we might be having on the environment. And just like our ability to find new sources of energy and ways of transforming matter increases faster than our thirst for them so will our ability to deal with whatever detrimental impact we might be causing before it becomes a serious nuisance.

The importance of private property needs to be stressed again. Respect for the two laws, "Do all you have agreed to do" and "Do not encroach on other persons or their property" are what turn chaotic little human ants into the world's most powerful supercomputer and transformation device. The last one hundred years have seen the human ant-farm transform itself with amazing speed and this has been greatly hampered by two world wars that destroyed a tremendous amount of productive order. Then Communism kept billions in Russia and China and the rest of the world in economic chaos unable to integrate themselves with and contribute to the social organism. Obviously it is impossible to predict what the world would be like today should the great wars and Communism have never occurred but at the very least I think a safe assumption is that if the market process would have had three times as many human brains and resources under its control for a period of time 3 times as long the world would have progressed into the future at least 10 times faster. If this would have been the case I seriously doubt that we'd be concerned with global warming today and we'd be more concerned about terraforming and planning vacations on the moon.

Having briefly discussed the solution to our worst case scenario, let us come back to reality and focus on what is more likely the case, that things are nowhere near as bad as the so called "experts"/enviromorons/economorons like former vice president Al Gore suggest. Let's once again refer to economist George Reisman:

"Perhaps of even greater significance is the continuous and profound distrust of science and technology that the environmental movement displays. The environmental movement maintains that science and technology cannot be relied upon to build a safe atomic power plant, to produce a pesticide that is safe, or even to bake a loaf of bread that is safe, if that loaf of bread contains chemical preservatives. When it comes to global warming, however, it turns out there is one area in which the environmental movement displays the most breathtaking confidence in the reliability of science and technology, an area in which, until recently, no one—not even the staunchest supporters of science and technology—had ever thought to exert very much confidence at all. The one thing, the environmentalist movement holds, that science and technology can do so well that we are entitled to have unlimited confidence in them is forecast the weather—for the next 100 years!

It is after all, supposedly on the basis of a weather forecast that we are being asked to abandon the Industrial Revolution or, as it is euphemistically put, "to radically and profoundly change the way we live"—to our enormous material detriment."[4]

If one understands that the progress of mankind is the cure for any global warming concerns, it becomes obvious to see how the major economic bottlenecks that are proposed by environmentalists, who are even more ignorant of economics than the already ignorant politicians and public, are the biggest harm to the very environment they want to protect. Ignorance of the market process is by far the greatest threat to our supply of natural resources, global warming, and just about every other thing human beings need to prosper. It seems like most "experts" fall into the category of scientists who see things like predation in the biological world, and make the same mistake Marx made by comparing the biological predation to a nonexistent predation of the working class by the capitalists. And also the constructivist view that the economy needs 'planning'. In that sense most scientists are as wrong as the public, they just think they are smarter because they can write about or compare this predation better than average folks. But just like all the experts were wrong about communism and unbelievably, the 20th century's greatest economist, Ludwig von Mises, could not even get a paid position in the US as a professor, the mass of scientists are once again blind to how the market process will solve our environmental concerns. The easy to absorb and instinctively appealing yet erroneous ideas like communism, which spread so easily amongst the public, are once again drowning out the powerful truths expounded by the likes of Mises, Hayek, Hazlitt, etc.

The conservation of species

Many people increasingly see human beings as a cancer that is growing and destroying the planet and selfishly and "unfairly" killing off other species. But this is not true, and the root of this mistake is due to our belief that we are somehow apart from nature and also to extending our egalitarian instincts to all living things, and of course, the usual culprit, our lack of an understanding of how the market process creates the social order. Once again it is important to keep in mind how flexible our minds are, we can brainwash ourselves to love and care greatly about fellow human beings but also things like our cars, favorite shirts, teddy bears, pets and especially for some biologists and nature lovers, all living things like bugs, grasses and so on, some of which unfortunately go extinct due to our flourishing. We are a new life form, not just a new kind of big-brained ape, we are parts of the new social organism. And species growing and changing the environment at the expense of others is fair game as far as natural selection is concerned. Actually, everything is fair game for natural selection. Our transition from social animal in our tribal world to market process coordinated social organism is as significant in the evolution of life and the continuous increase in complexity on this planet as the transition from single-celled to multicellular life which occurred about a billion years ago. Many people who absorb the environmentalist 'cultural book' might love the way beavers transform their environment when they build dams in rivers, yet they find our cities, skyscrapers, soaring planes, chemicals, pesticides, and world of concrete and pavement to be an environmental disaster and are completely unaware that these transformations of the world around us are precisely what create a better environment for human beings. One free of snakes, rotting and decaying animals and the countless microbes which would be praying on us.

I went through a huge biology/'nature-loving' phase which motivated me live off of my savings and go into debt while going back to college fulltime to study it. I can relate to people who love insects and grasses almost as much as human beings. Natural selection has created every creature to be so unique, with such a wonderful evolutionary story to tell. I love biology! One can even feel like other species besides human beings are sort of innocent because whatever seemingly "evil" things they need to do to survive are not done out of apparent malice like it might seem amongst us humans. Our wars and nuclear weapons can do so much damage; we could easily destroy the whole world and its amazing complexity which has taken natural selection billions of years to create. But even if this were the case, the evolutionary story of life has had many drastic extinctions and setbacks in the past, and perhaps a billion or two years in the future there will be big-brained roaches who reach our present level of civilization, it would just be an unfortunate change that I don't want to happen either. But preventing the continued economic progress of mankind is not the way to go about helping other species. Other species need us. We are the species that will take the life/order/complexity we have evolved here to other places like the nearby planets and who knows what the future might hold. It is just a matter of time before some asteroid or other major natural disaster takes us out and quite possibly all life in this planet. Assuming there are other planets with life out there, they too will all need a human-being-like species that will also become a social organism and be able to overcome inevitable cosmic disasters. Not only is it great that we are alive right now, but we are part of that special cosmological event where life consciously wakes up and is able to protect itself from cosmological disasters and continue to expand its order. We need to realize that when we work and trade and therefore integrate ourselves with the social organism we are becoming something wonderful, much more unique than the species that will die off and weren't able to achieve our order. Amongst the many good things we will be doing for all life is that thanks to rapid increases in biotechnology, within a relatively short time we will be able to sequence the genomes of any species we stumble upon with ease, helping save each specie's amazing evolutionary journey should they be displaced by our progress. Obviously the environments where such creatures have evolved is in many ways as important as their genomes but I think they'd still appreciate our effort. Perhaps someday in the future we could recreate the habitats of species that are dying now and bring them back to life. We are the saviors of all life in this planet, not the destroyers. We are natural selection's latest and greatest creation. As Spencer said:

> "Instead of civilization being artificial, it is a part of nature; all of a piece with the development of the embryo or the unfolding of a flower. The modifications mankind has undergone, and are still undergoing, result from a law underlying the whole organic creation."

Actually, I shouldn't speak so soon, we have all kinds of problems right now but all that is needed is a change in our 'cultural books', just a few simple ideas going "viral" on the Internet.

We really shouldn't get all worked up over species dying. Every time a species dies you are giving a helping hand to whatever that species ate. For the most part all that happens is that the balance of life/order changes, that's all. Besides, if we slow down the progress of mankind we will be denying the right of the countless of species that have adapted to leeching off of us to continue their evolution. By preventing the further expansion of human beings we are also preventing the further evolution of things like roaches and the various diseases that pray on us. What about their rights and intrinsic value? I love roaches, my parents tell me that they used to be one of my favorite treats as a young toddler.

Many people would also love to own some of these dying species but our governments make owning such animals illegal. If people were allowed to own the various monkeys, tigers, and so on that are going extinct it would never happen. Sure a tiger can run away from time to time and kill a loved one, but people would take the necessary precautions. The market process would discover the best way to make all of these things happen.

Conclusion

As if the steady march towards Socialism/Communism and therefore socioeconomic hardship via economic ignorance wasn't enough of a problem, the environmentalist movement and its ignorance of economics is yet another disastrous blow that humanity can't really afford. It is truly scary to see how fast the world's governments are being pressured into putting tremendous roadblocks to the only thing that can really save us, economic/technological progress. Freedom.

Having said all this with respect to the environment, I am not saying that the world is as simple as just following our two laws or that I am against all government regulation, especially as it relates to air pollution and things like that. I don't really care about figuring out which regulations might be tolerable or if maybe I want to fight for 0 regulations. I am not concerned about these things, because once enough people understand these important economic concepts I am sure that great solutions will emerge. And even if we don't come up with the perfect answers, whatever solutions or compromises humanity stumbles upon should easily solve our problems and enable use to continue on what should be an easy path to prosperity.

---

[1] Reisman, George. Capitalism: A Treatise on Economics. Published by Jameson Books. ISBN 0-915463-73-3, page 64.

[2] Energy: The Master Resource. By Robert L. Bradley, Jr. and Richard W. Fulmer. Published by Kendall/Hunt Publishing Company, ISBN 0-7575-1169-4, page 88-89

[3] Reisman, George. Capitalism: A Treatise on Economics. Published by Jameson Books. ISBN 0-915463-73-3, page 64

[4] Ibid. page 88.

V. Cultural Evolution

The intellectual backbone of this chapter is based on the ideas most commonly associated with Austrian School economist F.A. Hayek, but the concepts discussed here should not be lumped in with the Austrian School label and much less so with Dr. Paul. I want to make this distinction clear because there can be many people who accept the purely economics related discussions and might not accept what we will be discussing here, especially since this chapter looks at the evolution of religion.

Cultural evolution. Hayekian selection introduced

Human beings can be said to be made up of two books. One is our genome which contains the genes or sentences that describe how to create our biological order, and the other is our "cultural book" that fills our minds with language, concepts and the knowledge that ultimately shapes our understanding of the world and the actions we take based on it. This knowledge and the actions that people take based on it has an effect on the productivity and growth of societies and therefore their survival. If the rules and customs of society A lead to more growth or the better discovery and spread of productive knowledge compared to other societies or human ant-farms, then there is a higher chance that society A's rules and customs spread to other societies. Let's go over a few examples.

Let's make the safe assumption that men are better hunters than women and that women are just as good at gathering food as men. In our stereotypical tribal societies the men would hunt and the women would gather food, this rudimentary division of labor would be the most productive and therefore sustain the most growth and prosperity for the tribe. Let's assume that tribe A's traditional customs or rules divided its hunting parties as just previously described and tribe B had a religious rule or custom that mandated that women had an equal representation in hunting and because of this the tribe would end up with as much gathered fruits(because both men and women are equally good at this task) but with less meat(because a mixed sex hunting party would do worse than an all male hunting party), in other words, it would produce less than the optimal arrangement of having the men hunt while the women gathered. Given that tribe B would produce less than tribe A, tribe B would not be able to nourish as many mouths as tribe A, it would have a harder time dealing with famines and suffer other hardships, the point is that it would be overtaken by tribe A and eventually tribe B and its custom(rule) of having the men and women do the hunting equally would disappear. This is our first and highly simplified example of how culture contains knowledge that leads to a more productive arrangement of human beings. Given that groups are ultimately competing in our tribal zero-sum world, whether it be by conquest or having people migrating to the more successful groups, or copying and importing the rules that led to more productivity, the rules/customs/traditions/concepts that lead to more productivity will eventually spread and replace the rules/customs/traditions/concepts which did not lead to as much growth. The members of tribe A could be no different genetically than members of tribe B, natural selection is no longer selecting on the characteristics of the individuals themselves but on the rules of conduct/customs/traditions/concepts that lead to the more efficient and productive arrangements of human beings. The rules and customs we follow that give our societies order and ultimately help us be more productive than we would otherwise be without these rules, are not stored in our genes, they live in our culture and traditions, in our society, especially in our religions, in our written books, and most importantly for our modern societies, in our laws. This new type of selection, which acts on the rules or customs of groups of people as opposed to the people themselves and their genes is what we refer to as Hayekian selection.

Societies are made up of hundreds or thousands of such cultural rules and norms. We have marriage customs, customs about what is acceptable behavior, how to deal with people who do not follow such rules and many more. Every single rule or law has an effect in the productivity and growth and therefore survival of the social order. Given that a society is likely to have hundreds or thousands of such rules it is hard to know the particular impact of any one of them when considering the overall growth and stability of a society. Most of the rules and customs serve to restrict the selfish behavior of individual members of society, behaviors that although beneficial to the individual might weaken the group. For example, I cannot think of a single culture in today's world that does not have some religious edict/law/rule/moral value against theft. Why is this the case? Theft is something that in the short run benefits the person doing the stealing but leads to problems like lower productivity and retaliatory violence that weakens the group. Such a society would be naturally selected against and quickly cease to exist along with its lack of a rule against theft.

What about rules and customs relating to the punishment of crimes? What is the optimal punishment for certain crimes? If a man steals and he is killed it might prevent many acts of theft but killing people decreases the number of people in your group and all the productivity that this person might contribute to it in the future. If the steal-and-die policy results in many deaths the economic impact to the group might be bigger than the gains made by having less theft. How do we know what is the optimal punishment, the one that creates the best mixture of social stability and growth? One can only speculate as to how each custom grew or was born, and what exact impact on the social order it had but those are the small details one needs not be concerned about and are lost in our evolutionary past. The important thing is to understand that cultural norms/rules/laws impact the growth and spread of a society and that what at often times seem like silly laws or beliefs exist because they might have helped the group grow in ways that one cannot easily trace or understand. This last point will become especially important when we look at the evolution and impact of religions in a second.

What about nudity? Some people may ask "Why should I go to jail for being naked in public if I'm not harming anyone?" Why is it that the modern world has taboos or laws against public nudity? Sex is very important, we are all descendents of people that made reproduction a top priority, if the social rules and circumstances do not prevent people from spending all of their time and resources trying to compete with each other at the game of reproduction we might be stuck in our more tribal and barbaric past. You can't build a civilization when you have to spend most of your energy fighting over females. Sex and the competition and jealousy and all the turmoil that can come from it can weaken a group from within and lead to a less stable social order and less productivity and growth. Perhaps one of the benefits of covering up is that it led people to be less preoccupied with sex and that in turn led them to take on more productive activities which led to a more productive society which eventually outgrew and replaced other societies and their naked ways.

The reason why marriage for most of the world's cultures is a bond between a man and a woman and is often meant for life is because that particular arrangement might have been one of the key rules that led to increased productivity for the societies that enforced such values. Over our evolution we might have gone from an Alpha-male-type pattern where a single strong man does his best to shut out everyone else from the mating game, to our one man one woman deal. Too many women per man can leave a lot of angry guys around which can lead to internal conflict and so on. But sometimes it can work too. We have polygamous families where people are very happy. And in today's world we are seeing the family structure disintegrate into I-don't-know-what-just-yet. What I am brining up here is not to say which rules are best for society or even explain the effects of such rules. We just want to go over examples to train our minds to understand the way this simple selective process works.

What about prostitution? Prostitution is allowed in some places and not others and it is punishable by death in some Muslim countries. Prostitution, or again, pretty much anything related to sex just like our nudity example can be a source of fierce internal competition and conflict which can weaken a group. Or maybe not, maybe it helps release sexual frustrations which would be expressed in more socially detrimental ways and therefore it would be a positive thing. The effects of such rules on social growth and stability are often hard to predict and their impact can be dependent on man varying factors.

Today many of us look at the "bad" way single mothers were treated in the past with a little contempt and it is becoming increasingly politically incorrect to induce any shame on single mothers. This is probably a first for mankind. "The Scarlet Letter" comes to mind, a novel set in Puritan New England in the 17th century where the main character, a woman by the name of Hester Prynne, is made to wear the scarlet(red) letter "A" on her clothes to identify her as an adulteress so that she could bear public scorn for her adultery. Why was contempt for adultery part of people's cultural values? The answer seems instinctively obvious to most of us but let's briefly go over it from an evolutionary perspective. A woman who is raising a child on her own means that there is a man out there who does not have to spend part of his resources to raising this child so he has additional resources to have more kids with other women, this provides an advantage to this man over other men which breaks the equality and egalitarianism that we have sort of evolved to feel comfortable with. A woman raising a child by herself is also more likely to fall on hard economic times and need charity. Human beings have evolved with the capacity to be charitable and caring, we can easily calculate that the tables could be turned any day, but we hate being charitable in a way that we know benefits or relieves someone of their duties to their advantage and to our detriment, which would be the case for the man who does not take care of the child. Natural selection does not favor suckers. Because of this we put social pressure via shame/killing/stoning/etc. depending on your culture and the times, to create the kinds of incentives that will ensure women do not give in to their desire to have an adulterous relationship. Widows are obviously treated with charity because we know that their bad situation is one caused by true misfortune. And for a similar reasoning is why we force fathers to pay child support.

Why do we have this concept of "bad words"? What makes saying them so inappropriate? Even though it is actions that ultimately affect the world around us, words can change our mental ambience/setting/context and lead to thoughts which increase the probability of socially detrimental action. Again, anything related to sex fills our minds with imagery or incentives which increase the chances of sexual competition and all the instability that that can bring and this is why a lot of our bad words are related to sex. Besides bad words, proper gentleman in the traditional/conservative sense are to shun being loud or calling too much attention to themselves because this breaks our socially enforced egalitarianism. Again, all kinds of little things which can lead to differences in wealth, status, or anything that cannot be shared equally are 'egalitarianized' via our morals and social pressures. In more primitive cultures members of the tribe who do not show the proper level of resentment for not having shared or being too selfish would receive public shame or even be made social outcasts of the entire tribe. The word 'gentleman' briefly comes to mind. In a tribal world, such a word and the meaning that was traditionally associated with it would have done little good, in the tribal world we all wanted to be warriors, and being a warrior is something that appeals to our instincts much more than being a gentleman.

So to briefly recap. Our genomes are the books that describe our biological traits but our culture is like a book too, it is a book that is composed of the language, concepts, rules, traditions and ideologies that our brains assimilate as we grow up in our societies. Human beings are animals that depend on both books and have always lived with both. Obviously without our genome and genes we wouldn't exist but without culture and language we wouldn't exist either. Every human being has been raised by other human beings and has absorbed a language and countless cultural concepts that have led to enough productivity to be old enough to find a mate and reproduce. This unbroken chain of cultural absorption by our brains is as true and significant as the sexual intercourse which creates/transfers our genomes.

The easiest way to understand the role of our "cultural book" is to imagine what it would be like for a person to grow up without any human contact whatsoever. What would such a person be like? The closest thing to this is what are called feral children, children that grew up with little or no human contact. There are few known cases of such children and an even smaller number of well documented ones. The last one I am aware of is that of Sujit Kumar[1] who was confined to a chicken coop during early childhood until he was 8 years old and moved to a nursing home where due to his weird and aggressive behavior he was mostly confined to his room for another 22 years. The mimicking process which we go through as our brains absorb culture and language had Sujit making chicken sounds, pecking at his food and making other chicken-like mannerisms. He was not what we would classify as a rational human being. The environment around him which his mind absorbed did not train his brain to act in accordance with what most of us would consider to be reason.

Contrary to what many of us might instinctively think, the ability to reason is not something that we are born with, it is something our brains are trained to achieve. As we grow up our brains begin to interact and absorb our "cultural book" whose language, rules, traditions, concepts, morals, etc, can be seen as its pages and sentences. It begins with our parents and the language/rules/morals/traditions/concepts they teach us.

The constant interaction with them teaches our mind to think in ways that we consider to be more or less "rational" and our brains are obviously very good at picking this up, but "reason" and "rational" are concepts that do not have a concrete definition. Our actions are only considered "rational" from the perspective of the ideology or "cultural book" of the people judging whether an action is rational or not. For an atheist praying to what he considers a non-existing God is an irrational action yet for someone who does believe in God and feels like prayer is a way to reach him praying is a rational action. I hope that perhaps by the time the reader is finished with this book, people that do not understand the market process and act in ways that prevent it from working will be seen as unreasonable and irrational.

Culture is not designed by "rational" human beings. Most of the content of our "cultural books" was created by as almost as blind a process as that which shaped our biological genomes. Our "cultural books", the language/rules/concepts that they are composed of, are like the lemons out of which our brains can make lemonade with. Little by little, concepts are picked up, others are forgotten/erased, but our minds are limited to using the concepts they grew up with to piece together their thoughts, actions, and understanding of the world. As Karl Marx put it: "It is not the consciousness of men that determines their existence, but on the contrary their social existence determines their consciousness"[2]

The special role of language, which is one of the most important set of pages in our cultural books, needs at least a paragraph or two even in such a short talk-about-everything book. Language is not just about expressing ourselves, conveying and absorbing information, it is much more important than that. Language helps classify and give an efficient order to the information and concepts that a brain learns. For example, how do you think? I "talk" to my self in my head, or talk to my "conscience", or also envision myself talking to other people. Imagine a language that did not make use of nouns. How would this affect our ability to think and process information? Instead of easily being able to identify and recall a "spear" and "deer" and combine them into more complex and useful thoughts like "throw the spear at dear", we might have to use many adjectives in place of the noun. For example to refer to a spear one might think of "long, thin, sharp, killer" and "throw the spear at deer" might have to be expressed as follows "throw the long, thin, sharp, killer at fast, brown, furry, jumping". This "nounless" way of thinking is obviously much more cumbersome and requires more brainpower and speed to convey and piece together productive thoughts and ideas. What if we didn't have the concepts of nouns, or adjectives, or verbs? I get a headache just trying to think about this. As Hazlitt tells us:

> "[referring to man in general]He could not think at all(or only at the level of a chimpanzee) if he did not inherit from the society and civilization in which he was born the priceless gift of an already created language. Without this he would not only be unable to reason logically, he would have nothing worthy to be called a "concept". He could not frame a sentence; he could not even name things. We think in words, even in conversations. Our language, concepts, and logic are part of the social inheritance of all of us" ... "As the great nineteenth-century philologist Max Mueller put it: "To think is to speak low. To speak is to think aloud". The corollary of this is tremendously important. A man with a scant vocabulary will almost certainly be a weak thinker. The richer and more copious one's vocabulary and the greater one's awareness of the fine distinctions and subtle nuances of meaning, the more fertile and precise is likely to be one's thinking. Knowledge of things and knowledge of the words for them grow together. If you do not know the words, you can hardly know the thing. We are told that the Tasmanian method of counting is: "One, two, plenty." This points to a very significant truth. Man could not even count, certainly not beyond the number of fingers on his hands, until he had invented names and symbols for numbers. For in speaking of the need for language for thought, we must, of course, include symbols as an integral part of language. It is amazing how recent in human history are even the Arabic numerals, the denary system, and elementary signs for addition, subtraction, multiplication, and division..."[3]

The bottom line is that language is not just crucial for conveying and absorbing information but it is also a key element in our ability to think period.

Today we can find people following many "irrational" practices like astrology, and all kinds of superstitions. These things are just part of the cultural books which people absorb and they inevitably use. These people believe that how they see the world is reasonable and they might "reasonably" add new concepts or customs to their "cultural books" based on their current understanding of the world. For example, someone in a given culture might hold the common belief that God creates storms to punish society when they have not been pleasing him, and they might also believe that sacrificing virgins pleases God, then they might "reasonably" sacrifice some virgins in order to show their reverence for God after being hit by a storm. But as societies mold their "cultural books", even by what some might consider to be reason along the lines of our previous example, the real designing of culture is done by natural selection, which selects those human ant-farms whose customs/laws/concepts/'cultural books' just happened to lead to a more powerful/stable order. Just like genes are blindly selected based on the fitness they provide for the organisms that are built by them, cultural rules and concepts are naturally selected based on the strength of the social order they help produce.

Our modern world is not where it is today thanks to the reason and great thinking of specific individuals, the whole reason why these "great" men have been able to make such important contributions has a lot more to do to the cultural environment they inherited than their individual brains. There is no way Einstein, Hayek, or Newton would have been able to make the contributions they did if it weren't for the tremendous contribution in terms of language/technology/concepts they inherited from the environment they were born into. Supposedly Newton spent more time involved in various theological subjects and alchemy than he did making his great contributions, this was a sign of the times. Einstein too was a sign of his time, and his very smart and genius brain and what must have been a great ability to reason did not help prevent him from falling for Socialism/Communism. On his essay entitled "Why Socialism" Einstein provides a recipe for more death and suffering that any benefits his breakthroughs in physics might have given us:

> "Technological progress frequently results in more unemployment rather than in an easing of the burden of work for all. The profit motive, in conjunction with competition among capitalists, is responsible for an instability in the accumulation and utilization of capital which leads to increasingly severe depressions. Unlimited competition leads to a huge waste of labor...I am convinced there is only one way to eliminate these grave evils, namely through the establishment of a socialist economy, accompanied by an educational system which would be oriented toward social goals. In such an economy, the means of production are owned by society itself and are utilized in a planned fashion. A planned economy, which adjusts production to the needs of the community, would distribute the work to be done among all those able to work and would guarantee a livelihood to every man, woman, and child."[4]

This statement is obviously a recipe for the destruction of the market process and modern civilization.

It is thanks to our upbringing and interactions with other people that our minds are molded/brainwashed/programmed to think "rationally", and therefore it is only after we have absorbed a "cultural book" that is as old as our own evolution, and whose content in terms of language/laws/concepts has been shaped by natural selection that we can "reason" what might be called new cultural rules/laws/concepts. As Hayek puts it:

> "Learning how to behave is more the source than the result of insight, reason and understanding. Man is not born wise, rational and good, but has to be

taught to become so. It is not our intellect that created our morals; rather human interactions governed by our morals make possible the growth of reason and those capabilities associated with it."[5]

In today's modern industrialized countries what we consider to be reasonable thought is much more common than it would have been 20,000 years ago. We have many documented instances where early European anthropologists made contact with culturally primitive societies and they were treated as gods and so on. These people's level of rationality was based not on their brain's ability to reason but on the concepts and ideas which existed in the cultural books they absorbed as they grew up. Fortunately for most of us these days there is little doubt that taking a child from any of these primitive cultures and giving him a 21st century modern cultural book would allow it to be as reasonable as any one of us, and taking a child from our world and giving him a more primitive cultural book would greatly diminish his ability to reason as judged by our 21st century standards.

As our brains have evolved so has our ability to follow and absorb cultural rules/concepts, in other words, "cultural books" with more numerous and more complex customs and concepts that helped us maintain a more stable and productive social order. We are also not direct descendents of a single culture. "Cultural books" are constantly updating themselves as people stumble upon new rules or spread them into other cultures, and sometimes entire "cultural books" are wiped out in a war in which case one "cultural book" completely destroys another. "Cultural books" are best described by understanding our religions and their importance which we will deal with in the next section.

It is thanks to the great flexibility of our brains that we have been able to adapt our behavior to that which is required to follow the rules and customs that have made us more productive and therefore have led to our advanced social order. The farther back we go in the evolution of man the more rigid and inflexible our ability to alter our behavior was and this was due to our inferior and less flexible brains. If your behavior is very instinctual, in other words, more dictated by your genes, then any changes in such behavior that can lead to more productivity have to come about through the slow biological evolutionary process that alters genes, a process that can take thousands/millions of years. But if you have a very flexible brain that can quickly learn and change your behavior then you will be able to enjoy the benefits of increased productivity that come from following rules of conduct that lead to a better coordinated and productive society. How many of us have not liked being told what to do by our bosses, or have had to keep our cool when dealing with impatient customers? We hate following the very rules that help keep our world orderly. We hate waiting for green lights, waiting in lines at the supermarket, having to wait while the elevator stops at other people's floors, not being able to say exactly what we want in any given situation, paying bills on time, stopping when she says no, being on time and many more things. Our inherited instincts from the small group/tribal world are to rebel and to always want to do what is in our immediate best interest yet we are human beings, we are special in the sense that not only are we a lot smarter but we can sort of 'override' our instincts to follow rules which although we might not like, are responsible for the social order that nourishes our very lives. Again, no one consciously planned or designed all the cultural values which we follow and out of which our social order emerges. For reasons and circumstances that are as lost in our evolutionary past as the environmental factors which selected our genes, our cultural values/rules/customs emerged and our adherence to them inadvertently led to the growth and survival of our human ant-farms. As Hayek mentions:

> "Constraints on the practices of the small group, it must be emphasized and repeated, are hated. For as we shall see, the individual following them, even though he depend on them for life, does not and usually cannot understand how they function or how they benefit him."..."Disliking these constraints so much, we hardly can be said to have selected them; rather, these constraints selected us: they enabled us to survive."[6]

This is what growing up is all about, it is about programming/molding our flexible brains into learning all of these rules and rewiring them to be as happy as possible while doing so. We might not have a hard time reasoning how waiting in line at the supermarket helps give the world a more peaceful and productive order which benefits us all, but when it comes to losing our jobs to competition(especially when it is from another country/"tribe"), not being able to afford things that others can, and all of those things that go counter to our innate egalitarianism, yet are the foundations of our modern human ant-farms and we owe our very lives to, we definitely need more weaning. I hope that soon a man will not be considered an adult until he understands the market process. Our degree of brainwashing changes from person to person, some might get angry and honk at someone who cuts them off, yet others will pray that night so that God can fix whatever problem had the bad driver in such a rush, our brains are very flexible. Even if you could teach a monkey how to perform simple productive tasks, would you be able to train him in such a way that he would not run around and chase other monkeys and go "tribal" or "barbaric" from time to time? Maybe, put it would probably be a lot harder than with a human. Actually, monkeys are genetically very close to us and they too are very adaptable but obviously not as much as we are but I still wouldn't count them out for many "human" tasks.

The flexibility of our minds needs to be stressed again. A properly functioning human being is made in the womb and then the brain is constantly being rewired as the child grows. When we are young our brains are more flexible and better able to mold themselves as they learn whatever language and symbolism the surrounding culture contains. Our mind also learns when it should give itself positive reinforcement by learning when to sort of release the necessary 'happy chemicals' and other mental changes that lead to the feelings of happiness/pleasure/well-being. In other words, while some things like sexual orgasms are pleasurable by pure biology, as we grow up we also teach our brains to trigger pleasure/happiness by training it with positive reinforcement, and by doing this we brainwash/teach/rewire our brains to trigger happiness while doing things that would cause discomfort if it weren't for our previous positive reinforcement training/brainwashing/rewiring. For example, we are successful to varying degrees at enjoying things like sharing, helping others, even donating organs and raising other people's children, but most importantly, resisting the temptation to break the rules upon which the social order is built.

In a way our brains work following a very simple pattern, they make us happy when we do things they think are good for us, they cause discomfort when we do things they think are not good for us and they also causes discomfort in order to induce us to do things that they consider to be in our best interest. When we stand in line at the supermarket we need patience and restraint in order to overcome the desire to just skip people to get to the front of the line or just walk out with the goods. We need patience and restraint in order to follow and act according to the many rules we follow. There is always a little bit of discomfort when we restrain our behavior in order to follow these rules and this pain has to be bearable and manageable. When we envision a semi-tribal man, a caveman or some older ape-like ancestor we envision them as being brutes, brutes are not supposed to be patient and able to control their impulses. As we grow up, we learn to be patient and to master the art of restraint, we adapt our minds to be able to put up with patience and restraint in a way that does not cause as much discomfort. As parents we play a crucial role in this brainwashing. We reward the good actions by greeting them with smiles and other mannerisms associated with happiness. And we act with disgust and punish the bad actions. It takes a while to brainwash/wean a child to follow rules whose resulting actions he may not consider to be in his best interest and therefore might cause psychological discomfort which can lead to the usual temper tantrums, but eventually the brainwashing works. We learn to use reason, to be able to see how by following certain rules we can navigate the world in a way that gets us closer to achieving our goals. Some of us have been brainwashed better than others. Some people seem to enjoy being 'nice' and patient more than others. This ability to adapt our minds to be happy under many circumstances, especially while following rules that contradict or restrain a possible course of action that is seemingly very much in our best interest, like theft, seems like an important evolutionary adaptation.

The best examples of how cultural evolution work can be seen in the workings and evolution of our religions which we turn to next.

Understanding religion

Human beings have evolved to deal with other sentient beings, mostly fellow human beings and to a lesser extent other animals. This anthropomorphism, or attribution of human motivation or behavior to things that have nothing to do with human beings comes naturally to us, and so does the desire to relate events and the order/complexity we see in the world to sentient beings. In Hayek's words "This view is rooted originally in a deeply ingrained propensity of primitive thought to interpret all regularity to be found in phenomena anthropomorphically, as the result of the design of a thinking mind."[7] This is why simpler, more primitive religions have many animals and plants and natural phenomena(rain/wind/sun) for gods. There have been as many religions in the past as there have been isolated groups of people. Prior to the invention of writing these religions could not have been very complex because they were limited by the amount of information that could be passed down orally through the generations. Once religious thought could be written down the rules and stories could be more elaborate and more convincing to other brains looking to make sense out of the world. Having a holy book is pretty impressive. Regardless of how religious thought first emerged, religions are naturally selected for based on their ability to spread through the minds of people and the productive social order they help create and grow. So what are religions? After having discussed the evolution and importance of social norms/rules/customs/laws(Hayekian selection) it should be easy to realize that religions are identifiable collections of such rules. Religions are "cultural books".

Let's discuss some hypothetical as well as real major religions and see how the rules and values they preach and are composed of affect their growth and social order. Armed with an understanding of how the market process builds the most powerful human ant-farms, we can look for the kinds of rules in society that lead to a smooth working of the market process. Religions whose rules are favorable to a smoothly functioning market process will gain the benefits of having a more progressive social order. And by progressive I mean a society that constantly discovers new and more productive knowledge and grows in terms of population and technology faster than others. These rules are of course, respect for private property and individual freedom.

All doomsday type of religions where their members have to kill themselves to meet their God and so on cease to exist thanks to the piety of their members, so natural selection takes care of them pretty quickly. Others have such economically disastrous edicts that they are doomed to keep their society in backwardness and are quickly overtaken by more economically sound religions. Imagine a religion where people believe that once they died they needed to be buried with all of their possessions because they will need them in the afterlife. Instead of leaving behind wealth that could be used as a building block for the future, each generation has to reproduce all the wealth that people essentially destroy by burring it with them when they die. This would have a huge economic impact and make this society progress through time at a much slower rate than others and eventually suffer the consequences.

A religion that describes a world where your destiny is predetermined would have a detrimental effect on the motivation of its members to strive for better things since it is more likely that many will figure "why bother?". A God that is very involved in the real world also would lead to a reduced incentive to produce. For example, if you strongly believe that your piety and reverence for God is the determining factor in your spiritual as well as material well-being because God will just bring you wealth if you are good and pious, then you might spend more time praying and doing things you feel might please God as opposed to working and producing real wealth. How a man sees himself in the world is also an important factor. For example, in Christianity man is seen as God's ultimate creation, made in His image and the world is created by God for man to use for his purposes. As we learn from Genesis 1:26 "And God said, Let us make man in our image, after our likeness: and let them have dominion over the fish of the sea, and over the fowl of the air, and over the cattle, and over all the earth, and over every creeping thing that creepeth upon the earth.". Now compare this fundamental Judeo-Christian scripture and the effect it has on the minds that absorb it to other views like Hinduism where man is not God's ultimate creation but perhaps not much better than any other living thing and a monkey's soul might be respected almost as much as a man's. If you respect the sanctity of all other creatures then you will not use them to increase your well-being and therefore not progress as much as other religions where man can make use and "have dominion over" them.

Omnipresence, the ability to be everywhere at all times is another very useful concept that would provide a great benefit to religions that used it to describe their God. Without God's omnipresence you could get away with breaking the rules that give society order and only have to face the consequences brought upon you by fellow men. But if God is everywhere watching your every move you will be much more likely to follow those rules that give your society a productive social order. You might be able to steal and leech off of others and not get caught but God can see everything, not only is he everywhere all the time, he can even read your "impure" thoughts, so the idea of breaking the social rules that give society order are prevented from entering a brain before they can even lead to action. A similar case can be made for the concept of sin.

Since our egalitarian brains are suckers for equality then we can expect religions/"cultural books"/ideologies that preach such values to be able to attract more brains and therefore spread. Being equal under the eyes of God appeals to more people because there are more people under the power of rulers than there are rulers. Imagine a religion or set of beliefs that describes some people as being chosen by God to be the rulers and the rest to be servants. This "cultural book" would not be as appealing to the many brains out there that would end up being the servants, and would therefore have a harder time finding believers and eventually face cultural extinction. The idea that God is an Omnipresent and ultimate judge, not only prevents many selfish and socially detrimental acts as previously mentioned, but it might also prevent a cycle of vengeful violence by having some people believe that God will ultimately punish the wrong-doer as opposed to the injured party seeking immediate revenge. This helps eliminate costly internal violence which can weaken the group and it might be why "forgiveness" is a commonly preached value. Most religious individuals believe that God is "just" and in the end whatever injustices or inequalities exist in earth will be dealt with by God when the evildoer dies and either goes to heaven or hell or something along those lines. So one can see how this is all very appealing to our egalitarian brains and helpful at maintaining social order.

Unity and a sense of brotherhood too are important pages in our "cultural books". As previously discussed, our evolved egalitarian instincts contain a strong desire to belong to groups. We are very 'groupish', and religions have been naturally selected for based on their ability to harness such desires for solidarity. Most religions I can think of all have places of worship like churches, synagogues, temples, mosques, etc, to feel the strength of numbers. It is often times a source of jealousy, envy, and other dramas when people leave one church to go to another. Sermons and religious speeches often times are filled with unity and collective action, we feel great after an uplifting talk about brotherhood and how when we are all united nothing is impossible/etc. because in our tribal world unity was the most important element of many of the frequent tasks that required collective action, war/defense being the most important one.

Concepts like the idea that God is looking out for you and that there is an afterlife, invigorate people in ways that can lead to substantially better results. For example, willingness to fight and the confidence while doing so is greatly enhanced if you feel like God will help you and that if you die life will continue elsewhere. This also has its downside for those whose religious zeal has them fighting wars where they are hopelessly outnumbered. But as a whole, believing that God is on your side of the battle is a great plus, and is therefore another idea/concept/'page in our cultural books' that will spread through societies since it helps them compete with other groups, which lack such helpful ideological concepts.

The idea that God loves each and every one of us also gives us an additional source of confidence. Many people have been saved from suicide because they suddenly stumbled upon God's love for them and then went on to live happier and more productive lives. The concept of God and religion also provides a plan that lays out a path that will meet our needs like finding a mate and children. This sense of structure provides another psychological boost and ultimately helps the societies that have them have a more productive/powerful social order that inadvertently spreads such ideas.

To proselytize, to seek to convert others to your religion is another important "sentence/page" in our religious "cultural books". A religion that does not seek converts is likely to be a religion where its view of its members is something along the lines of "we are the chosen ones and the rest are beneath us" or worse. This is normal and a natural outcome of our tribal instincts and tendencies to see those outside of our group as enemies. Primitive religions were of this sort, where the religious values went hand in hand with the instincts that led to the most stable social order in our tribal zero-sum world. Our tribal zero-sum environment was a place where war really paid off and survival existed only for those who killed others in order to increase the size of the economic pie available to themselves. Since population size was limited by the more or less constant amount of food and resources that nature could replenish, the best way to increase your economic pie was to kill, subdue or enslave others. For most of our evolutionary past trading and the respect for private property would not have helped us much. We had not gotten smart enough to stumble upon farming or domesticating animals or coming up with a peaceful way of interacting that would somehow increase the economic pie beyond its natural replenishment rate. If there were no wars in the tribal world, we would all be living at the edge of subsistence in constant hunger, making the incentive to alleviate this hunger by wiping out the nearby tribe that much greater, until eventually it happened launching us back into tribal warfare. Being peaceful just made you an easier prey for the more aggressive minded folks and their more hostile values/religions/'cultural books'/ideologies. Given that war and pillage was the best strategy for survival, the social values/'cultural books'/ideologies of people at the time had to encourage and promote the us vs. them mentality which was crucial for our survival. No matter how brutal or backwards the religious values of tribal cultures, these ideologies/'cultural books' fostered the kinds of actions which were needed for survival in their respective cultures. As Herbert Spencer mentions:

> "The question to be answered is, whether these beliefs were beneficent in their effects on those who held them; not whether they would be beneficent for us, or for perfect men; and to this question the answer must be that while absolutely bad, they were relatively good.
>
> For is it not obvious that the savage man will be most effectually controlled by his fears of a savage deity? Must it not happen, that if his nature requires great restraint, the supposed consequences of transgression, to be a check upon him, must be proportionately terrible; and for these to be proportionally terrible, must not his god be conceived as proportionately cruel and revengeful?"[8]

As human ant-farms and their respective "cultural books" progressed to the point where the ability to increase the economic pie by market oriented means(the respect for private property and the inevitable peaceful trading that emerges from it) became more beneficial than through war, the more peaceful and market oriented human ant-farms started to displace the more warring ones and their respective "cultural books".

Little by little, religions that extended membership to bigger and bigger groups gained the benefits that come from less warfare and more opportunities for peaceful trade and therefore the better functioning of the market process and the more powerful social order that this would inadvertently bring. They would also gain a better ability to defend against other groups and to expand their social order by conquest. It should be no surprise that the world's two major religions Christianity and Islam are proselytizing religions that extend membership to people of all races. This has not always been the case because genocide/slavery/war has been common in both religions for most of their existence. Today's major religions were born in a tribal world and they therefore preached the kinds of values which would yield a stable social order given the circumstances. We definitely don't hear Sunday sermons teaching us that "When a man strikes his male or female slave with a rod so hard that the slave dies under his hand, he shall be punished. If, however, the slave survives for a day or two, he is not to be punished, since the slave is his own property." (Exodus

21:20-21). Passages such as these are cultural relics whose values and rules would have helped maintain a competitive social order in the past but are no longer useful and actually would be very detrimental to our social order. They are analogous to our genetic relics, genes in our genomes that are not used.

So to proselytize not only helps religions grow but it helps the most pro-growth and ultimately more pro-market process, pro-individual freedom values/laws/'cultural books' spread. Religions or human ant-farms that grow powerful will owe much of their power to having rules and customs that lead to a more powerful human ant-farm, and by proselytizing they are not just converting others to their religions they are spreading the very rules and customs that lead to a more powerful social order. If a religion or "cultural book" did not seek to spread itself by seeking converts even if this religion had the most pro-market process values it would be limited by the slow growth of the population of its members, and be an easy prey to more numerous and more aggressive minded "cultural books".

At the heart of most moral values we can see our egalitarian instincts at play. As already mentioned, equality is what we are most comfortable with, it is the "evolutionary stable strategy" that emerges out of the countless ways our instincts and incentives interact with the world and each other. If you are doing substantially better than others in some regard, in some regards you do not want equality, you want freedom from the social pressure which might force equality on you. If you are doing substantially worse you are for the enforcement of rules which lead to equality so that your relative position with everyone else is about the same as opposed to being a disadvantaged one. If the differences in wealth/females/etc. are too great, this leads to envy and subsequent internal conflict. Whether it is a few dominant males who are trying to shut out all the other males from the mating game, while the other males(since they are bound to be a larger group) gang up on the alphas, or some similar scenario whatever the resource might be, this causes internal conflict which is detrimental to the group and its ability to successfully compete in group competition. So on the one hand we have been naturally selected to be extremely selfish. Actually, it is not that we have been naturally selected to be extremely selfish, it is more like our minds are very susceptible to find it in their best interest to be very selfish. Again, there is no gene that specifically says we have to be selfish or want to do what we would consider "evil" acts, it just happens to be that our brains can easily calculate and reach the conclusion that "evil" acts are in our immediate best interest. So this kind of functioning on our part might have us always looking for ways to gain an advantage over others, but at the same time we know that the tables can be turned so in that case we like, and want, socially enforced egalitarianism.

Given these fundamental forces at play it is easy to see how many of our religious/cultural values were naturally selected for due to their ability to prevent such internal strife by ensuring a more or less comfortable level of internal egalitarianism.

Marriage between a man and a woman and the tendency for male/female relations to reach this pattern is an easy one to understand. Too many women per men leaves many men out of the mating game which will lead to a lot of internal strife/oppression and other things which can be detrimental to the productivity and stability of the group. This does not mean it doesn't happen, but the evolutionary stable strategy moves towards a single man/single woman pairing. Why are our traditional 'conservative' morals so hush-hush about sex, why did we dress so conservatively? Well, as already briefly discussed, the more we can create a 'cultural book' that helps us program ourselves as to not make sex such a central part of our lives, the more we will be able to devote our energies and efforts towards other things and avoid the fierce competition, waste of resources, time, conflict that can arise due to a strong preoccupation with sexual competition. Our minds make a strong association with sex and something that is very much in our best interest simply because of the strong pleasure we get from orgasms and other biological impulses that make its pursuit so tempting. But fortunately for us, since our minds are very flexible and are able to mold themselves into liking different things, our traditional morals, which included our conservative ways of dressing and many other cultural elements that were parts of our 'cultural books', shaped our minds in ways where the constant mimicking process and success-to-characteristic matching that our minds go through as we program ourselves as to what to like and what to find offensive or repulsive, reduced the relative importance of sex and all that goes with it. A great example of this can be found in the Islamic tradition of having women cover most of themselves. The Qur'an 24:30-31 states:

"And tell the believing women to subdue their eyes, and maintain their chastity. They shall not reveal any parts of their bodies, except that which is necessary. They shall cover their chests, and shall not relax this code in the presence of other than their husbands, their fathers, the fathers of their husbands, their sons, the sons of their husbands, their brothers, the sons of their brothers, the sons of their sisters, other women, the male servants or employees whose sexual drive has been nullified, or the children who have not reached puberty. They shall not strike their feet when they walk in order to shake and reveal certain details of their bodies."

There is a tremendous amount of embodied wisdom in this passage. By having women cover themselves and only revealing their beauty to those whose family relationships are too close to make the women available for sexual competition, costly internal social conflict is avoided. And also the last sentence "They shall not strike their feet when they walk in order to shake and reveal certain details of their bodies" is almost telling women not to show off, again, due to the problems this can bring like perhaps the feelings of jealousy and inferiority the less beautiful might feel, and how it distracts men. Contrary to what many Westerners might think, this form of dress is preferred by most Muslim women, even those who might be substantially prettier than others and would seem to be on the losing end of such equality of looks that the dress code would bring. It is true that beautiful women might be losing an advantage but it also makes it easier for them to not worry about their looks as they get older or worry about the looks of their children.

Let's briefly discuss how the idea of preference/beauty is formed in our minds. To some degree there is a certain biological component. I do not know to what extent a man can be programmed by upbringing into believing that 80 year old women are attractive. If a man grows up in a world where this is all he sees, to what extent would he find 80 year old women very beautiful? And then after living many years only knowing about the existence of 80 year old women how would he perceive or compare an 18 year old? A single very beautiful woman or a small group of them, especially in today's world of mass media where you don't even have to really see the beautiful women in person, can help reshape what a person's concept of beauty is. And if a few single very pretty women are what shape many men's ideas of what is beautiful, this would make many wives seem less attractive. I know, this is all pretty obvious. In today's modern world we deal with this by constantly striving to look like that which is considered attractive, we get fake boobs, spend tons in fashionable clothes, spend a considerable amount of time exercising and so on. Yet with all of these struggles the rate of unfaithfulness and divorces due to wondering eyes seem to be going up all the time.

Conservative/traditional values in all cultures seem to put a lot more emphasis on chastity and sexual restraint on the woman than in the man. If you are going to try to tame sex and the inevitably fierce competition that it brings, it is a much more effective strategy to apply pressure and instill chaste morals on the female than on the male. This just happens to be the case because it is a strategy that is more in synch with our biology. If women are lose, and willing to have an illegitimate child here and there with a stud, we already mentioned how it breaks our innate desire for equality, but the way it wreaks social havoc might be as follows. If a man does not make an effort to be the guy who has the additional sex with the promiscuous woman and he is a nice tame guy, it will be other men, with less tame genes that will gain a reproductive advantage, and eventually if society always allows women to just sort of sleep around it will be those men who competed for the extra sex the ones whose genes and extra competitive characteristics which spread, eventually replacing the tamer fellows until every male is of the type that will fiercely compete for the lose girls. This has been a very oversimplified explanation, there is so much more that can go on here, but this sort of speculation will have to do in such a short book. Bottom line, more reasons to understand why natural selection has selected so many restrictive morals to keep sex out of our minds.

Religious values just like everything else are subject to natural selection and we can see the process alive and well in today's America with issues like abortion, the acceptance of gays, women in the priesthood in the case of the Catholic Church and so on. "Cultural books" and their values ultimately survive and exist because they have human brains that absorb them. The pressure to be more inclusive to retain members and therefore remain relevant and survive ensures that religious values adapt to comply with whatever social values might have led to growth and stability. For example, the increased economic freedom of all human beings is something that leads to more productivity and will therefore help the human ant-farms that allow it, and religions have adapted their ways accordingly. Better treatment of human beings in general will seem more attractive to more people, who for the most part have been under the control of the powerful. In modern economies, where people of all walks of life realize how much alike all people are, this pressure to include all human beings and to be tolerant of some of their differences and tastes becomes even greater. Biblical passages like "You have heard that it was said, 'An eye for an eye, and a tooth for a tooth.' But I tell you, do not resist an evil person. If someone strikes you on the right cheek, turn to him the other also. And if someone wants to sue you and take your tunic, let him have your cloak as well. If someone forces you to go one mile, go with him two miles. Give to the one who asks you, and do not turn away from the one who wants to borrow from you." (Matthew 5:38-42, NIV), obviously cannot be followed too literally although it might have had a certain appeal which might have helped in attracting converts. The modern Western world is a cultural descendent of more war-like Christians. Let us also not forget our biological instincts and innate egalitarianism. Although the previous biblical passage dealing with the beating of slaves might be a cultural relic that would destroy our social order, Matthew 19:24 "Again I tell you, it is easier for a camel to go through the eye of a needle than for a rich man to enter the kingdom of God.", and other egalitarian/anti-capitalist ideas which are also detrimental to our social order are alive and well.

A family structure, as already mentioned has been important for keeping the peace and other things, and obviously respect for private property is the foundation of our modern socioeconomic orders.

Communism, good intentions and all, destroyed these two and suffered the consequences. As Hayek mentions:

> "Among the founders of religions over the last two thousand years, many opposed property and the family. *But the only religions that have survived are those which support property and the family.* Thus the outlook for communism, which is both anti-property and anti-family(and also anti-religion), is not promising. For it is, I believe, itself a religion which had its time, and which is now declining rapidly. In communist and socialist countries we are watching how the natural selection of religious beliefs disposes of the maladapted"[9]

Today religion is under attack. Although I have tried to show religion to be a naturally selected phenomenon whose validity in terms of what it preaches I do not believe, and in many ways everything I have described here about religion serves to diminish its influence, one has to realize that religion got us to where we are. Our religious 'cultural books' have evolved with us and have created a world for us in which our questions and concerns have been handled in ways that have met our socioeconomic and psychological needs. Our religious customs and values have been naturally selected for and have given us life in the process, and people who blindly criticize religion need to understand the beneficial and crucial role it has played in creating the social order we owe our very lives to. There are many people out there boosting their egos by believing that somehow they are smarter or more 'rational' than religious individuals and so on, as if somehow their "rationality" makes them superior. It is very much in our nature to constantly try to find ways to show off and make ourselves seem better/superior to others and this is one issue where the most ignorant of atheists suddenly feels and acts like an arrogant genius. Again, religion is what we owe our very lives to; its rules/customs/ideologies/'cultural books' have managed to tame what would otherwise have been a very nasty beast. I just would like to see less arrogant militant atheists I guess, and you never know...

Before finishing this section on religion we will briefly discuss a few more cultural concepts which have been crucial in our cultural evolution, they are the concepts of "good" and "evil", free will, and the "self".

As our tribal man was developing language and concepts which could be combined to make better sense of the world, and eventually lead to a more powerful social order, a concept which will help him sort, label, and communicate things that are good or bad to himself as well as the social order will provide a great advantage, and this is where the concepts of good/bad or good/evil come into play. Our human ant-farms can be seen as constantly working on the 'good and evil cycle', which works as follows: human beings grow up and associate a set of actions with the words or concepts good and evil. Practices that are "good" are usually good for the cooperation and stability of the human ant-farm as a group, but might put the breaks on actions that are in the immediate best interest of individual human ants and the continued copying of their genes, like rape, theft and so on, which are classified as "evil". Brains that do evil and get caught are terminated/punished, and those that do good are allowed to survive and praised.

The concept of 'free will' is one that is losing its importance the more we tend to accept the important role that upbringing and the environment plays, especially as it relates to things like the punishment of crimes and poverty. I guess these days in the US the perfect example is that of a black teenage male who grows up with no productive role models in a crime/drug/'semi-tribal machismo' infested environment. Our culture provides the lemons out of which our brains can make lemonade with. This young black man's lemonade is much more likely to land him in jail due to criminal behavior. Did he really have free will? Not really. Is he specifically responsible for his action? I don't think so either. Should he be punished for his crimes. Yes[10]. This is unfortunate in some ways but anything but this will bring the entire social order down with it. The point I want to make is one I believe most people accept these days, that our free will is sort of constrained by the incentives, consequences, "cultural book" a person absorbs.

Finally we'll briefly mention the concept of the "self". I wonder at what point in our evolution did we begin using things like names to call each other? At some point referring to people by name was needed to help the internal division of labor("Ug do this. Guga do that") which would have yield tremendous benefits. At some point we began teaching this language and referring by name to our kids, and the mind would begin forming a stronger sense of all that is associated with the body it controls. We have an idea of who we are and as we grow up we brainwash ourselves into adhering to whatever cultural values are considered good and lead to a prosperous social order as opposed to bad/evil which might lead to conflict. But deep down inside we are all the same.

Comments on drug prohibition, its history, and race relations

Mind altering substances have been a constant part in our recent evolutionary history. Such drugs have helped our minds ease their powerful soberness, and by screwing up that reality-minded functioning of our brains, drugs have helped us interact, or better said, create, the spiritual world which as already discussed has been such a key factor in our evolution. Some drugs make us more relaxed and better able to bond with others, some drugs excite us and give us a feeling of invincibility which might have been helpful in overcoming our fear in preparation for an always brutal war/confrontation. The bottom line is that when one looks at the evolutionary history of mankind, mind altering substances have been a common trait in our cultures. Besides the obvious reasons that people do drugs because they like them, drug use has been a cultural trait that has been naturally selected for. If it was so detrimental and played such an important and negative role in society, it is a trait that would have been damaging to those societies that had it and would have led to their cultural extinction, but again, the fact that it has been common in all cultures gives some powerful evidence that it has had a net beneficiary effect.

Some might say that on the contrary, that the tough drug war and moral depravity associated with drug use has been a key ingredient in creating a better society. In today's world we can't get high around some fire and then drive a car. But this is non-sense, the vast majority of drug users are easily able to understand and control such risks. Alcohol is a far worse drug than marijuana yet millions of human beings incorporate it into their functioning without any problems. And probably the biggest problem with alcohol, drunk driving related accidents, are more the result of our bad laws. A person who is high on a drug easily knows that he/she is impaired and should this person need to drive he could compensate by driving a lot slower and say with blinkers or some other signal letting people know that "I am impaired". But given our laws this would ruin your life so you have no choice but to surrender your good judgment which is more than capable of dealing and planning for its future impaired state. Anyways, this is not the book to make an in-depth case for ending our war on drugs.[11]

The real reason why I am including this seemingly off-topic subject here is for the following. An important factor in our drug prohibition is rooted in our desire to restrain the actions of others, actions which we feel might put us at a disadvantage in some regard. For example, one of the things we like about marriage between a man and a woman and all the social pressures we use to push for this, is because we fear a guy who is a stud who will do better with many women, and likewise, women fear other women luring their men away and so on. The strict adherence to our traditional marriage customs is the "evolutionary stable strategy" that pleases the most, and might have helped create the most stable social order.

The ideologies which we adhere to have a lot to do with incentives and how we see ourselves succeeding or failing given the ideology. For example. If you see yourself as being very beautiful with a killer body compared to others, you might be ok with people wearing skimpy dresses and would be less likely to shun such behavior. If on the other hand you are fat and ugly, you might shun such behavior and have your mind inadvertently gravitate towards ideologies which associate such behavior with bad things. If you are the nerdy kid who for whatever reason never managed to absorb the much more fun culture of recreational drug use and sex, your mind might inadvertently gravitate more towards an ideology that restricts such behavior.

People who tend to be more tolerant of freedom are less likely to feel threatened by what others might do with such freedom. And similarly, people who tend to be less tolerant of freedom are more likely to feel threatened by what others do with their freedom. This applies perfectly to drug prohibition. The prohibition of drugs is a strategy for preventing others from perhaps succeeding at being more social and gaining the benefits that come from this at our expense, and the history of drug prohibition clearly shows this to have been the motivating factor. Let me explain.

In the Western world Asian men are not usually regarded as sex symbols for the simple fact that they happen to be shorter on average. But fortunately for all of mankind, sex appeal has more to do with being happy and confident and being associated with fun than it does with how tall you are, and this was the case with "chinamen" in San Francisco in 1875 when the City of San Francisco passed the first laws aimed at prohibiting drug use. They did this because white women where finding their way to the opium dens where the high, happy and down to earth chinamen were showing them a better time. The terminology the jealous white men in power would use is "lured" but the women weren't "lured" they just went where the fun was.

The same applies but in a much more important way with blacks and deserves special mention. Harry J. Anslinger, the nation's first Drug Czar, before Congress in 1937 he said "There are 100,000 total marijuana smokers in the U.S. and most are Negroes, Hispanics, Filipinos and entertainers. Their satanic music, jazz and swing, result from marijuana use. This marijuana causes white women to seek sexual relations with Negroes.". Sure Mr. Anslinger… What was happening was that jazz music was the cool music and blacks were just having more fun, and just like with the chinamen, the pretty down to earth white girls wanted to be where the fun was, and that was in the jazz scene, and quite naturally there were plenty of happy and high black guys looking to score with a pretty white girl.

Race relations in the United States obviously play a huge role in our politics, especially in the motivation and justification for our disastrous welfare/public spending, and attempts to have government socially engineer morality. The rise and dominance of Hip-Hop culture is something that affects politics and society in ways that don't get enough attention and are swept under the rug. The worst fears which motivated the above statements by Mr. Anslinger have in many ways become true. The rise of Hip-Hop culture and complete domination of professional sports by black athletes is a huge thorn for many white Americans. From some perspectives their children are "white boys", who can't make the basketball team, or be the star football player, or draw upon the confidence that comes from knowing that you could be like those role models that play such a key role in defining what is cool or not. The Internet is full of pornography and one of its most popular genres is interracial pornography, where by far the most popular of this kind is black men have sex with white women. I believe that the rise of Hip-Hop culture played a role in increasing American's religious fervor which ultimately helped create the disastrous second Bush presidency. I will not go into more detail about this in this book. All I will say here is that all human beings are essentially the same and that government intervention motivated by fears and political correctness are what have lead to such a polarized society and are preventing freedom from evolving a more optimal racial harmony.

While we are at this, let's quickly discuss why the drug war is so awful and truly racist. Economics and our inability to understand the workings of the modern world play a key role here as well. In a simpler tribal world, if you had a drug problem like we do today and wanted to get rid of it by killing the bad guys, you would gather the necessary resources, which would be synonymous with increasing taxes to fund the drug war today, find the bad guys, kill them, problem solved. So in today's world we create our government tentacle/bureaucracy and get it to root out the bad guys, and believe that that will make things better at some point. But this is not what happens. Let's begin with the source of the "problem". People like drugs, humanity has for all of mankind, this is reflected in their desire to trade money for them. Since drugs are illegal, if you sell them you can go to jail for a long time, so this greatly reduces the incentive to create and sell the drugs. The average price of a drug will tend to be the total amount of money being offered by society divided by the total amount of drugs available for sale. Since society wants the drugs, and is offering lots of money for them, and there is few drugs because it is illegal to make/sell them, the amount of money that goes to each unit of drug is very high, so the price of drugs is very high. This high price of drugs, simply motivates people to break the law and go into the drug trafficking business, especially if you are from a poorer country and can sell drugs for top dollar in the U.S. Every drug bust that the police makes, does two things. First it reduces the supply of drugs which simply means that their price will go up or stay high, once again increasing the incentive for more people to get into the drug trafficking business. And the second thing that a bust does is simply to remove a competitor and make it easier for a new competitor to sell the drugs. So a cycle that never ends takes place. Drug traffickers enter the market to exploit the high profits, busts are made which remove competitors and drives up the price of drugs, which motivates new competitors to enter the drug trafficking business and the cycle just continues.

As this is happening the social order and economic pie are being destroyed in many ways. Meet Doug, a 28 year old computer programmer, who uses cocaine about once every couple of months at parties. Like your average recreational drug user, he is not some desperate, jobless, petty criminal living from high to high. He is an average human being who has ambitions, family, and a productive job that adds wealth to society. He just wasn't a nerd who bought into the whole "fear" of drugs when he was in high school. He had good friends that did it from time to time, they seemed to be enjoying life better and were in control of what they were doing. They were happier, more relaxed and confident, which made them more attractive to the girls. The girls enjoyed being with happy cool guys and the guys enjoyed the girls. They had more sex and fun.

It is ironic how today's baby boomer generation politicians play the fear card, trying to get America's youth not to do drugs, when so many of them did them in their youth(Gore, Bush, Clinton, Gingrich…). The real reason why politicians have to seem so tough on drugs, is because they have to appeal to that large segment of the population that is resentful, or a bit fearful, of the fun others have. These people have an additional incentive to gravitate towards more religious fervor than others. I'm not saying that all people who are for the drug war are these resentful people, or that religious individuals are of this type. Many people envision the real dangers which drug abuse might lead to and want to help prevent them. I just want to bring attention to this important "competitive-behavior-suppressing" role that our religious institutions have evolved to carry out. Something similar to this but in a grater scale took part during the Iranian Islamic Revolution of 1979. Prior to the revolution, Iran had been westernized to the point where it had many bars that sold alcohol, discos, cinemas that even showed nudity, and was in many ways indistinguishable from Europe and America. But eventually a pent up resentment and various other factors exploded in the revolution and such symbols of "decadence" were burnt down and destroyed. Who knows, if the Hip-Hop world keeps growing the US might have a great Christian Revolution.

So Doug gets stopped for a broken taillight and eventually busted for carrying 10 grams of cocaine and gets a mandatory 5 year sentence. The social order now loses Doug's productivity as a computer programmer plus $125,000 in wealth like cars, homes, food, etc., that will have to be consumed in order to feed and clothe for 5 years[12] an ever expanding U.S. criminal-industrial-complex made up of inmates, jailors, cops, jail building companies, etc. From 1984 to 1996, California built 21 new prisons, and only one new university[13]. In 2006 there were a whopping 1,889,810 drug related arrests[14], of which almost 830,000 were related to marijuana[15], which is completely harmless, and much more so than alcohol. Just try to imagine all the wealth that is consumed from society as we feed, clothe and equip, the criminal-industrial-complex as it does this useless function. There is also Gina, a high school mate of Doug's who due to upbringing and many other factors was not one of the popular girls who had enough common sense to do drugs responsibly and grew up resentful. Her ideology drifted more towards those of people who think drug users are "bad" people, and are more inclined to think that there is something "wrong" with them. She got a degree in psychology and became a counselor at our jails, "counseling" people like Doug, helping them overcome their "problems" which turned them to drug use. I once met a woman who was getting a PhD in psychology and wanted to do her doctoral dissertation in children with mystical powers. She told me that even if it seems a little far-fetched she had read a lot about them and research needed to be done to verify such things and what could be learned form them. She had a high-paying part-time job-counseling people in a Miami jail, helping them understand why theft was bad and overcome whatever was wrong with them. Doug and countless others, have to agree and admit that there is something "wrong" with themselves in front of the Ginas of the world, who make up the majority of our parole boards and employees of the criminal-industrial-complex. One should also keep in mind that if a taxpayer refuses to pay the taxes that go to feed this socially destructive drug-war, the taxpayer will be locked up too, causing yet another $25,000 per year to be further consumed by force from the social order to feed an army of politically correct zombies.

One of the examples of out current drug laws' more blatant racism comes from the discrepancy in sentencing between being busted for crack cocaine and powdered cocaine. Crack cocaine is cheaper and more predominantly used by lower income blacks yet the punishment for using crack is much more severe. For example, you might get a mandatory 5 year sentence for carrying 5 grams of crack cocaine, yet you would need to carry maybe 500 grams of the powdered cocaine to get hit with same sentence. As mentioned in drugwarfacts.com :

"In 1986, before mandatory minimums for crack offenses became effective, the average federal drug offense sentence for blacks was 11% higher than for whites. Four years later following the implementation of harsher drug sentencing laws, the average federal drug offense sentence was 49% higher for blacks."[16]

Ideology. Democrats, Republicans and Libertarians

What is the difference between Democrats and Republicans, and the lesser-known Libertarians? What causes some people to gravitate and associate themselves with each of these ideologies? How have our cultural books evolved over the last century in a way that causes so many people to segregate themselves into these categories? The following pages are very brief and can be misleading in many ways but for brevity's sake, we continue.

Libertarians and traditional conservatives

Libertarians are the ones who for the most part just want the government to adhere to our two fundamental laws. Libertarians are probably the most diverse group. There are libertarians like myself, who come to believe in such views via an understanding of economics. There are also many people who are just gun-ho about freedom without necessarily understanding anything about economics. Many came to libertarian views via the literary works of Ayn Rand. Then there is a large group of Libertarians who come to hold such views due to their Christian morals. For the most part, these type of libertarians can also be referred as "traditional conservatives", and the rest of my discussion focuses on them.

People who are more likely to label themselves conservatives are likely to do so because of their religious values. These people tend to have a stronger sense of the "self" and the idea that people should be responsible for their actions. This sort of viewpoint is a central theme in the Christian cultural book that Americans inherited and has led to America's great success, because it inadvertently leads to a well functioning market process and therefore an increasingly productive social order. According to traditional Christian values it is the role of the individual to be responsible and hard working, to provide for the family/etc., and the role of the young and able in the family to take care of the elderly. This is really no different than in Islam and most other "cultural books" out there. For thousands of years, individual responsibility and families have been the center of moral values. Only with the rise of our modern industrial civilizations and the tremendous amount of wealth and social complexity that they have created, has the idea that it is the government that is responsible for providing for people taken such a stronghold.

Traditional "conservative" positions like being pro-life are easy to understand from a religious point of view. To take a life is obviously a sin and awful. One does not have to be religious and fear God's wrath, we are human beings, very caring, compassionate and susceptible to putting ourselves in other people's shoes/etc. Conservatives are also for free-trade and a strong respect for private property. This is really an outgrowth of the central theme of personal responsibility, that a man has a sort of God-given free will and that his success/failures come from his decision to exercise that free-will. God sees all men as being equal and therefore some men cannot boss others around.

Since these people take God more seriously than most, they are very likely to see all the taxation that goes on to be clear violations of "thou shalt not steal" and other Christian values. Given our current big-government ideology, a person who does not want to pay taxes to fund a public education system they want no part of can be sent to prison, or killed should they resist by using force. The same applies to people who would rather spend their money on their children's education, instead of paying for some people to have a great time trying to put people on the moon, i.e., funding NASA. These people are obviously crazy right? How dare they not want to contribute to such wonderful social causes? These very pious Christian's faith and absorption of the Christian "cultural book" is far stronger than the aforementioned tendencies that has the rest of America falling for Socialism.

Modern day Republicans

Today's mainstream "Conservative" or Republican, is a whole different animal than what true, traditional conservatism as just discussed is. If George W. Bush was a true or traditional conservative, a Christian who felt like it was immoral and against God's law to threaten to imprison a Christian for wanting to spend his money on his moral duty of family and community instead of government, there should have been all kinds of cuts in the size of government. But obviously this is not what happened. Why? First of all, because of the aforementioned reasons that lead society to believe that we need a big government. America's religious principles have been bent or thwarted due to the new complexities of our modern industrialized world, and this has caused Americans to believe that it is government management of the social order that helps bring prosperity, as opposed to following their traditional Christian values of individual freedom and personal responsibility. In other words, today's modern "conservative"/Republican is a Christian who puts government above true Christian values to various degrees.

It should be obvious to any Christian, or even any non-Christian who knows just a little about the Christian faith, that threatening to incarcerate someone for refusing to pay into a social security system that they don't want, or space research that they don't want, or have their money given to farmers or welfare recipients or to foreign nations, etc. goes against Christian values, period. Have a Christian not pay his income taxes, then go to court and explain that he feels it is morally wrong to take his hard earned money to give it to an unwed mother who keeps having kids. There is a good chance that the judge who sends him to jail is a so called "Christian Conservative" who votes republican, same can be said about the police officers that jail him and countless other individuals who will go along with this man's troubles and watch his story unfold on T.V. thinking he is some overtly religious fool. So the mainstream Christian faith has sort of evolved with the times. Our tendency to believe that we need this huge government has evolved the Christian faith in a way that many of its current actions go counter to its most basic principles. But this makes sense anyways, "cultural books" and religions evolve with time and how the majority sees the world.

The modern Republican party has also sort of become, what your average black guy in the street will tell you, the "white man" 's party or tribe. Although religion also helps us be more inclusive of other people, it has usually been the ideological glue that bonds a tribe and helps shape its identity. And in this respect it is definitely the "white man" 's tribe. We can clearly see this on an election results map, with the heavily white-populated states usually going red for republican, while those with larger immigrant and black populations tend more to be Democrats associated with the color blue. With slower birthrates than Hispanics and the already mentioned thorny relations with blacks, there has been more incentive to inadvertently seek unity, and a stronger sense of identity and collective action to somehow turn the trend. Being tough on immigration seems like a bigger deal for these folks than for democrats whom we will discuss next. Although republicans still talk about small government and traditionally conservative values, one might get the impression that many don't preach such values out of Christian and moral principles, but more so out of the fact that they hate feeling like they are subsidizing the minorities, and with good reason, there is nothing wrong about being upset about having your money taken from you to give to someone else.

While the traditional conservative or Libertarian Christian is pious enough in a direction that can sort of overcome our tribal nature, the modern Republican is less so. For example, I see Dr. Paul as a true conservative Christian, who often times brings up the Christian inspired concept of Just War Theory when he talks about when a war is justified. The mainstream republican masses are much more likely to let our tribal nature see the Muslim world as "evil", and is willing to ignore Christian principles in order to meddle in their affairs. The fact that Jews are white like the "Republican Base", and our religious histories are so intertwined, makes them our natural sort of tribal allies, especially compared to the darker Arabs and North African blacks. Not that I'm labeling all republicans as being blatant racists, it is just that these things do matter in the general psyche of individuals as we inadvertently segregate ourselves.

With the exception of Dr. Paul, all Republican presidential candidates are for the continuation of the Iraq war and are very pro-military, completely blinded to the historical nuances of the Middle East and the unintended consequences of their ideological pursuits.

So far I have been talking about things that might lure a mind into labeling itself as a Republican, but I have not really talked about the Republican party itself, which is the political structure that arises out of this ideology. In some ways the Republican party itself has evolved to be a sort of militant Christian tribe, where powerful evangelical leaders exert tremendous influence. In 2004, 41 out of 51 Republican senators, over 80% of them, voted with the powerful Christian Coalition 100% of the time[17], which is actually a good thing in many ways because they want to keep government smaller than the democrats. The real problem comes with foreign policy and especially our current troubles in the Middle East. There are Senators like Jim Inhofe(R-Okla) who believe that American foreign policy in the Middle East should be based on the Bible[18]. And then there are the Christian Zionists like mega-church pastor John Hagee who are eagerly awaiting the second coming of Christ and believe that our support of Israel and our meddling in the Middle East must continue in order for this prophesy to come true in the near future[19]. In an interview given by Max Blumenthal of Tom Delay(the former House Majority Leader and therefore top Republican in congress from 2003-2005) at John Hagee's "Christians United for Israel Tour" , when asked by Max "How much of an inspiration is the second coming in your support for Israel?" Tom said : "Obviously it is what I live for and I hope it comes tomorrow... And obviously we have to be connected to Israel in order to enjoy the second coming of Christ".[20]

The tribal nature of human beings and how religion plays into all this is of crucial importance. It seems like I have gone a little off topic here but that's all right. I would also like to add that all of this even relates to our military. The Republican Party is the party of the U.S. Military, and this powerful mixture of religious zeal and military, especially with our troops in a Muslim country is also leading to a dangerous militant Christianity. Lt. Col. Brandl, a man who commands over 800 troops said while leading his attack of Fallujah: "The enemy has got a face. He's called Satan. He's in Fallujah, and we're going to destroy him." [21]

Karen Kwiatkowski, a retired U.S. Air Force Lieutenant Colonel who worked in the Pentagon and has commented in the ideological extremism of the Pentagon mentioned how she was advised by a college that "if I wanted to be successful here, I'd better remember not to say anything positive about the Palestinians."[22]

Democrats / Liberals

Liberals/Democrats are in some ways a little more enlightened than conservatives in their understanding of the world. If you strongly believe in "free will"/"individualism" then a criminal is more likely to be "evil" and deserving of punishment. But Liberals tend to be seen as "progressive". "Progressive" from what? Well, from tradition of course, and tradition is our religious values. People who label themselves Liberal feel like they have a better understanding of human nature and the important role that the environment plays in shaping people. Here the "Liberal", and probably wiser view is that criminals are sort of products of their environment and that we should not be as hard on them. The modern "Liberal" view is to try to use the government to take from the "haves"/"fortunate ones" to socially engineer environments where people grow up "right". Given this "enlightened" liberal view the punishment of criminals can even be seen by some to be a crime itself because it is the "social injustices" and differences in wealth, the exploitation of the workers by the rich/haves/etc. that creates the conditions that leads to crime in the first place, and that given that we know that all human beings are equal, those factors that have minorities caught in a web of higher crime and poverty are "obviously" outgrowths of such "social injustices"/etc. From the "Liberal" point this whole concept of "free will" might be true but to a much smaller degree than a "conservative" viewpoint might accept.

Most US university faculty are "Liberals" and are sort of descendents of the scientific revolution which gives us the feeling that we can use science and the coercive power of government to mold a better society. "Liberal" university professors are much more likely to be atheists and many look upon religion as being antiquated, which in many ways it is. With the rise of science and so much new knowledge about fields like biology, we were freed from our religious traditions and dogmas and we could experiment. All kinds of social theories emerged, Freud/etc. and entire new branches of study became prominent like Sociology/Anthropology and Psychology. Our modern cultural books suddenly were no longer limited to concepts like the soul, good, evil, the devil, possessed, bad spirits, etc., with which to piece together an understanding of man. Now we had chemistry, brains, early childhood development, and a whole slew of psychobabble. The "conservative" cultural book is weary of all this, especially when it contradicts tradition and scripture but the Liberal cultural book is expanding and attracting more and more brains as science and reason expand.

The Liberal/Democratic mindset's tamer religious fervor can be seen in its pro-choice views when it comes to abortion and tolerance of social freedoms like gay rights. This further departure with religious traditions are also reflective in its economic ideology. While the Republicans at least talk about free-trade, low taxes, personal responsibility and God as being the ultimate source of what is right and wrong, in other words, Republicans *seem* to have more Natural Law, the Liberals/Democrats don't mind violating "thou shalt not steal" at all, as long as it is done from the haves to bring about their well intentioned Socialism. Given our sort of egalitarian tendencies and zero-sum view of the world, minorities like African Americans and Hispanics feel like it is perfectly justifiable to have higher tax rates, and sort of share the wealth, since it is taken from the rich white man who is greedy. This is just the usual mindset that so easily spreads Socialism/Communism all over the world.

Review

In this section we have looked at the evolution of culture, and subsets of culture like religion and political ideology. Our "cultural books" contain the lemons out of which our brains can make lemonade with. Our cultural books and their pages and concepts are shaped by group selection. Each set of laws/customs/ideas which make up a cultural book is responsible for the social order that it helps create. As societies grow or perish their cultural books spread/adapt/perish. The two most important factors in cultural books is their ability to prevent internal conflict as well as their ability to guide the actions of people in the most productive way that will ultimately lead to higher population growth and social order. This higher productivity inadvertently comes about as the cultural books respect individual freedom more and more, inadvertently creating the market process.

When we take an honest look at human beings, we see just how flexible our nature is. We have all sorts of sexual combinations like gays, lesbians, polygamy, gangbangs, and yes, even people who have sex with animals. Things like birth control have had a great impact on our cultural books. Soon genetic engineering will play a big role. I'm guessing that things like being able to have a child that is a clone of oneself will become possible. Have a child where his genes come form 3 people. How incentives, fears, technology and so much more interact to shape our actions is impossible to foretell. As Hayek mentions at the end of one of his final works:

"Man is not and never will be the master of his fate: his very reason always progresses by leading him into the unknown and unforeseen where he learns new things."[23]

Unfortunately, the way things are going these days in the US, should our socioeconomic conditions continue to deteriorate and launch us into social chaos and transform us into a second or third world nation, people will look at our pornography, drugs, promiscuity, etc. as the reason for our downfall, yet these are harmless compared to what really destroys the social order and causes chaos. Government and its spending, taxation, regulation, etc, its interferences in the workings of the market process. The lack of individual freedom.

---

[1] http://www.sujitfoundation.com/

[2] http://www.marxists.org/archive/marx/works/1859/critique-pol-economy/preface.htm

[3] "The Wisdom of Henry Hazlitt" published by The Foundation for Economic Education, Inc., March 1993, page 51.

[4] This essay was originally published in the first issue of Monthly Review (May 1949) http://www.monthlyreview.org/598einst.htm

[5] F.A. Hayek, The Fatal Conceit. The University of Chicago Press, published 1989, ISBN 0-226-32066-9 page 21

[6] ibid, page 14

[7] F.A. Hayek, Law Legislation and Liberty, Volume I Rules and Order. The University of Chicago Press, published 1983, page 9

[8] Herbert Spencer's Essay "The Use of Anthropomorphism" in his book "Illustrations of Universal Progress"

[9] F.A. Hayek, The Fatal Conceit. The University of Chicago Press, published 1989, ISBN 0-226-32066-9 page 137. Words in italics are that way in original text.

[10] Well, not necessarily. If people paid restitution to their victims things might be different. But a discussion on our criminal system is beyond our scope for now so I'll just leave it at "Yes"

[11] For this I recommend "Saying Yes" by Jacob Sullum

I also forgot where I read about this example I just mentioned. Must have been either some mises.org daily article or in lewrockwell.com

[12] It costs 25,000 dollars per inmate to maintain our criminal-industrial-complex-bureaucracy running

[13] http://www.drugwarfacts.org/prison.htm

[14] http://www.fbi.gov/ucr/cius2006/data/table_29.html

[15] 43.9 % of arrests were marijuana related   39.1 for possession and 4.8 for sale/manufacture

[16] http://www.drugwarfacts.org/racepris.htm

Source: Meierhoefer, B. S., The General Effect of Mandatory Minimum Prison Terms: A Longitudinal Study of Federal Sentences Imposed (Washington DC: Federal Judicial Center, 1992), p. 20.

[17] www.theocracywatch.org

[18] Inhofe said:

"I believe very strongly that we ought to support Israel; that it has a right to the land. This is the most important reason: Because God said so. As I said a minute ago, look it up in the book of Genesis. It is right up there on the desk.

In Genesis 13:14–17, the Bible says:

The Lord said to Abraham, "Lift up now your eyes, and look from the place where you are northward, and southward, and eastward and westward: for all the land which you see, to you will I give it, and to your seed forever. . . . Arise, walk through the land in the length of it and in the breadth of it; for I will give it to thee." That is God talking.

The Bible says that Abraham removed his tent and came and dwelt in the plain of Mamre, which is in Hebron, and built there an altar before the Lord. Hebron is in the West Bank. It is at this place where God appeared to Abram and said, "I am giving you this land — the West Bank". This is not a political battle at all. It is a contest over whether or not the word of God is true."

[19] http://www.lewrockwell.com/orig/north7.html Excellent article by Gary North explaining the evolution of this powerful and dangerous ideological movement.

[20] http://www.youtube.com/watch?v=mjMRgT5o-Ig . Max's youtube profile with many more great videos http://www.youtube.com/mblumenthal

Also check out http://tinyurl.com/27qlhq

[21] Robert H. Reid "Over 30 Killed in Iraq Insurgent Attacks", Associated Press, November 6, 2004

[22] Karen Kwiatkowski's article in Salon.com titled "The new Pentagon papers: A high-ranking military officer reveals how Defense Department extremists suppressed information and twisted the truth to drive the country to war." http://dir.salon.com/story/opinion/feature/2004/03/10/osp_moveon/index.html

[23] F.A. Hayek , Law Legislation and Liberty Volume 3 ISBN 0-226-32090-1 Page 176

VI. The Ron Paul Revolution

The fallacy of needing to "protect our interests" overseas and police the world. Non-interventionism

In our tribal world, the social order was not built on trade, you either got possession of the banana tree, or you didn't. If the person who got to the banana tree was in your tribe, great, he had to share. If he was from another tribe, you fought over it. But this is not how the modern market-process coordinated world works. In the modern world we have human ant-farms that ultimately work in a way that transforms a virtually limitless amount of matter into new wealth, we do not live in a zero-sum world where there is a fixed amount of wealth and we need to acquire anything by force. All you have to do is be productive, and use that which you produce to trade for everything else you want. In our complex societies we don't do this in an obvious way by each person producing a physical good. That which we produce is our labor which is then combined in complex ways to ultimately create the physical goods and services we consume.

Let's take for example oil which is the main reason why the United States occupies the Middle East to protect its "interests" in the region. Let's assume the worst possible scenario. We leave the Middle East and chaos ensues, the oil stops flowing, and the price goes to $300 per barrel. This high price creates an incentive so strong for a social order to emerge and exploit the high profits that it will inevitably emerge. We would not want it to be some cruel dictatorship, but eventually, the incentives created by such a high price in the millions of people who live in that region will grow a stable social order built on the right mixture of alliances/intimidation/whatever, to ultimately exploit such a high price by getting the oil flowing once again. One has to understand that given the cultural values and histories of conflict and so much more, perhaps some form of dictatorship is the superior way to bring about a stable social order in some places.

The possibility of making high profits is all that is needed to lure brains and create social order around it. No visible entity has to be the one that creates the social order.

Let us now assume that the "evil" Iranians or Russians or Chinese go in there and fill the power vacuum so the U.S. no longer controls the area. So what? What are the Iranians, Russians, or Chinese going to do with the oil? They are going to trade it with us just like the Arabs used to do.

What difference does it make to an American whether the money he pays for gas goes to sustain the Arab gene pool or the Chinese one or that of a fellow American? Only our tribal instincts and zero-sum mentality get in the way of allowing this to happen. We tend to see "Americans", "Chinese", "Russians" as if we were tribes fighting to control an essential life-sustaining banana tree which we won't share because we are from different tribes, or better yet, a resource which we will purposely hoard to ensure the others starve and once they die there will be less competition for the other remaining banana trees.

The monopolization of resources was a key survival strategy in our evolution, and is probably one of the reasons why we might have a propensity to dislike the concept of private property. This idea that something belongs exclusively to someone else, especially if it is something our lives might someday depend on or give them a great advantage, is something that we might instinctively rebel against and helps further explain our share-the-wealth/communist tendencies.

As long as the United States or any other country has a free economy at home, the market process will make it a very productive and technologically advanced human ant-farm with nothing to fear from anyone. Even in the ridiculous case that one of our so called potential enemies controls the oil. Would they prevent other countries from reselling the oil they get to us? A worldwide black market devoted to selling oil to the U.S. would emerge **even in this ridiculous scenario**. Moreover, chances are that the trillions we would save in military spending would more than offset whatever higher prices might come about due to this arrangement. So again, as long as the U.S. economy is productive, the goods and services that it produces will lure whoever has oil or whatever resource we could possibly want. And when it comes to energy, another heavily regulated sector of the economy, the moment we get rid of the regulations and the market process is free to do its thing, it will inevitably discover superior knowledge, eventually driving down the cost of all competing alternatives like oil. The riches that allow unproductive and oppressive "cultural books" to survive in the Middle East, will dry up, and inevitably bring about the kind of social change that can compete, which will mean more freedom and equal treatment of human beings.

The key to our foreign policy is to have the freest and most productive economy at home. All the wealth we create is everything we need in order to lure the rest of the world into giving us whatever we want by trade. We do not have to fear the rest of the world being overtaken by some "evil" power. Countries that try to use force to spread their empires are not free economies so they collapse from within as was the case with the former Soviet Union and is unfortunately happening to us as will be discussed in more detail shortly.

Ron's desire to bring all the troops home from all over the world is something that scares most who hear this message, but this fear is also rooted in our tribal nature and completely ignores economic reality. Based on our tribal understanding of the world, we think the big ape has the moral responsibility of protecting the others, but this is not how things work in the modern world. Freedom greatly helps eradicate the reasons for violence as well as the possibility of it happening. Here is what I mean. On Dec. 23rd 2007 Dr. Paul was asked by Tim Russert if his desire to bring the troops home from all over the world included bringing all troops from South Korea. He asked this to Dr. Paul as if implying that removing the troops would be like leaving a helpless child to fight an invading hoard of savages. This tribal, economically ignorant view could not be further from the truth. The minute the US is serious about removing its 30,000 troops and billions worth of military equipment from South Korea, South Korea can take just a tiny fraction of its 1 trillion dollar GDP and arm itself to the teeth. It could just buy the military base from the US, or as the US leaves, it can buy the same armament from US arms manufacturers, or just buy them from the countless other countries that already have the latest and greatest US military stuff. North Korea has a GDP of only 40 billion dollars. It has nothing to offer the rest of the world to trade for the necessary military technology needed to attack anyone, or the food with which to feed its army in a battle for longer than probably a week. And the food that currently helps it avoid mass starvation comes from aid by China and South Korea itself. It basically has a large number of badly nourished bodies and old weapons, with little in the way of replacement parts and other means with which to launch any kind of serious threat compared to what South Korea can do. The same applies to Japan, Germany and the countless other rich nations where the hapless US taxpayer is raped by our big-protector-ape-ideology and the ambitions of the Military Industrial Complex. So again, Japan, South Korea, Germany, France, and everyone else, just because they don't make the weapons themselves it does not mean that they can't defend themselves. THEY JUST TRADE FOR WHAT THEY NEED. And this is the piece that just does not occur to the economically ignorant mind and 100% of the mainstream media and our politicians. They are still living in a tribal world. Free nations can produce more, and therefore they can trade more for the necessary technology to keep themselves safe from aggressors. So not only do free nations provide more incentives for peace, they can defend themselves better when they need to.

But all of this is unneeded. The Internet, coupled with the proper understanding of the socioeconomic world, as especially provided by the "Austrian School", is a new lemon in our ideologies/"cultural books" which should continue to spread quickly and help overcome our old tribal order. Instead of people worrying about international conflicts we should just be looking for the most creative ways of spreading this knowledge as quickly as possible.

The nonsense of mainstream economists

Alan Greenspan tries to save face and our needed return to the gold standard

In a recent interview, Alan Greenspan, the head of our nation's central bank from 1987 to 2006 was asked[1]:

Fox: "So then, why do we need a central bank?"

Greenspan: "Well, the question is a very interesting one. We have at this particular stage a fiat money. Which is essentially money printed out of thin air by a government and it's usually the central bank which is authorized to do so. Some mechanism has got to be in place that restricts the amount of money that is produced, either a gold standard or currency board or something of that nature because unless you do that, all of history suggests that inflation will take hold with very deleterious effects on economic activity."

Yes. It is so simple. With the help of central banking, elected ideologues create trillions with which to fund the bureaucracies they intend to use to help out society. The bureaucracies/tentacles and whatever help they try to provide is what is *visible*, but what we don't see, is how as the bureaucracies trade the new money for wealth from the private sector, they end up consuming much more than whatever wealth in terms of services they might add to society, leaving society poorer and closer to socioeconomic chaos.

What really brings prosperity? It is an arrangement of the social order that produces more wealth than it consumes. The knowledge needed to achieve such order resides in the minds of billions of free individuals/entrepreneurs/businessmen who are already part of profitable, or nearly profitable, business plans, and as we have already discussed, such knowledge can only come about and efficiently spread via the market process in the private sector.

Money is the means by which we morph the social order. Ideally every brain in the social supercomputer would have access to an amount of money/resources proportional to the pie-increasing profitability of its ideas. Why is Microsoft a very wealthy company? Because the knowledge embodied by Microsoft has guided human ants in a very productive way that has greatly improved society, and such improvement to society is reflected in the amount of wealth society has traded with Microsoft making it rich.

Central banking and our "fiat" government created money, allows the stupidest and most tribal brains, our elected ideologues who are the embodiment of our tribal nature, to arrange the social order in disastrous ways that would have been impossible for them to do otherwise. Central banking has been the enabler of countless stupid wars and incalculable socioeconomic hardship. As Dr. Salerno mentions in one of his many great lectures at the Ludwig von Mises Institute:

> "Wars have invariably been financed by printing money since the invention of paper money. Indeed, it might be said that paper fiat money and central banks were invented mainly to finance wars. The first irredeemable paper currency in the Western world was issued in 1690 by the British colony of Massachusetts in order to pay its soldiers in its sporadic wars of plunder against the French colony of Quebec. The first central bank in history, the Bank of England, was established in 1694 to finance the mercantilist and imperialist foreign policy of the Whig party that had gained control of the British government."[2]

It is not just wars obviously. It is the regulations, welfare, and overall destruction of a much more prosperous social order that would have otherwise taken shape if it weren't for all the government created nonsense.

We must abolish central banking and go back to the gold standard. Just like the market process was not consciously invented by human beings, neither was the decision to use gold for its preferred source of money. Gold became the worldwide standard because it naturally emerged as the best money. Society did not go off the gold standard because we found a better alternative; we went off the gold standard due to economic ignorance.

For hundreds of years, the time-honored idea/obligation that money was backed by gold inadvertently provided tremendous benefits to the social order, the biggest one being that it prevented ideologues from distorting the social order to finance their silly plans(wars/welfare/etc). But by breaking this tradition, we opened the door to the type of damaging central planning via inflation that would not have been possible before and has gotten us into countless messes. As Jesús Huerta De Soto tells us:

> "The original neglect of this obligation led to all the banking and monetary issues which have given rise to the current financial system, with its high level of government intervention.
> The idea is ultimately to apply a seminal idea of Hayek's to the field of money and banking. According to this idea, whenever a traditional rule of conduct is broken, either through institutional government coercion or the granting of special privileges by the state to certain people or organizations, sooner or later grave, undesirable consequences always ensue and cause serious damage to the spontaneous process of social cooperation."[3]

We have such a mess today with different countries creating their own paper currencies, everyone inflating at different rates, wreaking havoc on their local economies and messing up what would otherwise have been smooth cooperation between people all over the world. Remember, there are no countries, only individuals trading in various ways. Trade barriers, different currencies, etc., all prevent the market process from smoothly organizing the entire global human ant-farm into the leanest and meanest matter to human usable wealth transformation machine possible. We must go back to the gold standard to once again obtain these benefits, but more importantly, to prevent the damaging effects of government planning and regulation.

In the same interview by Greenspan quoted earlier, Greenspan continues:

"There are numbers of us, myself included, who strongly believe that we did very well in the 1870-1914 period with an international gold standard."

Wow! Of course we did well, as the picture on book's cover shows. Then why did Greenspan create so much money and set us up for the housing bubble and oh so much more we are currently facing? As Dr. Paul says in one of his speeches before Congress:

"In the ten years that Greenspan has held the Fed, 2 trillion of new credit has been created..."[4] (and this was half way through Greenspan's 20 years)

Murderers like Stalin and Mao were trying to implement a communist ideology that they and those around them certainly believed in, in their own self absorbed sort of way, but they certainly did not purposely destroy their countries. A great mystery to many libertarians and people who know a bit about the history of economic thought is how Greenspan could have gone from someone who clearly understood the evils of central banking and benefits of gold, to being one of the greatest inflators and destroyers of prosperity of all time. In his famous "Gold and Economic Freedom" published in Ayn Rand's "Objectivist" newsletter in 1966, and reprinted in her book, "Capitalism: The Unknown Ideal", in 1967, Greenspan said:

"In the absence of the gold standard, there is no way to protect savings from confiscation through inflation...

...This is the shabby secret of the welfare statists' tirades against gold. Deficit spending is simply a scheme for the confiscation of wealth. Gold stands in the way of this insidious process. It stands as a protector of property rights. If one grasps this, one has no difficulty in understanding the statists' antagonism toward the gold standard."[5]

How could Greenspan have written this and believe that the gold standard would be a better solution, yet lead to the inflationary policies that have allowed our mega-cancer government to bankrupt our future, finance ideological wars and create so much socioeconomic harm? Anyways, now we even have "the Maestro" 's blessing for going back to the gold standard.

Bernanke's economic nonsense and his "stimulus" package

Next let's include another statement, this time by current head of the Federal Reserve Ben Bernanke. Check out this absurdity:

"…the U.S. government has a technology, called a printing press (or, today, its electronic equivalent), that allows it to produce as many U.S. dollars as it wishes at essentially no cost. By increasing the number of U.S. dollars in circulation, or even by credibly threatening to do so, the U.S. government can also reduce the value of a dollar in terms of goods and services, which is equivalent to raising the prices in dollars of those goods and services. We conclude that, under a paper-money system, a determined government can always generate higher spending and hence positive inflation."[6]

He is right, a determined government can always print money with which to rob productive citizens of their wealth and leave them with higher prices. And "positive inflation"? That's like saying "delightful headache". The excerpt came from a speech titled "Deflation: Making Sure "It" Doesn't Happen Here". In a prospering economy under a gold standard, as the picture on the cover shows, we should expect to see a slight downward trend in prices because the productivity tends to increase faster than the money supply. Lower prices are a sign of progress. Your savings last you longer, etc. The speech should have been titled "Progress: We the government will give you paper and you give us this progress so we can feed a bigger bureaucracy while you stay running in place or falling behind with higher prices." Ok, reworked title was too long but one gets the point. Our misguided economic policies do not just harm us via the inflation we can clearly see on a graph, even if prices would remain stable, it would still be robbing us of progress because prices would most likely be going down, and inflation would rob us of this progress.

Right now our bureaucrats and Bernanke are working on a "stimulus" package. They envision giving money to people and then seeing people spending the money and businesses working and producing to get people's money. They talk about consumer confidence, about psychology, about "consumer spending", as is getting people to spend money and seeing the human ant-farm moving around is all that is needed to create prosperity. What they will never talk about, because they do not understand it, is that all the activity and "stimulating" in the world needs to be part of a delicate cycle that increases production over consumption. Just because you see people moving around and working/buying/selling does not mean that their actions will lead to prosperity. On the contrary, if their actions lead to more consumption than production you are making things worse, and that is exactly what will happen when the government borrows/prints another 150 billion for its "stimulus" package. The economy is in trouble because its human ants are misaligned, and giving money here and there will not help create the necessary incentives to help discover and spread the knowledge with which to realign our messed up social order.

When one realizes that what is needed is for the right knowledge to spread throughout society in a way that it can coordinate pie-increasing/profitable human action, it becomes easier to see that simply giving money here and there has nothing to do with accomplishing this goal. Only things like interest rate coordination and the competitive knowledge discovery process inherent in the market process can accomplish such a task. These mechanisms can only work in the private sector, in a private sector that is not burdened and thwarted by taxation, regulation, and inflation.

Notice how they don't talk about cutting spending, i.e., consumption by some government bureaucracy. This would "put people out on the streets" which is a tribal sin and therefore political suicide, but it is exactly what we need and the only thing that will save us. The former public sector employees would cease being part of a consumptive social cancer as they are laid off, and by joining the private sector they would incorporate themselves into a profitable social order which would increase the economic pie.

John Maynard Keynes. The grandfather of our mainstream economorons

John Maynard Keynes was the most important economoron of the 20th century. Keynes was a British economist whose book "The General Theory of Employment, Interest and Money" published in 1936 became the intellectual foundation upon which our mainstream economics establishment stands on. Keynesian economics can be summarized very briefly, Henry Hazlitt accomplishes this in a few sentences when he tells us, "John Maynard Keynes was, basically, an inflationist."…"In other words, the Keynesian solution to every slow-down in business or rise in unemployment was still another dose of inflation."[7] So essentially get the government to print some money and provide a "stimulus" which will "jump-start" things and get the "economy moving" and all the usual nonsense that one hears the economically ignorant establishment talking about. Again, as already mentioned, getting the economy moving is not the solution, you have to get it moving in a cycle that produces more than it consumes, but Keynes could not see that far. I am sure that he could if he really wanted to, all he had to do was honestly discuss things with his friend

F.A. Hayek, but Hayek had already torn to pieces some of his earlier published nonsense.

In many ways Keynes seemed like a pompous arrogant fool. A good example of someone who is born into British high status and believed that his supposedly superior blood inevitably leads to greatness in all his endeavors[8]. As wrong as this might be, the confidence that one gets from believing this lie can take you places, especially when your economic nonsense is lightly peppered with always-seemingly-impressive mathematicobabble and allows and encourages politicians to do exactly what they want: attempt to use government to fix or improve the economy. Hayek knew Keynes very well and said this of him:

"There were of course extraordinary gaps in his knowledge. His knowledge was aesthetically guided, with the result that he was completely ignorant of nineteenth-century economic history. Totally ignorant. He just disliked it.

I had to tell him every day, not so much about economic history, but even about earlier English economists…if I had introduced him to English inflationists of the nineteenth century, that might have put him off.

…if you take his time of study, I don't think he spent more than a year learning economics… I like to say, I liked Keynes and in many ways admired him, but do not think he was a good economist"[9]

Just like Marx's communist ideas appealed to the Russian and Chinese ideologues and public for various reasons, Keynes' ideas appealed to those who believed that the world needed the big-ape-government to steer it in the right direction and prevent what would surely be great injustices, which was pretty much everyone in the Western world as well. The Anglo-Saxon world might have had too strong a legal tradition of respect for private property and individual rights, so full-blown revolutionary Communism at the point of a gun might not have cut it, but Socialism via inflation inadvertently evolved to be the perfect tool. This is what the ghost of Keynes essentially left us with, with well intentioned 'government control'/Socialism, not at the point of a gun, but by essentially using inflation to create the necessary money with which to allow the government to rearrange the social order nonetheless.

Next, a nice quote by Keynes:

"The ideas of economists and political philosophers, both when they are right and when they are wrong, are more powerful than is commonly understood. Indeed the world is ruled by little else. Practical men, who believe themselves to be quite exempt from any intellectual influences, are usually the slaves of some defunct economist. Madmen in authority, who hear voices in the air, are distilling their frenzy from some academic scribbler of a few years back. I am sure that the power of vested interests is vastly exaggerated compared with the gradual encroachment of ideas…But, soon or late, it is ideas, not vested interests, which are dangerous for good or evil."[10]

Yes. Keynes himself is one of those defunct economists. He is also famously known for having said, "In the long run we are all dead." The problem is that shortsighted defunct economists' "long run" is our present.

Let's go over a few brief quotes by Keynes to see how his fallacies still haunt us today:

"…whenever you save five shillings, you put a man out of work for a day. Your saving that five shillings adds to unemployment to the extent of one man for one day—and so in proportion. On the other hand, whenever you buy goods you increase employment…For if you buy goods, someone will have to make them. And if you do not buy goods, the shops will not clear their stocks, they will not give repeat orders, and some one will be thrown out of work.

Therefore, oh patriotic housewives, sally out to-morrow early into the streets and go to the wonderful sales which are everywhere advertised. You will do yourselves good…And have the added joy that you are increasing employment, adding to the wealth of the country because you are setting on foot useful activities…

…Surely all this is the most obvious common sense. For take the extreme case. Suppose we were to stop spending our incomes altogether, and were to save the lot. Why, every one would be out of work. And before long we should have no incomes to spend."

Wow! First of all, when most people save their money they invest it, which for the general case here we'll just assume that it is loaned out at interest. The money still gets spent! As Henry Hazlitt stresses in his classic "Economics in One Lesson", *""Saving," in short, in the modern world, is only another form of spending. The usual difference is that the money is turned over to someone else to spend on means to increase production."*[11] That's right. When you save and lend your money, the borrowers still spend it but they have to spend it in a way that increases the economic pie enough for them to not only pay back the loan, but to also pay the interest on it, which means that they are increasing the economic pie. This is how the world progresses, by saving and investing.

If we assume that society is ordered in such a way that it *produces as much as it consumes*, then taking your paycheck and spending it will just keep society in the same sort of cycle, with people doing more or less the same thing. Since there would be little to no savings, there is not enough wealth to fund new restructurings of the social order. Where would a new company get the funds/wealth to sustain itself as it builds the manufacturing plant and cannot yet create wealth? Interest rates would be very high, and only few ideas, those with very high returns on investment would be able to borrow profitably at such high interest rates. So as previously discussed in the economics section, society would be more or less stuck with little technological progress.

If we assume that society is ordered in a way that *consumes more than what it produces*, then the economic situation is deteriorating, the economic pie would be shrinking, we would be in a depression. So again, just because people are working/spending/buying and we have a "dynamic" economy does not mean that we are headed towards prosperity. Society needs to be properly ordered, its millions of human ants need to be coordinated by the only thing that can do so, individual freedom, the market process. Keynes obviously did not see this. He was a bad economist who only looked at the immediate results of his ideas. Keynes as well as the politicians eager to usher in a new utopia only saw people working and making money and things being built under their wonderful leadership, but they could not see all the consumption going on which would inevitably shrink or slow down the economy if the social order was not properly aligned. As people produce they also consume, if a thousand men drive to work every day and wear out 1,000 cars in order to produce 100 cars then they are making things worse.

Keynes continues with more nonsense:

"…activity of one kind or another is the only possible means of making the wheels of economic progress and of the production of wealth go round again.

Nationally, too, I would like to see schemes of greatness and magnificence designed and carried through. I read a few days ago of a proposal to drive a great new road…That is the right sort of notion. But I should like to see something bigger still. For example, why not pull down the whole of South London from Westminster to Greenwich, and make a good job of it…Would that employ men? Why, of course it would! Is it better that the men should stand idle and miserable, drawing the dole? Of course it is not."

Again, more of the same fallacy, "activity of one kind or another." This is nonsense, one cannot just act, one has to produce more than one consumes. Next, he gives the green light for the usual massive public works projects that governments are prone to fall for. Politicians/economorons can envision some great new road bringing great benefits, but they do not see all the wealth that is consumed in terms of the stuff that society really needs like cars, homes, food, medical services, etc., as this road is being built by those who build it. Next comes an even bigger fallacy, he wants to "pull down", in other words, demolish wealth, in order to put people to work and rebuild "South London from Westminster to Greenwich."

In a recent front-page article in yahoo news:

"The House quickly adopted a $161 billion economic stimulus plan this week that would send $600-$1,200 rebates to more than 100 million Americans in hopes they would spend the money quickly and give the flagging economy a shot in the arm."[12]

Thank God the revolution will put an end to this quickly.

Franklin Delano Roosevelt: America's drastic turn towards Socialism

The obvious truth that Americans are no different from Russians and Chinese easily manifested itself in our own path to Socialism, especially under Franklin Delano Roosevelt's presidency. Let's briefly say a couple of things about this important period in our history.

The Federal Reserve created boom of the 1920s finally began to visibly bust[13] with the stock market crash of 1929, but the Hoover administration at the time did not just let the crash and necessary correction take its place. We had an emergency, our bureaucrats had to act, right? Hoover further aggravated the problem by doing stupid things like confiscating and consuming even more wealth from the private sector by raising taxes and creating bureaucracies aimed at curing the evils the government itself was responsible for. As Hoover stated in 1932: "I have waged the most gigantic program of economic defense and counter-attack ever evolved in the history of the Republic." What would have been an economic correction needed to properly realign the social order, which would have been followed by normal economic growth, turned into the Great Depression as FDR took office and did even more economic damage. If one harebrained government intervention did not work, you just have to keep trying, right? What kind of leader just gives up and decides to do nothing and leave the private sector alone, especially when the people are begging the leader to take action? As FDR said "The country needs and, unless I mistake its temper, the country demands bold, persistent experimentation. It is common sense to take a method and try it; if it fails, admit it frankly and try another. But above all, try something" Every "something" attempted by FDR created yet another government tentacle aimed at curing a visible social ill, benefiting a visible few, while consuming and destroying more social order leading to unproductive chaos. As leading businessman Lamont du Pont mentioned with respect to the government created chaos in 1937:

"Uncertainty rules the tax situation, the labor situation, the monetary situation, and practically every legal condition under which industry must operate. Are taxes to go higher, lower or stay where they are? We don't know. Is labor to be union or non-union?…Are we to have inflation or deflation, more government spending or less?…Are new restrictions to be placed on capital, new limits on profits?…It is impossible to even guess at the answers."[14]

How can the social order arrange itself in a sustainable and prosperous cycle which produces more wealth than it consumes, in other words, a profitable cycle, when the government makes it impossible to predict the future and plan accordingly?

Governmental foreign aid does not help

Take your average poor African country, say Ethiopia. Why is it poor? Because its human ants are not ordered in a way that produces enough wealth to *trade* for all the things that we associate with the good life like affordable cars, medicines, etc. The only way Ethiopia can be wealthy is if it figures out a way to give its 75 million human ants a highly efficient and productive order. An order that produces enough desirable wealth so that the rest of the world is willing to trade cars, medicines, planes, etc. for it. How do they do this?

First of all, central planning does not work. If the foreign aid money is spent by the governments in an attempt to order their human ants in a cycle that produces more than it consumes they will inevitably fail. It might work for a while as they burn the loaned funds, but given the inevitable inefficiencies in central planning, their socially planned order will become another unproductive social cancer. Only the businessmen, both domestic to Ethiopia and potential foreign investors, who are already running profitable businesses know how to incorporate more labor in pie-increasing/profitable ways. The key to building a prosperous social order for the poorer countries is to let foreign investors hire them and invest in their countries directly, or make it easy for native entrepreneurs to do business and get loans from the outside. Kiva.org is a new popular site that makes it easy to lend to people in poor countries and seems to be having some success.

Poor African nations, the European and American intellectuals ultimately export their socialist well-intentioned ideas to Africa and keep it screwed up. Then many people quite naturally think that the reason that Africa is always stuck in a shit-hole is because Africans must be biologically inferior in some way. Nothing could be farther from the truth. Someone once asked me what single power I would like to have, I replied with "the ability to place knowledge in people's minds". If one could suddenly place the proper understanding of economics in the mind of every African inhabitant, I have little doubt in my mind that within a couple of generations Africa would be the economic and intellectual powerhouse of the world. That is, assuming that the rest of the world continues in its semi-socialist big government boom-bust/"evil"-seeking-tribalism, because obviously the modern Western world has a huge lead.

African leaders get educated in European universities. This naturally makes them "smart" and therefore the most suitable central planners. They inevitably fail of course. Since governments exert so much power and control in Africa, people have no choice but to riot if their buddy is not in power as we are seeing right now in Kenya where the machete is the weapon of choice. If government only takes about 2-5% of your wealth and its regulatory tentacles do not interfere with you, there is little need to be too concerned with politics. But the more it takes and controls, the more people inevitably have to fight over how the wealth is distributed and who the regulations will hurt or benefit.

Whatever the government does and the law are ultimately two sides of the same coin. In order for the government to do something new, it has to alter the law, i.e., mandate a new tax, a new regulation, etc. In a free society, the law protects the freedom of the individual and is less likely to change, it does this by mostly enforcing our two fundamental laws. Once you feel like big government has to solve problems, the law goes from protecting the freedom of the individual, to forcing the human ants down whatever the solution to some "social problem" the elected ideologues want to implement. Since we know that such top-down solutions just create more problems, this mentality inevitably ushers in an uncontrollable torrent of laws and regulations, sort of like a dog chasing after its own tail. Referring to 19th century America and its proper legal sphere at the time, Frederic Bastiat mentions:

"There is no country in the world where the law is kept more within its proper domain: the protection of every person's liberty and property. As a consequence of this, there appears to be no country in the world where the social order rests on a firmer foundation."

When large multinational companies employ people in poor nations they are using their superior knowledge and tools to give a productive order to the poorer nation's social orders, but since they are making a profit and not sharing it equally, many people and the local governments, fueled by our egalitarian instincts see it as exploitation, make it unprofitable for businesses so they leave(or never come in the first place), and the poorer nations remain without that which they need most, profitable knowledge and tools with which to give their human ant-farms a productive and self sustaining order.

Terrorism and national security

Government monopolies cannot protect us

Given that we instinctively think that some visible entity has to keep us safe, we inevitably believe that the government has to do it, and that we have to give up our freedoms for it to be able to do so. If the government is going to solve the problem, then it must be able to move the "different pieces upon a chess-board" and we have to give up our freedom. But what we don't realize is that we have over 300 million sets of eyes, whose freedom to protect themselves is far more powerful than a central bureaucracy. If airlines would have had the freedom to manage how they want to protect themselves there would have been the usual competitive process to discover the best ways of achieving security and 9/11 would not have happened. But since the government regulates airline safety, we just get countless of baggage screeners searching through the bags of old, harmless ladies, taking our liquids away, paying exorbitant amounts of money for screening equipment from politically connected companies. And with all of this, airline security is virtually inexistent. For example, in a recent test of security at Newark Liberty International Airport, undercover agents "were able to smuggle through an array of fake bombs and guns in 20 of 22 tests at checkpoints through the hub's three terminals" [15]. The last time I was on an airplane, I remember the plane taxing after landing and it went over a bridge where there was free-flowing traffic just a few feet underneath. I remember thinking just how easy it would have been for a disgruntled person to just drive by and throw a grenade from their passing car.

Safety, like any other good or service requires figuring out the best way to provide it, and since it is knowledge we are after, only freedom and competition can properly provide it in our modern world. If safety is a concern, this would reflect itself accordingly in the willingness of airline passengers to trade their money for safer airlines. A market for airline safety would naturally arise and be shaped by the market process as competition discovered and spread the best ways of providing such safety. But since the government completely took over the airline safety market, it turned it into a monopoly, where the knowledge would come from a single inevitably inefficient bureaucracy, leading to the obvious results of high prices for utterly useless labor, more comfy pensions, jobs people never lose, long lines, pomposity by those who think they are the heroes who protect us, etc., and little in terms of safety in return. Simply allowing the pilots to carry firearms would have gone a long way in preventing 9/11. If the government monopolizes some service, i.e. 'airline safety'/'roads and highways', or regulates the private sector as in the case of the healthcare sector, it just destroys the market process' competitive knowledge discovery process that creates the best solutions, ultimately leading to ever growing consumptive bureaucracies. We just see the government as being the big bad ape that has all the resources and feel like that is all that is needed to fix problems. This might have worked in a tribal past where pretty much everything came down to force and numbers, but it won't work today. It should also be noted that when the bureaucracies inevitably fail, we just think they need even more resources and more regulation, continuing our "road to serfdom" and the inevitable socioeconomic collapse.

Why do they hate us

Why is the Muslim world so susceptible to the radicalization that led to the 9/11 attacks? As Dr. Paul keeps reminding us, it is the occupation and long history of meddling in the region. As the European powers were in a race to colonize the world due to their misguided zero-sum fears, which led them to believe that they had to control natural resources; they plundered, mistreated, took favorites in regional disputes and so much more. This created plenty of reasons for some to get upset at the foreign players, mostly the British, who ruled much of the world in the early 20th century. For example, the Arabian Peninsula used to be just that, a geographic area that was populated by many Arab tribes, but one powerful Arab family headed by Ibn-Saud, backed by the British, finally conquered the large chunk of land that is now called Saudi Arabia. As Richard Maybury points out, this would be like the Ferguson family subduing all of Canada and calling it Ferguson Canada. Mr. Saud had 150 wives and today the country is run by his extended family. It is nepotism at its best. Recently Saudi Arabia's human rights abuses once again made the news when a woman was gang raped and found to be guilty and punished to 200 lashings. It was her fault for being in a car with someone she was not supposed to be with. Fortunately for her, enough media attention seems to have pressured the king to pardon her.

Saudi Arabia contains the two holiest cities in Islam. Mecca, the birthplace of Muhammad, and Medina, Muhammad's burial place. A lot of people do not like the way the country is run, there are political and religious conflicts that go back hundreds of years, and everyone probably has good reason to hate someone else, including the nepotistic ruling establishment. But the U.S.'s economically ignorant tribal minded ideologues believe that the U.S. has "vital interests" in the region, so they picks a side to aid and then that side has the money and military backing to keep everyone else in check and continue a status quo that many do not like. This pisses people off, especially the fact that the United States has military bases in their holy lands, supporting the system they want changed. One of these people is Osama bin Laden, who has been fighting what he considers a bad Saudi government. Let's just read a little of what he says. From his 1996 fatwa[16].

Here he criticizes the government's mismanagement of the economy:

"People are fully concerned about their every day livings; every body talks about the deterioration of the economy, inflation, ever increasing debts and jails full of prisoners ... They complain that the value of the Riyal is greatly and continuously deteriorating among most of the main currencies."

"The financial and the economical situation of the country and the frightening future in the view of the enormous amount of debts and interest owed by the government; ... while imposing more custom duties and taxes on the nation."

Hum, looks like bin Laden knows a thing or two about economics. He does, he knows too much as we will soon discuss. Next he gets to the U.S. presence in "Holy Places":

"The latest and the greatest of these aggressions... is the occupation of the land of the two Holy Places... by the armies of the American Crusaders and their allies."...

"The crusaders were permitted to be in the land of the two Holy Places...The land was filled with the military bases of the USA and the allies. The regime became unable to keep control without the help of these bases. You know more than any body else about the size, intention and the danger of the presence of the USA military bases in the area."...

Next is a very important statement:

"More than 600,000 Iraqi children have died due to lack of food and medicine and as a result of the unjustifiable aggression (sanction) imposed on Iraq and its nation. The children of Iraq are our children. You, the USA, together with the Saudi regime are responsible for the shedding of the blood of these innocent children. Due to all of that, what ever treaty you have with our country is now null and void."

These 600,000 Iraqi children are the same ones that Medeleine Albright, then US ambassador to the United Nations, was asked about in a "60 Minutes" interview in 1996. With respect to these sanctions imposed on Saddam's Iraq[17] by the UN, with heavy pressure from the US, the question was "We have heard that half a million children have died. I mean, that's more children than died in Hiroshima. And, you know, is the price worth it?" and Albright's answer "I think this is a very hard choice, but the price — we think the price is worth it."[18]

Later in her autobiography, Mrs. Albright discussed how she regretted using those words as soon as she spoke them. But it doesn't matter how bad she must have felt or how she worded things, what mattered was the deaths of thousands of innocent people due to misguided foreign policy.

Doesn't everyone know that sanctions just hurt innocent civilians? Let's hear it from Dr. Paul:

"I oppose economic sanctions for two very simple reasons. First, they don't work as effective foreign policy. Time after time, from Cuba to China to Iraq, we have failed to unseat despotic leaders by refusing to trade with the people of those nations. If anything, the anti-American sentiment aroused by sanctions often strengthens the popularity of such leaders, who use America as a convenient scapegoat to divert attention from their own tyranny. History clearly shows that free and open trade does far more to liberalize oppressive governments than trade wars. Economic freedom and political freedom are inextricably linked--when people get a taste of goods and information from abroad, they are less likely to tolerate a closed society at home. So while sanctions may serve our patriotic fervor, they mostly harm innocent citizens and do nothing to displace the governments we claim as enemies."[19]

Doesn't everyone know that the last people to get whatever resources are in short supply are the civilians who are not part of the ruling establishment? Did Saddam and his political structure suffer because of the sanctions? Of course not. But our tribal ideologues only think about the evil Saddam. No matter how small the chance that he might get a nuclear weapon to create a mushroom cloud over here might be, it justifies pretty much anything, especially when our top ideologues are so ignorant about human nature, economics, and many are heavily influenced by religious ideology that can easily detach Muslim deaths and suffering from their minds. It is true that Saddam was a bad guy, but our elected ideologue's misguided foreign policy led to the deaths of more people than Saddam might have killed with his gassings, etc. But obviously our elected ideologues did not have bad intentions so this makes it alright through our eyes.

In another statement by Ayman Al-Zawahiri, close friend of bin Laden and Al-Qaeda #2, he explains[20] their justification for attacking civilian targets. According to Al-Zawahiri, Islam classifies people into enemy combatants and non-combatants. Combatants are people who either directly harm Muslims or *enable* those that do Muslims harm. He makes the point that since we freely elect our leaders and fund them as their policies harm Muslims, we are enemy-combatants and therefore fair game. An argument I do not support, but more on this in a second.

With respect to the 1993 World Trade Center bombings, bin Laden was asked by John Miller[21], "What about the World Trade Center bombing. It's not like fighting the Russians on the field of battle. This is targeting innocents and civilians." And bin Laden replied, "This is a very strange question coming from an American. Was it not your country that bombed Nagasaki and Hiroshima? Were there not women and children and civilians and noncombatants there? You were the people who invented this terrible game and we as Muslims have to use those same tactics against you."

Bin Laden makes a seemingly good point. Although I doubt bin Laden knows the details of the U.S.'s dropping of the bombs, it is common knowledge amongst many historians that the nuclear bombs were dropped for political reasons that had nothing to do with saving American lives(not that this would have justified dropping the bombs anyways). Months before the bombs were dropped the Japanese had been trying to negotiate surrender in a way where they could keep their emperor, who according to their religion was a holy figure. As historian, John V. Denson mentions "Since President Truman, in effect, accepted the conditional surrender offered by the Japanese as early as May of 1945, the question is posed, "Why then were the bombs dropped?""[22]. Long before the bombs were dropped Japan had already been completely devastated by our B-29 bombers. For example, on the single day of March 9, 1945, 279 B-29s incinerated Tokyo killing over 185,000 Japanese[23]. Mostly women and children for sure, at a cost of 14 US planes.

Our elected ideologues during the time wanted to intimidate the Russians by showing off their new weapon, justify their expenditures on the research to Congress, and another factor was the good'ol tribalism that makes us look at our human enemy as subhuman beasts. As president Truman mentions in a letter to Samuel McCrea Cavert, General Secretary of The Churches of Christ in America:

"The only language they seem to understand is the one we have been using to bombard them.
When you have to deal with a beast you have to treat him as a beast. It is most regrettable but nevertheless true." [24].

Obviously there must be great genetic differences between Americans and the Japanese and therefore their ability to understand things. And the genetic differences are very big because they are "beast". Luckily for us, we live in the 21st century and our great religious ideologue, Mr. Bush, would never think of Muslims in the same way, right?

Although Al-Zawahiri and bin Laden make some very good points, I do not believe that their arguments justify the killing of innocent Americans in terrorist attacks. I will not go into some lengthy rebuttal of their arguments but will just rebuke one thing that will lead us to another point. Just because some elected ideologues decided to view others as "beast"s, and for other political reasons needlessly drop atomic bombs killing innocent civilians, this does not give justification for killing innocent people that had nothing to do with it. This reminds me of Dr. Paul's constant and important reminder that the real culprit in our troubles is NOT the American people, but our foreign policy. This is yet another example of how our groupish tribal mentality gets us into trouble, especially as it relates to war and dealing with foreigners. What comes to mind was the heated exchange between Dr. Paul and Mike Huckabee during a presidential debate where Dr. Paul explains how the American people were not to blame for the Iraq war debacle:

<u>Dr. Paul</u> : "The American people didn't go in. A few people advising this administration, a small number of people called the neoconservatives hijacked our foreign policy. They are responsible, not the American people. They are not responsible, we shouldn't punish them."

<u>And Huckabee, representing the American tribe:</u> "Congressman we are one nation. We can't be divided. We have to be one nation under God, and that means that if we make a mistake we make it as a single country, the United States of America, not the divided states of America."

America did not drop the bombs on Japan, it was the ideologues that had the means to do it. The point I want to make is that all human beings are equal. What sets the reader, myself, Truman, and bin Laden apart, is a sequence of thoughts and circumstances that leads our actions one way or the other. This is sort of obvious and is something our ideologues understand when they talk about putting pressure in various Muslim governments to close the more radical-minded schools.

Bin Laden is not "evil", he was once a little boy who played and loved. He has wives and children that he loves and is little different from any other human being. Unfortunately, the religious lemons in his head inevitably make a lemonade that has a holy fervor about our occupation of their holy lands and involvement in their politics. But he does this with logical reasons and moral justification from a perspective shared by millions of other human beings, and is far, far away from being this concentration of "evil" that our politicians make him out to be.

Bin Laden is a hero to millions, a man who willingly put himself in the front lines against the invading Russians to inspire his people. He is viewed favorably by 65% of people in Pakistan, 55% in Jordan, and 45% in Morocco[25]. We are not fighting bodies, we are fighting ideologies. Sequences of thoughts and socioeconomic circumstances that can lead a mind to rationalizing that terrorist acts are a good thing. Our tribal economically ignorant foreign policy and history of blunders(Abu Ghraib, etc.) has created more than enough facts and stupidities for the unfortunate sequences of thoughts that lead to terrorism to easily spread through thousands of minds.

By around March 6, 2006 according to this[26] U.K. Guardian Unlimited story based on a report by Amnesty International titled "Iraq: Beyond Abu Ghraib: Detention and torture in Iraq"[27] the US had 14,000 detainees held without trial, out of which 3,800 had been held over a year and 200 for over 2 years. By today the US detains almost twice as many, 26,000[28], and the resentment caused by such reckless judiciary is transforming such detention centers into breeding grounds for more extremism[29]. According to Brig. Gen. Janis Karpinski, one of the Americans demoted due to the Abu Ghraib scandal, one of the top brass giving out orders Gen. Wodjakowski said, "I don't care if we're holding 15,000 innocent Iraqis, we're winning the war."[30] . Thousands of these detainees are the parents, brothers, uncles of an already malnourished population that desperately needs whatever help and love these people provide to their families.

Let us momentarily forget the fact that no one in Iraq had anything to do with 9/11 and continue with the assumption that there were in fact some bad people in Iraq that we wanted to kill because they were the evil bad guys. How upset would you be if some foreign country occupied your country, bombed your buildings, and inadvertently killed one of your family members as it tried to get a few bad guys? Even if you agreed with the invading army that the guys they were after were bad people, how can they put their desire to get some bad guys above your safety and material well-being? When we are out there, destroying property and inadvertently killing civilians, we are in some ways saying, "we care more about getting the bad guys than your life". We do not say it that way, and we don't mean this, but this is a factual representation of our current policy in Iraq. Remember, we want to "fight them over there, so we don't have to fight them over here". This is how our ideologues see things. The majority of Iraqis want us out of there and feel like our presence there is causing more harm than good[31]. But their wishes and suffering are secondary to our "winning the war on terror".

Marine Corporal Grant Collins, now a member of Iraq Veterans Against the War(www.ivaw.org) painfully describes in this[32] video how he gave the order to bomb a building which upon entering they saw a frantic mother who had lost her children and husband. Mr. Collins began to cry and the woman, who had just lost her family, understood he did not mean to do this and consoled him. This experience made it obvious to Mr. Collins that this war was doing far more harm than good.

One of the many disturbing things about our war in Iraq is the increasing "coolness" of being in the military these days.

It is in our nature to love violence. As a recent Live Science article[33] aptly titled "Humans Crave Violence Just Like Sex" discusses, mice have been found to love to fight and gain pleasure in a similar manner to how we love food and sex. When you have spent most of your evolutionary time in a zero-sum world where other people's loss is your gain, killing and causing harm to others should feel as good as eating and having sex and we all know it. This is obvious, and it is the reason why guns and fighting are so appealing to men. We shouldn't be shocked when men murder and rape, the real miracle that has taken thousands of years of cultural evolution to create, are the modern cultural values we absorb that brainwash us into respecting the rights of all human beings regardless of age, sex, and race. So let's not kid ourselves with political correctness and "my people would never do such a thing" kind of talk. It is worrisome to look at the many youtube videos showing footage of the war with loud heavy metal music full of testosterone[34] as well as countless comments glorifying all the destruction and the taking out of the bad guys. It is young macho tribalism at its best.

We like to tape ourselves doing cool things, like having sex for some people, and this carries over to blowing things up with all the cool weaponry that is a sign of power. Our armed forces have lowered their standards for the acceptance of recruits to all time levels. In a matter of hours an ill educated and maladapted youth who might even have a rap sheet[35] can suddenly become one of "Americas finest", a "hero". This type of move by our military is yet another slap in the face to the thousands who were lied into fighting this ideological war for the right moral reasons. Then we have over 100,000 military contractors who are not accountable to any court for their actions and can get away with pretty much anything. Over 2 million Iraqis have left their country, even more have been displaced, over a million people have had their lives cut short either directly due to the violence or other factors…there is little need to bring up statistics.

The point of all this is that there are more than enough facts, atrocities and wrongdoings by this war to create the necessary sequence of thoughts needed to have thousands of regular human beings rise up against our troops.

A so-called "insurgent" is just one of these human beings that has absorbed such a sequence of thoughts. A sequence of thoughts that has inadvertently been created by our own misguided foreign policy and ultimately the tribalism of a few ideologues at the top of our government. It is also wrong to just say that our elected ideologues are 100% of the problem. Human nature is the problem. I remember knocking on doors weeks prior to the Iowa caucus telling people about Ron Paul, and running into one nice elderly man who told me we should kill all the Muslims. Do I think this old man is evil? Of course not. Did I simply have bad luck and stumble upon the one crazy old militant in Council Bluffs, Iowa? I don't think so either.

Little do Americans realize that when they join the armed forces, they are not fighting to protect our freedoms, they are simply surrendering their freedom and agreeing to become part of the largest chain of command whose sole purpose is to do what the elected ideologues want. In George W. Bush's case, "My administration has a job to do... We will rid the world of the evil-doers." "This will be a monumental struggle of good versus evil. But good will prevail."

With respect to Bush's decision-making process, Jacob Weisberg in his book "The Bush Tragedy" discusses Bush Jr.'s ignorant and cowboy decision making:

"This Bush did not want to host debates in his office or hear a range of opinions. He would begin a foreign policy discussion by stating his own views—and would bristle if someone had the temerity to challenge them. He did not intend to use his national security adviser as a filter for differing opinions. He definitely did not want to read long, boring memos... He rejected rethinking, micromanaging, or getting too absorbed in the details."[36]

With respect to Mr. Rumsfeld, Weisberg tells us:

"Rumsfeld wanted to go to war with Iraq for his own reasons. He saw invading Iraq as an opportunity to demonstrate the theory of "military transformation." With new technology, the defense secretary believed the Pentagon could fight wars cheaply and easily, with many fewer troops. By proving the efficacy of new technology and tactics, Rumsfeld thought he would leave an important legacy in his second turn at Defense Department"[37]

One could go on and on, many books have been written that go into excruciating detail describing the many lies and manipulations that allowed our elected and appointed ideologues to use our nation's resources and lives to attempt to implement their well-intentioned ideas.

Unlike reaching the top of a company in the free-market, where such a position of leadership can only come about through the kinds of good decisions and values that increase profits, and therefore how much wealth is added to the economic pie. The democratic process launches to the top of the most powerful enterprise, the U.S. government, people who are reflective of our tribal nature and unfortunate economic ignorance.

Our invasion and massive occupation of Muslim holy lands in Iraq is a constant source of hatred and moral inspiration. Since our invasion, there have been far more terrorists attacks and recruiting people for martyrdom has never been easier. Here bin Laden comments on his happiness with respect to the US occupation of Iraq:

> "Be glad of the good news: America is mired in the swamps of the Tigris and Euphrates. Bush is, through Iraq and its oil, easy prey. Here is he now, thank God, in an embarrassing situation and here is America today being ruined before the eyes of the whole world."[38]

And sadly, America is being "ruined". Which brings us to our next section.

The destruction of the American social order via military spending

It costs a few disgruntled Iraqis a couple hundred dollars to make a bomb, while it is costing us millions to protect our soldiers against them. The disgruntled Iraqis, thanks to our limited tribal understanding of the world, are destroying the American social order, not via the direct blowing up of our buildings, but via the economic destruction that the military industrial complex is doing to our social order. Let's look at this further.

According to one wikipedia article[39], the economic damages incurred by hurricane Katrina were about 150 billion dollars. So about 150 billion dollars in human usable wealth, in terms of buildings, property, etc. were destroyed. Society lost this wealth. It is as if it were traded for nothing, and as if 150 billion dollars in wealth would have to be consumed in order to feed, clothe and equip thousands of people to rebuild that which was lost. If the loss is not replaced, then Louisiana and Mississippi remain without such wealth, but if it is replaced, 150 billion worth of wealth will still have to be removed from the economic pie in order to recreate the lost wealth. Either way, 150 billion in wealth has disappeared. In 2008, the total expenditure in national security will be over 1,000 billion dollars[40]. Over a trillion dollars worth of wealth will be consumed from the economic pie to sustain and expand our national security related social order. We will trade over a trillion dollars worth of homes, cars, energy, etc. to sustain millions of people, from the thousands stationed in our 700 plus bases in over 130 countries, to those who work in our large politically connected military contractors like Lockheed Martin and Bechtel, and everyone they do business with and so on. All for the ability to prevent another major power from crossing either the Pacific or Atlantic oceans with enough troops to occupy us, and to defend other wealthy countries and police the world, which as previously shown, can do fine without the hapless US taxpayer. This is just way too much when one considers the actual probability that something like this will happen. With the right understanding of economics one can easily come to the conclusion that our *yearly* "national security" spending is a far bigger disaster than having 5 Katrina-like disasters. And again, every year!

Just the Iraq war by itself has already cost over half a trillion dollars. Every day that we are in Iraq the American private sector loses 275 million dollars worth of wealth that are needed to feed/clothe/cure everyone who is involved in this disaster. If our military wasn't so needlessly huge, most of these people would be in the private sector, adding wealth to it instead of being enormous drains on society. Every million dollar missile or bomb we fire to destroy some building and inadvertently kill civilians, also destroys a million dollar building over here which was never allowed to come into existence because the food/clothes/medicine needed to sustain the people building it had to be diverted to the manufacturing of the missile/bombs. Every dollar we spend above that which is truly needed to protect ourselves is a dollar we spend destroying ourselves and our future.

Our military spending does not make us any safer. Anyone with half a brain can understand how our foreign policy has in fact made us much more likely to have another major terrorist attack, the kind of attack that our billions worth of tanks, aircraft carriers, fighter jets, etc. are utterly useless against.

Having discussed economics well enough by now, we should realize that the Military-Industrial-Complex is one of the largest monopolies in the entire world. No job probably has more stability than a job in the armed forces. In Iraq 12 billion dollars suddenly went unaccounted for[41]. Only in a monopoly as bureaucratic and protected by secrecy as the Military-Industrial-Complex could inefficiencies like this and worse happen on a regular basis, especially when we are trying to manage a war thousands of miles away. We have a hard time knowing where the money goes once it makes it to Washington D.C., so one can just imagine how much easier it is for the billions to disappear when the money is shipped even further away. Sharon Weinberger's "Imaginary Weapons: A Journey Through the Pentagon's Scientific Underworld" details how even crackpot scientists can get millions of dollars spent on their wild ideas. This gigantic monopoly can grow so large because it is protected by our patriotic tribalism as well as the need for secrecy.

As the United States continues its socioeconomic decline, other countries like China and Russia get to grow their economies. While our ideologues want to inadvertently cripple our already deteriorating economy via more military consumption and threatening Iran, other powers like Russia and China increase their economic pies by trading with Iran. As we are doing this, we have presidential candidates, like John McCain, who are talking about continuing our occupation of holy Muslim lands for 100 years[42], and Rep. Tom Tancredo who propose retaliatory nuclear strikes on Muslim holy cities. Think about this: some overtly religious nuts manage to nuke one of our cities, and we retaliate by killing millions of innocent people and destroying a spiritual center to over 1.5 billion of people. The Muslim world is hearing all of this. But obviously this has nothing to do with motivating someone, a human being, with an already strong territorial instinct, to attack American troops and look forward to the death of many Americans who fund such occupations via their taxes and ideology.

Next, I thank Mr. Jeffrey St. Clair from counterpunch.org for giving me permission to include his following article[43] that gives us just one tiny example of what our Military-Industrial Complex is like.

Lockheed and Loaded: The Company that Runs the Empire. By Jeffrey St. Clair

**********************Part I****************************

Lockheed is headquartered in Bethesda, Maryland. No, the defense titan doesn't have a bomb-making factory in this toney Beltway suburb. But as the nation's top weapons contractor, it migrated to DC from southern California because that's where the money is. And Lockheed rakes it in from the federal treasury at the rate of $65 million every single day of the year.

From nuclear missiles to fighter planes, software code to spy satellites, the Patriot missile to Star Wars, Lockheed has come to dominate the weapons market in a way that the Standard Oil Company used to hold sway over the nation's petroleum supplies, before being broken up for being a monopoly. And it all happened with the help of the federal government, which steered lucrative no bid contracts Lockheed's way, enacted tax breaks that encouraged Lockheed's merger and acquisition frenzy in the 1980s and 1990s and turned a blind eye to the company's criminal rap sheet, ripe with indiscretions ranging from bribery to contract fraud.

Now Lockheed stands almost alone. It not only serves as an agent of US foreign policy, from the Pentagon to the CIA; it also helps shape it. "We are deployed entirely in developing daunting technology," Lockheed's new CEO Robert J. Stevens told *New York Times* reporter Tim Weiner. "That requires thinking through the policy dimensions of national security as well as technological dimensions."[44]

Like many defense industry executives, Stevens is a former military man who cashed in his Pentagon career for a lucrative position in the private sector. The stern-jawed Stevens served in the Marines and later taught at the Pentagon's Defense Systems Management College, an institution which offers graduate level seminars in how to design billion dollar weapons deals. From the Marines, Stevens landed first at Loral, the defense satellite company. Then in 1993 he went to work for Lockheed, heading its "Corporate Strategic Development Program". There Stevens wrote the game plan for how Lockheed would soar past Boeing, General Dynamics, Northrop Grumman and the others, as the top recipient of Pentagon largesse.

The plan was as simple as it proved profitable. Instead of risking the competition of the marketplace, Lockheed, under Steven's scheme, would target the easy money: federal contracts. The strategy was also straightforward: flood the congress with PAC money to get and keep grateful and obedient members in power. Those friendly members of congress would also be surrounded by squads of lobbyists to develop and write legislation and insert Lockheed-friendly line items into the bloated appropriations bills that fund the government. It also called for seeding the Pentagon and the White House with Lockheed loyalists, many whom formerly worked for the company.

"We need to be politically aware and astute," said Stevens. "We need to work with the congress. We need to work with the executive branch. We need to say: we think it is feasible, we think this is possible. We think we have invented a new approach."

The scheme succeeded brilliantly. By the end of the 1990s, Lockheed had made the transition from an airplane manufacturer with defense contracts to a kind of privatized supplier for nearly every Pentagon weapons scheme, from the F-22 fighter to the Pentagon's internet system. Then 9/11 happened and the federal floodgates for spending on national security, airline safety and war making opened wide and haven't closed. Lockheed has been the prime beneficiary of this gusher of federal money.

Since September 2001, the Pentagon's weapons procurement program has soared by more than $20 billion, from $60 billion to $81 billion in 2004, Lockheed's revenues over the same time period jumped by a similar 30 percent. And, despite the recession and slumping Dow, the company's stock tripled in value.

Almost all of this profiteering came courtesy of the federal treasury. More than 80 percent of Lockheed's revenue derives directly from federal government contracts. And most of the rest comes from foreign military sales to Israel, Saudi Arabia, South Korea and Chile. Israel alone spends $1.8 billion a year on planes and missile systems purchased from Lockheed. Lockheed sells weaponry, from F-16 fighters to surveillance software, to more than 40 nations. "We're looking at world domination of the market," gloats Bob Elrod, a senior executive in Lockheed's fighter plane division.

And there's little risk involved. Nearly all of these sales are guaranteed by the US government.

After 9/11, Bush tapped Lockheed's Stevens to lead his presidential commission on the Future of the US Aerospace Industry, a body which, not surprisingly, wasted little time pounding home the importance of sluicing even more federal dollars in the form of defense and air traffic control contracts to companies such as Lockheed.

But Steven's position was just the icing on a very sweet cake. Former Lockheed executives and lobbyists toil every day on behalf of the defense giant from the inside the administration and the Pentagon. At the very top of the list is Steven J. Hadley, recently tapped to replace Condoleezza Rice as Bush's national Security Advisor. Prior to joining the Bush administration, Hadley represented Lockheed at the giant DC law firm of Shea and Gardner. Other Lockheed executives have been appointed to the Defense Policy Board and the Homeland Security Advisory Council. Bush's Transportation Secretary, Norman Mineta, and Otto Reich, the former deputy Secretary of State for the Western Hemisphere, both once worked as Lockheed lobbyists.

But the revolving door swings both ways for Lockheed. On its corporate board reposes E.C. Aldridge, Jr. Before retiring from the Defense Department, Albridge served as the head of the Pentagon's weapon procurement program and signed contracts with Lockheed to build the F-22, the world's most expensive airplane.

When insiders don't get you everything you need, there's always political bribery. In the US, politicians who serve Lockheed's interests get annual dispensations of corporate swill courtesy of the company's mammoth political action committee. Each year Lockheed's corporate PAC doles out more than $1 million, mainly to members of the crucial defense and appropriations committees.

Overseas, Lockheed has often resorted to a direct bribe of government officials. In the 1970s, Lockheed famously handed out $12.5 million in bribes to Japanese officials(and organized crime figures) to secure the sale of 21 Tristar aircraft to Nippon Airlines. The ensuing scandal brought down Japanese Prime Minister Kakuei Tanaka, who was convicted of being on the receiving end of Lockheed's payola. Even though the imbroglio lead the enactment of the Foreign Corrupt Practices Act in 1977 which set stiff penalties for bribery, Carl Kochian, Lockheed's CEO at the time, defended the practice of handing out covert cash inducements as a cost-effective way of securing billions in contracts for the company. Bribery was just a cost of doing big business.

And indeed the Corrupt Practices Act didn't deter Lockheed from handing out financial incentives to foreign officials to speed things along. In the 1990s, Lockheed admitted to stuffing the pockets of an Egyptian official with $1.2 million dollars in order to grease the sale of Lockheed-made C-130 transport planes to the Egyptian military.

The clunky old C-130 Hercules continues to bring millions to Lockheed, which sells the cargo plane to Jordan, Egypt, and Israel. But the biggest profits continue to derive from sales to the Pentagon, even though the latest model of the transport has been plagued with operational problems and cost overruns. Of course, in the funhouse economics of defense contracts "cost over-runs" simply mean more millions of taxpayer money going into the accounts of the very defense contractors that performed the untimely or shoddy work in the first place.

Since 1999, the Air Force has purchased 50 of the new C-130J prop planes from Lockheed. But none of these planes have performed well enough to allow the Air Force to put them into service. An audit of the C-130 contract by the Inspector General of the Air Force revealed a host of problems with the new plane that had been gilded over by Lockheed and Pentagon weapons buyers.

One of the biggest problems with the plane is an ineptly designed propeller system that keeps the C-130 from being flown in bad weather. The C-130J is powered by six propellers covered in composite material that becomes pitted or even dissolves under sleet, hail or even heavy rain. Ironically, many of the first batch of planes were delivered to an Air Force reserve unit in Biloxy, Mississippi, where they were supposed to function as "Hurricane Hunters," plying through thunderstorms and heavy winds in search of the eye of the storm. The planes proved useless for the task. As a result, most of the C-130Js have been use only for pilot training.

"The government fielded C-130J aircraft that cannot perform their intended mission, which forces the users to incur additional operations and maintenance costs to operate and maintain older C-130 mission-capable aircraft because the C-130J aircraft can be used only for training,"[45] the IG audit concluded.

Nevertheless, the Air Force paid Lockheed 99 percent of the contract price for the useless planes.

"This is yet another sad chapter in the history of bad Pentagon weapons systems acquisitions," said Eric Miller, a senior Defense Investigator at the Project of Government Oversight. "For years, the Air Force has known it was paying too much for an aircraft that doesn't do what it's supposed to. Yet it has turned a blind eye. The aircrews who have to fly these aircraft should be very angry. They've been betrayed by the very government that should be ensuring that the weapons they receive are safe and effective."[46]

The profits from the C-130 are mere pittance compared to what Lockheed stands to make from its contracts to produce the two costliest airplanes ever envisioned: the Joint Strike Fighter and the F-22 Raptor.

The Joint Strike Fighter, also known as the F-35, is slated to replace the venerable F-16. Even though the initial designs for the F-35 proved faulty(there continue to be intractable problems with the weight of the plane), the Pentagon, under prodding from influential members of Congress, awarded the Lockheed a $200 billion contract to build nearly 2,000 of the still unairworthy planes. Lockheed plans to sell another 2,500 planes at a sticker price of $38 million apiece to other nations, starting with Great Britain. Once again, most of these sales will be underwritten by US government loans.

The F-35 contract was awarded on October 16, 2001. Already, costs have soared by $45 billion over the initial estimate with no end in sight.

But the F-22 Raptor stands in a class of its own. With a unit price of more than $300 million per plane, the Raptor is the most expensive fighter jet ever designed. One congressional staffer dubbed it, "Tiffany's own wings." Conceived in the 1980s to penetrate deep into the airspace of the Soviet Union, the F-22 has no function these days, except to keep a slate of defense contractors in business, from Lockheed, which runs the project, to Being which designed the wings, to Pratt-Whitney which designed the huge jet engines.

The F-22 was supposed to be operational a decade ago. But the latest incarnation of the plane continues to suffer severe problems in fight testing. Its onboard computer system is mired with glitches and its Stealth features haven't prevented the plane from popping up "like a fat strawberry" on radar. Even worse, several test pilots have gotten dizzy to the point of nearly passing out while trying to put the fighter through evasive maneuvers at high altitudes.

Even so, the doomed project moves forward, consuming millions every week, and no one with power to do so seems to show the slightest inclination to pull the plug.

******************Part II************************

By one account, Lockheed garners $228 in federal tax money from every household in the US each year. But when it comes time to paying taxes Lockheed pleads poverty. By taking advantage of a bevy of designer loopholes, Lockheed's legion of accountants has reduced the corporation's annual tax bill to 7 percent of its net income. By comparison, the average federal tax rate for individuals in the US is around 25 percent.

Of course, these kinds of special dispensations don't come cheaply. Lockheed spends more money lobbying congress than any other defense contractor. In 2004, a banner year for the company, it spent nearly $10 million on more than 100 lobbyists to prowl the halls of congress, keeping tabs on appropriations bills, oversight hearings and tax committees. Over the past five years, only Philip Morris and GE spent more money lobbying congress.

With Lockheed, it's sometimes difficult to discern whether it's taking advantage of US foreign policy or shaping it. Take the Iraq war. Lockheed's former vice-president, Bruce Jackson, headed an ad hoc group called the Committee for Liberation of Iraq. This coven of corporate executives, think tank gurus and retired generals includes such war-mongering luminaries as Richard Perle, Jeane Kirkpatrick, Gen. Wayne Downing and former CIA director James Woolsey. The Washington Post reported that group's goal was to "promote regional peace, political freedom and international security through replacement of the Saddam Hussein regime with a democratic government that respects the rights of the Iraqi people and ceases to threaten the community of nations."

This supposedly independent body seems to have gotten its marching orders from inside the Bush White House. Jackson and others met repeatedly with Karl Rove and Steven Hadley, Condoleezza Rice's number two at the National Security Council and a former Lockheed lobbyist. The group eventually got a face-to-face meeting with the dark lord himself, Dick Cheney. After meeting with White House functionaries, members of the Committee would fan out on cable news shows and talk radio to inflame the fever for war against Saddam.

Jackson has long enjoyed close ties to the Bush inner circle. In 2000, he chaired the Republican Party's platform committee on National Security and Foreign Policy and served as a top advisor to the Bush campaign. Naturally, the platform statement ended up reading like catalogue of Lockheed weapons systems. At the top of the list, the RNC platform pledged to revive and make operational the $80 billion Missile Defense program supervised by Lockheed.

In 2002, the Bush administration called on Jackson to help drum up support in Eastern Europe for the war on Iraq. When Poland and Hungary came on board, Jackson actually drafted their letter supporting an invasion of Iraq. His company was swiftly rewarded for his efforts. In 2003, Poland purchased 50 of Lockheed's F-16 fighters for $3.5 billion. The sale was underwritten by a $3.8 billion loan from the Bush administration.

Lockheed also made out quite nicely from the Iraq war itself. It's F-117 Stealth fighters inaugurated the start of the war with the "Shock and Awe" bombing of Baghdad. Later, the Pentagon stepped up orders of Lockheed's PAC 3 Patriot missile. The missile batteries, designed for use against SCUD missiles that Iraq no longer possessed, sell for $91 million per unit.

After the toppling of Saddam, Lockheed executives saw an opportunity to gobble up one of the big private contractors doing business in Iraq, Titan Corporation. The San Diego-based company was awarded a $10 million contract to provide translators for the Pentagon in Iraq. Two of these translators, Adel Nakhl and John Israel, were later accused of being involved in the torture of Iraqi prisoners at Abu Ghraib prison. Titan translators, who are paid upwards of $107,000 a year, were also implicated in a scandal at Guantanamo prison.

Like Lockheed, after 9/11 Titan jettisoned almost all of its commercial operations and began to focus entirely on government work. By 2003, 99 percent of its $1.8 billion in corporate income came courtesy of government contracts. The firm also went on a buying spree of other smaller defense contractors. Since 2001, Titan gobbled up ten other defense-related companies. The most lucrative acquisition proved to be BMG, Inc., a Reston, Virginia based company that specializes in information collection and analysis for the Pentagon and the CIA. BMG alone held Pentagon contracts worth $650 million.

The abuse scandals didn't deter Lockheed from pursuing Titan. Indeed, Christopher Kubasik, Lockheed's chief financial officer, told the *Los Angeles Times* that the torture allegations "were not significant to our strategic decision."

The merger was later delayed for other reasons by the Justice Department, which was looking into allegations that Titan executives and subsidiaries paid bribes to government officials in Africa, Asia and Europe in order to win contracts—a method of doing business that Lockheed executives must have admired.

Titan, which was formed amid the Reagan defense build up of the early 1980s, saw itself as a new kind of defense contractor, a weapons company that didn't make weapons. Instead of building missiles or planes, Titan concentrated on developing software and communication packages for Pentagon programs. Its first big contract was for the development of a communications package for the guidance system of a Minuteman missile. Since then Titan has become a major player in the lucrative information technology market.

In recent years, Lockheed has begun to aggressively pursue the same types of "soft defense" programs. In the past decade, Lockheed's Information Technology sales have increased by more than four hundred percent. The bonanza began during the Clinton administration, when Al Gore's "reinventing government" scheme auctioned off most of the data-management tasks of the federal government to the private sector. Now nearly 90 percent of the federal government's Information Technology has been privatized, most of it to Lockheed, which is not only the nation's top arms contractor but also its top data-management supplier.

This opened vast new terrains of the government to conquest by Lockheed. It now enjoys contracts with the Department of Health and Human Services, Department of Energy and EPA. Lockheed also just corralled a $550 million contract to take over the Social Security Administration's database. The privatization of Social Security has already begun.

But even in the IT sector, the big bucks are to be made in the burgeoning surveillance and Homeland Security business. Lockheed now runs the FBI's archaic computer system, which took some much deserved heat for letting the 9/11 hijackers slip through its net without detection. It also won the $90 million contract to manage the top secret computer network for the Department of Homeland Security, a system that is supposed to function as a kind of "deep web", linking the system of the FBI, CIA, and Pentagon.

All of this is a precursor to even bigger plans hatched by Lockheed and its pals in the Pentagon to develop an all-encompassing spying system called Global Information Grid, an internet system that is meant to feed real time tracking information on terrorist suspects directly into automated weapons systems, manufactured, naturally, by Lockheed.

"We want to know what's going on anytime, any place on the planet," pronounced Lorraine Martin, Lockheed's vice-president for Command, Control and Communications Systems. And eliminate them, naturally.

On the battlefield of defense contractors, Lockheed has now achieved full-spectrum dominance.

May, 2005

----- End of article by Jeffrey St. Clair -----

The coming mushroom cloud?

As time goes by and technology improves, some new technology will arise and make the manufacturing of powerful weapons a cheap reality to any disgruntled group of people. As I write this book, it is very hard and expensive to come up with a weapon that can create as much damage as a nuclear bomb. But what will happen when they become cheaper and easier to make? Are we going to have a government bureaucracy grow to the point where a large portion of the world's production goes to feed a network of spies who monitor the actions of every human being hoping to catch someone trying to assemble this new weapon? This is what our economically ignorant tribal nature calls for, and is occurring in the United States, and is the main motivating fear for the Iraq war. As president Bush said while trying to rally Americans into the inevitable path of the Iraq war: "America must not ignore the threat gathering against us. Facing clear evidence of peril, we cannot wait for the final proof -- the smoking gun -- that could come in the form of **a mushroom cloud**." But even this bureaucracy, for reasons already mentioned, will lack the knowledge with which to be truly effective and simply lead to socioeconomic hardship and foreign policy blunders as has been the case, and therefore create even more reasons for some disgruntled group to do a lot of damage.

The simple truth is that only if every human being grows up in an environment where he can easily understand how peace and prosperity really work, will the incentives to cause such damage not become a part of his calculating brain. Everyone in the world needs to understand how freedom works. Before discussing how to go about preventing such terrorist attack without creating a bigger evil via a prosperity destroying police-state bureaucracy that will be useless anyways, let us discuss the worst possible scenario.

What if a major terrorist attack like a nuclear bomb did happen? Without an understanding of the market process, our own governments are going to do far more damage than the terrorists. As previously mentioned, in our modern worlds, we do not owe our lives and well-being to hard work, to the good intentions of leaders, to pretty much anything that is an individual trait. We owe our existence to the workings of the market process, to individual freedom. To destroy the market process, or hamper it greatly, is to destroy the social order that gives us life. The hardest working, honest, intelligent person in a communist created famine in China or Russia would have died regardless of such traits, while a lazy, and perhaps immoral American saw his living standard rise. So again, it is to the market process, to individual freedom that we owe everything. So let us imagine that the unlikely event that a "mushroom cloud" does occur in a major US city and kills 500,000 people and injures another 500,000. As horrible as this might be, 1 million people is 0.33% of the American population and a tiny fraction of the entire global economy. Thanks to free trade, we are not an American human ant-farm, we are a global human ant-farm. The more free-trade we have, the more integrated the social order will be in a way that the effects of disasters like this will have a smaller impact. It will obviously be a tremendous calamity for those who died, the injured, their families and the emotions of billions. But if the market process is allowed to function, in other words, if the millions of free individuals are allowed to do the best they can with their humanity and good will, their billions of calculations and subsequent actions will help those in need better than a centrally planned bureaucracy ever will, and the effect on the rest of the economy will be much smaller as well. We cannot eradicate all ill intent, the world is not perfect, all we can do is the best we can, and that best comes from the market-process-coordinated private sector. We saw the horrendous failure of FEMA's handling of Katrina which is still in chaos. The failure here would be even greater. The government will once again want to execute some great master plan, its tentacles will want to control and see everything to better handle the crisis and prevent future ones, "which are now sure to happen" and "no price will be too high" to prevent such a thing of course, according to those who will be in power. And obviously anyone who refuses to go along with the countless new laws and regulations will be seen as an "enemy of the people", "someone who does not understand the gravity of the situation and simply cannot be allowed to prevent the master plan from working and we will have no choice but to make the tough decision of locking him up." More power and resources will be taken away from the social supercomputer(the private sector) and put in the hands of militant bureaucrats and police chiefs. All of this will continue to prevent our already devastated private sector from continuing its complex cycle of production and take us further into socioeconomic collapse. And I will not even discuss our social and racial problems. As long as the economic pie is big enough, racial problems can be swept under the rug by political correctness/religion/tolerance/etc., but someday, when things get bad enough, we might have the kinds of riots that are frequently burning cars in "civilized" places like Paris, France[47].

So as bad as it might be in a human toll, it would still only be one third of a percent of the US human ant-farm, and unless the government paralyzes the market process in its attempts to control everything, for the most part life will go on as usual. Ok, definitely not as usual, but a whole lot better than how it would go if economically ignorant, tribal-minded ideologues tried to manage the situation. The last time something really bad happened to the US, in 9/11, our elected ideologues invaded and destroyed a country that had absolutely nothing to do with the attack, and fully knowing it ahead of time[48]. And one should always keep in mind that which is not seen. The economic damage that our own military consumption is doing to us.

Our maladapted nature when it comes to our modern world and the terrorist fear is especially visible when one considers the probability of being affected by a terrorist attack. A terrorist attack killing 100 people each day in the U.S. would still kill far fewer people than our socialized highway system where about 114 died per day in 1999[49]. Yet for such a small probability the entire American economy and millions of people all over the world are harmed by our government's economic ignorance.

So unfortunately the reaction by our very own government would end up leading to more destruction and chaos. And this is assuming the worst case scenario of a nuclear blast. Just a few smaller terrorist attacks that injure a couple hundred people here and there in a few cities simultaneously, and some leaked fake news about some bio-terrorist attack can have a similar effect. Terrorists have little need to kill that many people in order to destroy the American social order. You just have to play your fear cards right, and human nature, via the US government, will destroy the social order for you.

Bin Laden's embarrassing victory. Brought to you by American tribalism and economic ignorance

Having discussed how our Military-Industrial-Complex is destroying us from within, we can now understand how bin Laden is winning the war. Understanding the economics of the war is the key. Just a few disgruntled, overtly religious Muslims can spend a couple hundred dollars and cause the Military-Industrial-Complex to consume several million in wealth from the US economy. They are bleeding us into socioeconomic collapse, just like they did with the Russians. It could not be more obvious. Here is bin Laden himself giving it away[50]:

"We, alongside the mujahedeen, bled Russia for 10 years until it went bankrupt and was forced to withdraw in defeat,"

"We are continuing this policy in bleeding America to the point of bankruptcy. Allah willing, and nothing is too great for Allah,"

"All that we have to do is to send two mujahedeen to the furthest point east to raise a piece of cloth on which is written al Qaeda, in order to make generals race there to cause America to suffer human, economic and political losses without their achieving anything of note other than some benefits for their private corporations,"

"Every dollar of al Qaeda defeated a million dollars, by the permission of Allah, besides the loss of a huge number of jobs,"

"As for the economic deficit, it has reached record astronomical numbers estimated to total more than a trillion dollars."

"And it all shows that the real loser is you,"..."It is the American people and their economy."

What an embarrassment to what remains of freedom and Capitalism in our nation. Some guy in a cave thousands of miles away has managed to let American tribalism help destroy us from within.

A few answers

So how do we deal with national security and the potential terrorist attack from radical Muslims?

The most important thing is the proper understanding of the socioeconomic world by as many people as possible right here in the US, which is something that will quickly export itself to the rest of the Western world. But some concrete steps are doing what Dr. Paul wants to do. Bring the troops home to help avert the economic crisis and related turmoil.

When people think about the United States, they think about that entity that represents the United States, the US government and its president and powerful ideologues. On the other hand, what comes to mind when people think about Europe? They are less likely to see it as a single entity with a single sort of "social character" to be either hated or loved. It is a collection of individual countries that has yet to be personified by a single entity. It is getting there though, as it goes through our tribal centralization of decision-making power via the European Union's legislative body, much like our own United "States" did in the past. In reality, there is no such thing as countries, only individuals. Our countries and notional borders are vestiges of our tribal mindset. I'm not saying that we should just abolish all national borders overnight, but as the proper understanding of how the world works spreads, this is what will eventually occur, and to the great benefit of all mankind. The angry Muslims hate the United States, much more than they hate Jane who lives in Wichita. The more we do as Dr. Paul says, and dismantle our useless federal bureaucracies, the more the US will be seen as a land of free individuals who don't bother anyone. This will greatly reduce the probability that a brain can get worked up enough to want to harm us. One needs to keep in mind that terrorist attacks are not just carried out by one person, many people have to be convinced and supported by many other people to commit such acts. The more peaceful as a nation we become the less of the supporting people will exist, making it even harder for the smaller number of extremists. We are not fighting extremists, we are fighting sequences of thoughts that enter people's minds that lead to extreme behavior, so again, the less we bother, the more prosperous our economy becomes, the more the ideas of freedom and tolerance will spread and overtake the poverty and fear that lead to more extreme ideology. This in no way means giving up our defense needs: we just need to focus them here and with more common sense.

Leaving Iraq, bringing the troops home from all over the world, and transitioning them into private sector jobs would be the quickest way to begin to steer away from our socioeconomic decline. Instead of consuming 1,000 billion to ineffectively police the world, we can spend 200 billion, still have by far the most powerful and technologically advanced armed forces in the world, and increase the economic pie by the additional 800+ billion dollars worth of wealth that would now be created by the additional private sector labor force.

Another tremendously important reason to stop our ideologue's stupid exportation of democracy is the fact that it is not democracy that brings prosperity, it is Capitalism, which is something none of our ruling ideologues understands! If our bureaucrats in Washington DC do not understand freedom and the market process, how in the world are we going to expect them to export economic prosperity when they are the ones that are destroying economic prosperity right here at home? They openly talk about their centrally planned share-the-wealth ideas like sharing Iraq's oil wealth, and having the government provide jobs for the people which would inadvertently bring about Socialism. The Iraqi government, probably learning from American and European economorons, feeds its own useless bureaucracy via the printing press creating 50%+ inflation rates. Creating more social hardship and more incentives for radical ideology to spread.

And who are our enemies anyways? Besides a few religious fanatics, who unlike our American religious fanatics have little influence and means with which to cause much damage, who remains? The Chinese and the Russians? These are just governments, who like our very own, are a maladapted and mostly unneeded social growth. Thanks to the Internet, young people everywhere are absorbing a more common and much more tolerant culture. If we could just prevent our stupid governments from continuing to screw things up. But again, it is not really our government's faults, they are simply the embodiment of our maladapted tribalism.

We are truly in a perilous situation. After the cold war, compared to the United States, the world was still licking its wounds from the communist nightmare. But now China, Russia, India, and much of the rest of the world has been growing, and the perceived zero-sumness of the world is increasing like never before, especially as it pertains to oil and the environment. We are already in the midst of a socioeconomic decline. It has not happened fast enough for us to clearly see it in terms of a drastic collapse of the stock markets, or hyperinflation, or an astronomical jump in interest rates. It has been happening slower than this but happening nonetheless and with a good chance of a truly visible crisis happening in the near future. That saying about the frog being boiled alive without jumping from the pan suits humanity perfectly. Just like the frog has not evolved to sense slow changes in temperature, we have not evolve to understand slow changes towards Socialism and socioeconomic disasters. Ultimately Dr. Paul is correct. We will destroy ourselves from within via our destruction of the economy.

The real motivation for the Ron Paul Revolution

Human beings have more or less evolved to do what is in our best interest. The reason why most of us don't make a conscious effort to strive for a more capitalist society is because we simply don't know what Capitalism is or how it really works and is in everyone's best interest, especially for the "poor" in the United States, and much more so for the really, really, poor in African nations. If someone offers to give you a nice free car for pushing a button, it is trivial to realize how pushing the button is in your best interest. The intelligence and effort required to understand this is something a small child can achieve. Unfortunately, understanding what the market process is, how it works, and how it has created civilization and the material prosperity that has allowed so much human life to flourish is not as trivial. Not only does it require a little more thinking than our button-for-a-car example, but some aspects of the market process/Capitalism are counter intuitive to our evolved human nature, making them a bit harder to understand and easy to instinctively hate. At the same time, Socialism/Communism are destructive, yet our brains are suckers for those ideologies and their policies, causing them to quickly spread through our minds even though we have an entire 20th century filled with their failures to serve as examples. Again, as briefly discussed at various times throughout the book, this is due to our mal-or-ongoing-cultural-adaptation from tribal world to modern market-process-coordinated world. Fortunately, how Capitalism and the whole world more or less works is not that hard to understand and definitely within the reach of regular folks.

Once an individual clearly understands economics he can easily see how important it is and how everything else pales in comparison. Economics is the difference between having to eat your children out of hunger as happened in communist Russia and China, and having even the "poorest" members of society be able to afford things like transportation, TVs, clothes and food as is the case in modern countries. Once a properly functioning brain understands this, it is almost inevitable that it works with much of its might to spread such an understanding. This is essentially what happened to Dr. Paul early in his career as mentioned in the introduction. It is easy, or should I say, almost inevitable, that once a mind stumbles upon the proper understanding of economics it becomes a great fighter for individual freedom. It is disappointing to run into so many libertarians who go around insulting people for their big-government views without realizing that if it weren't for the understanding of economics that they were just lucky to stumble upon, they too would be just as wrong. All human beings are equal, and equally susceptible to fall for big government ideology. For the most part this sort of ideology can only be overcome by very strong religious ideology, as briefly discussed in the last chapter while talking about Christian Libertarians, or via a sound understanding of economics. And in many ways the strong religious influence as protector of freedom is not really all that great a case to make. Piety can lead to some bad results too, it is great when it protects freedom, as in the true "Christian Conservative" or "Christian Libertarian" tradition which has been so key to America's success but it could just as well create a lot of harm. There are plenty of "Christian Socialist" political parties out there[51].

The salvation of mankind depends on this knowledge spreading through enough brains in society to turn the tide. Unfortunately, the rate at which such ideas could spread from brain to brain has been much slower than the rate at which economic fallacies, our mal-adapted nature, and our government's ignorance moves us towards Socialism. But the Internet changed this. Countless individuals, some with more success than others, took their message to the web and suddenly the speed at which the right ideas can spread from brain to brain has greatly increased. Probably the most successful of these sites, especially as it relates to the Ron Paul Revolution and my own understanding of economics and so much more is the Ludwig von Mises Institute's www.mises.org, and the institute's founder, Lew Rockwell's www.lewrockwell.com.

I do not know what sequence of thoughts eventually led to the decision by Dr. Paul and his close friends to launch a presidential bid. But I am 99.999% sure that based on the tremendous growth of mises.org and lewrockwell.com, they figured that at the very least it would be a great way to help spread their message of freedom and sound economics. Which brings me to a few important criticisms of the Ron Paul Revolution.

Common libertarian ideological mistakes

Government is not evil. Hayek's most alarming lesson of modern history

Many Libertarians and Ron Paul supporters greatly harm their cause when they vilify the mainstream establishment. It is true that the policies of all the other candidates and the supporting chatter of the mainstream media are the usual recipe for Socialism and international conflict, but this is not because they are "evil" or have bad intentions.

Socialist ideology did not spread because its adherents were "bad people", it just made sense to our egalitarian/socialist tendencies. Let's hear it from Hayek once again:

> "Most people are still unwilling to face the most alarming lesson of modern history: that the greatest crimes of our time have been committed by governments that had the enthusiastic support of millions of people who were guided by moral impulses. It is simply not true that Hitler or Mussolini, Lenin or Stalin, appealed only to the worst instincts of their people: they also appealed to some of the feelings which also dominate contemporary democracies."[52]

Yes... Hitler, Mussolini, Stalin, Mao and the like, whose actions brought us so much death and destruction were feverishly followed and admired by large segments of their populations. To this day one can go to villages or towns in their respective countries and find portraits and old supporters of these men. Actually, it is much worse, there are still entire political parties with the support of thousands still idolizing them. These people were not "evil", they were simply the embodiment, or executioners, of the ideologies held by a large portion of the very masses that put them in power and tolerated their actions, socialist ideologies that are like candy to our tribal instincts.

The concept of "Americans" is just a word that refers to the people living in a large chunk of land. A group of human beings biologically no different from the Chinese and Russians who were swayed by socialist ideology that created so much misery. **We are not fighting a battle of "good" vs. "evil", we are fighting a battle against economic ignorance and our tribal cultural heritage!** An ignorance for which no one is really to blame. Understanding the human animal and the economic world is new to mankind. I have little doubt in my mind that if one could travel back in time and spend a good month or two with Hitler and Stalin, teaching them how the market process works and so on, that they would have been able to see things differently. Maybe not, maybe it would take more time but one gets the point. These people did not have "evil" genes. They were a sign of their times. We have to accept this truth in order to stop blaming particular individuals for problems and look at the socioeconomic forces that create such monstrous regimes.

Government is composed of average human beings who for the most part have good intentions given the ideologies that shape their minds. Sure there are many blatantly corrupt people in government that use their influence to benefit themselves at the expense of society[53], but for the most part our huge government is not out there to "oppress us" and "take our liberties away" like so many Libertarians and Ron Paul supporters seem to portray. One cannot stress this enough, the overwhelming factor is our tribal nature and ignorance of the relatively new economic forces that shape our modern worlds. The number of such "bad" individuals is an insignificant factor compared to those who just don't know better and end up playing the big government game because that is all they can imagine. Our bureaucrats, the media, and Wall Street, are much better labeled as misguided than "evil", "the enemy" and so on. Evil does not really exist, it is a cultural relic from more theistic times.

The biggest threat to prosperity is our tribalism and lack of an understanding of economics that feeds government, not government itself. If society expects the government and public sector to solve problems, those who want to dismantle much of the public sector will easily be seen as a bunch of dangerous ideologues. Dr. Paul says that "Freedom is popular", but it is not, Libertarianism and its philosophy of freedom scares people. It is becoming popular now because people are beginning to educate themselves to the point where they can overcome such fears, but freedom by itself is definitely not popular and is usually seen as a recipe for chaos and anarchy. For example, in an infamous segment on Glenn Beck's cable tv program he tried to associate the Ron Paul Revolution with some kind of domestic terrorism threat. His guest on the show, David Horowitz said the following with respect to the growing disenfranchisement with government in general and more specifically about the Ron Paul Revolution:

"there is a strain of isolationism and anarchy…There are plenty of unfortunately libertarian websites which are indistinguishable from the anti-American left these days. Lewrockwell.com and others like that. They are totally in bed with the Islamofascists and have turned against this country."

Wow! This is a perfect example of what we are dealing with. "anarchy"… this is what people fear from Ron Paul's message of freedom and his attacks on government. Saying that lewrockwell.com, Lew Rockwell's site, a man who put together one of the greatest educational institutions ever, the Ludwig von Mises Institute(mises.org), is in bed with the Islamofascists, has to be the most ridiculous thing I have ever heard. In many ways, Glenn and Mr. Horowitz are good examples of how the ignorant masses, and the media which reflects their ignorance, inevitably see freedom as something bad, as "anarchy", and supporters of freedom as potential terrorists because in order to have more freedom you inevitably have to be against the government.

This treatment and fringe status is in many ways a result of how the Ron Paul Revolution carries itself. If the Ron Paul Revolution goes around referring to the government as "evil" and out there to "oppress us" and "rob us", then it is inevitable that the mainstream establishment reacts the way that it does. For example, in Dr.Paul's encouraging message to supporters on Jan 10th, he says:

> [54]"But now is the time to stick together like the brothers and sisters we are, to stand side by side in this fight against the media toadies, warmongers, and Wall Street rip-off artists who stand against us, and who always remind me of Tolkien's Orcs."
> "beating back the enemy"...
> "not let the enemy divide us"...
> "our neocon[55] enemies"...

I'll assume that some of this is just pep talk but I think we have too much of it. Wall Street and the "media toadies" simply have no clue how the socioeconomic world works and cannot envision a world without big government and its tentacles attempting to maintain/fix the social order. For example, with respect to the financial sector, something like the stock market was not invented by the government. Just like language, money, and the market process, the stock market is a social growth. The role that stock markets play in our economies is the result of human action, but not of human design. This is like if the government created a Department of Speech, regulated speech for 100 years, and then people feared that abolishing the Department of Speech would lead to linguistic chaos and the inability of people to communicate. Since the government has been regulating the financial sector for what to everyone alive today seems like forever, we believe that if the government regulation of the financial sector goes away, that our financial institutions might dissolve into chaos and bring down society with it.

We are so used to living in a big-government world that we inevitably see the small-government freer world as a recipe for chaos, and look at those that preach for such freedom as a bunch of nuts, especially when Libertarians/Ron Paul supporters refer to the establishment as "evil" and out there to "oppress us".

This back and forth vilifying is especially dangerous with today's new "war on terrorism". Popular Fox news host Bill O'Reilly, a man who I believe has very good intentions and in many ways seems like a very tolerant and exemplary human being, referred to the American Civil Liberties Union(ACLU) as "I think they're a terrorist group. ... I think they're terrorists"[56], for their opposition to the tremendous expansion in power of the executive branch over the freedoms of individuals. This growth in government power is obviously done with good intentions. So what happens when a group of educated citizens inevitably view their very government as the main cause of the problems? And at the same time, the public at large(the bureaucrats, the media, regular folks) are convinced that our government bureaucracies are not this great evil that the freedom ideologues portray them as. And that to them, anyone who opposes them is obviously a dangerous crazy ideologue that will someday be responsible for anarchy or a "mushroom cloud"?

To most people government is good, it is what manages the social order, it is what supposedly prevents the strong from abusing the weak, it is the embodiment of our national tribal identity. It educates us, protects us, is staffed by good people with good intentions and does pretty much everything these days. This is what is visible. With the right understanding of economics we can see the great harm that government creates, that it creates far more harm than most can imagine, that it is in fact THE source of most of our problems. But without this understanding we are left with the ideology that government is good, that to be against that which is good is bad, and therefore to be against the government is to be for the bad, for the "evil" terrorists, for greedy selfish people, for the social chaos that would "obviously" occur. If you are against Social Security, you are evil and against the elderly. If you are against welfare, you are for the starvation of the poor etc.

Paul Craig Roberts, a Republican who worked in the Reagan administration, recently discussed his fears that some major terrorist attack would once again occur before the 2008 presidential election which would allow our elected ideologues to justify their continued stewardship and expansion of our government. He envisioned Bush giving the following speech:

"My administration knew that there would be more attacks from these terrorists who hate us and our way of life and are determined to destroy every one of us. If only more of you had believed me and supported my war on terror these new attacks would not have happened. Our security efforts were impaired by the democrats' determined attempts to surrender to the terrorists by forcing our withdrawal from Iraq and by civil Libertarian assaults on our necessary security measures. If only more Americans could have trusted their government this would not have happened"[57]

The bureaucrats will reason that they have no choice but to lockup the pesky freedom ideologues, especially when like many Ron Paul supporters and Libertarians in general, they refer to the mainstream politicians and media as evil warmongers and all kinds of other nasty things, which the politicians and mainstream media are thoroughly convinced that they are not. I agree 100% that with the exception of Dr. Paul, our entire congress' lack of an understanding of how freedom works leads to death and destruction, but again this is mostly the result of mass ideological error and not ill intent. I know, I am way too nice.

This brings us to "H.R. 1955: Violent Radicalization and Homegrown Terrorism Prevention Act of 2007" which contains the following definitions:

`(2) VIOLENT RADICALIZATION- The term `violent radicalization' means the process of adopting or **promoting an extremist belief system for the purpose of facilitating ideologically based violence to advance political, religious, or social change.**

`(3) HOMEGROWN TERRORISM- The term `homegrown terrorism' means the use, planned use, or threatened use, of force or violence by a group or individual born, raised, or based and operating primarily within the United States or any possession of the United States to intimidate or coerce the United States government, the civilian population of the United States, or any segment thereof, in furtherance of political or social objectives.

`(4) IDEOLOGICALLY BASED VIOLENCE- The term `ideologically based violence' means the use, **planned use, or threatened use of force or violence by a group or individual to promote the group or individual's political, religious, or social beliefs.**

Essentially, you can no longer even think, much less say, "I wish someone would kill those incompetent idiots in the white house". This right, the right to the kind of free speech that allows citizens to curse and wish the death of their incompetent politicians, something that has been such a symbol of true freedom no longer exists. With this bill, the Patriot Act, and the continued growth of the executive branch over personal freedom that takes us on Hayek's "Road to Serfdom", all the pieces seem to be in place to lawfully take a rightly disgruntled American to a secret prison in some other country, torture him, and all without the knowledge of a judge.[58]

To the tribal and economically ignorant establishment, freedom leads to chaos, it is an "extreme belief system". The Ron Paul Revolution and Libertarians in general should understand this situation and act accordingly. It should change its tone to be one of more ridicule and intellectual dialogue as opposed to vilification. I don't want to sort of pigeonhole everyone here obviously, Dr. Paul and maybe even the majority of his supporters certainly know that our Socialism is a well intentioned one and that we are battling ignorance for the most part, but this fact needs to be better expressed as part of the general movement.

Just like our foreign policy in the Middle East is what aggravates the problems there, the Ron Paul Revolution's vilification and negative portrayal of the mainstream world is largely responsible for its reaction to it. Getting people who do not understand economics to accept freedom is tough enough as it is, but by vilifying the current establishment, we are only making things worse.

Another example of the Ron Paul Revolution harming itself is the following video[59] where a mob of Ron Paul supporters shouted anti-Fox news chants as they followed Fox news commentator Sean Hannity. Fox news is the mainstream media mouthpiece for our current brand of big-government "Conservatism". Mr. Hannity is not a bad guy that is part of some mass conspiracy to trample our freedoms and ruin our country. His respect for our current republican administration is based on good'ol human tribalism. He might believe that Mr. Bush and his administration are "good" people and that the Islamofascists will blow us up. Since he has no understanding of economics, he too probably feels like abolishing the Federal Reserve and the many other bureaucracies that Ron Paul wants to abolish is a recipe for chaos. Like most people, he might believe that it's good people with "good morals" that makes a difference. I do not know the man and do not want to put words in his mouth but the point I want to make is that instead of insulting and treating people like Mr. Hannity and Mr. O'Reilly as mouthpieces for an "evil" empire, the Ron Paul Revolution would do tremendously better if it engaged these individuals amicably. Vilifying the current "Conservative" establishment is only making it harder to engage them in an intellectual conversation which is what is needed to alleviate their fears of freedom, and help them understand just how disastrous all other candidates and policies really are.

To resume this section: Government is not "evil", and neither is the establishment. Both are the embodiments of our usual economic and mal-adapted ideological fallacies. Even what to many "crazy" Ron Paul supporters is the great dark lord himself, Dick Chaney, is a human being no different than you and I. A man who married his high school sweetheart and has children and grandchildren. That his ideology and certain traits in his character has created incredible hardships and suffering for millions of human beings compared to alternatives, I have no doubt about it, but he is not a "bad" person. I hope the Ron Paul Revolution changes its tune. But I am not 100% opposed to it either. Let's face it, the Ron Paul Revolution has also gotten a tremendous boost of energy and passion from such "vilifiers".

Preaching freedom for freedom's sake and ignoring economics as part of the freedom message.

The content of this section has already been discussed several times before but I just wanted to stress the point again. To the vast majority of people, individual freedom and very small government is a recipe for chaos. If people ask the public sector to solve problems, then getting rid of it will lead to the aggravation of those very same problems and fears they wanted the government to fix in the first place. People's thoughts will go along the lines of the usual fears that lead to Socialism like:

> "Won't the rich exploit the poor? Won't employers pay less than the minimum wage to exploit the workers? Won't the poor go uneducated and lead to all kinds of social problems? Won't the "white man" hoard all the wealth and oppress the minorities? Won't the drug companies exploit us even more? Who will help the less fortunate?…Surely we will have chaos!"

This relates to preaching the Constitution as well. The Constitution is a recipe for individual freedom and therefore the constraint of government power. Most people believe that so much freedom might have worked well in the simpler past, but the complexities of our modern world and the aforementioned fears lead us to think that so much freedom and so little government is antiquated, and again, a recipe for social chaos and "great injustices". Only an understanding of economics can really help someone see how individual freedom, as opposed to leading to social chaos, is the key ingredient to a prosperous social order. Most people see the Constitution just like their elected ideologue Bush Jr. who said, "The Constitution is just a Goddamn piece of paper".

I cringe every time I think about the millions of dollars that the campaign is spending telling people about freedom and the Constitution, in other words, letting them know that Dr. Paul will bring about chaos and anarchy. Dr. Paul has done a great job of bringing up economics but I believe that the movement, as well as the official campaign, needs to stress economics much, much more. Teaching economics to America should be the campaign's goal, especially to young people. The campaign is putting millions of dollars trying to get votes via ads tailored to that "Republican Base" of old white folks. I know we need their votes but 30-second ads will not affect a tribal mind that has been hardened by generations of big government ideology. We already got every person that will go along with the libertarian message of freedom based on either religious beliefs or anger about politicians. From time to time one runs into some libertarians who are experts in the Constitution and its history and try to convince others about the unconstitutionality of our big government world. Although these individuals have done a great job of learning about history, it is an ineffective way of spreading the message of freedom. As long as people believe that trampling over the constitution and creating a big ape government is needed to keep society from falling apart and preventing great injustices, most folks will not give a damn about right or wrong as defined by the constitution or religious beliefs. Using moral and constitutional arguments is not going to cut it in today's secular world. So again, freedom has to be defended in a way that shows why it is in everyone's best interest, and this can only be done via economic reasoning.

What sets Dr. Paul apart from other politicians is not his morality/etc., Dr. Paul is a human being like any other, what has made him such a great asset to all of us is his understanding of economics. Max Raskin, a blogger for lewrockwell.com made the following important point:

> "Without the Mises Institute and LRC, Ron Paul is just another politician, devoid of any principle and intelligence.
> Thankfully this is not the case. Ron Paul is great, but let's not forget he is standing on the shoulders of giants."

I know this sounds a little harsh, and it is wrong in some ways because Dr. Paul was a great economist long before the Ludwig von Mises Institute came into existence, but Mr. Raskin was just blogging and the point he is making is just as valid. People are pretty much the same for all the things we need to be concerned about, what truly sets us apart is the "cultural books" we absorb as we grow up. This should be a humbling point.

Going after young people, even those who cannot vote is a much better strategy. They have parents and grandparents and all the time and energy to let their new ideological fervor convince the entire family. In many ways, this is what is happening. From the little I currently know about Dr. Paul's new book "The Revolution: A Manifesto", it looks like it will be the perfect bit-sized book needed to quickly spread a good understanding of economics to many minds. Dr. Paul's previous book "Pillars of Prosperity" is great, but it is a 475 page collection of speeches that does not start from scratch, and this is way beyond what the layperson would be willing to tackle and need to overcome their fear of freedom. His previous book, "A Foreign Policy of Freedom", 372 pages of foreign policy related speeches was yet another great book, but even more beyond what is needed to go "viral" and quickly spread the needed ideas through millions of minds. But his new book, at less than 200 pages and beginning from scratch, should deal a devastating blow to our national ignorance. I only wish it would have been put together sooner. But even in his new book I fear the tone might put off a lot of people. In the preface, with respect to the message of freedom Dr. Paul mentions:

> "But as we've learned through hard experience, we are not going to hear a word in its favor if our political and media establishments have anything to say about it"

This is true, but the mainstream establishment does not ignore and try to stamp out freedom because they are evil warmongers who want to bankrupt our nation. They ignore freedom because they think it leads to chaos and cannot imagine a world where there would be no need for their quackery and "leadership". Again, this is just reflective of how society sees the world. Statements like these just turn people off. When the average American reads something like this the thought that goes through their minds is "why would our politicians and media want to prevent our freedom?" It gives the impression that there is some kind of ill intent while there really isn't, and this rightly turns people off. The missing ingredient is economics and an understanding of our evolutionary tribal inheritance, but this last part might be a hard pill to swallow for a movement that has strong roots in Christian morality.

Having said all this I am obviously a huge supporter. I know enough about economics to understand that this Ron Paul Revolution is one movement I want to support with all of my might regardless of my ideological differences with various parts of the movement.

So for the last time, economics, patience, and understanding of people's fear of freedom is the key. Ron Paul supporters should try to become an educational army or evangelicals spreading the econogospel. We should try to reach everyone: movies stars, athletes, etc. It is just a matter of time before the econogospel becomes truly popular and the cool thing amongst people. Young democrats/'caring socialists' make great converts because once they are brought over to the dark side of Capitalism they can use the same motivation for consciously creating a prosperous social order as opposed to inadvertently destroying it. The ideas are what matter not necessarily getting Dr. Paul in the White House. I think a great strategy is to also try to reach the other candidates and their supporters. Obama and Hillary are not evil socialists, if they really did understand the socioeconomic forces that shape our lives they too would make the right decisions.

Teaching economics to every American is the key, as Dr. Reisman so powerfully expresses in this quote, which is printed three times in this book:

"The solution to the present problem of massive, overwhelming poverty is nothing other than the science of economics. As should be increasingly clear, economics is a science which can make possible the construction of a social and political system in which human success is a feature of normal, everyday life everywhere. It is truly the humanitarian science, and only those who have studied it well and who are prepared to implement its teachings deserve to be called friends of mankind. The most important charity which true friends of mankind can pursue is to disseminate knowledge of this vital subject as widely and as deeply as they know how."[60] —George Reisman

Some final thoughts

The US, as well as the entire world, is just misaligned, that's all. The more the government does, the more it screws things up, leading to further attempts to do more, and more problems.

As we understand economics our fears of a more privatized and therefore freer world will wither away and be replaced by confidence, enthusiasm, and excitement for the future. The millions of public sector employees and those who work in heavily regulated sectors of the economy will fear losing their jobs as the economy transitions into a more fully privatized and prosperous society. This fear of losing one's job is what is visible. But hopefully with the right understanding of economics people will be able to foresee the huge increases in real wages, technology, and overall prosperity that will come as the human ant-farm begins clicking on all cylinders in the market-process-coordinated private sector. As this is happening those in the private sector should also become more adamant about keeping the fruits of our labor therefore forcing the public sector ants to eventually become useful.

Soon enough, working for the government, or being part of a heavily regulated industry will be shun upon, be "uncool", and the subject of ridicule. I can't wait to see rappers making fun of our Federal Reserve and quoting people like Menger, Mises, Hayek, Spencer, and Hazlitt in their songs. If the lyrics of the latest and greatest rap song can make it through the minds of millions in a matter of weeks, I don't see how the proper understanding of the world can take too much longer. We are just a few really good videos on youtube going viral from having this happen. I am just as convinced that someday I will drive a top of the line Hayek class automobile or something along those lines. These men and a whole bunch of other intellectuals of freedom will become mainstream cultural icons.

A culture of freedom and understanding of economics is already brewing within the Ron Paul Revolution. Whether Ron Paul succeeds or not, the Ron Paul Revolution, which is really an Austrian Economics revolution, should triumph soon. Either that or tribal social turmoil will keep the world in constant conflict. The market process and freedom is what has created our social order, and if our continued ignorance of it keeps messing it up, the social order that has been built upon it will be messed up accordingly to the detriment of billions. But I for one am extremely optimistic and see little chance of something getting in the way of this intellectual revolution.

Henry Hazlitt's inspirational words

The following is the last third of a speech given by Henry Hazlitt on his 70th birthday, November 29th, 1964. He gave this speech in front of many of his friends including the great Ludwig von Mises. The entire speech can be found in Chapter 4, "Reflections at 70", of a great book titled "The Wisdom of Henry Hazlitt"[61]. Whenever I get a little discouraged, this is what I read.

"...Those of us who place a high value on human liberty, and who are professionally engaged in the social sciences —in economics, in politics, in jurisprudence— find ourselves in a minority (and it sometimes seems a hopeless minority) in ideology. There is a great vogue in the United States today for "liberalism." Every American leftist calls himself a liberal! The irony of the situation is that we, we in this room, are the true liberals, in the etymological and only worthy sense of that noble word. We are the true adherents of liberty. Both words —liberal and liberty— come from the same root. We are the ones who believe in limited government, in the maximization of liberty for the individual and the minimization of coercion to the lowest point compatible with law and order. It is because we are true liberals that we believe in free trade, free markets, free enterprise, private property in the means of production; in brief, that we are for capitalism and against socialism. Yet this is the philosophy, the true philosophy of progress, that is now called not only conservatism, but reaction, the Radical Right, extremism, Birchism, and only Bill Buckley here knows how many other terrible things it's called.

Now this is no petty or narrow issue that ties us in this room together. For on the outcome of the struggle in which we are engaged depends the whole future of civilization. Our friend, Friedrich Hayek, in his great book, *The Road to Serfdom*, which was published 20 years ago, pointed out that it was not merely the views of Cobden and Bright that were being abandoned, or even of Hume and Adam Smith, or even of Locke and Milton. It was not merely the liberalism of the 18th and 19th centuries that was being abandoned; it was the basic individualism that we had inherited from Christianity and the Greek and Roman world, and that was reflected in the writings of such figures as Pericles and Thucydides. This is what the world is in danger of abandoning today. Why? Why, if, as we like to think, reason is on our side? Why are we drifting deeper and deeper into socialism and the dark night of totalitarianism? Why have those of us who believe in human liberty been so ineffective?

We Haven't Been Good Enough

I am going to give what is no doubt a terribly oversimplified answer to that question. In the first place, we are almost hopelessly outnumbered. Our voices are simply drowned out in the general tumult and clamor. But there is another reason. And this is hard to say, above all to an audience of this sort, which contains some of the most brilliant writers and minds in the fields of economics, of jurisprudence, of politics, not only of this age but of any age. But the hard thing must be said that, collectively, we just haven't been good enough. We haven't convinced the majority. Is this because the majority just won't listen to reason? I am enough of an optimist, and I have enough faith in human nature, to believe that people will listen to reason if they are convinced that it is reason. Somewhere, there must be some missing argument, something that we haven't seen clearly enough, or said clearly enough, or, perhaps, just not said often enough.

A minority is in a very awkward position. The individuals in it can't afford to be just as good as the individuals in the majority. If they hope to convert the majority they have to be much better; and the smaller the minority, the better they have to be. They have to think better. They have to know more. They have to write better. They have to have better controversial manners. Above all, they have to have far more courage. And they have to be infinitely patient.

When I look back on my own career, I can find plenty of reasons for discouragement, personal discouragement. I have not lacked industry. I have written a dozen books. For most of 50 years, from the age of 20, I have been writing practically every weekday: news items, editorials, columns, articles. I figure I must have written in total some 10,000 editorials, articles, and columns; some 10,000,000 words! And in print! The verbal equivalent of about 150 average-length books!

And yet, what have I accomplished? I will confess in the confidence of these four walls that I have sometimes repeated myself. In fact, there may be some people unkind enough to say I haven't been saying anything new for fifty years! And in a sense they would be right. I have been preaching essentially the same thing. I've been preaching liberty as against coercion; I've been preaching capitalism as against socialism; and I've been preaching this doctrine in every form and with any excuse. And yet the world is enormously more socialized than when I began.

There is a character in Sterne or Smollett—was it Uncle Toby? Anyway, he used to get angry at politics, and every year found himself getting angrier and angrier and politics getting no better. Well, every year I find myself getting angrier and angrier and politics getting worse and worse.

But I don't know that I ought to brag about my own ineffectiveness, because I'm in very good company. Eugene Lyons has been devoting his life to writing brilliantly and persistently against Communism. He now even has the tremendous circulation of the Reader's Digest behind him. And yet, at the end of all these years that he has been writing, Communism is stronger and covers enormously more territory than when he started. And Max Eastman has been at this longer than any of the rest of us, and he's been writing a poetic and powerful prose and throwing his tremendous eloquence into the cause, and yet he's been just as ineffective as the rest of us, so far as political consequences are concerned.

Yet, in spite of this, I am hopeful. After all, I'm still in good health, I'm still free to write, I'm still free to write unpopular opinions, and I'm keeping at it. And so are many of you. So I bring you this message: Be of good heart: be of good spirit. If the battle is not yet won, it is not yet lost either.

Our Continuing Duty

I suppose most of you in this room have read that powerful book, George Orwell's 1984. On the surface it is a profoundly depressing novel, but I was surprised to find myself strangely encouraged by it. I finally decided that this encouragement arose from one of the final scenes in it. The hero, Winston Smith, is presented as a rather ordinary man, an intelligent but not a brilliant man, and certainly not a courageous one. Winston Smith has been keeping a secret diary, in which he wrote: "Freedom is the freedom to say that two and two makes four." Now this diary has been discovered by the Party. O'Brien, his inquisitor, is asking him questions. Winston Smith is strapped to a board or a wheel, in such a way that O'Brien, by merely moving a lever, can inflict any amount of excruciating pain upon him (and explains to him just how much pain he can inflict upon him and just how easy it would be to break Smith's backbone). O'Brien first inflicts a certain amount of not quite intolerable pain on Winston Smith. Then he holds up the four fingers of his left hand, and says, "How many fingers am I holding up? Winston knows that the required answer is five. That's the Party answer. But Winston can't say anything else but four. So O'Brien moves the lever again, and inflicts still more agonizing pain upon him, and says, "Think again. How many fingers am I holding up?" Winston Smith says, "Four. Four. Four fingers." Well, he finally capitulates, as you know, but not until he has put up a magnificent battle.

None of us is yet on the torture rack; we are not yet in jail; we're getting various harassments and annoyances, but what we mainly risk is merely our popularity, the danger that we will be called nasty names. So, before we are in the position of Winston Smith, we can surely have enough courage to keep saying that two plus two equals four.

This is the duty that is laid upon us. We have a duty to speak even more clearly and courageously, to work harder, and to keep fighting this battle while the strength is still in us. But I can't do better than to read the words of the great economist, the great thinker, the great writer, who honors me more than I can say by his presence here tonight, Ludwig von Mises. This is what he wrote in the final paragraph of his great book on socialism 40 years ago:

"Everyone carries a part of society on his shoulders; no one is relieved of his share of responsibility by others. And no one can find a safe way out for himself if society is sweeping towards destruction. Therefore, everyone, in his own interests, must thrust himself vigorously into the intellectual battle. None can stand aside with unconcern; the interests of everyone hang on the result. Whether he chooses or not, every man is drawn into the great historical struggle, the decisive battle into which our epoch has plunged us."

Those words -- uncannily prophetic words -- were written in the early 1920's. Well, I haven't any new message, any better message than that.

Even those of us who have reached and passed our 70th birthdays cannot afford to rest on our oars and spend the rest of our lives dozing in the Florida sun. The times call for courage. The times call for hard work. But if the demands are high, it is because the stakes are even higher. They are nothing less than the future of human liberty, which means the future of civilization."[62]

---

[1] http://www.youtube.com/watch?v=ZjMQG3qUFKo

² Dr. Joseph Salerno's lecture titled "War and Inflation: The Monetary Process and Implications" available at http://www.mises.org/multimedia/mp3/misescircle-ny06/Salerno.mp3 , beginning seconds.

³ De Soto, Jesús Huerta. "Money Bank Credit, and Economic Cycles" Published by the Ludwig von Mises Institute ISBN 978-0-945466-39-0 also freely available here

http://www.mises.org/books/desoto.pdf

⁴ Paul, Ron . Speech titled "The Bubble" from his new book "Pillars of Prosperity" isbn 978-1-933550-24-4 Published by the Ludwig von Mises Institute www.mises.org Page 183

⁵ http://www.constitution.org/mon/greenspan_gold.htm

⁶ http://www.federalreserve.gov/boardDocs/speeches/2002/20021121/default.htm

⁷ "The Wisdom of Henry Hazlitt" Published by the Foundation for Economic Education www.fee.org . ISBN910614-83-0

⁸ See Murray N. Rothbard's "Keynes, the Man"

http://www.mises.org/etexts/keynestheman.pdf

⁹ F.A. Hayek. Hayek on Hayek: An Autobiographical Dialogue. The University of Chicago Press. ISBN 0-226-32062-6

¹⁰ John Maynard Keynes, The General Theory of Employment, Interest and Money. Last paragraph.

http://www.marxists.org/reference/subject/economics/keynes/general-theory/ch24.htm

¹¹ Henry Hazlitt's "Economics in One Lesson" ISBN 0-930073-19-3 page 164

¹² BEN FELLER, Associated Press Writer "Bush sees 'troubling signs' for economy"

http://tinyurl.com/yoz2hd

¹³ Jim Cox's The Concise Guide to Economics is an awesome introduction to economics with great bits of history and is freely available online at http://www.conciseguidetoeconomics.com. Below is link to great bite sized overview of 1929's black Tuesday where the market crashed and is commonly regarded as the beginning of the Great Depression

http://www.conciseguidetoeconomics.com/book/blackTuesday/

¹⁴ Herman E. Krooss, *Executive Opinion: What Business Leaders Said and Thought on Economic Issues, 1920s-1960s* (Garden City, N.Y.: Doubleday and Co., 1970), p. 200.

I originally found this quote on Robert Higg's excellent "Neither Liberty Nor Safety: Fear, Ideology, and the Growth of Government"

¹⁵ According to this Associated Press story found here http://tinyurl.com/yw5s92. Titled "Tests find passenger screening troubles at Newark airport" October, 27, 2006

¹⁶ From PBS website http://www.pbs.org/newshour/terrorism/international/fatwa_1996.html

¹⁷ http://en.wikipedia.org/wiki/Iraq_sanctions

¹⁸ http://en.wikipedia.org/wiki/Madeleine_Albright

¹⁹ Speech given before congress on July 26, 2001 titled ""Lift the United States Embargo on Cuba". Speech is included in this book's Appendix.

[20] http://www.memritv.org/clip/en/1269.htm

[21] Bergen, Peter L. "The Osama bin Laden I know" ISBN 978-0-7432-7892-8, page 216

[22] John V. Denson. Article titled "The Hiroshima Myth" http://www.lewrockwell.com/orig2/denson7.html

[23] I read this point in Richard Maybury's World War II ISBN 978-09420617436 but reference to specific facts Mr Maybury gets from "History of the Second World War" by B.H. Liddell Hart, Perigree Books, NY, 1982, p691. I would like to add that Mr. Maybury's World War II book is a MUST READ.

[24] The letter can be found here:

http://www.nuclearfiles.org/menu/library/correspondence/truman-harry/corr_truman_1945-08-11.htm

I originally found the quote on Dr. Denson's previously mentioned article.

[25] "A Year After Iraq War: Mistrust of America in Europe Ever Higher, Muslims Anger Persists", The Pew Global Attitudes Project, March 16, 2004. I originally saw this in Peter L. Bergen's "The Osama bin Laden I know" ISBN 978-0-7432-7892-8, page XXVIII

Bergen, Peter L. "The Osama bin Laden I know" ISBN 978-0-7432-7892-8, page XXVIII

[26] http://www.guardian.co.uk/Iraq/Story/0,,1724837,00.html

[27] http://www.amnesty.org/en/alfresco_asset/59ee55f3-a49b-11dc-bac9-0158df32ab50/mde140012006en.html

[28] http://en.wikipedia.org/wiki/Detainees_in_Iraq

[29] http://www.memritv.org/clip/en/1650.htm

[30] Jen Banbury's story at salon.com titled "Rummy's Scapegoat" http://dir.salon.com/story/books/int/2005/11/10/karpinski/index.html

[31] WorldPublicOpinion.org poll. "The Iraqi Public on the US Presence and the Future of Iraq"

http://www.worldpublicopinion.org/pipa/pdf/sep06/Iraq_Sep06_rpt.pdf

Do you think the US military in Iraq is currently:

A stabilizing force: 21%

Provoking more conflict than it is preventing: 78%

"More broadly, 79 percent of Iraqis say that the US is having a negative influence on the situation in Iraq, with just 14 percent saying that it is having a positive influence. Views are especially negative among the Sunnis (96% negative), and the Shias (87% negative)."

[32] http://www.youtube.com/watch?v=D0mCydl8KP0

[33] http://www.livescience.com/health/080117-violent-cravings.html

[34] Here is just one youtube user that has many such videos http://www.youtube.com/profile?user=ADLCHRIS3

If the link does no longer work just do a search on youtube for Iraq, or "Iraq war", or "Marines" and you will stumble upon many. Reading the comments is also reflective of the obvious macho tribalism shared by many young men who are part of this increasingly popular culture. Just a few minutes ago I looked at video http://www.youtube.com/watch?v=2sCmj0CemF8 posted by the user I linked to above and here are some of the comments on the very first page:

Someguy1: why the fuck iraq has not be annexed is beyond me. these people are to stupid to govern themselves. all they have ever done is fight and kill each other, they are a blight on humanity

To which Someguy2 replies: Thank you Someguy1. you hit it right on the head. My sentiment exactly.

A couple comments further below Someguy3 says: Awesome video, great job in Iraq guys. Too bad you could not have included some shots of the Apaches (:39-:45) firing the Hellfire missile. Watching one of those killing machines in action is the ultimate, and flying one was the best job I ever ahd.

Iraqis are just like us. It is pathetic to see our politicians blame the Iraqis for not controlling their situation as the reason for this were in their genes. Our politicians don't create our order and stability, they are its main destroyers.

[35] By Bryan Bender, Globe Staff, July 13, 2007 "More entering Army with criminal records"
http://www.boston.com/news/nation/washington/articles/2007/07/13/more_entering_army_with_criminal_records/

Also good reads are http://www.slate.com/id/2127487/ "The Dumbing-Down of the U.S. Army" and http://www.slate.com/id/2133908/ "GI Schmo: How low can Army recruiters go?" by Fred Kaplan

[36] Jacob Weisberg's "The Bush Tragedy" ISBN 978-1-4000-6678-0 Page 171

[37] ibid. Page 201

[38] Message to Iraqis on October 2003.

http://english.aljazeera.net/English/archive/archive?ArchiveId=40703

[39] http://en.wikipedia.org/wiki/Economic_effects_of_Hurricane_Katrina

[40] Robert Higgs' article "The Trillion-Dollar Defense Budget is Already Here" http://www.independent.org/newsroom/article.asp?id=1941

[41]
http://www.bloomberg.com/apps/news?pid=20601103&sid=aRfRyhT0yHzU&refer=us

[42] John McCain "Maybe 100!..." http://www.youtube.com/watch?v=vf7HYoh9YMM

[43] Article can be found online here
http://www.counterpunch.org/stclair01222005.html

[44] Tim Weiner's New York Times article "Lockheed and the Future of Warfare" Nov. 28, 2004. http://www.nytimes.com/2004/11/28/business/yourmoney/28lock.html

[45] http://www.dodig.osd.mil/audit/reports/fy04/04102sum.htm

[46] Eric Miller. POGO Statement on C-130J Inspector General Audit , July 23, 2004
http://www.pogo.org/p/defense/da-040702-C130J.html

And on a side note. One can look at this article by Miller "Five Weapons That Bilk the Taxpayer" http://www.counterpunch.org/fiveweapons.html and here is another great article by Jeffrey St. Clair http://www.counterpunch.org/f22.html that looks at perhaps the greatest example of how the Military Industrial Complex rapes the US taxpayer via the world's most expensive and unnecessary plane, the F-22 Raptor. 187 planes should be built for the 62 billion spent at a cost of 332 million dollars per plane. But that is assuming that there aren't any further cost overruns. So far 108 have been built. On Feb 11 2007 while on their first overseas deployment 6 planes experienced computer crashes leading to total loss of navigation instrumentation amongst other things.

[47] http://en.wikipedia.org/wiki/Paris_Riots

[48] Craig Unger's "The Fall of the House of Bush: The Untold Story of How a Band of True Believers Seized the Executive Branch, Started the Iraq War, and Still Imperils America's Future" is a great book that seems to put the latest and greatest knowledge of how and when things happened as well as a great background on the ideological makeup of our current ruling ideologues.

[49] http://www.ntsb.gov/Publictn/2000/SPC0003.pdf

[50] Article on cnn.com titled "Bin Laden: Goal is to Bankrupt U.S." November 1, 2004 which can be found here:

http://www.cnn.com/2004/WORLD/meast/11/01/binladen.tape/index.html

Text of complete speech can be found here http://www.memri.org/bin/articles.cgi?Area=sd&ID=SP81104

[51] http://en.wikipedia.org/wiki/Christian_Social_Party

[52] F.A. Hayek, Law Legislation and Liberty, Volume II The Mirage of Social Justice. The University of Chicago Press, published 1976, page 134

[53] Especially our banking elite who control the nation's money supply via the Federal Reserve. Just like our politicians lie to us in order to bring about their ideological wars and well-intentioned socialist ideas, our banks meet secretly to determine FED policy via the Federal Open Market Committee(FOMC) and surely their decisions are influenced by their interests. Ron Paul has been fighting to get some transparency as to what exactly goes on in these meetings without much success. In one of Dr. Paul's speeches included in the appendix titled "Federal Reserve has Monopoly over Money and Credit in United States", he mentions, "Mr. Speaker, I serve on the Committee on Banking and Financial Services and I am on the Subcommittee on Domestic and International Monetary Policy, and I myself cannot attend the open market committee meetings. I have no access to what really goes on... The recent news revealed that the chief of the janitorial services over at the Federal Reserve makes $163,000 a year, and yet we have no authority over the Federal Reserve because it is a quasi-private organization that is not responding to anything the Congress says."

While our politicians are economically ignorant and come and go with the times, these bankers might be the closest thing we have to a real conspiracy theory from the top. But at the same time, how much of a conspiracy theory can they be when our economics educational establishment truly believes in central banking and the role they play.

In Dr. Paul's excellent book "Freedom Under Siege" on page 104 section titled "The Origins of the Fed" he has a nice overview of how the Fed came to existence.

Book can be found here for free http://www.dailypaul.com/freedom-under-siege/Freedom-Under-Siege-complete.pdf

[54] http://ronpaul2008.typepad.com/ron_paul_2008/2008/01/message-from-ro.html

55 "Our neocon enemies" are a group of "intellectuals" who basically expound a very simple ideology. It is as tribal and obvious as it gets, here is the one sentence version. After Communism fell and we were the remaining big ape, we should expand our military, continue to police the world and spread democracy and our values at the point of a gun. I like Dr. Paul's foreign policy better. Here is what it would be like. Dr. Paul gains the prestige of the US presidency, the world is intrigued about the man, he goes on diplomatic trips spreading the Austrian Economic gospel. Ideologues learn enough economics to get over their socialist fears and bullshit. World peace follows in a matter of months. The neocons are not "enemies" they are people with good intentions(from their standpoint) that have a different ideology and calling them enemies just turns people off in a weird way. That they are dangerous ideologues? Very much responsible for our Iraqi debacle, the suffering of millions, and who knows what other calamities in the future due to the disastrous Bush presidency? I have no doubt about that. For example, Norman Podhoretz, one of the senior neocons, man who believes in "good" and "evil" and wants to bomb Iran, said that Bush Jr. is *"...a man who knows evil when he sees it and who has demonstrated an unfailingly courageous willingness to endure vilification and contumely in setting his face against it."* Yesss. I am sure that our great religious ideologue has no problems seeing evil in many places, especially Muslim ones, and his great ability to endure vilification and "contumely"(new word for me, a humiliating insult) is just what we need to leave a stubborn path of destruction and unintended consequences that will guarantee the eventual mushroom cloud over here.

Mr. Podhoretz's quote about Bush can be found in his article titled "The Case for Bombing Iran" https://www.commentarymagazine.com/viewarticle.cfm/The-Case-for-Bombing-Iran-10882?page=all

I do not dislike Mr. Podhoretz, again, it is just ideology. Mr. Podhoretz actually wrote a very candid and courageous article about his feelings with respect to race relations titled "Our Negro Problem – And Ours" I do not see things as Mr. Podhoretz does in the article but it was nonetheless a great article.

56 Media Matters for America, "O'Reilly on ACLU: "I think they're a terrorist group. ... I think they're terrorists" http://mediamatters.org/items/200503030007

57 On Thom Hartman show on 7/19/2007 Here is audio : http://tinyurl.com/yqlz3l

58 see Judge Napolitano's great speech for Reason Magazine here http://reason.tv/video/show/178.html

59 http://www.youtube.com/watch?v=NNZS9ZuZcrg

60 Reisman, George. Capitalism: A Treatise on Economics. Published by Jameson Books. ISBN 0-915463-73-3, page 335

61 This is a fantastic book. It is a collection of some of Hazlitt's articles and can be read here for free http://tinyurl.com/2eae5u

62 Reprinted with permission of the publisher, Foundation for Economic Education, Irvington-on-Hudson, NY 10533, www.fee.org. All rights reserved.

Appendix

A few speeches by Dr. Paul before congress

These are some of the many great speeches given before congress by Dr. Paul. Some can be found in Dr. Paul's great new book "Pillars of Prosperity: Free Markets, Honest Money, Private Property" published by the Ludwig von Mises Institute(www.mises.org) and also freely available here http://www.mises.org/books/prosperity.pdf

Has Capitalism Failed?

July 9, 2002

It is now commonplace and politically correct to blame what is referred to as the excesses of capitalism for the economic problems we face, and especially for the Wall Street fraud that dominates the business news. Politicians are having a field day with demagoguing the issue while, of course, failing to address the fraud and deceit found in the budgetary shenanigans of the federal government- for which they are directly responsible. Instead, it gives the Keynesian crowd that run the show a chance to attack free markets and ignore the issue of sound money.

So once again we hear the chant: "Capitalism has failed; we need more government controls over the entire financial market." No one asks why the billions that have been spent and thousands of pages of regulations that have been written since the last major attack on capitalism in the 1930s didn't prevent the fraud and deception of Enron, WorldCom, and Global Crossings. That failure surely couldn't have come from a dearth of regulations.

What is distinctively absent is any mention that all financial bubbles are saturated with excesses in hype, speculation, debt, greed, fraud, gross errors in investment judgment, carelessness on the part of analysts and investors, huge paper profits, conviction that a new era economy has arrived and, above all else, pie-in-the-sky expectations.

When the bubble is inflating, there are no complaints. When it bursts, the blame game begins. This is especially true in the age of victimization, and is done on a grand scale. It quickly becomes a philosophic, partisan, class, generational, and even a racial issue. While avoiding the real cause, all the finger pointing makes it difficult to resolve the crisis and further undermines the principles upon which freedom and prosperity rest.

Nixon was right- once- when he declared "We're all Keynesians now." All of Washington is in sync in declaring that too much capitalism has brought us to where we are today. The only decision now before the central planners in Washington is whose special interests will continue to benefit from the coming pretense at reform. The various special interests will be lobbying heavily like the

Wall Street investors, the corporations, the military-industrial complex, the banks, the workers, the unions, the farmers, the politicians, and everybody else.

But what is not discussed is the actual cause and perpetration of the excesses now unraveling at a frantic pace. This same response occurred in the 1930s in the United States as our policymakers responded to the very similar excesses that developed and collapsed in 1929. Because of the failure to understand the problem then, the depression was prolonged. These mistakes allowed our current problems to develop to a much greater degree. Consider the failure to come to grips with the cause of the 1980s bubble, as Japan's economy continues to linger at no-growth and recession level, with their stock market at approximately one-fourth of its peak 13 years ago. If we're not careful- and so far we've not been- we will make the same errors that will prevent the correction needed before economic growth can be resumed.

In the 1930s, it was quite popular to condemn the greed of capitalism, the gold standard, lack of regulation, and a lack government insurance on bank deposits for the disaster. Businessmen became the scapegoat. Changes were made as a result, and the welfare/warfare state was institutionalized. Easy credit became the holy grail of monetary policy, especially under Alan Greenspan, "the ultimate Maestro." Today, despite the presumed protection from these government programs built into the system, we find ourselves in a bigger mess than ever before. The bubble is bigger, the boom lasted longer, and the gold price has been deliberately undermined as an economic signal. Monetary inflation continues at a rate never seen before in a frantic effort to prop up stock prices and continue the housing bubble, while avoiding the consequences that inevitably come from easy credit. This is all done because we are unwilling to acknowledge that current policy is only setting the stage for a huge drop in the value of the dollar. Everyone fears it, but no one wants to deal with it.

Ignorance, as well as disapproval for the natural restraints placed on market excesses that capitalism and sound markets impose, cause our present leaders to reject capitalism and blame it for all the problems we face. If this fallacy is not corrected and capitalism is even further undermined, the prosperity that the free market generates will be destroyed.

Corruption and fraud in the accounting practices of many companies are coming to light. There are those who would have us believe this is an integral part of free-market capitalism. If we did have free-market capitalism, there would be no guarantees that some fraud wouldn't occur. When it did, it would then be dealt with by local law-enforcement authority and not by the politicians in Congress, who had their chance to "prevent" such problems but chose instead to politicize the issue, while using the opportunity to promote more Keynesian useless regulations.

Capitalism should not be condemned, since we haven't had capitalism. A system of capitalism presumes sound money, not fiat money manipulated by a central bank. Capitalism cherishes voluntary contracts and interest rates that are determined by savings, not credit creation by a central bank. It's not capitalism when the system is plagued with incomprehensible rules regarding mergers, acquisitions, and stock sales, along with wage controls, price controls, protectionism, corporate subsidies, international management of trade, complex and punishing corporate taxes, privileged government contracts to the military-industrial complex, and a foreign policy controlled by corporate interests and overseas investments. Add to this centralized federal mismanagement of farming, education, medicine, insurance, banking and welfare. This is not capitalism!

To condemn free-market capitalism because of anything going on today makes no sense. There is no evidence that capitalism exists today. We are deeply involved in an interventionist-planned economy that allows major benefits to accrue to the politically connected of both political spectrums. One may condemn the fraud and the current system, but it must be called by its proper names- Keynesian inflationism, interventionism, and corporatism.

What is not discussed is that the current crop of bankruptcies reveals that the blatant distortions and lies emanating from years of speculative orgy were predictable.

First, Congress should be investigating the federal government's fraud and deception in accounting, especially in reporting future obligations such as Social Security, and how the monetary system destroys wealth. Those problems are bigger than anything in the corporate world and are the responsibility of Congress. Besides, it's the standard set by the government and the monetary system it operates that are major contributing causes to all that's wrong on Wall Street today. Where fraud does exist, it's a state rather than federal matter, and state authorities can enforce these laws without any help from Congress.

Second, we do know why financial bubbles occur, and we know from history that they are routinely associated with speculation, excessive debt, wild promises, greed, lying, and cheating. These problems were described by quite a few observers as the problems were developing throughout the 90s, but the warnings were ignored for one reason. Everybody was making a killing and no one cared, and those who were reminded of history were reassured by the Fed Chairman that "this time" a new economic era had arrived and not to worry. Productivity increases, it was said, could explain it all.

But now we know that's just not so. Speculative bubbles and all that we've been witnessing are a consequence of huge amounts of easy credit, created out of thin air by the Federal Reserve. We've had essentially no savings, which is one of the most significant driving forces in capitalism. The illusion created by low interest rates perpetuates the bubble and all the bad stuff that goes along with it. And that's not a fault of capitalism. We are dealing with a system of inflationism and interventionism that always produces a bubble economy that must end badly.

So far the assessment made by the administration, Congress, and the Fed bodes badly for our economic future. All they offer is more of the same, which can't possibly help. All it will do is drive us closer to national bankruptcy, a sharply lower dollar, and a lower standard of living for most Americans, as well as less freedom for everyone.

This is a bad scenario that need not happen. But preserving our system is impossible if the critics are allowed to blame capitalism and sound monetary policy is rejected. More spending, more debt, more easy credit, more distortion of interest rates, more regulations on everything, and more foreign meddling will soon force us into the very uncomfortable position of deciding the fate of our entire political system.

If we were to choose freedom and capitalism, we would restore our dollar to a commodity or a gold standard. Federal spending would be reduced, income taxes would be lowered, and no taxes would be levied upon savings, dividends, and capital gains. Regulations would be reduced, special-interest subsidies would be stopped, and no protectionist measures would be permitted. Our foreign policy would change, and we would bring our troops home.

We cannot depend on government to restore trust to the markets; only trustworthy people can do that. Actually, the lack of trust in Wall Street executives is healthy because it's deserved and prompts caution. The same lack of trust in politicians, the budgetary process, and the monetary system would serve as a healthy incentive for the reform in government we need.

Markets regulate better than governments can. Depending on government regulations to protect us significantly contributes to the bubble mentality.

These moves would produce the climate for releasing the creative energy necessary to simply serve consumers, which is what capitalism is all about. The system that inevitably breeds the corporate-government cronyism that created our current ongoing disaster would end.

Capitalism didn't give us this crisis of confidence now existing in the corporate world. The lack of free markets and sound money did. Congress does have a role to play, but it's not proactive. Congress' job is to get out of the way.

Statement on Ending US Membership in the IMF

Feb. 27th, 2002

Mr. Speaker, I rise to introduce legislation to withdraw the United States from the Bretton Woods Agreement and thus end taxpayer support for the International Monetary Fund (IMF). Rooted in a discredited economic philosophy and a complete disregard for fundamental constitutional principles, the IMF forces American taxpayers to subsidize large, multinational corporations and underwrite economic destruction around the globe. This is because the IMF often uses the $37 billion line of credit provided to it by the American taxpayers to bribe countries to follow destructive, statist policies.

For example, Mr. Speaker, the IMF played a major role in creating the Argentine economic crisis. Despite clear signs over the past several years that the Argentine economy was in serious trouble, the IMF continued pouring taxpayer-subsidized loans with an incredibly low interest rate of 2.6% into the country. In 2001, as Argentina's fiscal position steadily deteriorated, the IMF funneled over 8 billion dollars to the Argentine government!

According to Congressman Jim Saxton, Chairman of the Joint Economic Committee, this "Continued lending over many years sustained and subsidized a bankrupt Argentine economic policy, whose collapse is now all the more serious.

The IMF's generous subsidized bailouts lead to moral hazard problems, and enable shaky governments to pressure the IMF for even more funding or risk disaster."

Argentina is just the latest example of the folly of IMF policies. Only four years ago the world economy was rocked by an IMF-created disaster in Asia. The IMF regularly puts the taxpayer on the hook for the mistakes of the big banks. Oftentimes, Mr. Speaker, IMF funds end up in the hands of corrupt dictators who use our taxpayer-provided largesse to prop up their regimes by rewarding their supporters and depriving their opponents of access to capital.

If not corrupt, most IMF borrowers are governments of countries with little economic productivity. Either way, most recipient nations end up with huge debts that they cannot service, which only adds to their poverty and instability. IMF money ultimately corrupts those countries it purports to help, by keeping afloat reckless political institutions that destroy their own economies.

IMF policies ultimately are based on a flawed philosophy that says the best means of creating economic prosperity is through government-to-government transfers. Such programs cannot produce growth, because they take capital out of private hands, where it can be allocated to its most productive use as determined by the choices of consumers in the market, and place it in the hands of politicians. Placing economic resources in the hands of politicians and bureaucrats inevitably results in inefficiencies, shortages, and economic crises, as even the best intentioned politicians cannot know the most efficient use of resources.

In addition, the IMF violates basic constitutional and moral principles. The federal government has no constitutional authority to fund international institutions such as the IMF. Furthermore, Mr. Speaker, it is simply immoral to take money from hard-working Americans to support the economic schemes of politically-powerful special interests and third-world dictators.

In all my years in Congress, I have never been approached by a taxpayer asking that he or she be forced to provide more subsidies to Wall Street executives and foreign dictators. The only constituency for the IMF is the huge multinational banks and corporations. Big banks used IMF funds- taxpayer funds- to bail themselves out from billions in losses after the Asian financial crisis. Big corporations obtain lucrative contracts for a wide variety of construction projects funded with IMF loans. It's a familiar game in Washington, with corporate welfare disguised as compassion for the poor.

The Argentine debacle is yet further proof that the IMF was a bad idea from the very beginning- economically, constitutionally, and morally. The IMF is a relic of an era when power-hungry bureaucrats and deluded economists believed they could micromanage the world's economy. Withdrawal from the IMF would benefit American taxpayers, as well as workers and consumers around the globe. I hope my colleagues will join me in working to protect the American taxpayer from underwriting the destruction of countries like Argentina, by cosponsoring my legislation to end America's support for the IMF.

Lift the United States Embargo on Cuba

July 26, 2001

Mr. Speaker, encouraged in part by a recent resolution passed by the Texas State Legislature, I rise again this Congress to introduce my bill to lift the United States Embargo on Cuba.

On June 29, 2001, the Texas state legislature adopted a resolution calling for an end to U.S. economic sanctions against Cuba. Lawmakers emphasized the failure of sanctions to remove Castro from power, and the unwillingness of other nations to respect the embargo. One Texas Representative stated:

"We have a lot of rice and agricultural products, as well as high-tech products, that would be much cheaper for Cuba to purchase from Texas. All that could come through the ports of Houston and Corpus Christi."

I wholeheartedly support this resolution, and I have introduced similar federal legislation in past years to lift all trade, travel, and telecommunications restrictions with Cuba. I only wish Congress understood the simple wisdom expressed in Austin, so that we could end the harmful and ineffective trade sanctions that serve no national purpose.

I oppose economic sanctions for two very simple reasons. First, they don't work as effective foreign policy. Time after time, from Cuba to China to Iraq, we have failed to unseat despotic leaders by refusing to trade with the people of those nations. If anything, the anti-American sentiment aroused by sanctions often strengthens the popularity of such leaders, who use America as a convenient scapegoat to divert attention from their own tyranny. History clearly shows that free and open trade does far more to liberalize oppressive governments than trade wars. Economic freedom and political freedom are inextricably linked--when people get a taste of goods and information from abroad, they are less likely to tolerate a closed society at home. So while sanctions may serve our patriotic fervor, they mostly harm innocent citizens and do nothing to displace the governments we claim as enemies.

Second, sanctions simply hurt American industries, particularly agriculture. Every market we close to our nation's farmers is a market exploited by foreign farmers. China, Russia, the middle east, North Korea, and Cuba all represent huge markets for our farm products, yet many in Congress favor current or proposed trade restrictions that prevent our farmers from selling to the billions of people in these areas. The department of Agriculture estimates that Iraq alone represents a $1 billion market for American farm goods. Given our status as one of the world's largest agricultural producers, why would we ever choose to restrict our exports? The only beneficiaries of our sanctions policies are our foreign competitors.

Still, support for sanctions continues in Congress. The House International Relations committee last week considered legislation that will extend existing economic sanctions against Iran and Libya for another 5 years. While I certainly oppose this legislation, I did agree with the

I certainly understand the emotional feelings many Americans have toward nations such as Iran, Iraq, Libya, and Cuba. Yet we must not let our emotions overwhelm our judgment in foreign policy matters, because ultimately human lives are at stake. For example, 10 years of trade sanctions against Iraq, not to mention aggressive air patrols and even bombings, have not ended Saddam Hussein's rule. If anything, the political situation has worsened, while the threat to Kuwait remains. The sanctions have, however, created suffering due to critical shortages of food and medicine among the mostly poor inhabitants of Iraq. So while the economic benefits of trade are an important argument against sanctions, we must also consider the humanitarian argument. Our sanctions policies undermine America's position as a humane nation, bolstering the common criticism that we are a bully with no respect for people outside our borders. Economic common sense, self-interested foreign policy goals, and humanitarian ideals all point to the same conclusion: Congress should work to end economic sanctions against all nations immediately.

The legislation I introduce today is representative of true free trade in that while it opens trade, it prohibits the U.S. Taxpayer from being compelled to subsidize the United States government, the Cuban government or individuals or entities that choose to trade with Cuban citizens.

I submit for inclusion in the record, a copy of the Sense of Congress Resolution passed in Austin in late June.

SENATE CONCURRENT RESOLUTION NO. 54

Whereas, The relationship between the United States and Cuba has long been marked by tension and confrontation; further heightening this hostility is the 40-year-old United States trade embargo against the island nation that remains the longest-standing embargo in modern history; and

Whereas, Cuba imports nearly a billion dollars' worth of food every year, including approximately 1,100,000 tons of wheat, 420,000 tons of rice, 37,000 tons of poultry, and 60,000 tons of dairy products; these amounts are expected to grow significantly in coming years as Cuba slowly recovers from the severe economic recession it has endured following the withdrawal of subsidies from the former Soviet Union in the last decade; and

Whereas, Agriculture is the second-largest industry in Texas, and this state ranks among the top five states in overall value of agricultural exports at more than $3 billion annually; thus, Texas is ideally positioned to benefit from the market opportunities that free trade with Cuba would provide; rather than depriving Cuba of agricultural products, the United States embargo succeeds only in driving sales to competitors in other countries that have no such restrictions; and

Whereas, In recent years, Cuba has developed important pharmaceutical products, namely, a new meningitis B vaccine that has virtually eliminated the disease in Cuba; such products have the potential to protect Americans against diseases that continue to threaten large populations around the world; and

Whereas, Cuba's potential oil reserves have attracted the interest of numerous other countries who have been helping Cuba develop its existing wells and search for new reserves; Cuba's oil output has increased more than 400 percent over the last decade; and

Whereas, The United States' trade, financial, and travel restrictions against Cuba hinder Texas' export of agricultural and food products, its ability to import critical energy products, the treatment of illnesses experienced by Texans, and the right of Texans to travel freely; now, therefore, be it

Resolved,

Statement Opposing the use of Military Force against Iraq

October 8, 2002 The words that appear in bold also appear in bold in original publication.

Madam Speaker, I rise in opposition to this resolution. The wisdom of the war is one issue, but the process and the philosophy behind our foreign policy are important issues as well. But I have come to the conclusion that I see no threat to our national security. There is no convincing evidence that Iraq is capable of threatening the security of this country, and, therefore, very little reason, if any, to pursue a war.

But I am very interested also in the process that we are pursuing. This is not a resolution to declare war. We know that. This is a resolution that does something much different. This resolution transfers the responsibility, the authority, and the power of the Congress to the President so he can declare war when and if he wants to. He has not even indicated that he wants to go to war or has to go to war; but he will make the full decision, not the Congress, not the people through the Congress of this country in that manner.

It does something else, though. One-half of the resolution delivers this power to the President, but it also instructs him to enforce U.N. resolutions. I happen to think I would rather listen to the President when he talks about unilateralism and national security interests, than accept this responsibility to follow all of the rules and the dictates of the United Nations. That is what this resolution does. It instructs him to follow all of the resolutions.

But an important aspect of the philosophy and the policy we are endorsing here is the preemption doctrine. This should not be passed off lightly. It has been done to some degree in the past, but never been put into law that we will preemptively strike another nation that has not attacked us. No matter what the arguments may be, this policy is new; and it will have ramifications for our future, and it will have ramifications for the future of the world because other countries will adopt this same philosophy.

I also want to mention very briefly something that has essentially never been brought up. For more than a thousand years there has been a doctrine and Christian definition of what a just war is all about. I think this effort and this plan to go to war comes up short of that doctrine. First, it says that there has to be an act of aggression; and there has not been an act of aggression against the United States. We are 6,000 miles from their shores.

Also, it says that all efforts at negotiations must be exhausted. I do not believe that is the case. It seems to me like the opposition, the enemy, right now is begging for more negotiations.

Also, the Christian doctrine says that the proper authority must be responsible for initiating the war. I do not believe that proper authority can be transferred to the President nor to the United Nations.

But a very practical reason why I have a great deal of reservations has to do with the issue of no-win wars that we have been involved in for so long. Once we give up our responsibilities from here in the House and the Senate to make these decisions, it seems that we depend on the United Nations for our instructions; and that is why, as a Member earlier indicated, essentially we are already at war. That is correct. We are still in the Persian Gulf War. We have been bombing for 12 years, and the reason President Bush, Sr., did not go all the way? He said the U.N. did not give him permission to.

My argument is when we go to war through the back door, we are more likely to have the wars last longer and not have resolution of the wars, such as we had in Korea and Vietnam. We ought to consider this very seriously.

Also it is said we are wrong about the act of aggression, there has been an act of aggression against us because Saddam Hussein has shot at our airplanes. The fact that he has missed every single airplane for 12 years, and tens of thousands of sorties have been flown, indicates the strength of our enemy, an impoverished, Third World nation that does not have an air force, anti-aircraft weapons, or a navy.

But the indication is because he shot at us, therefore, it is an act of aggression. However, what is cited as the reason for us flying over the no-fly zone comes from U.N. Resolution 688, which instructs us and all the nations to contribute to humanitarian relief in the Kurdish and the Shiite areas. It says nothing about no-fly zones, and it says nothing about bombing missions over Iraq.

So to declare that we have been attacked, I do not believe for a minute that this fulfills the requirement that we are retaliating against aggression by this country. There is a need for us to assume responsibility for the declaration of war, and also to prepare the American people for the taxes that will be raised and the possibility of a military draft which may well come.

I must oppose this resolution, which regardless of what many have tried to claim will lead us into war with Iraq. This resolution is not a declaration of war, however, and that is an important point: this resolution transfers the Constitutionally-mandated Congressional authority to declare wars to the executive branch. This resolution tells the president that he alone has the authority to determine when, where, why, and how war will be declared. It merely asks the president to pay us a courtesy call a couple of days after the bombing starts to let us know what is going on. This is exactly what our Founding Fathers cautioned against when crafting our form of government: most had just left behind a monarchy where the power to declare war rested in one individual. It is this they most wished to avoid.

As James Madison wrote in 1798, "The Constitution supposes what the history of all governments demonstrates, that the executive is the branch of power most interested in war, and most prone to it. It has, accordingly, with studied care, vested the question of war in the legislature."

Some- even some in this body- have claimed that this Constitutional requirement is an anachronism, and that those who insist on following the founding legal document of this country are just being frivolous. I could not disagree more.

Mr. Speaker, for the more than one dozen years I have spent as a federal legislator I have taken a particular interest in foreign affairs and especially the politics of the Middle East. From my seat on the international relations committee I have had the opportunity to review dozens of documents and to sit through numerous hearings and mark-up sessions regarding the issues of both Iraq and international terrorism.

Back in 1997 and 1998 I publicly spoke out against the actions of the Clinton Administration, which I believed was moving us once again toward war with Iraq. I believe the genesis of our current policy was unfortunately being set at that time. Indeed, many of the same voices who then demanded that the Clinton Administration attack Iraq are now demanding that the Bush Administration attack Iraq. It is unfortunate that these individuals are using the tragedy of September 11, 2001 as cover to force their long-standing desire to see an American invasion of Iraq. Despite all of the information to which I have access, I remain very skeptical that the nation of Iraq poses a serious and immanent terrorist threat to the United States. If I were convinced of such a threat I would support going to war, as I did when I supported President Bush by voting to give him both the authority and the necessary funding to fight the war on terror.

Mr. Speaker, consider some of the following claims presented by supporters of this resolution, and contrast them with the following facts:

Claim: Iraq has consistently demonstrated its willingness to use force against the US through its firing on our planes patrolling the UN-established "no-fly zones."

Reality: The "no-fly zones" were never authorized by the United Nations, nor was their 12 year patrol by American and British fighter planes sanctioned by the United Nations. Under UN Security Council Resolution 688 (April, 1991), Iraq's repression of the Kurds and Shi'ites was condemned, but there was no authorization for "no-fly zones," much less airstrikes. The resolution only calls for member states to "contribute to humanitarian relief" in the Kurd and Shi'ite areas. Yet the US and British have been bombing Iraq in the "no-fly zones" for 12 years. While one can only condemn any country firing on our pilots, isn't the real argument whether we should continue to bomb Iraq relentlessly? Just since 1998, some 40,000 sorties have been flown over Iraq.

Claim: Iraq is an international sponsor of terrorism.

Reality: According to the latest edition of the State Department's Patterns of Global Terrorism, Iraq sponsors several minor Palestinian groups, the Mujahedin-e-Khalq (MEK), and the Kurdistan Workers' Party (PKK). None of these carries out attacks against the United States. As a matter of fact, the MEK (an Iranian organization located in Iraq) has enjoyed broad Congressional support over the years. According to last year's Patterns of Global Terrorism, Iraq has not been involved in terrorist activity against the West since 1993 – the alleged attempt against former President Bush.

Claim: Iraq tried to assassinate President Bush in 1993.

Reality: It is far from certain that Iraq was behind the attack. News reports at the time were skeptical about Kuwaiti assertions that the attack was planned by Iraq against former. President Bush. Following is an interesting quote from Seymore Hersh's article from Nov. 1993:

Three years ago, during Iraq's six-month occupation of Kuwait, there had been an outcry when a teen-age Kuwaiti girl testified eloquently and effectively before Congress about Iraqi atrocities involving newborn infants. The girl turned out to be the **daughter of the Kuwaiti Ambassador to Washington, Sheikh Saud** Nasir al-Sabah, and her account of Iraqi soldiers flinging babies out of incubators was challenged as exaggerated both by journalists and by human-rights groups. (**Sheikh Saud was subsequently named Minister of Information in Kuwait, and he was the government official in charge of briefing the international press on the alleged assassination attempt against George Bush.**) In a second incident, in August of 1991, Kuwait provoked a special session of the United Nations Security Council by claiming that twelve Iraqi vessels, including a speedboat, had been involved in an attempt to assault Bubiyan Island, long-disputed territory that was then under Kuwaiti control. The Security Council eventually concluded that, while the Iraqis had been provocative, there had been no Iraqi military raid, and that the Kuwaiti government knew there hadn't. What did take place was nothing more than a smuggler-versus-smuggler dispute over war booty in a nearby demilitarized zone that had emerged, after the Gulf War, as an illegal marketplace for alcohol, ammunition, and livestock.

This establishes that on several occasions Kuwait has lied about the threat from Iraq. Hersh goes on to point out in the article numerous other times the Kuwaitis lied to the US and the UN about Iraq. Here is another good quote from Hersh:

The President was not alone in his caution. Janet Reno, the Attorney General, also had her doubts. "The A.G. remains skeptical of certain aspects of the case," a senior Justice Department official told me in late July, a month after the bombs were dropped on Baghdad...Two weeks later, what amounted to open warfare broke out among various factions in the government on the issue of who had done what in Kuwait. Someone gave a Boston Globe reporter access to a classified C.I.A. study that was highly skeptical of the Kuwaiti claims of an Iraqi assassination attempt. **The study, prepared by the C.I.A.'s Counter Terrorism Center, suggested that Kuwait might have "cooked the books" on the alleged plot in an effort to play up the "continuing Iraqi threat" to Western**

interests in the Persian Gulf. Neither the Times nor the Post made any significant mention of the Globe dispatch, which had been written by a Washington correspondent named Paul Quinn-Judge, although the story cited specific paragraphs from the C.I.A. assessment. The two major American newspapers had been driven by their sources to the other side of the debate.

At the very least, the case against Iraq for the alleged bomb threat is not conclusive.

Claim: Saddam Hussein will use weapons of mass destruction against us – he has already used them against his own people (the Kurds in 1988 in the village of Halabja).

Reality: It is far from certain that Iraq used chemical weapons against the Kurds. It may be accepted as conventional wisdom in these times, but back when it was first claimed there was great skepticism. The evidence is far from conclusive. A 1990 study by the Strategic Studies Institute of the U.S. Army War College cast great doubts on the claim that Iraq used chemical weapons on the Kurds. Following are the two gassing incidents as described in the report:

In September 1988, however – a month after the war (between Iran and Iraq) had ended – the State Department abruptly, and in what many viewed as a sensational manner, condemned Iraq for allegedly using chemicals against its Kurdish population. The incident cannot be understood without some background of Iraq's relations with the Kurds...throughout the war Iraq effectively faced two enemies – Iran and elements of its own Kurdish minority. Significant numbers of the Kurds had launched a revolt against Baghdad and in the process teamed up with Tehran. As soon as the war with Iran ended, Iraq announced its determination to crush the Kurdish insurrection. It sent Republican Guards to the Kurdish area, and in the course of the operation – according to the U.S. State Department – gas was used, with the result that numerous Kurdish civilians were killed. The Iraqi government denied that any such gassing had occurred. Nonetheless, Secretary of State Schultz stood by U.S. accusations, and the U.S. Congress, acting on its own, sought to impose economic sanctions on Baghdad as a violator of the Kurds' human rights.

Having looked at all the evidence that was available to us, we find it impossible to confirm the State Department's claim that gas was used in this instance. To begin with. **There were never any victims produced.** International relief organizations who examined the Kurds – in Turkey where they had gone for asylum – failed to discover any. Nor were there ever any found inside Iraq. **The claim rests solely on testimony of the Kurds who had crossed the border into Turkey, where they were interviewed by staffers of the Senate Foreign Relations Committee...**

It appears that in seeking to punish Iraq, the Congress was influenced by another incident that occurred five months earlier in another Iraqi-Kurdish city, Halabjah. In March 1988, the Kurds at Halabjah were bombarded with chemical weapons, producing many deaths. Photographs of the Kurdish victims were widely disseminated in the international media. Iraq was blamed for the Halabjah attack, even though it was subsequently brought out that Iran too had used chemicals in this operation and **it seemed likely that it was the *Iranian* bombardment that had actually killed the Kurds**.

Thus, in our view, the **Congress acted more on the basis of emotionalism than factual information**, and without sufficient thought for the adverse diplomatic effects of its action.

Claim: Iraq must be attacked because it has ignored UN Security Council resolutions – these resolutions must be backed up by the use of force.

Reality: Iraq is but one of the many countries that have not complied with UN Security Council resolutions. In addition to the dozen or so resolutions currently being violated by Iraq, a conservative estimate reveals that there are an additional 91 Security Council resolutions by countries other than Iraq that are also currently being violated. Adding in older resolutions that were violated would mean easily more than 200 UN Security Council resolutions have been violated with total impunity. Countries currently in violation include: Israel, Turkey, Morocco, Croatia, Armenia, Russia, Sudan, Turkey-controlled Cyprus, India, Pakistan, Indonesia. None of these countries have been threatened with force over their violations.

Claim: Iraq has anthrax and other chemical and biological agents.

Reality: That may be true. However, according to UNSCOM's chief weapons inspector 90-95 percent of Iraq's chemical and biological weapons and capabilities were destroyed by 1998; those that remained have likely degraded in the intervening four years and are likely useless. A 1994 Senate Banking Committee hearing revealed some 74 shipments of deadly chemical and biological agents from the U.S. to Iraq in the 1980s. As one recent press report stated:

One 1986 shipment from the Virginia-based American Type Culture Collection included three strains of anthrax, six strains of the bacteria that make botulinum toxin and three strains of the bacteria that cause gas gangrene. **Iraq later admitted to the United Nations that it had made weapons out of all three...**

The **CDC, meanwhile, sent shipments of germs** to the Iraqi Atomic Energy Commission and other agencies involved in Iraq's weapons of mass destruction programs. It sent samples in 1986 of botulinum toxin and botulinum toxoid — used to make vaccines against botulinum toxin — **directly to the Iraqi chemical and biological weapons complex** at al-Muthanna, the records show.

These were sent while the United States was supporting Iraq covertly in its war against Iran. U.S. assistance to Iraq in that war also included covertly-delivered intelligence on Iranian troop movements and other assistance. This is just another example of our policy of interventionism in affairs that do not concern us – and how this interventionism nearly always ends up causing harm to the United States.

Claim: The president claimed last night that: "Iraq possesses ballistic missiles with a likely range of hundreds of miles; far enough to strike Saudi Arabia, Israel, Turkey and other nations in a region where more than 135,000 American civilians and service members live and work."

Reality: Then why is only Israel talking about the need for the U.S. to attack Iraq? None of the other countries seem concerned at all. Also, the fact that some 135,000 Americans in the area are under threat from these alleged missiles is just makes the point that it is time to bring our troops home to defend our own country.

Claim: Iraq harbors al-Qaeda and other terrorists.

Reality: The administration has claimed that some Al-Qaeda elements have been present in Northern Iraq. This is territory controlled by the Kurds – who are our allies – and is patrolled by U.S. and British fighter aircraft. Moreover, dozens of countries – including Iran and the United States – are said to have al-Qaeda members on their territory. Other terrorists allegedly harbored by Iraq, all are affiliated with Palestinian causes and do not attack the United States.

Claim: President Bush said in his speech on 7 October 2002: " Many people have asked how close Saddam Hussein is to developing a nuclear weapon. **Well, we don't know exactly, and that's the problem**..."

Reality: An admission of a *lack* of information is justification for an attack?

Arguments Against the Iran Sanctions Enabling Act of 2007

July 30, 2007

Mr. Speaker, I strongly oppose any move to initiate further sanctions on Iran. Sanctions are acts of war, and expanding sanctions on Iran serves no purpose other than preparing the American people for an eventual attack on Iran. This is the same pattern we saw in the run up to the war on Iraq: Congress passes legislation calling for regime change, sanctions are imposed, and eventually we are told that only an attack will solve the problem. We should expect the same tragic result if we continue down this path. I urge my colleagues to reconsider.

I oppose economic sanctions for two very simple reasons. First, they don't work as effective foreign policy. Time after time, from Cuba to China to Iraq, we have failed to unseat despotic leaders or change their policies by refusing to trade with the people of those nations. If anything, the anti-American sentiment aroused by sanctions often strengthens the popularity of such leaders, who use America as a convenient scapegoat to divert attention from their own tyranny. History clearly shows that free and open trade does far more to liberalize oppressive governments than trade wars. Economic freedom and political freedom are inextricably linked--when people get a taste of goods and information from abroad, they are less likely to tolerate a closed society at home. So sanctions mostly harm innocent citizens and do nothing to displace the governments we claim as enemies.

Second, sanctions simply hurt American industries, particularly agriculture. Every market we close to our nation's farmers is a market exploited by foreign farmers. China, Russia, the Middle East, North Korea, and Cuba all represent huge markets for our farm products, yet many in Congress favor current or proposed trade restrictions that prevent our farmers from selling to the billions of people in these areas.

We must keep in mind that Iran has still not been found in violation of the Non-Proliferation Treaty. Furthermore, much of the information regarding Iran's nuclear program is coming to us via thoroughly discredited sources like the MeK, a fanatical cult that is on our State Department's terror list. Additionally, the same discredited neo-conservatives who pushed us into the Iraq war are making similarly exaggerated claims against Iran. How often do these "experts" have to be proven wrong before we start to question their credibility?

It is said that we non-interventionists are somehow "isolationists" because we don't want to interfere in the affairs of foreign nations. But the real isolationists are those who demand that we isolate certain peoples overseas because we disagree with the policies of their leaders. The best way to avoid war, to promote American values, and to spread real freedom and liberty is to engage in trade and contacts with the rest of the world as broadly as possible.

I urge my colleagues to reconsider this counterproductive and dangerous move toward further sanctions on Iran.

Repeal Sarbanes-Oxley!

April 14, 2005

Mr. Speaker, I rise to introduce the Due Process and Economic Competitiveness Restoration Act, which repeals Section 404 of the Sarbanes-Oxley Act. Sarbanes-Oxley was rushed into law in the hysterical atmosphere surrounding the Enron and WorldCom bankruptcies, by a Congress more concerned with doing something than doing the right thing. Today, American businesses, workers, and investors are suffering because Congress was so eager to appear "tough on corporate crime." Sarbanes-Oxley imposes costly new regulations on the financial services industry. These regulations are damaging American capital markets by providing an incentive for small US firms and foreign firms to deregister from US stock exchanges. According to a study by the prestigious Wharton Business School, the number of American companies deregistering from public stock exchanges nearly tripled during the year after Sarbanes-Oxley became law, while the New York Stock Exchange had only 10 new foreign listings in all of 2004.

The reluctance of small businesses and foreign firms to register on American stock exchanges is easily understood when one considers the costs Sarbanes-Oxley imposes on businesses. According to a survey by Kron/Ferry International, Sarbanes-Oxley cost Fortune 500 companies an average of $5.1 million in compliance expenses in 2004, while a study by the law firm of Foley and Lardner found the Act increased costs associated with being a publicly held company by 130 percent.

Many of the major problems stem from section 404 of Sarbanes-Oxley, which requires Chief Executive Officers to certify the accuracy of financial statements. It also requires that outside auditors "attest to" the soundness of the internal controls used in preparing the statements-- an obvious sop to auditors and accounting firms. The Public Company Accounting Oversight Board defines internal controls as "controls over all significant accounts and disclosures in the financial statements." According to John Berlau, a Warren Brookes Fellow at the Competitive Enterprise Institute, the definition of internal controls is so broad that a CEO possibly could be found liable for not using the latest version of Windows! Financial analysts have identified Section 404 as the major reason why American corporations are hoarding cash instead of investing it in new ventures.

Journalist Robert Novak, in his column of April 7, said that,

"[f]or more than a year, CEOs and CFOs have been telling me that 404 is a costly nightmare" and *"ask nearly any business executive to name the biggest menace facing corporate America, and the answer is apt to be number 404…a dagger aimed at the heart of the economy."*

Compounding the damage done to the economy is the harm Sarbanes-Oxley does to constitutional liberties and due process. CEOs and CFOs can be held criminally liable, and subjected to 25 years in prison, for inadvertent errors. Laws criminalizing honest mistakes done with no intent to defraud are more typical of police states than free societies. I hope those who consider themselves civil libertarians will recognize the danger of imprisoning citizens for inadvertent mistakes, put aside any prejudice against private businesses, and join my efforts to repeal Section 404.

The US Constitution does not give the federal government authority to regulate the accounting standards of private corporations. These questions should be resolved by private contracts between a company and its shareholders, and by state and local regulations. Let me remind my colleagues who are skeptical of the ability of markets and local law enforcement to protect against fraud: the market passed judgment on Enron, in the form of declining stock prices, before Congress even held the first hearing on the matter. My colleagues also should keep in mind that certain state attorneys general have been very aggressive in prosecuting financial crimes

Section 404 of the Sarbanes-Oxley Act has raised the costs of doing business, thus causing foreign companies to withdraw from American markets and retarding economic growth. By criminalizing inadvertent mistakes and exceeding congressional authority, Section 404 also undermines the rule of law and individual liberty. I therefore urge my colleagues to cosponsor the Due Process and Economic Competitiveness Restoration Act.

Federal Reserve has Monopoly over Money and Credit in United States
April 28, 1997

Mr. Speaker, today I would like to talk about the subject of monopolies. The American people historically have been very much opposed to all monopolies. The one thing that generally is not known is that monopolies only occur with government support. There is no such thing as a free market monopoly. As long as there is free entry into the market, a true monopoly cannot exist.

The particular monopoly I am interested in talking about today is the monopoly over money and credit, and that is our Federal Reserve System.

The Federal Reserve System did not evolve out of the market, it evolved out of many, many pieces of legislation that were passed over the many years by this Congress. Our Founders debated the issue of a central bank and they were opposed to a central bank, but immediately after the Constitutional Convention there was an attempt to have a central bank, and the First Bank of the United States was established. This was repealed as soon as Jefferson was able to do it.

Not too long thereafter the Second National Bank of the United States was established, another attempt at centralized banking, and it was Jackson, who abhorred the powers given to a single bank, that abolished the Second National Bank.

Throughout the 19th century there were attempts made to reestablish the principle of central banking, but it was not until 1913 that our current Federal Reserve System was established. Since that time it has evolved tremendously, to the point now where it is literally a dictatorship over money and credit.

It works in collaboration with the banking system, where not only can the Federal Reserve create money and credit out of thin air and manipulate interest rates, it also works closely with the banks through the fractional reserve banking system that allows the money supply to expand. This is the source of a lot of mischief and a lot of problems, and if we in the Congress could ever get around to understanding this issue, we might be able to do something about the lowering standard of living which many Americans are now suffering from. If we are concerned about repealing the business cycle, we would have to finally understand the Federal Reserve and how they contribute to the business cycle.

Recently it has been in the news that Alan Greenspan had raised interest rates, and he has received a lot of criticism. There were some recent letters written to Greenspan saying that he should not be raising interest rates. That may well be true, but I think the more important thing is, why does he have the power? Why does he have the authority to even be able to manipulate interest rates? That is something that should be left to the market.

Not only is this a monopoly control over money and credit, unfortunately it is a very secret monopoly. Mr. Speaker, I serve on the Committee on Banking and Financial Services and I am on the Subcommittee on Domestic and International Monetary Policy, and I myself cannot attend the open market committee meetings. I have no access to what really goes on. I have no authority to do any oversight. There is no appropriation made for the Federal Reserve.

The recent news revealed that the chief of the janitorial services over at the Federal Reserve makes $163,000 a year, and yet we have no authority over the Federal Reserve because it is a quasi-private organization that is not responding to anything the Congress says. Yes, they come and give us some reports about what they are doing, but because Congress has reneged, they no longer have much to say about what the Federal Reserve does.

This, to me, is pretty important when we think how important money is. If they have the authority to manipulate interest rates, which is the cost of borrowing, which is the price as well as the supply of money, this is an ominous power because we use the money in every single transaction.

It is 50 percent of every transaction. Whether it is the purchase of a good or whether it is the selling of our labor, it is denominated in terms of what we call the dollar, which does not have much of a definition anymore, and yet we have reneged on our responsibility to monitor the Fed to determine whether or not this dollar will maintain value.

Things have not always been this bad, and it did not happen automatically in 1913 when the Federal Reserve was established. It took a while. But it is worse now than it has ever been. Matter of fact, a well-known former Chairman of the Federal Reserve, William McChesney Martin, had interesting comments to make about this very issue in 1953. Mr. Martin said this: `Dictated money rates breeds dictated prices all across the board.'

Well, it is abhorrent to those who believe in free enterprise and the marketplace. He goes on to say, `This is characteristic of dictatorship. It is regimentation. It is not compatible with our institutions.'

So here we have a former Chairman of the Federal Reserve System coming down very hard on the concept of control of money and credit, and yet today it is assumed that the Federal Reserve has this authority. And so often it gravitates into the hands of one individual.

So those who are levying criticism toward the Federal Reserve today are justified, but if it is only to modify policy and not go to the source of the problem, which means why do they have the power in the first place, it is not going to do much good. So we will have to someday restore the integrity of the monetary system, and we have to have more respect for the free market if we ever expect to undertake a reform of a monetary system which has given us a great deal of trouble, and it is bound to give us a lot more trouble as time goes on.

How will this be done? Some argue that the Federal Reserve is private and out of our control. That is not exactly true. It is secret, but it is a creature of Congress. Congress created the Federal Reserve System and Congress has the authority to do oversight, but it refuses and has ignored the responsibility of really monitoring the value of our currency and monitoring this very, very powerful central bank.

There is no doubt in my mind and in the minds of many others that this has to be done. To say that we must just badger a little bit to the Fed and to Mr. Greenspan, and say that interest rates should be lowered or raised or whatever, and tinker with policy, I think that would fall quite short of what needs to be done.

What is the motivation behind a Federal Reserve System and a central bank? Indeed, there is some very interesting motivation because it does not happen accidentally. There is a good reason to have a central bank that has this power to just with a computer create billions of dollars. It is not an accident that

Congress more or less closes their eyes to it.

Between 1913 and 1971 there were a lot more restrictions on the Federal Reserve to do what they are doing today, because at that time we were still making a feeble attempt to follow the Constitution. The dollar was defined as the weight of gold. There were restrictions in the amount of new money and credit one could create because of the gold backing of the currency.

Although Americans were not allowed to own gold from the 1930's to 1971, foreigners could. Foreigners could come in and deliver their dollars back onto the United States and say, `Give us $35 an ounce.' But that was a fiction, too, because by that time we had created so many new dollars that the market knew that it took more dollars to get one ounce of gold. In the process, we gave up a large portion of our gold that was present in our Treasury.

Why would the Congress allow this and why would they permit it? I think the reason is Congress likes to spend money, and many here like to tax, and they have been taxing. But currently, today, the average American works more than half the time for the Government. If we add up the cost of all the taxes and the cost of regulations, we all work into July just to support our Government, and most Americans are not that satisfied with what they are getting from the Government.

The taxes cannot be raised much more, so they can go out and borrow money. The Congress will spend too much because there is tremendous pressure to spend on all these good things we do; all the welfare programs, and all the military expenditures to police the world and build bases around the world. It takes a lot of money and there is a lot of interest behind that to spend this money.

So, then, they go and spend the money and, lo and behold, there is not enough money to borrow and not enough tax money to go around, so they have to have one more vehicle, and that is the creation of money out of thin air, and this is what they do. They send the Treasury bills or the bonds to the Federal Reserve, and with a computer they can turn a switch and create a billion or $10 billion in a single day and that debases the currency. It diminishes the value of the money and alters interest rates and causes so much mischief that, if people are concerned about the economy or their standard of living or rising costs of living, this is the source of the problem.

So it is not only with the Federal Reserve manipulating the money and the interest rates, but the responsibility falls on the Congress as well because the Federal Reserve serves the interests of the Congress in accommodating the Congress as we here in the Congress spend more than we should.

Before 1971, when there were still restraints on the Federal Reserve, there was not as much deficit spending. Since that time, since the breakdown of the final vestiges of the gold standard in 1971, we have not balanced the budget one single time. So there is definitely a relationship. Now we have a national debt built up to $5.3 trillion, and we keep borrowing more and more.

We have a future obligation to future generations of $17 trillion, and this obligation is developed in conjunction with this idea that money is something we can create out of thin air. Now, if it were only the accommodation for the excess spending that was the problem, and we just had to pay interest to the Federal

Reserve, that would be a problem in itself but it would not be the entire problem that we face today and that we face in the future.

As the Federal Reserve manipulates the economy by first lowering interest rates below what they should be and then raising interest rates above what they think they should be, this causes the business cycle. This is the source of the business cycle. So anybody who is concerned about unemployment and downturns in the economy and rising costs of living must eventually address the subject of monetary policy.

As a member of the Committee on Banking and Financial Services, I am determined that we will once again have a serious discussion about what money is all about and why it is so important and why we in the Congress here cannot continue to ignore it and believe that we can endlessly accommodate deficits with the creation of new money. There is no doubt that it hurts the working man more so than the wealthy man. The working man who has a more difficult time adjusting to the rising cost of living is now suffering from a diminished standard of living because real wages are going down.

There are many, many statistics now available to show that the real wage is down. Between 1973 and 1997, the wages of the working man has gone down approximately 20 percent. This has to do with the changes in the economy, but it also has to do with changes in the value of the currency and the wages do not keep up with the cost of living.

The increase in the supply of money is called inflation, even though there are not very many people in the news world or here in the Congress would accept that as a definition, because everybody wants to say that inflation is that which we measure by the Consumer Price Index.

The Consumer Price Index is merely a technique or a vehicle in a feeble attempt to measure the depreciation of our money.

It is impossible to measure the money's value by some index like the Consumer Price Index. There are way too many variables because the individual who is in a $20,000 tax bracket buys different things than the individual who is in a $200,000 tax bracket. Wages are variable and the amount of money we borrow, the amount of money we spend on education as well as medicine varies from one individual to another. So this Consumer Price Index which we hang so much on is nothing more than a fiction about what we are trying to do in evaluating and accommodating and adjusting to the depreciating value of the dollar.

The critics of the Fed are numerous, as I said. The recent criticism has erupted because a few weeks ago, after warning of about 3 or 4 months by the Chairman of the Federal Reserve that interest rates were going to go up and, lo and behold, he did. The overnight interest rates that banks pay to borrow money just to adjust their books went up one-fourth of 1 percent. This is very disturbing to the markets. But Alan Greenspan mentioned this for 3 or 4 months. He started talking about the threat to the marketplace and the threat to the stock market back in December. But instead of him being entirely in control as he would pretend to be, actually market interest rates were already rising. Because if we look carefully at the monetary statistics from December up until the time he raised interest rates, he actually was doubling the growth of the money supply.

What does this mean? This means that there were pressures already on rising interest rates, and the way to keep interest rates down is to create more and more money. It is the supply-and-demand effect. So if you have more money, make it more available, interest rates come down. So this was his attempt to keep interest rates down rather than him saying, today we have to have higher interest rates.

But the real problem is why does the Federal Reserve have this much power over interest rates? In a free market, interest rates would be determined by savings. People would be encouraged to work, spend what they want, save the rest. If savings are high, interest rates go down, people then are encouraged to borrow and invest and build businesses. But today we have created an environment that there is no encouragement for savings, for tax reasons and for psychological reasons, very, very little savings in this country. Our country saves less money than probably any country in the world. But that does not eliminate the access to credit. Because if the banks and the businesses need money, the Federal Reserve comes along and they crank out the credit and they lower the interest rates artificially, which then encourages business people and consumers to do things that they would not otherwise do.

This is the expansion or the bubble part of the business cycle, which then sets the stage for the next recession. So people can talk about how to get out of the next recession when the next recession hits and they can talk about what caused it, but the next recession has already been scheduled. It has been scheduled by the expansion of the money supply and the spending and the borrowing and the deficits that we have accumulated here over the last 6 to 8 years. And so, therefore, we can anticipate, and we in the Congress will have to deal with it, we anticipate for the next recession.

But unfortunately, because we do not look at the fundamentals of what we have done and the spending and the deficits, the next stage will be what we have done before. That is, if unemployment is going up, the government has to spend more money, there has to be more unemployment insurance. We cannot let people suffer. So the deficits will go up, revenues will go down and as we spend more money to try to bail ourselves out of the next recession, we will obviously just compound the problems because that is what we have been doing for the past 50 years. We have not solved these problems.

As a matter of fact, what has happened, because we eventually get the economy going again, what we do is we continue to build this huge financial bubble which exists today. It is a much bigger bubble than ever existed in the 1920's, it is international in scope and it is something never experienced in the history of mankind. Yet we have to face up to this, because when that time comes, we have to do the right things.

The 64 Members of Congress recently that signed the letter to Alan Greenspan said, Mr. Greenspan, you should not raise interest rates. Of course I just mentioned that maybe interest rates were rising, anyway, maybe he was accommodating the market pressures. But when 64 Members of Congress write to Greenspan and say do not let interest rates rise, or lower interest rates, what they are really saying is crank out more money, because if there is a greater supply of money, then interest rates will be lower and everybody is going to be happy. That is true, for the short run. On the long run, it causes very serious problems.

Stiglitz, who used to be the chairman of the council of economic advisers, is a very strong critic of Alan Greenspan right now. He said that there are no problems, there is no cliff we are about to go over, do not worry about the future. I do not fault Mr. Greenspan's concern, believe me. I think he knows what is coming and why adjustments have to be made. But his critics are saying, when they talk about do not raise interest rates, what we have to remember is what they are saying to him is make sure there is more inflation, more money, lower interest rates and, of course, that will add to our problems in the future.

Not only do we have Members of Congress telling the Fed what to do, and the former Chairman of the Council of Economic Advisers telling them, many others all have an opinion on what to do, but nobody really asks the question, why are they doing all this in secret and where did they get all this power and why do we tolerate this system of money?

Even the IMF, something I am very much concerned about is the internationalization of our credit system, the IMF now has issued a recent report, but they do not agree with the 64 Members of Congress and they do not agree with the critics who say lower interest rates, create more money. They are saying to our Federal Reserve, you are creating too much money and you are having too much growth. Who ever heard of anything like too much growth? What is wrong with too much growth? Some people think that too much growth causes inflation, which is an absolute fallacy. If there is a lot of growth and a lot of production, prices would come down. Prices go up when the value of the money goes down. But the IMF is saying that should not even be involved in our domestic policy, and they are more involved than ever before, they are telling our Fed, this is good, what you are doing is good, keep raising your interest rates, turn off the economy, have a little slump here.

We do not need that kind of advice from somebody. We have enough problems taking advice from our own people and our own Congress about what has to happen, but we certainly do not need the advice from the IMF telling us that we ought to have more inflation, that we should involve overheating and that for some reason growth is bad. In a free market, sound monetary system, growth is good. If you have sound money and you have economic growth of 6 or 7 or 8 percent a year, you do not have inflation. That does not cause the inflation. It is only the debasement of the money that causes prices to rise.

Why do we hear so much concern about interest rates and price? Well, there is a specific reason for this according to some very sound economic thinkers, and, that is they would like for us here in the Congress to think only about prices, either the price of money, which is the interest rate, or other prices, because so often it leads to the conclusion that, well, maybe what we ought to do is have price controls, which they tried in the early 1970's and it was a total disaster, but this is essentially what we have in medicine today.

We create new credit, the money goes in certain areas, the Government takes this money and channels it into education in medicine, so you have more price inflation. So what do you do? You have price controls. That is what is going on. That is what we are having today in medicine, rationing of health care. That is what managed care is all about. Patients suffer from this because they have less choices, and they do not have as much decision making on what care they are going to get. This is a consequence of Government manipulation of money and credit.

Those who want to perpetuate this system do not want us to think of the real cause, and that is, the real cause is the monetary system. They would like us to think about the symptoms and not the cause, because it is not in the interest of a lot of people, not only not in the interest of the big spenders here in the Congress who love the idea that the Federal Reserve is able to accommodate them on deficits, but there are business and banking interests and international interests and even some military production interests who like the idea that the credit is readily available and that they will be accommodated. The little guy never benefits. The little guy pays the taxes, he suffers from the inflation, he suffers from the unemployment, but there is a special group of people in an inflationary environment that benefits. Today of course there are a lot of people on Wall Street benefiting from this environment.

If this type of system were real good, we would all be very, very prosperous, and if we listened to the Government statistics, we would say there are no problems in this country. But I know differently. A lot of people I talk to, they tell me they are having a lot of problems making ends meet. Sometimes they work two and three jobs to get their bills paid. It is not all feminism that makes women go to work. A lot of women go to work because they have to do it to make ends meet and take care of their families. So there are a lot of problems.

But one key point that I think is important and, that is economic growth. If we have no economic growth and there is no productivity growth, we cannot maintain the standard of living, we cannot have increasing wages. If you do not produce more, you cannot have wages going up.

Unfortunately, that is where we are really hurting in this country. We are living prosperously because we borrow a lot of money, by individuals, by corporations, and our Government borrows a lot from overseas. But we are not producing. Productivity growth in the last 5 years has averaged 0.3 percent. This is very, very low. It is equivalent to what happened before the Industrial Revolution, and it is going to lead to major problems in this country unless we understand why we are not producing as we had in the past. We need to address this if we have any concern about the people who suffer from these consequences.

The economic growth is slow. Predictions are that they, according to the Government statistics, are going to slow even more in time, whether it is the end of this year or next. We will have a recession. Even by some Government statistics now, we are seeing signs that there is a rising price level in some of our commodities. There is belief that these prices will go up and we will be suffering more so, even measured by the Consumer Price Index. This story that is being passed out here in the Halls of Congress and in other places in Washington that we do not have to worry about the Consumer Price Index, it overstates inflation, therefore we can make the adjustment, I do not think that is correct at all. I think the Consumer Price Index probably way underestimates inflation. If you have private sources, there are many people who suffer the cost of living much higher than the 3 or 4 percent that the Government reports. But there are some commodity indices that in the past 2 years have gone up over 50 percent. This is a sign of the consequence of the inflating of the money supply and it is starting to hit, or will hit some of our consumer products, because it is already hitting our commodities.

This idea that if there is a sign that prices are increasing, what we have to do is take it under control and we have to suppress economic growth and raise interest rates, this says something about our policy that shows the lack of understanding. Because if we look at all the recessions that we have had since World War II, in spite of the seriousness of many of these recessions, prices still go up.

The one that we remember most clearly is in the 1970's, where they even coined the word `stagflation.' This is not an unheard of economic phenomenon. It is very frequent in many other nations, where you have a lot of inflation and poor economic growth. We have not had a serious problem with that, but it is very likely that that is eventually what we will get, because we have absolutely no backing and no restraint on our monetary system.

When we have an economic and monetary system as we have today, I mention how it encourages Congress to spend beyond its means. It spends too much, it borrows too much, it inflates too much, and it leads to serious long-term problems, that as long as you can borrow again and borrow again, you sort of hide the problems, delay the consequences of the problem and prevent the major correction that eventually comes.

But what have the American people been doing? Well, they have been encouraged by this. They see the credit is available out there. They keep borrowing, living beyond their means. Government lives beyond their means, and individuals live way beyond their means.

But some of the statistics are not very good about what is happening with our consumers, the American citizens. In 1996 personal bankruptcies were up 27 percent. It is at record high; well over a million bankruptcies were filed in 1996. This is a reflection of loose credit policies, but it also is a reflection of a moral attitude.

There was a time in our history where bankruptcy was looked down upon, that we had a moral obligation to do our very best. If we have a bad turn in our businesses, what we did was we notified everybody, we went back to work, and we systematically did our very best to pay off all our debts. There is no incentive for that today. So it is very easy today to see the bankruptcies filed, and they are increasing rapidly. I suspect that they are going to continue to increase even more dramatically.

Credit card delinquencies are at an all time high. They were at 3.72 percent in 1996, and those who are late payments, they are also a historic high, well over 5 percent. So the credit conditions of this country are not very good.

Now what do we see as the signs of things changing to sort of take care of this problem? So far, not too many good things happening. In 1995, the latest year we have measurements for, we find out that credit card issuers, credit card companies, issued 2.7 billion credit cards, pre-approved. Pre-approved credit cards, 2.7 billion, and it was equivalent to sending every single American between the ages of 18 and 64, 17 pre-approved credit cards. Nothing like throwing out the temptation there, and many Americans fall into the temptations. Congress does it. They keep borrowing, and they exist. So the individual keeps borrowing, takes another credit card, rolls them over.

Eventually, though, the banker will call. The banker will call the individual. Who calls the Congress? Who calls a country when it spends beyond its means and it is way past the time when they should be cutting back? The problem that develops then is not so much that the Government, our Government, quits taxing and quits paying the bills. We will always do that. We have control over that because we now have this authority by Federal Reserve to create the money. The checks will always come.

The one thing that we do not have in the Congress and we do not have in the Federal Reserve, and the President does not have, is to guarantee the value of the money, and that is the problem. Today all we hear about is the strength of the dollar, but if you look at the dollar from 1945 on, the dollar is on a downward spiral, and we are on a slight upward blip right now. Ultimately the dollar will be attacked by the marketplace, and it will be more powerful than any of the policy changes that our Federal Reserve might institute.

There is a couple other things that have happened in our financial system that is different than in the other ones. Some would argue with me and say you are concerned about the supply of money and credit. Well, I can show you a statistic measured by M-1, M-2 and M-3, and the money supply is not going up all that rapidly. And this is the case compared to other times, that money supply as measured by the more conventional methods are not--those measurements are not going up as rapidly as they have in the past. But there are other things that can accommodate the lack of expansion of money as measured by, say, M-2 and M-3.

First, if an individual has an incentive not to hold the money and save the money, but spend their money the day they get it, that is called the velocity or the propensity to spend the money, and if you use it more often, it is like having more dollars, and that is one statistic that has gone up dramatically. Between 1993 and 1996 it has gone up 45 percent, so there is more desire to take the money and spend it, and it acts as if there is a lot more money, and we will also put pressure on the marketplace and cause the distortions that can be harmful.

The other thing that we have going that is different than ever before is that because there is no definition of the money, the dollars, no definition of the dollar, we have introduced the notion of all kinds of hedges and all kinds of speculation, and some serve financial and economic interests to do hedging, but because there is no soundness to the currency there is a greater need all the time to hedge and to try to protect against sudden changes. Some of that would be economically driven, but other activity of that sort is driven by speculation.

So in an age when you have tremendous excessive credit, money and credit, you have more speculation. Consumers speculate they spend too much money, a businessman speculates, invests in things he probably should not, but also governments do the same thing. They spend money that they should not have.

But in this area of derivatives, we have things like swaps and futures and options, repos, and the foreign currency market. Right now there is $20, $21 trillion worth of these derivatives floating around out there outside of the measurement by our conventional money supply, which means that this participates in this huge financial bubble that exists around the world.

There is also a measurement that we make on a daily basis which is called through the clearinghouse interbank payment system, and this is all the electronic money that is traded throughout the world every single day, and this again reflects how quickly we are spending our money and how fast we are circulating and how quickly it moves among and through our computers. Today it is estimated that $1.4 trillion is transferred over the wire service.

Now, if there were a sound dollar and it was created only with a proper procedure rather than out of thin air, this would not be as bad, but the fact that this is contributing toward a financial bubble I think is a very, very dangerous condition.

We live in an age called the Information Age; we live in a computer age, and this technology is all very, very helpful to us. As a matter of fact, it has served us in many ways to accommodate this age of the paper money systems of the world. No money is sound today in history in the entire world. So there is what we call the fluctuating currency rates. Every single day, every single minute, the value of the dollar versus the yen, versus the mark, versus the pound is changing instantly.

Now in the old days each currency was defined by a weight of gold. There was less speculation even though under those conditions governments manipulating, and there were periodic times when certain countries would have to devalue. But now the computer system has really been a free market answer to those individuals who like the system, and it does work, it does work to a large degree for a time. But it also allows the system to last longer, and it allows us to create more of this financial bubble.

This is why we have been able to go along with the system of government where we have made commitments to our future generations of $17 trillion; otherwise we could not have made these commitments that would have had to be a correction. We would have had to cut back and live within our means, just as individuals do; they have to live within their means, and they have to live probably less high than they were when they were borrowing all the money. A country will have to do that, too, that has lived way beyond its means, and this is why what we are doing is so dangerous.

The fact that we had these floating exchange rates for years has permitted many of our paper currencies to last a lot longer than they otherwise would have. We in the United States have a dollar which is considered the reserve currency in the world which lends itself to even more problems because the dollar is held in higher esteem and it is considered the reserve that other countries are more willing to hold, and this came out of the World War II because we had essentially all the gold, the dollar was strong, our economy was strong, so the dollar was good as gold. So people took dollars and they would hold them, and they still do that to a large degree today.

So what does that encourage us to do? It encourages here in the Congress and elsewhere to create this debt, and then as the money circulates, we go and we say, oh, we have a lot of credit, we can borrow this money, we will buy foreign products, and that is what we do. We buy a lot of foreign products, and everybody is decrying, you know, this foreign deficit. We owe more money to foreigners and we have a greater foreign deficit than any other country in the world, and it is encouraged because they are willing to take our dollars, and we are willing to spend the money and we are willing to run up these deficits and not worry about the future.

But where do these dollars go? They go into the central banks, they buy our Treasury bills, and they are quite satisfied at the moment. But when they get unsatisfied and dissatisfied with it, they are going to dump these dollars, and they will come back. But the trade deficit is running more than a hundred billion dollars a year, which means we buy more products from overseas than we sell to the tune of a hundred billion dollars.

This in many ways has allowed our Federal Reserve to get off the hook a bit because if we had a $100 billion that nobody wants to loan us and they had to create that new money, that would be very, very damaging to the psychology of our market, and it would be very, very inflationary. So it is still inflationary, but it is delayed. So as long as foreigners will take our dollars and let us buy their goods and we live beyond our means and hold our dollars and we keep creating new money and paying the interest, this thing could go on for a while. But eventually though in all monetary systems which are based on fiat, the creation of money out of thin air, eventually comes to an end, and when it comes to an end, there is the rejection of the dollar, and then the dollars come home, interest rates will go up, inflation will be back with a vengeance, and there will come a time, and nobody knows when that time will come, it will not be because of us in the Congress being very deliberate and very wise to all of a sudden live within our means, but we will be forced to live within our means because those who want to loan the money to us and the value of the money will change, that there will just not be enough wealth.

What promotes all this? Well, what is the grand illusion that allows us to get ourselves into such a situation? Well, the grand illusion of the 20th century, especially in the latter half of the 20th century, has been that prosperity can come from the creation of credit. Now if you think about it, it does not make any sense if you take a Monopoly game and you create more Monopoly money and pass it out, everybody knows it has no value. But we have literally endorsed the concept that if we just print money and pass it out, everybody is going to be wealthy, and because it is government and because it was related to a gold standard and because foreigners will take money, this system continues to work because there is still trust in the money.

But eventually this trust will be lost. The wealth cannot be created by creating new money. Yes, if the Federal Reserve prints more money today and hands it to me, I can go spend it and I can feel wealthier. But in the grand scheme of things, you do not create wealth that way, and that is also the reason why productivity growth is down. We do not create it. We have to have incentives, we have to encourage work and effort. That is the only place you can get wealth.

So our taxes are too high, the regulations are too high, we borrow too much money, interest rates are too high, and we discourage savings all because of this monetary system. So eventually we are going to be required to do something about that to restore trust in the money so we do save money so we work harder. But we have to lower taxes, we have to get rid of regulations, we have to get rid of taxes on capital gains and get rid of taxes on savings and interest and get rid of taxes on inheritance. Then people will have more of an incentive to work rather than just to borrow. So the illusion of wealth today is that which comes from a fiat or paper monetary system.

We need today a very serious debate on what the monetary system ought to be all about. It cannot be a debate which is isolated from the role of government. If we have a role of government which is to run the welfare state, to give anything to anybody who needs something or wants something or claims it is an entitlement or claims it is a right, if that is a system of government that we want to perpetuate, it is going to be very difficult to have any reform. If we continue to believe that this country is the policeman of the world, that we must police the world and build bases overseas at the same time we neglect our own national defense, our own borders, our own bases here at home, but we continue to spend money on places, on Bosnia and Africa, and pay for the defense of Japan and Europe; as long as we accept those ideas, there is no way we can restore any sanity to our budget.

So I am suggesting to my colleagues here in the Congress that what we must do is address the subject of what the role of government ought to be. There should be a precise role for government. That is what the whole idea and issue was of the Constitutional Convention as well as our Revolution. We did not like the role of government that the English and the British had given us, and we here in the United States decided that the role of government ought to be there for the preservation of liberty.

The role of government ought not to be to redistribute wealth, it ought not to be the counterfeiter of the world, to create money out of thin air. It is illegal for you or I to counterfeit money. Why do we allow the Government to counterfeit the money and make it worthless all the time?

As long as we accept that, we are going to have big problems. But there will be a time coming, and I suggest to all of my colleagues that we be ready for it, because it is so serious. Not only is it a serious threat to our physical and economic well-being, the greater threat is the threat to our individual liberty. As conditions worsen, and when we have to face up to our problems, so often the response is, all we need is another government program. And that is still an attitude that I see all the time around here: if we just have a little more tax money.

Already in this very early Congress, we have had tax increases in spite of the rhetoric against taxes. We have been raising taxes. We have increased the amount of regulations. We have done nothing to really address the subject.

That comes from the fact that we never really ask the right questions. What should the role of government be? The Founders, as they concluded after the Revolution, as they wrote the Constitution, it very clearly was stated that the role of government, especially at the Federal level, ought to be there to protect the individual liberties of all individuals, no matter what. But today, we have lost that as a goal and as a target. We concentrate, whether it is a businessman or the person that is receiving welfare benefits, the concentration is on the material benefits that usually come from a free society in a voluntary way. But today, if anybody wants something or they need something or they think they have a right to it, what do they do; they order a political action committee and come to Washington.

I was gone for a few years. I was here in the Congress in 1976, and, after returning, there is one dramatic difference. There are more lobbyists than ever, more commands, more people coming and more people wanting things. I have more demand from the business community than I do from those who are from the poor end of the spectrum. There is a vicious maldistribution of wealth in a society that destroys its money. Inevitably, if a country destroys its money, it destroys its middle class.

This is what is happening in this country already. The poor, middle class individual who is still proud enough not to go on the dole and not to take welfare, that is the individual who suffers the very most; and he is the one that is most threatened by the loss of a job in the next downturn.

Currently right now, Wall Street, are they suffering from this financial bubble that I see? No. If you are in the stock market or the bond market or borrowing overseas, they are doing quite well. People say: You worry too much. There is no inflation. No matter what you say about the money supply and all of these things you talk about, there is no inflation, do not worry about it. Inflation deals with money, not prices.

So as I said earlier, I believe prices are going up much faster than people will admit; but at the same time, the supply of money and credit continues to expand. So we will have to eventually address these problems. I think it will be up to us as Members of Congress to at least make some plans. Because if we do not, if we do not make the plans, I see this as a serious, serious threat to our personal liberties.

Mr. Speaker, it will not be a simple reform that we need. We have to do something more than that. We have to start thinking about what do we need to do to really change the course. Is there anything wrong with addressing the subject of individual liberty? Is there anything wrong with talking about the value and the importance of sound money? I claim there is nothing wrong with that, but there is very little debate. There is very little debate among our committee members and in our committees to address this. It is usually, how do we tide ourselves over? How do we modify this so slight a degree?

But the time will come, the time will come, because we will go bankrupt, because no country has ever done this before. No country can live beyond its means endlessly. No country can spend and inflate and destroy its money. There will be this transfer of wealth. It happened in many, many countries in this century. Of course, one example of the 20th century was the German inflation, and then there has to always be a scapegoat. The middle class suffers the most. Somebody has to be blamed.

Currently today, I see a trend toward those of us who advocate limited government, those who detest big government as becoming the scapegoat saying, oh, you individuals who are against big government, you are the people who cause trouble, you cause unhappiness. That is not the case. People are unhappy. I meet them all the time because they are having a difficult time making it in this day and age. Who knows who the next scapegoat will be, but there will be one.

Mr. Speaker, the middle class in America will have to eventually join in the reforms that we need. The reforms can be all positive. There is nothing wrong with advocating limited government. There is nothing wrong in the American spirit to advocate the Constitution. There is nothing wrong with the American tradition that says work is good. And there is something wrong with a system that endorses and encourages and pushes the idea that we have the right to somebody else's life and somebody else's earnings. I do not believe that is the case. I think that is morally wrong. I do not believe it has been permitted under the Constitution, and it also leads to trouble. If it led to prosperity, it would be a harder argument for me. But if it leads to trouble and it leads to people being undermined in their financial security and in their economic security, then we have to do something else.

I would like to invite those who expressed deep concern about the poor and those who advocate more programs, more welfare programs, I would like to suggest they need to look at monetary policy. They need to look at deficits, and they need to realize that wealth has to be created. And if we truly do care about the poor people in this country, and if we do care about the people trying to build homes, public housing obviously has not worked. We have been doing public houses now and spent nearly $600 billion, and there is no sign that we have done much for the people that we have given public housing to.

We have spent $5 trillion on welfare. There are more homeless than ever. The educational system is worse than ever. Yet we do not really say, well, what should we do differently? Sometimes we will say, well, let us take the management and change the management. Let us take the bureaucrats from Washington and put them in the States. Let us do block grants. Let us make a few minor adjustments and everything is going to be OK, and it will not be.

We will not make it OK until we address the subject of what kind of a society we want to live in. I want to live in a free society. Fortunately for me, as a Member of Congress, and as one who has sworn to uphold the Constitution, this is an easy argument. It should be an easy argument for all of my colleagues who would say, yes, I have sworn to uphold the Constitution, I believe in America, I believe in hard work. But why do you vote for all of these other programs? Why do you vote for all of the deficits? Why are we getting ready to vote for more taxes soon? Why are we voting a supplemental appropriation? Why are we doing these things if we really are serious? I have not yet seen any serious attempt to cut back on spending and cut back on taxes.

Mr. Speaker, someday we will have to do it. The sooner, the better. If we do it in a graceful manner, there is no pain and suffering. The American people will not suffer if we cut their taxes. The American people will not suffer if we lower the amount of regulations. The American people will not suffer if we get out of their lives and not give them 100,000 regulations to follow day in and day out. The American people will not suffer if the Federal Government gets out of the management of education and medicine. That is the day I am waiting for and the day I am working for. Hopefully, I will get other Members of Congress here to join me in this effort to support the concepts and the principles of individual freedom.

INDEX

The numbers in the index are a little off. The higher the number the higher the chance that the page entry will reside about a page earlier than mentioned in index.

Albright, Medeleine, 220
Al-Zawahiri, Ayman, 221, 222
American Medical Association, 138, 139, 143
Anslinger, Harry J., 192
Austrian Economics, 14, 253
Bastiat, Frederic, 121, 122, 217
Bechtel, 227
Beck, Glenn, 245
Bernanke, Ben, 16, 34, 210
bin Laden, Osama, 219, 221, 222, 223, 227
Blumenthal, Max, 199
Böhm-Bawerk, Eugen von, 30
Bono, 161
Bush, George W., 155, 193, 222, 226, 231, 247, 250
Castro, Fidel, 155
Chaney, Dick, 249
Churchill, Winston, 152
Darwin, Charles, 113
De Soto, Jesús Huerta, 208
DeLauro, Rosa(Rep. D-Connecticut), 137
Delay, Tom, 199
Denson, Jonh V., 222
Einstein, Albert, 176
FDA, 136, 137, 141, 143
Friedman, Milton, 16
Ghraib, Abu, 224
Great Depression, 16, 215
Greenspan, Alan, 207, 209
H.R. 1955: Violent Radicalization and

Homegrown Terrorism Prevention Act of 2007, 248
Hadley, Steven J., 231
Hagee, John, 199
Hannity, Sean, 249
Hayek, F.A., 14, 17, 84, 101, 107, 110, 156, 165, 176, 178, 180, 201, 208, 212, 244, 248, 253
Hazlitt, Henry, 116, 122, 165, 175, 253
Hitler, Adolf, 152, 244
Horowitz, David, 245
Huckabee, Mike, 223
Hussein, Saddam, 221
Inhofe, Jim (Rep.Okla), 199
Jefferson, Thomas, 108, 119, 152, 153
Johnson, Lyndon B., 85
Katrina, Hurricane, 25, 127, 227, 238
Kennedy, Edward M., 142
Kepler, Johannes, 111
Kerry, John V., 142
Kwiatkowski, Karen, 199
Lenin, Vladimir, 27, 113, 142, 152
Litvinov, Maxim, 111
Martin, Lockheed, 227, 229
Marx, Karl, 20, 165, 174
Maybury, Richard J., 34, 114, 152, 157, 219
McCain, John, 228
Menger, Carl, 41, 47, 48, 101, 253

Miller, John, 222
Mises, Ludwig von, 14, 20, 80, 83, 134, 165, 253
Muhammad, 42, 219
Mussolini, Benito, 244
Newton, Isaac, 111, 176
Nixon, 15, 150
O'Reilly, Bill, 246, 249
Obama, Barack, 142
Paine, Thomas, 118
Paul, Ron, 14, 198, 206, 209, 223, 240, 242, 246, 247, 248, 251, 253
    Pillars of Prosperity, 251
    The Revolution
        A Manifesto, 251
Rand, Ayn, 196
Raskin, Max, 251
Read, Leonard E., 102
Reisman, George, 30, 130, 159, 164, 252
Rice, Condoleezza, 231
Roberts, Paul Craig, 247

Rockwell, Lew, 34, 243, 245
Roosevelt, Franklin Delano, 111, 150, 157, 215
Rothbard, Murray N., 34
Rumsfeld, Donald, 226
Russert, Tim, 206
Saint-Simon, Henri de, 113
Salerno, Joseph, 208
Smith, Adam, 113
Spencer, Herbert, 126, 128, 135, 145, 146, 147, 152, 167, 184, 253
St. Clair, Jeffrey, 229
Stalin, Joseph, 21, 244
Stevens, Robert J., 229, 230
Stevens, Ted (Senator), 127
Tancredo, Tom, 229
Tocqueville, Alexis De, 119
Truman, Harry S., 222
Walker, David (US Comptroller General), 13
Washington, George, 118
Weisberg, Jacob, 226

Printed in the United States
104646LV00003B/166-174/P